Online Social Sciences

Online Social Sciences

Edited by

Bernad Batinic

Ulf-Dietrich Reips

Michael Bosnjak

Hogrefe & Huber Publishers

Seattle • Toronto • Bern • Göttingen

Library of Congress Cataloging-in-Publication Data

is now available via the Library of Congress Marc Database under the
LC Catalog Card Number 2002105139

Canadian Cataloging in Publication Data

Main entry under title:

Online social sciences

Includes bibliographical references.
ISBN 0-88937-257-8

1. Social sciences—Computer network resources. 2. Social sciences—Research. 3. Internet.
I. Batinic, Bernad, 1969–, II. Reips, Ulf-Dietrich, 1964–, III. Bosnjak, Michael, 1971–

H61.95.O54 2002   025.06'3   C2002-900022-X

Copyright © 2002 by Hogrefe & Huber Publishers

USA: P.O. Box 2487, Kirkland, WA 98083-2487
                  Phone (425) 820-1500, Fax (425) 823-8324
CANADA: 12 Bruce Park Avenue, Toronto, Ontario M4P 2S3
                  Phone (416) 482-6339
SWITZERLAND: Länggass-Strasse 76, CH-3000 Bern 9
                  Phone (031) 300-4500, Fax (031) 300-4590
GERMANY   Rohnsweg 25, D-37085 Göttingen
                  Phone (0551) 49609-0, Fax (0551) 49609-88

Printed and bound in Germany

ISBN 0-88937-257-8

Table of Contents

Preface

Since its inception, the Internet has created opportunities previously unimagined. One such opportunity is the use of the Internet for exploring and understanding various social science phenomena. *Online Social Sciences* seeks to provide insight into just such possibilities. Readers will learn about foundation-level knowledge concerning online methodology, technical approaches to data collection, and the quality and limitations of data collected online.

Online studies can address many questions that are asked by social scientists. For instance: Do virtual teams lead to a decrease of commitment and personal communication in comparison to traditional teams? How are "online tests" with various applications to be judged regarding their efficiency? Do virtual courses in universities have the desired effect? In what respect are "lurkers" different from other Internet users? What is the quality of online relationships?

This is only a small selection of Internet-specific questions that can be examined by online research methods. In addition to Internet-specific questions, the medium can also be used for the analysis of classical problems in the social sciences. The twenty-three chapters which follow investigated the implementation of reactive and nonreactive methods of data collection. The studies reported utilize Web-based questionnaires, Web experiments, observations of virtual worlds, case narration, content analysis, and analysis of mailinglists and other log data.

In addition to featuring various fields of research in the online environment and reporting the results of such studies, this book also seeks to bridge a gap between Internet scientists in Europe and the US. In the past, researchers have tended to work on similar projects without collaboration. This book represents a joint effort among these researchers.

Principal editing responsibilities and much of the contact with authors were distributed as follows: Batinic chapters 8-9, 16-19, and 21-22; Reips chapters 5, 7, 10-13, and 20; Bosnjak 1-4 and 6. Responsibility for chapters 14, 15, and 23 was shared. Main responsibility for timing, contact with the publisher, and organization of the final manuscript rested with Batinic.

Last but not least, we would like to acknowledge the following people. Without their help this book would not have been possible. First of all, thanks go out to all authors for their excellent work, supportive attitude, and patience. Tracy Tuten checked all chapters for language errors – the book improved immensely. Our thanks go to Roman Soucek for his help to fit the book into a nicely formatted shape. The aid of Bernad Batinic, Lorenz Graef, Wolfgang Bandilla and Andreas Werner in an earlier state of the editing process is gratefully acknowledged. We also thank Klaus Moser, Friedrich Wilkening, and Wolfgang Bandilla, who as our supervisors and gave us a lot of support, despite the toll such a book project takes on other tasks that had to be done in our workplaces. We gratefully acknowledge the German Society for Online Research (D.G.O.F.; http://www.dgof.de/) for supporting this book as part of its mission to support activities that serve to advance, and improve the quality of, online research methods in the social sciences.

April, 2002
Bernad Batinic, Ulf-Dietrich Reips, and Michael Bosnjak

1 Web Surveys – An Appropriate Mode of Data Collection for the Social Sciences?

Wolfgang Bandilla

According to estimates of August 2001, there are about 513 million Internet users world wide: the USA and Canada alone account for 180 million, whereas in Europe 154 million people are online (Nua Internet surveys, http://www.nua.ie/). These numbers prove that the Internet cannot be considered a fringe phenomenon. Even if at present, the majority of the population does not have access to the Internet, we must ask ourselves whether it is already viable to use the opportunities of the Net for acquiring sociological data – i.e., by conducting surveys via the Internet.

The advantages of such a venture are obvious. In comparison to mail surveys, the financial expenditure of surveys on the Internet is smaller, and surveys can be conducted within short periods with an extremely high number of cases. However, these advantages are confronted by serious methodical problems. Above all, difficulties in determining population and random samples need to be mentioned. Primarily, these problems concern World Wide Web (WWW) surveys, i.e., surveys in which anyone with Internet access can participate, and where a sample selection cannot be compiled according to a well-defined design. However, today there are already numerous applications in which the advantages of the Net can be used in accordance with the usual methodological standards. These include, for example, employee surveys in globally dispersed and networked corporations, surveys on particular populations (see amongst others Schaefer & Dillman, 1998) or experts, as well as surveys of registered Internet users in defined areas – in other words, surveys in areas where the respective populations are clearly defined, and either total censuses or random samples are possible. Such methodically harmless surveys are not the subject of this contribution.

In the following section the difficulties involved in using data acquired in this manner to make general statements on the Internet user population will be pointed out in a short outline based on what could be called the most famous WWW survey, the GVU User surveys.

1.1 The GVU's WWW User Surveys

The Graphics, Visualization, & Usability (GVU) Center at the Georgia Institute of Technology started conducting WWW surveys at the beginning of 1994 (http://www. cc.gatech.edu/gvu/user_surveys/). Anybody who had access to the Internet and the usual Browser software could, without further restrictions, take part in these surveys. The first survey took place in January 1994 and included more than 1,500 participants. In October of 1994, more than 4,000 participants took part in the second survey. Since 1995, the surveys have taken place on fixed dates every 6 months, annually in April/May and in October/November. Each time the field periods have amounted to 4 weeks. The surveys were publicized by means of appropriate references in newsgroups and mailing lists, as well as in the form of advertising banners on large search engines and on other frequently visited sites (e.g., Netscape).

The main methodological problem of these surveys lay in the recruitment of participants, since the samples were not actively selected (i.e., the problem of self-selection, Bandilla & Hauptmanns, 1998). The announcement of the surveys via advertising banners on large search engines alone is extremely problematic due to the fact that usually less than one percent of those viewing the request ultimately decide to participate in a Web survey (see Bandilla, Bosnjak, Schneid, & Stiegler, 1999; Tuten, Bosnjak, & Bandilla, 2000).

Despite the generally small click rate, the absolute numbers of participants in the GVU inquiries were very high. In the surveys conducted between the spring of 1995 and fall of 1997 the numbers lay between 10,000 and 20,000. Only in the surveys conducted in 1998 could a drastic drop be observed in the numbers of participants, down to only 5,000. Almost without exception, the participants involved in these surveys were always different: on average only 1% of all participants confirmed having already participated once in a previous survey.

If one regards the classic demographic variables "age", "education" and "sex", to which population descriptions are usually referred, in the course of time very homogeneous pictures come to light: the age distribution of the participants is quite skewed (left- or youth-shifted) and deviates clearly from the normal population. The average age values in the individual surveys lie between 32.7 and 35.2 years. The median varies accordingly between 31 and 34. Trends over time are not apparent. In the April 1995 survey, the average value was 35 years of age. One year later, it was 33, only to rise again slightly in the following surveys. On the whole, therefore, a dominance of the younger age groups was apparent in all surveys. A clear bias in education level was also evident in comparison to the normal population: participants with degrees in higher education were clearly over-represented almost identically in all surveys. With the exception of the first survey (16%), the proportion of women was almost constant in all surveys at about 31%.

How, then, can these results be assessed? For this purpose, the GVU findings will be compared to the development of computers attached to the Internet. This comparison is based on the "Internet Domain survey" carried out by Mark Lottor since 1987. According to this survey, there has been a disproportionate increase in computer (host) registration since 1995 (see Figure 1.1).

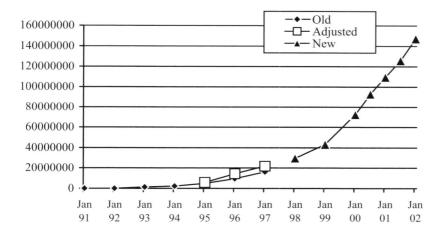

Figure 1.1: Host count from January 1991 until January 2002;
source: Internet Software Consortium (http://www.isc.org/)

Particular attention should be paid to the fact that Lottor had to apply a new measurement technique at the beginning of 1998, since the procedure used until then had increasingly underestimated the number of Internet computers due to technical restrictions (see detailed description of different techniques under the following URL: http://www.nw.com/). Therefore, in Figure 1.1 the lower line refers to the old and the upper line to the new procedure and to the correspondingly adjusted numbers. Even if it is not possible to project the total number of Internet participants based on the number of Internet computers, since the number of persons with access to the Internet per computer is unknown, (Batinic & Bosnjak, 2000), one must assume that – regardless of which measuring procedure is applied – between 1995 and 2002 the number of persons with access to the Internet, and equally the increase in hosts grew disproportionately[1].

---

[1]   This comparison is based on the assumption that the factor "users per computer" remains constant over time.

With regards to the GVU, the over proportional increase in computers should have been noticeable within this period in relation to the question of how long participants in these surveys had already been using the Internet. With the exception of the October 1997 survey, it is obvious (see Table 1.1) that the percentage of Internet beginners among the participants ("less than 6 months' experience on the Internet") decreased during the period from 28% in October 1995 to only 5% in October 1998.

If, on the basis of the absolute host numbers in the Internet Domain survey, the semi-annual percentages of newly introduced hosts is calculated and compared with the GVU survey findings (that took place three months later) with regards to the proportion of Internet beginners ("less than 6 months' experience"), clear discrepancies are continually evident – according to both old and new measurement procedures.

Table 1.1: "Internet beginners" in comparison to host increase
(all data in percent)

	October 95	April 96	October 96	April 97	October 97	April 98	October 98
Less than 6 months on the Internet	28	24	18	12	18	8	5
Increase on host "old" procedure	37	43	36	25	21		
Increase on host "new" procedure	40	75	14	30	19	14	24

Whilst according to the "old" measurement procedure, the number of the computers (hosts) with access to the Internet increased to approximately 37% in the first half of 1995, only 28% of the participants in the October 1995 GVU survey indicated having accessed the Internet within the last six months (i.e., between April and October 1995). If one were to apply the – in this case – "new" and adjusted measurement procedure (40%), the deviation is even stronger. That means that clearly fewer persons with little Internet experience participated in the GVU survey of autumn 1995 than was to be expected on the hosts' side in almost the same period. With the exception of the survey conducted in October 1997, where the proportion of Internet beginners (18%) is relatively close to the increase in computers in the first half of 1997 (21% and/or 19%), Internet beginners are clearly underrepresented in the GVU surveys. Such distortions cannot be excluded in the other variables which describe the participants of these surveys (e.g., age, education, and gender). The main cause for these discrepancies is to be found in the self-selection effects described earlier which are especially notable in WWW surveys.

For example, when comparing the age distribution of participants in a WWW survey conducted in Germany (W3B) with the results of a representative telephone survey on online use conducted in an equivalent period (GfK Online Monitor), severe deviations come to light between the age structure of people using the Internet in the self-selected W3B survey and those figures obtained representatively by the GfK Market Research Institute (see Figure 1.2).

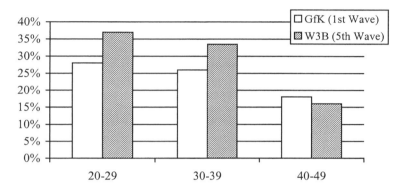

Figure 1.2: W3B vs. GfK survey – age of respondents

Similar deviations have also been reported by CommerceNet/Nielsen (1995). These methodically-based discrepancies in the findings are also the reason why the GVU surveys in their original form have been postponed.

1.2   Conclusion

It was pointed out that WWW surveys (still) do not represent a serious alternative to the prevailing data acquisition techniques employed in empirical social research: "face-to-face" and "telephone". The distortions, which can occur in the data due to uncontrollable sample selection and self-selection effects, are too strong. On the basis of this, further systematic basic research is required. Already, WWW surveys might be suitable for a number of special questions. One need only think of the opportunities for Pretest studies (Gräf, 1997). A wide field is also opened for experimentally oriented studies (Reips, 2000). WWW surveys also represent an alternative for studies that are explorative in nature. Coomber (1997) describes such a study. He conducted a survey on the Internet aimed at dealers of hard drugs (cocaine and heroin), on questions of distribution, and on this group's specific behavior patterns. The data obtained in this manner was used as an additional form of data from interviews which he had already personally conducted beforehand in prisons, and in the related scene.

References

Bandilla, W. & Hauptmanns, P. (1998). Internetbasierte Umfragen als Datenerhebungstechnik für die Empirische Sozialforschung? *ZUMA Nachrichten, 43*, 36-53.

Bandilla, W., Bosnjak, M., Schneid, M., & Stiegler, A. (1999). Interaktive Medien als Gegenstand und Instrument der empirischen Sozialforschung. In M. Berghaus (Ed.), *Interaktive Medien* (pp. 129-148). Opladen: Westdeutscher Verlag.

Batinic, B. & Bosnjak, M. (2000). Fragebogenuntersuchungen im Internet [Questionnaire studies in the Internet]. In B. Batinic (Ed.), *Internet für Psychologen* (2nd ed.) (pp. 287-317) [Internet for psychologists]. Göttingen: Hogrefe.

CommerceNet/Nielsen (1995). *The CommerceNet/Nielsen Internet demographic survey, executive summary.* [Online]. Available: http://www.nielsenmedia.com/.

Coomber, R. (1997). *Using the Internet for survey research. Sociological Research Online, 2.* [Online]. Available: http://www.socresonline.org.uk/socresonline/2/2/2.html.

Gräf, L. (1997). Pretest of online questionnaires. In D. Janetzko, B. Batinic, D. Schoder, M. Mattinley-Scott, & G. Strube (Eds.), *CAW-97* (pp. 51-62). Freiburg: Universität, IIG-Berichte.

Reips, U. D. (2000). Das psychologische Experimentieren im Internet [Psychological experimentation in the Internet]. In B. Batinic (Ed.), *Internet für Psychologen* (2nd ed.) (pp. 319-343) [Internet for psychologists]. Göttingen: Hogrefe.

Schaefer, D. R. & Dillman, D. A. (1998). Development of a standard e-mail methodology: Results from an experiment. *Public Opinion Quarterly, 62*, 378-397.

Tuten, T. L., Bosnjak, M., & Bandilla, W. (2000). Banner-advertised web surveys. *Marketing Research, 11*, 17-21.

2 Internet Surveys and Data Quality: A Review

Tracy L. Tuten, David J. Urban, & Michael Bosnjak

The many advantages of collecting survey data via the Internet have been well-documented. Internet surveys are inexpensive due to the elimination of postage, printing, and data entry. A vast improvement in response speed over traditional mail surveys is widely reported (e.g., Bachmann, Elfrink, & Vazzana, 1996; Sproull, 1986; Mehta & Sivadas, 1995), and the Internet provides ready access across geographic boundaries and time zones (Schmidt, 1997). Despite such disadvantages as potential sample bias and system incompatibility, Internet surveys represent an exciting new method for researchers. This is evidenced by numerous Web-based surveys and experimental Web laboratories[1]. Consequently, the Internet as a tool for research has become a popular topic in magazines and journals.

Up to the present, the literature on Internet surveys mainly tends to be one of two types. The first type is made up of "how to do it" articles. These articles document technological procedures for the development and administration of Internet-based surveys, mention the method's advantages and disadvantages, like those described above, and often provide new solutions to commonly encountered problems. For example, Morrow and McKee (1998) describe a process for conducting between-subjects experimental designs on the Web using Common Gateway Interface (CGI) scripts. Schmidt (1997) explains the benefits and potential problems of Internet surveys and describes the importance of an appropriate procedure in protecting against multiple submissions and incomplete responses. Such articles are valuable problem-solving tools for Internet researchers but do not evaluate the reliability or validity of the method itself. The second type of literature, though, has sought to establish the viability of Internet surveys as a data collection method in terms of response rates and data-quality issues.

While standardized methods for using Internet surveys have not yet been developed fully (Schaefer & Dillman, 1998), several authors have begun this process by evaluating issues including response rates, response speed, and data quality in Internet surveys. Consequently, they have established the initial research stream regarding

---

[1] e.g., http://www.olemiss.edu/PsychExps and http://www.psych.unizh.ch/genpsy/Ulf/Lab/WebExpPsyLab.html.

Internet surveys as a data collection method. This paper reviews this literature on electronic mail (e-mail) surveys and Web-based surveys and discusses remaining gaps in the evaluation of Internet surveys as a data collection method. Implications for future research are discussed.

2.1   Response Rates and Data Quality

Methodological studies of Internet surveys can be categorized into two general areas: those designed to measure or increase response rates and those designed to evaluate the response quality associated with the mode of data collection. Response rates are of critical interest, because the greater the response the more likely it is that the study will accurately estimate the parameters of the population sampled. Unlike mail (Dillman, 1978, 2000) and telephone surveys (Frey, 1976), researchers still have limited knowledge of prescriptive techniques that may improve response rate to Internet surveys.

Instinct may suggest that techniques similar to those used in mail surveys would be useful for improving response rates in Internet-based surveys. Yet, the situational variables surrounding the activities of using the Internet and e.g., reading e-mail may be different from those of reading and responding to traditional mail. Little is known about the behaviors and the behavioral determinants of individuals as they use the Internet. In other words, there may exist a "psychology of Internet usage". For example, Tuten (1998) found that individuals tend to open electronic mail messages based on familiarity of the name identified in the mailbox, and to delete those messages from individuals they did not know. Bosnjak and Batinic (this volume) identified four categories of motive for participation in Internet surveys: curiosity, opportunity to contribute to research, self-knowledge, and material incentives. While mail surveys have an opportunity to be opened by using official cues and sponsorship, Internet surveys may not lend themselves to such cues. Likewise, some tools developed for traditional mail surveys may be relevant, while others may not be.

Tools to increase response rates for traditional mail surveys can be classified by timing and by technique (Kanuk & Berenson, 1975). In other words, the timing of communication may have an effect, as in the case of preliminary notification and reminders. Techniques are part of the survey itself and include such variables as survey length, sponsorship, return envelopes, postage, personalization, cover letters, anonymity, size and color, monetary incentives, and deadline dates (Kanuk & Berenson, 1975; Dillman, 1978). Whether these variables will have a similar effect of increasing response rates in Internet surveys is yet unknown, but some variables are likely to be more important than others in an Internet environment.

A variable related to response rates and response quality is that of response speed. Nonresponse and response bias are noted as key weaknesses inherent in using Internet surveys for research. Specifically, one can only make generalizations about a population if those who do not respond are not significantly different from those that do respond. Traditional mail surveys utilized speed of response as one method of estimating nonresponse bias (Kanuk & Berenson, 1975). In other words, early responders may differ from later responders. Respondents who answered later are thought to be more similar to nonresponders than to responders. These responses can then be used to weight the final nonresponse.

The constructs "response" and "data-quality" are a diverse area made up of at least three dimensions: item omission, response error, and completeness of answer (McDaniel & Rao, 1980). Though, it also includes such issues as equivalence of response. In other words, it assesses whether response content similar between modes of data collection. Related to response equivalence is the potential for different modes to introduce the presence of context effects, and socially desirable responding (SDR). Because traditional mail survey methods are well established, the equivalence of response is important for ensuring that mode of data collection is not a moderator of response content. The validity of Internet surveys, as a form of self-report survey, is threatened by context effects, the potential for various contextual cues to affect response, which could ultimately result in misleading estimates of relationships among constructs (Harrison, McLaughlin, & Coalter, 1996).

Empirical studies of Internet surveys have generally described one or more of these three topics: response rates, response speed, and some additional data quality issues. The paper will now review the literature on two forms of Internet surveys: electronic mail surveys and Web-based surveys. Some gaps in the literature will be identified and discussed.

2.2   Electronic Mail Surveys

In using electronic mail surveys, a survey is sent to a person's electronic mail (e-mail) address. Individuals can then read, scroll down the message, answer the questions and then simply "reply" or send the survey back to the researcher. Individuals who do not want to answer online may also print the survey out and then answer it like a paper questionnaire and mail or fax it back to the researcher.

Electronic mail as a data collection tool offers many notable benefits: 1) it is easy to send; 2) it is easy to reply; 3) it is low in cost compared to mail or phone or in person interviews; 4) it offers speed of response – responses can begin immediately; and 5) it eliminates time zone hassles for individuals in different geographic areas (Parker, 1992; Mehta & Sivada, 1995; Schmidt, 1997). At the same time, many drawbacks exist. First, data editing or even data entry is sometimes still required; thereby, restricting one of the key benefits of electronic data collection in general. Second, systems used by different e-mail users must be compatible for an e-mail form to be displayed and filled out correctly (Smith, 1997; Parker, 1992). Third, because many people do not have e-mail, may prefer not to use it, or may be unfamiliar with some of the more advanced functions that may be necessary in answering a questionnaire online, sample coverage and therefore sample bias is an issue. And, fourth, even when a population of e-mail users is chosen, e-mail addresses may be incorrect or inactive, thereby preventing the survey from reaching the intended individual (Comley, 1996). These challenges, though, are being lessened daily as technology continues to improve, as individuals increasingly adopt new technology, as organizations seek to improve databases of e-mail addresses, and as researchers develop new tools and processes for handling these new methods.

While a standardized methodology does not yet exist for this method of data collection, several studies have laid the groundwork for using e-mail surveys. The discussion is organized around the three themes of response rates, response speed, and several indicators of data quality.

2.3   Response Rates

Some studies reporting on response rates have indicated positive experiences with e-mail (e.g., Parker, 1992; Sproull, 1986; Mehta & Sivadas, 1995), while others have confirmed that e-mail is not yet on a par with traditional mail surveys (e.g., Tse, Tse, Yin, Ting, Yi, Yee, & Hong, 1995; Swoboda, Muehlberger, & Schneeweiss, 1997). For example, Parker (1992) conducted an e-mail survey at AT&T. The electronic mail survey met several objectives for AT&T including a response rate of 68%, a tight deadline, the need to reach people conveniently in multiple time zones, and a budget. Parker attributed the high response rate to the e-mail version to the amount of "junk mail" present in company mailboxes. Anderson and Gansneder (1995) reported a response rate of 68% to their 72-item e-mail survey. Bachmann, et al. (1996) also achieved a respectable response rate exceeding 50%. While Sproull (1986) reported a lower response rate for electronic mail (76%) than the traditional format (87%), Sproull noted that it was still sufficiently high to encourage electronic mail surveys.

While these studies support the utility of electronic mail surveys, e-mail has not met the standard established by mail studies. With the exception of Parker (1992), who reported a 68% response rate for e-mail as opposed to a 38% response rate to mail, all studies comparing e-mail to mail report higher response rates to the traditional mail version of the survey (Schuldt & Totten, 1994; Kittleson, 1995; Mehta & Sivadas, 1995; Tse, et al., 1995; Bachmann, et al., 1996; Comley, 1996; Good, 1997,

Smith, 1997; Treat, 1997; Schaefer & Dillman, 1998; Couper, Blair, & Triplett, 1999). Further, many have reported exceptionally low response rates. In a study of newsgroup users, Swoboda, et al. (1997) achieved a low response rate of only 20%. Tse, et al. (1995) achieved a response rate of only 6% for e-mail in a study of faculty and staff at the Chinese University of Hong Kong. Vogt (1999) compared an e-mail survey to a survey using disk-by-mail (DBM). The e-mail version attained a lower response rate (48% compared to 78%) in this case as well. Specific response rates for each study cited are reported in Table 2.1.

While the studies cited above have compared response rates for e-mail and mail surveys, the studies did not specifically evaluate the effects of timing and technique on response rate. In other words, mail survey methods developed the ability to achieve adequate response rates by timing, including preliminary notification and reminders, and by technique, including incentives and other concurrent information. All timing and technique factors may not apply to e-mail surveys, but many are likely to have an effect on response rates.

Mehta and Sivadas (1995) included timing and technique variables in their comparison of electronic mail and traditional mail survey response. The following groups were compared:

1) electronic mail with prenotification, incentives, and reminders;
2) electronic mail with no prenotification, incentives, and reminders;
3) electronic mail for international users;
4) traditional mail with prenotification, incentives, and reminders, and
5) traditional mail with no prenotification, no incentives, and no reminder.

In their study, traditional mail with prenotification, incentives, and reminder had the highest response rate. However, electronic mail used with the same prenotification, incentive, and reminder showed the second highest response rate.

These findings are further supported by Good (1997). She also compared electronic mail surveys to traditional mail and included such treatments as notifications, personalization, incentives, and reminders. Again, the response rate was highest for the traditional mail method but electronic mail was almost equal when combined with personalization and reminders.

Schaefer and Dillman (1998) also included prenotification and reminders in their study of e-mail survey response rates. In addition, the study addressed the issue of e-mail usage by including multi-mode groups in the experimental design. They emphasized the efficiency of e-mail when appropriate, but noted that a multi-mode strategy can accommodate individuals who do not have e-mail accounts, are not using existing e-mail accounts, or are temporarily unavailable via e-mail.

Table 2.1: Electronic mail studies

Authors	N	Sample	Methods compared	Response rate e-mail - mail	Response speed, e-mail - mail	Response quality
Sproull (1986)	30 EM/ 30 PP	Professionals in R&D and product development	e-mail vs. in person and paper-pencil	73%-87%	5.6-12	Missing data higher in e-mail survey, no differences in response content
Parker (1992)	100 EM/ 40 M	AT&T employees	e-mail vs. company mail	63%-38%	N/A	N/A
Schuldt & Totten (1994)	343 EM/ 200 M	Marketing and MIS university faculty	e-mail vs. mail	19.3%-56.5%	e-mail noted as faster	N/A
Anderson & Gansneder (1995)	600	Cross-sectional	e-mail only	68%	Within 2 weeks total	N/A
Kittleson (1995)	153 EM/ 153 M	Health educators international directory	e-mail vs. mail	28.1%-76.5%	2.88-12.6	N/A
Mehta & Sivadas (1995)	354 EM/ 309 M	Newsgroups readers	e-mail vs. mail (also with/out notification, incentives, reminder)	64%-83% 43%-45%	2-21	No difference
Opperman (1995)	665 EM	AA of geographers	e-mail only	48.8%	N/A	N/A

Note: em = e-mail, m = mail, pp = paper-pencil, N/A = not available

Table 2.1: Electronic mail studies

Authors	N	Sample	Methods compared	Response rate e-mail - mail	Response speed, e-mail - mail	Response quality
Tse, Tse, Yin, Ting, Yi, Yee, & Hong (1995)	200 EM/ 200 M	Faculty / staff Chinese university of Hong Kong	e-mail vs. mail	6%-27%	8.09-9.79	No difference
Bachmann, Elfrink, & Vazzana (1996)	224 EM/ 224 M	US business school deans	e-mail vs. mail	52.5%-65.6%	4.68-11.18	Higher item non-response for e-mail, answers to open-ended quest. longer in e-mail
Comley (1996)	795 EM/ 2769 M/	Subscribers to UK Internet magazine	e-mail vs. mail	13.5%-15%	4.2-10.8	Longer answers to open-ended quest., missing items slightly higher in e-mail
Bosnjak (1997)	99	Panel	e-mail vs. reported retest reliab. of psy. tests reported in manuals	N/A	N/A	No sig. difference between e-mail and reported reliabilities in manuals
Good (1997)	528	University faculty and staff	e-mail vs. mail (also with/out notifications, incentives, reminders)	51%-67%, e-mail with pers. & follow-up achieved same resp. rate as traditional mail.	3-15	N/A

Note: em = e-mail, m = mail, pp = paper-pencil, N/A = not available

Table 2.1: Electronic mail studies

Authors	N	Sample	Methods compared	Response rate e-mail - mail	Response speed e-mail - mail	Response quality
Smith (1997)	150 EM/150 EI	Members of web consultants association	e-mailed survey vs. e-mailed request to send e-mail survey	8%-13.3%	N/A	N/A
Swoboda, Muehlberger, & Schneeweiss (1997)	1713	Newsgroups users	e-mail only	20%	4	N/A
Treat (1997)	8500	Federal employees	e-mail vs. mail	51.46%-75.46%	N/A	Higher item nonresponse for e-mail. Nonresponse related to demographic questions.
Schaefer & Dillman (1998)	904	Faculty of Washington state university	e-mail vs. mail vs. multi-mode	48.2%-57.5%-53.5%	9.16-14.39	Longer answers, lower item nonresp. for e-mail
Couper, Blair, & Triplett (1999)	8253	Employees of US statistical agencies	e-mail vs. mail	42.6%-70.7%	N/A	No differences in missing data for attitudinal quest., but higher missing data for the mail version on background data.
Vogt (1999)	308	Net, compuserve and t-online users	e-mail vs. disk-by-mail	48%-78%	N/A	No differences in question-order effects

Note: em = e-mail, m = mail, pp = paper-pencil, N/A = not available

The experimental design in the study by Schaefer and Dillman (1998) compared an all paper group, an all e-mail group, a group with a paper prenotification and then all e-mail communication, and a group with all e-mail communication followed by a paper reminder if an individual had not responded. The control group of all paper achieved a response rate of 57.5%, the all e-mail group responded at a rate of 58%, the paper prenotice group achieved a 48.2% response rate, and the paper reminder group achieved a 54.4% response rate. The authors estimated that the multi-mode strategy led to a 5.3% higher response rate than if electronic mail had been used alone. Further, the all e-mail format showed a response rate almost equal to that of a traditional survey when prenotifications and reminders were included.

These studies suggest that timing of communication may have an effect, as in the case of preliminary notification and reminders. Techniques are part of the survey itself and include such variables as survey length, sponsorship, return envelopes, postage, personalization, cover letters, anonymity, size and color, monetary incentives, and deadline dates (Kanuk & Berenson, 1975; Dillman, 1978). Some evidence exists to support the relationship between technique and response behavior, but the techniques examined are few and the designs not as thorough. Length of survey, sponsorship, personalization, and incentives are likely to affect response behavior.

For example, anecdotal evidence suggests that Internet users tend to lose interest quickly (Krasilovsky, 1996). Smith (1997) compared response rates between a long survey and a short poll and found response to be much higher to the short poll. She further noted that many individuals requested information about her and checked references before answering the survey, suggesting that sponsorship will be critical to Internet surveys. Good (1997) used personalization as one treatment in an e-mail survey and found a higher response rate in that treatment group. Mehta and Sivadas (1995) and Good (1997) included incentives and achieved acceptable response rates for e-mail surveys; however, the incentives were not expressly separated from a treatment of timing and so conclusions about the effectiveness of incentives cannot be made.

2.3.1 Response Speed

Several studies have also reported a comparison of the speed at which responses are returned for e-mail surveys and traditional mail surveys (Sproull, 1986; Kittleson, 1995; Mehta & Sivadas, 1995; Tse, et al., 1995; Bachmann, et al., 1996; Comley, 1996; Good, 1997; Schaefer & Dillman, 1998). These studies consistently report a faster response speed for e-mail when compared to traditional mail. Response speed is an important benefit to Internet surveys as faster response provides a researcher with an opportunity to begin data analysis and/or new phases of a study earlier. The response speed in days for each study is reported in Table 2.1.

2.3.2   Data Quality Issues

In addition to response rates and speed, several studies cited above also included discussion of data quality. Sproull's (1986) comparison examined data completeness and equivalence of response as indicators of data quality. This study reported no differences in response content for closed-ended questions, but differences did exist in that responses were longer and more detailed for open-ended questions in e-mail surveys. This finding is mirrored in results reported by Bachmann, et al. (1996), Comley (1996), and Schaefer and Dillman (1998). A comparison of electronic mail and a traditional mailed paper-and-pencil survey by Mehta and Sivadas (1995) found no differences in either completeness of response or equivalence of response.

However, results are mixed with regard to differences in item omissions for e-mail and mail surveys. Couper, et al., (1999) reported no significant differences between e-mail and mail for missing data of attitudinal items, but noted that traditional mail did show a significantly higher rate of missing data for background items. Bachmann, et al. (1996) reported higher item nonresponse for the e-mail survey as did Sproull (1986), Comley (1996), and Treat (1997); however, Schaefer and Dillman (1998) reported a lower item nonresponse for the e-mail survey. Bosnjak (1997) compared e-mail and Web-based surveys. While responses were equivalent with regard to internal consistency, results suggested a higher incident of socially desirable responding (SDR) in the e-mail version of the survey.

2.4   Web Surveys

Web surveys represent a growing segment of Web sites. Sites such as Nua Internet surveys[1], with direct links to companies doing research on the Web, and the APS (American Psychological Society) site[2], with links to a variety of Web projects in psychology, indicate a strong affinity to Web-based research. Its benefits are extensive, including elimination of time and space boundaries, data entry, and postage and copying expenses. It is fast and inexpensive. Cleland (1996) reported that online research costs about half that of traditional methods, and went on to predict that the Internet will replace telephone and mail surveys as the primary medium for conducting research. While it does create challenges for researchers, perhaps the most difficult challenge being sample bias, many of its problems (e.g., multiple submissions) can be solved via careful programming and/or data cleaning by hindsight. Like electronic mail, many researchers and organizations are utilizing the Web as a data col-

---

[1]   http://www.nua.ie/surveys
[2]   http://www.psych.hanover.edu/APS

lection tool. Also like electronic mail, most work in the area has used the tool without systematically investigating its viability.

While many firms have adopted the Web as a primary tool for conducting market research, it is unlikely that Web research will become widely accepted for scientific communities in the short term. The primary drawback of using the Web to collect survey data is the presence of sample bias. The population of individuals with access to the Web is small as compared to those with mail addresses and telephones. To respond to a Web survey, an individual must find the survey through links or search engines or, if an individual knows the survey address, she or he can choose to go directly to the survey. The sample is self-selected by those individuals visiting the Web site. Thus, it is difficult to compare nonrespondents to respondents to ascertain key differences between the groups or to control the quality of the sample of respondents participating in the survey.

To many, sample bias and a limited population of Web users do not represent reasons for collecting data in traditional means rather than using the Web. Rather, these researchers recognize the value of Web survey administration for small, known populations (as opposed to general public surveys) and admit that sample bias is ultimately a limitation of any form of self-report survey data (Schonland & Williams, 1996, Smith, 1997). Schonland and Williams (1996) described a research project utilizing a Web survey of travelers. While Schonland and Williams (1996) openly discussed the significant drawback of sample bias and an unknown population in using Web surveys, respondents to their survey were similar to general descriptions of travelers. Thus, in their specific situation, sample bias did not represent a negative factor. Response appeared strong with 17,700 responses over one year of data collection.

The population of Web users, while different from that of the general public, changes constantly. Graphics, Visualization, & Usability (GVU) WWW user surveys[3] described the following average characteristics of the Web user. Web users are 70% male and 30% female. Fifty-six percent of Web users hold a college or advanced degree. Eighty-three percent of the users are in the US. The average age is 35 and the average income is just above $60,000. This is consistent with the picture painted by others of young, educated, male, wealthy users (Schonland & Williams, 1996; Davis, 1997). However, it is recognized that the population will develop to better represent the average public as technology becomes increasingly adopted and decreases in price and availability (Smith, 1997).

Aside from the major challenges of sample bias, many smaller hurdles face a Web researcher. It may be difficult to attract potential respondents to a survey site. Davis (1997) stated that banners located on frequently visited sites and the use of incentives

---

[3]   http://www.cc.gatech.edu/gvu/

have been successful in attracting and retaining respondents, but such techniques can be costly for a researcher. Further, Tuten, Bosnjak, & Bandilla (1999) report that intrinsic appeals in banner ads generated higher click-through rates to a Web survey than incentives (like prizes) in an extrinsic appeal banner ad. Many authors note that click-through rates to banner ads are often very disappointing (Tuten, Bosnjak, & Bandilla, 1999; Briggs & Hollis, 1997).

Schonland and Williams (1996) identified another major challenge for all Web researchers: keeping a respondent's attention when another surprise is just a keystroke away. In other words, drop-out rates are high for Web-based surveys. Anecdotal evidence suggests that respondents tend to lose interest after 25-30 questions and then quit the survey (Krasilovsky, 1996). Tom Miller, Vice-President of Find/SVP, stated that online interviews gather less than 10% of the information that can be gathered in a telephone interview, because online respondents typically only answer one wave of questions (Krasilovsky, 1996). Dillman, Tortora, and Bowker (1999) have proposed several principles to guide Web survey design, such as including a welcome screen, presenting questions in a traditional format, and providing specific instructions for computer actions necessary in answering each question. However, there is a lack of evidence as to the effectiveness of such principles. Drop-outs may also be high due to system problems. Smith (1997) emphasized a problem of servers crashing and, thus, preventing survey completion. This problem and a related issue of slow page loading as an impetus to drop-out effects was further noted by Dillman, Tortora, Conradt, and Bowker (1998).

Thus, popular literature concludes that Web-based surveys have many benefits including the ability to reach respondents anywhere in the world, the potential to reach a very large sample, speed of response, and low cost. This literature also concludes that respondents are fickle, must be invited to a Web survey through sales promotions, banner advertisements, and incentives, and will only stay for a few questions before dropping out. Yet, benefits to Web-based data collection seem to outweigh these challenges.

While many studies are using Web-based surveys, the empirical study of the method of Web-based data collection is limited. Table 2.2 summarizes the studies on Web-based surveys. As before, the discussion will focus on response rates, response speed, and some additional indicators of data quality.

Table 2.2: Web-based survey studies

Authors	N	Sample	Methods compared	Response rate	Response speed	Response quality
Bertot & McClure (1995)	46	Public libraries	Web-based vs. mail (choice)			Mixed results, some indicated no access to www.
Bosnjak (1997)	305 WB/ 150 EM	Internet panel	Web-based vs. e-mail	N/A	N/A	No differences in reliab. (internal consistency). Sig. higher socially desirable resp. in e-mail version.
Smith (1997)	161	Announcement posted to www oriented mailing lists	Web-based only	U/K: 161 total useable responses	Most within initial 24-48 h	N/A
Dillman, Tortora, Conrad, & Bowker (1998)	9,522	Computer product buyers	Web-based only, fancy format vs. plain format	41.1% plain – 36.29% fancy	N/A	Completion higher for plain version.
Stanton (1998)	50 WB/ 181 M	Employees of several organizations	Web-based vs. mail	U/K: 50 total responses to web-based	N/A	Fewer missing data in www survey, no differences in factor structure or variability, measurement error higher in www
Rietz & Wahl (1999)	105 WB / 45 PP	Psychologists	Web-based vs. paper-and-pencil	N/A	N/A	Higher evidence of socially desirable resp. in paper-and-pencil version than in www survey

Note: em = e-mail, wb = web-based, pp = paper-pencil, N/A = not available

2.4.1 Response Rates

Like the known research evaluating electronic mail survey methods, only a small stream of research exists to evaluate the viability of Web-based survey methods. E-mail surveys may be sent to a known population and, consequently, response rate can be calculated as a percentage of those individuals receiving the survey. However, Web-based surveys are not addressed to a particular sample of individuals but rather are available to a larger group of potential, but unknown respondents. Individual responses may be counted, but the rate cannot be calculated as the survey was not addressed to a set sample initially. Even in situations where a sample of respondents is invited to participate, intruders may stumble upon the survey and distort the results. Consequently, most articles reporting Web-based survey results have reported total useable responses (Smith, 1997; Stanton, 1998) or have partially relied upon a panel of participants (Bosnjak, 1997).

The one exception to the lack of evidence on response rates to Web-based surveys is an article by Dillman, et al. (1998) in which they compared the effect of a fancy versus plain format for a Web-based survey. The sample was drawn from a list of computer buyers who were then contacted by telephone and invited to participate in the Web survey. Participants were then randomly assigned to a condition of plain or fancy format. The authors found that a fancy format was associated with a lower response rate (36.3%) while a plain format resulted in a higher response rate (41.1%). Further, the completion rate was higher for the plain group (93.1%) than the fancy group (82.1%). Specifically, while fancy formats may entertain a respondent, such formats also require more time in transmission and processing by browsers. In such a situation, Web pages load slower and systems may crash, ultimately encouraging an individual to not respond to a survey or to drop out of a survey. Thus, while Web surveys utilizing the latest programming advances may be more attractive and entertaining in order to acquire and retain respondents, the end result may be fewer useable responses.

The study by Dillman, et al, (1998) also addressed the effect of timing and technique for increasing response rates to Web-based surveys by including an incentive (technique) and reminder (timing). In addition, individuals were not able to conclude how many questions were left in the survey during participation (to minimize any negative effect caused by survey length). However, conclusions cannot be drawn about the effectiveness of these tools because the variables were not part of the study's experimental design (all respondents received incentives and reminders).

Related to the issue of response rates in Web-based survey, though, is the idea of mode preference on the part of respondents. In other words, response to Web-based surveys may be affected by preference for other modes of response, particularly in multi-mode studies. Bertot and McClure (1995) conducted a study of public libraries.

Each respondent could choose to complete their questionnaire by paper-and-pencil or to answer the questions on a Web site. While most individuals used the paper-and-pencil format, many stated that they chose paper-and-pencil when they could not access the Web site. This reaction confirms the suggestion by Smith (1997) and Dillman, et al (1998) that technology can create response difficulties that can ultimately affect nonresponse and drop-out effects.

2.4.2   Response Speed

Similar to response rates, response speed is also difficult to evaluate in Web-based surveys. Individuals must be made aware of the survey posting and choose to visit the survey site. While researchers have a measure of the date a mail survey is mailed and the date it is returned, Web-based researchers know only the date of posting to the Internet and, under conditions of prenotification via e-mail, the date the notification was sent out, but not the date of exposure to or "survey awareness" of the potential respondent. Anecdotal evidence, however, suggests that those individuals who will respond tend to respond within the first few days with responses decreasing rapidly after the first week (Batinic & Bosnjak, 2000). Response speed as a dependent variable has not been expressly examined.

2.4.3   Data Quality

Initial results reporting measures of data quality are positive for Web-based surveys. Stanton (1998) compared a Web-based survey with a paper-and-pencil version and found fewer missing data in the Web survey and no differences in variability, factor structure or measurement error. Rietz and Wahl (1999) also compared a paper-and-pencil version to a Web-based version. They found higher evidence of socially desirable responding (SDR) in the paper-and-pencil version than in the Web-based version. Thus, self-report data may be more accurate in a Web environment. Bosnjak (1997) compared a Web-based version and an electronic mail survey version and found higher SDR in the e-mail version. This conclusion makes intuitive sense in that individuals may feel more anonymous in a Web environment than when using a personal e-mail account. Bosnjak (1997) also examined seven psychometric scales for reliability between reported reliabilities in the test documentation administered via paper-and-pencil, and the internal consistency present in the e-mail and Web-based versions. No differences were found. Dillman, et al (1998) used total boxes checked and write-ins as measures of data quality in their fancy versus plain version experiment. The plain version showed more total boxes and write-ins than did the fancy version. These results are promising as the Web continues to be explored as an efficient data collection tool.

2.5   Gaps in the Literature and Implications for Future Research

In summary, a small but growing stream of literature is developing to assess the effectiveness of Internet surveys as a data collection method. With regard to response rate, electronic mail surveys have a lower response rate than its traditional mail counterpart. However, studies have illustrated that response to e-mailed surveys can be improved with timing and techniques commonly used for traditional mail surveys. Web-based surveys are still more unknown in terms of how to improve response. This mystery is compounded by the difficulty in measuring response rate for Web-based surveys.

For response speed, Internet surveys, both e-mail and Web-based, appear to offer the clear advantage of speed. E-mail's response speed is documented in many articles. The evidence is not as clear for Web-based surveys, but anecdotal evidence suggests that Web-based surveys can exhibit this characteristic of speed as well.

In considering response quality, there are mixed results with regard to item nonresponse and response errors in electronic mail surveys. Context effects appear to be no different than in traditional mail surveys. Responses to open-ended questions are documented as longer and more complete than responses to open-ended questions in a traditional mail survey. The lack of anonymity associated with e-mail surveys, though, seems to create more socially desirable responding (SDR) when compared to Web-based surveys. Existing reports on Web-based surveys indicate that data quality (missing data, errors, and item nonresponse) is comparable or better than that of traditional mail surveys. Reliabilities show no difference to either e-mail or paper-and-pencil surveys. These results indicate that Web-based surveys have great potential for becoming a mainstream data collection method in the 21st century.

While the existing literature is promising, many challenges still face researchers seeking to establish the use of Internet surveys as a reliable and valid data collection tool. These challenges represent gaps in the literature that should be addressed through future research. With regard to response rates, the remaining gaps essentially address the questions of how and why. How can response rates be improved? Many articles cited previously indicated that timing (e.g., prenotification and reminders) and technique (e.g., incentives, sponsorship, and personalization) may improve response to Internet surveys. What are the effects of survey length, purpose of research, type of appeal, and other variables on response rate? These tools should be systematically investigated with the goal of determining standardized guides for the implementation of Internet surveys.

Given the difficulty in assessing Web-based survey response rate, some attention must be paid to other measures of response, nonresponse, and drop-out effects. For example, how many individuals view a Web survey page, but choose not to participate? How many begin a survey but do not complete it? How can these different forms of nonresponse be explained and predicted? In other words, response to Web-based surveys may have various levels of commitment on the part of the participant. If so, it is possible that individuals can be categorized into respondent types that can explain response behaviors in Internet surveys. Such a typology may also have implications for data quality. In addition, there exists an entertainment factor on the Internet which may affect response to surveys. Do some individuals possess an affinity to respond to Internet surveys? If so, this affinity may create bias in results.

Further, the effect of confidentiality and anonymity (or the lack thereof) on response rate and response content should be investigated both for e-mail surveys (which have shown evidence of socially desirable responding) and Web-based surveys. Web-based surveys have shown lower SDR than e-mail surveys but have not been compared to traditional mail surveys. Do individuals feel equally protected participating in Web-based surveys and traditional mail surveys? How will changes and advances in the Web environment (like the use of cookies) affect response content and data quality in Web-based surveys? While some research has begun to assess errors and item nonresponse, mixed results have made conclusions difficult to assess.

2.6   Conclusions

While a strong case is being built for the use of Internet surveys as a data collection method, many questions still must be answered before Internet surveys can gain widespread use like that of traditional mail surveys. Future research must seek to fill the gaps in the literature. Generally, researchers must learn more about how to use Internet surveys and why various tools work to improve response rate and quality. In other words, we must not only know the rules for good implementation but must also understand the underlying *psychological processes* that explain why the rules work. Knowing how and why will provide a strong basis for the growth of Internet surveys in research as both an efficient and effective tool. One thing is certain: even a few months ago, despite its attractiveness as an efficient way to reach a potentially large sample of respondents, Internet data collection seemed almost unattainable as a reliable and valid method. With each passing day, more is known about this new and exciting format and the likelihood that Internet surveys will become a widely used tool for both small, defined populations, and, ultimately, for general public surveys increases.

References

Anderson, S. & Gansneder, B. (1995). Using electronic mail surveys and computer-monitored data for studying computer-mediated communication systems. *Social Science Computer Review, 13*, 33-46.

Bachmann, D., Elfrink, J., & Vazzara, G. (1996). Tracking the progress of e-mail vs. snail mail. *Marketing Research, 8*, 31-35.

Bertot, J. C. & McClure, C. (1996). Electronic surveys: Methodological implications for using the www to collect survey data. *Journal of the American Society for Information Science, 33*, 173-185.

Batinic, B. & Bosnjak, M. (2000). Fragebogenuntersuchungen im Internet. In B. Batinic (Ed.), *Internet für Psychologen* (2nd ed.) (pp. 287-317) [Internet for psychologists]. Göttingen: Hogrefe.

Bosnjak, M. (1997). *Internetbasierte, computervermittelte psychologische Fragebogenuntersuchungen.* St. Augustin: Gardez.

Briggs, R. & Hollis, N. (1997). Advertising on the web: Is there response before click-through? *Journal of Advertising Research, 37*, 33-45.

Cleland, K. (1996). Online research costs about half that of traditional methods. *Advertising Age's Business Marketing, 81*, B8-9.

Comley, P. (1996). *The use of the Internet as a data collection method.* [Online]. Available: http://www.sga.co.uk/esomar.html.

Couper, M., Blair, J., & Triplett, T. (1999). A comparison of mail and e-mail for a survey of employees in U.S. statistical agencies. *Journal of Official Statistics, 15*, 39-56.

Davis, G. (1997). Are Internet surveys ready for prime time? *Marketing News, 31*, 31.

Dillman, D. (1978). *Mail and telephone surveys: The total design method.* New York: Wiley and Sons.

Dillman, D. (2000). *Mail and Internet surveys: The tailored design method.* New York: Wiley.

Dillman, D., Tortora, R., Conradt, J., & Bowker, D. (1998). *Influence of plain vs. fancy design on response rates for web surveys.* [Online]. Available: http://survey.sesrc.wsu.edu/dillman/papers/asa98ppr.pdf.

Dillman, D., Tortora, R., & Bowker, D. (1999). *Principles for constructing web surveys.* [Online]. Available: http://survey.sesrc.wsu.edu/dillman/papers.htm.

Frey, J. (1976). *Survey research by Telephone.* Beverly Hills: Sage.

Good, K. (1997). *A study of factors affecting responses in electronic mail surveys.* Dissertation, Western Michigan University, DAI, vol 58-10A pg. 3899, 119 pages.

Harrison, D. A., McLaughlin, M. E., & Coalter, T. M. (1996). Context, cognition, and common method variance: Psychometric and verbal protocol evidence. *Organizational Behavior and Human Decision Processes, 68*, 246-261.

Kanuk, L. & Berenson, C. (1975). Mail surveys and response rates: A literature review. *Journal of Marketing Research, 12*, 440-453.

Kittleson, M. (1995). An assessment of response rate via the postal service and e-mail. *Health Values, 18*, 27-29.

Komsky, S. H. (1991). A profile of users of electronic mail in a university. *Management Communication Quarterly, 4*, 310-340.

Krasilovsky, P. (1996). Surveys in cyberspace. *American Demographics, Supplement, Nov-Dec*, 18-22.

McDaniel, S. & Rao, C. P. (1980). The effect of monetary inducement on mailed questionnaire response quality. *Journal of Marketing Research, 17*, 265-275.

Mehta, R. & Sivada, E. (1995). Comparing response rates and response content in mail versus electronic mail surveys. *Journal of the Market Research Society, 37*, 429-439.

Morrow, R. H. & McKee, A. (1998). CGI scripts: A strategy for between-subjects experimental group assignment on the world wide web. *Behavior Research Methods, Instruments, and Computers, 30*, 306-308.

Opperman, M. (1995). E-mail surveys: Potentials and pitfalls. *Marketing Research, 7*, 29-33.

Parker, L. (1992). Collecting data the e-mail way. *Training and Development, July*, 52-54.

Rietz, I. & Wahl, S. (1999). Vergleich von Selbst- und Fremdbild von PsychologInnen im Internet und auf Papier. In B. Batinic, A. Werner, L. Gräf, & W. Bandilla (Eds.), *Online Research. Methoden, Anwendungen, und Ergebnisse* (pp. 77-92). Göttingen: Hogrefe.

Schaefer, D. R. & Dillman, D. (1998). Development of a standard e-mail methodology: Results from an experiment. *Public Opinion Quarterly, 62*, 378-397.

Schmidt, W. C. (1997). World wide web survey research: Benefits, potential problems, and solutions. *Behavior Research Methods, Instruments, & Computers, 29*, 274-279.

Schonland, A. & Williams, P. (1996). Using the Internet for travel and tourism survey research: Experiences from the Net traveler survey. *Journal of Travel Research, 35*, 81-87.

Schuldt, B. & Totten, J. (1994). Electronic mail vs. mail survey response rates. *Marketing Research, 6*, 36-39.

Smith, C. (1997). Casting the NET: Surveying an Internet population. *Journal of Communication Mediated by Computers, 3*. [Online]. Available: http://www.usc.edu/dept/annenberg/vol3/issue1.

Sproull, L. (1986). Using electronic mail for data collection in organizational research. *Academy of Management Journal, 29*, 159-169.

Stanton, J. (1998). An empirical assessment of data collection using the Internet. *Personnel Psychology, 51*, 709-725.

Swoboda, W., Muehlberger, N., & Schneweiss, S. (1997). Internet surveys by direct mailing. *Social Science Computer Review, 15*, 242-255.

Treat, J. (1997). The effects of questionnaire mode on response in a federal employee survey. *American Statistical Association, Survey Research Methods Section*, 600-604.

Tse, A. C. B., Tse, K. C., Yin, C. H., Ting, C. B., Yi, K. W., Yee, K. P., & Hong, W. C. (1995). Comparing two methods of sending out questionnaires: e-mail versus mail. *Journal of the Market Research Society, 37*, 441-446.

Tuten, T. (1998). Getting a foot in the electronic door: The process of reading and deleting electronic mail. *The Journal of Technical Writing and Communication, 28*, 271-284.

Tuten, T., Bosnjak, M., & Bandilla, W. (2000). Banner-advertised web surveys. *Marketing Research, 11*, 17-22.

Vogt, K. (1999). Verzerrungen in elektronischen Befragungen? In B. Batinic, A. Werner, L. Graef, & W. Bandilla (Eds.), *Online Research Methoden, Anwendungen, und Ergebnisse* (pp. 127-143). Göttingen: Hogrefe.

3 Online Panels

Anja S. Göritz, Nicole Reinhold, & Bernad Batinic

The promise of the Internet to quickly and inexpensively examine large samples and the need to assess special and low-incidence populations have incited a great interest in online data collection. Due to accelerated market dynamics, information about new trends and feedback on released products are required at short notice. With traditional methods it can be difficult and expensive to reach trendsetters and early adopters of new technologies. Surveys among the staff of expanding companies need to be real snapshots, otherwise the results are outdated before the data are analyzed.

An Online Panel (OP) is a pool of registered persons who have agreed to take part in online studies on a regular basis. With the further spreading of the Internet, OP's have become increasingly attractive to researchers from both marketing and academic backgrounds because they have the potential to serve those new needs. At the same time, they have additional advantages over other forms of online data collection.

At the beginning of this chapter, the reader is presented with an introduction into the methodological background of the classical panel approach. We take a closer look at the transitions that occur when the traditional panel methodology meets the Internet. An outline is given of how a prototypical OP is operated on a practical level and what IT is needed. Later in this text, the standing of the OP method with respect to other techniques of online data gathering is investigated. The chapter informs about the advantages of the OP method and describes different forms of OP's. Finally, the results of a recent survey among panel operators give insight into the status quo of research with OP's.

3.1 Before There Were Online Panels: Methodological Background of Classical Panels

In the classical sense, a panel design is a longitudinal study in which information is collected from the same participants at different time points on the same dependent variables. The points in time when data are collected are referred to as *panel waves*. Like other longitudinal designs, panel analyses can depict change, be it social, economic, or political because they uniquely allow one to test time-related hypotheses.

With regard to temporal analysis different observation plans are feasible. *Time-series* data record the state of a dependent variable at many points in time for one member of a population. Panel data, therefore, can be viewed as time-series data for more than one sample unit. In contrast to time-series data, the number of collection points is smaller (often two or three time points) whereas the number of sample units is higher. *Multiple time-series* data refer to data collected on a small number of individuals at many dates. Multiple time-series and panel data differ primarily in the relative amount of temporal variation versus intra-unit variation, which affects the kinds of questions that can be addressed effectively with one rather than the other (Tuma & Hannan, 1984). Panel data can also be gathered *retrospectively* with a cross-sectional design. The determining characteristic of the retrospective approach is a lag between the time of data gathering and the point in time to which the measurement refers. For example, respondents may be asked whether they were unemployed last year, five years ago, and ten years ago.

In a *trend design,* data on the same dependent variables are collected from different but statistically comparable individuals at multiple time points. This approach is analogous to a series of cross-sections on the same topic. Panel studies' advantages over trend designs are twofold. Fieldwork costs are reduced because the fixed costs for the recruitment and the selection of a sample incur only once – namely at the first wave of the panel. Secondly, costs to reach persons who were sampled but are not willing to participate are higher in cross-sections than in panel studies. In other words, the drop-out rate is generally lower with panel studies than with cross-sections. With panel studies, however, there arise also panel specific expenses in the form of following costs to reach participants who live farther away, costs to track respondents who have moved house, and, last but not least, considerable outlays resulting from measures of panel maintenance.

Panel designs and trend designs merely represent the extreme poles on a continuum of designs with overlapping consecutive samples. While the overlap in a static panel is 100%, it is 0% in a pure trend design. Observation plans that lie between those ends are referred to as rotating panels. Their defining characteristic is that a certain number of sample units, but not all, are examined repeatedly. The purpose of such a dynamic panel is to maintain generalizability while constantly adapting to a changing universe. Rejuvenation is achieved through regularly recruiting a proportion of fresh, and expelling stale, panelists while maintaining structural equivalence.

Panel analyses are more informative than trend analyses. In panel data, one can analyze change with a higher resolution than with trend data. Since in a panel study the same sample units are observed, change can be analyzed on the level of the individuals whereas by means of a trend design change can only be registered in an aggregated fashion. Put differently, panel data cannot only inform about the Net change as trend data can but also about the turnover and the direction of the change between different time points. Further advantages of the panel approach are:

- It is possible to distinguish between cohort, age, and period effects. These normally confounded influences can be isolated by taking different analytical perspectives on panel data.
- In the course of a panel study, a trustful relationship with the respondents can be built. This rapport can allow one to ask more intimate questions than would have been possible in the first wave or in a one-time survey.
- The measurement of change with the help of a panel design is less prone to sample error because the same sample units are examined. Yet in panel designs, measurement errors such as situational factors, interviewer effects, or coding and counting inaccuracies are more detrimental than in trend designs. While in trend designs errors of that kind partly cancel each other out, in panel designs they can mistakenly lead to the covering-up of actual change or the appearance of change where there is stability (Hanefeld, 1987, p.23).

That does not mean, however, that panel designs should always be preferred to trend designs. A trend design should be favored if the objective of a study is to inform about the Net change over a series of time points while ensuring representativeness at each point of data collection. The great strength of a trend design is the dynamic adjustment to a changing universe.

This points to certain critical factors inherent in the panel approach. First, there is the risk of inordinate *selection bias*. Panelists need to invest far more time and effort than participants in one-time surveys. It has been demonstrated that the initial refusal rate is twice as high when recruiting for a panel as opposed to a representative cross-sectional study (Roth, 1993, p.287).

Drop-out threatens the external validity of both cross- and longitudinal sections because, as has been demonstrated, participants and nonrespondents differ in a number of characteristics (Rosnow & Rosenthal, 1976). In the panel context the systematic and nonsystematic drop-out of sample units is called *panel attrition*. One can differentiate between a temporary (wave drop-out) and a permanent drop-out (panel drop-out). The number of panelists can dwindle for a multitude of reasons such as natural mortality, moves or other reasons of nonaccessibility, refusal due to losing interest, an ever changing interviewer, or concerns with data security. Other influences have to do with the analyzed variables and can result in education biases, age biases, and class biases of the remaining sample. Attrition tends to be high at the beginning of a panel study and slopes with an increasing amount of waves (Rendtel, 1990). After the first wave of the panel, the bias of the panel sample can be gauged by comparing relevant characteristics of the loyal and the unfaithful participants.

The term *panel maintenance* refers to all the undertakings that are aimed at reducing panel attrition. Panel maintenance can roughly be divided into three components: the motivation of the respondents, the tracking of straying participants, and the motivation of the interviewers. The motivation of the respondents involves measures to waken interest, facilitate participation, and create an atmosphere of mutual trust. This can be achieved through personalized cover letters, birthday, Christmas cards, brochures or other information on the research subject, payment or give-aways, or lotteries. Certain strategies (e.g., paid participation or passing on survey results) have the potential to promote sample bias or can lead to uncontrollable panel bias. The respondents can be unburdened through lean questionnaires, a reasonable frequency of panel waves, and a careful selection of questions with regard to wording, complexity, and invasion. Trust can be enhanced by ensuring that the participants are informed about issues of data confidentiality. Personal contact is helpful if sought by a panelist. Employing a constant interviewer is equally conducive to the stability of the panel sample (Rendtel, 1990).

Panel bias is another threat to the validity of panel data. The term panel bias denotes a change of the behavior of the respondents as a consequence of their participation in the panel. Natural reactions of panelists are altered due to their awareness of being part of the panel (Hawthorne effect), repeated exposures to the survey topic and the interviewer, similar questionnaires, and measures of panel maintenance. Typical panel bias occurs due to reinterview effects, freezing effects (exaggerated consistency of reactions), and over reporting. It is conceivable, however, that taking part in a panel does not necessarily compromise a panelist's responses, but, in fact, can cause the responses to become closer to the "true values". For example, practice reduces the unfamiliarity with the survey material or uneasiness with the interviewing situation. Panel bias can be made visible by paralleling a given panel wave with an independent cross-sectional survey. One attack on panel bias is to rotate the measurement of the dependent variables through the panelists so that all the information is not collected every time from the same panelists, but alternately from different subgroups of the panel sample.

Finally, there is a problem of *data security*. Because the collected information from every wave needs to be traced back to the individual panelists, panel analyses cannot be conducted with fully anonymized data. Despite all the efforts to ensure confidentiality, there remains a risk of identification, which can lead to nonparticipation (Laatz, 1993, p.546).

It should be noted that both the temporal design of a study (cross-sectional or longitudinal) and the design for variance control (experimental or quasi-experimental) are independent of the applied method of data collection. Panel data, for instance, can be collected through reactive and nonreactive observation with and without technological aids, telephone surveys, self-administered questionnaires, and one-on-one interviews. The chosen method and medium of data collection, however, affect panel bias and attrition and also determine which measures of panel maintenance are feasible.

3.2   What Does the Transfer of the Classical Panel Approach to the Internet Entail?

An OP is a pool of registered persons who have agreed to take part in online studies on a regular basis. As pointed out above, the classical panel approach implies data-gathering from the same participants at multiple time points on the same dependent variables. With an OP, this traditional understanding is widened because it can also be employed as a sampling source for diverse studies. Contemporary OP's closely resemble so-called "Access Panels". In the offline world, most commercial market research institutes have at their disposal such a reservoir of registered participants. Access Panels, therefore, are not a specific online phenomenon. The unique aspect of online Access Panels is that the special advantages of the Net can be brought to bear. Such an Access Panel, be it online or offline, can be worked with from different analytical perspectives. It is possible to examine static relationships among variables with cross-sectional designs as well as to carry out temporal analyses, which depict change over time.

The methodological deviation from the classical panel concept has generated some confusion among researchers as to whether the name "panel" still applies. We would like to suggest a negative definition for what an OP is. As a methodological demarcation, the term "OP" should not be used for respondent-banks, which, in principle, cannot comply with the notion of a classical panel and, therefore, do not make possible longitudinal designs. In those pseudo OP, respondents select themselves for the surveys they are interested in, whereas in a "real" OP, panelists select themselves for the panel in its entirety but not for individual surveys. In respondent-banks, the respondents' addresses are stored in a database for identification purposes only because it has to be guaranteed that they are compensated for their participation. Due to the self-selection of panelists, a complete association of earlier responses with repeated questions at a later wave cannot be accomplished. That is why recording comprehensive profile data and a history is superfluous. Two examples for such pseudo OP we found on the Web are "Greenfield Online"[1] and "Technologypanel.com"[2].

---

[1] http://www.greenfieldonline.com/
[2] http://www.technologypanel.com/

In addition to the methodological distinction, the differentiation into online[3] versus offline panel is somewhat blurry. One can roughly break down the stages of a panel into recruitment resulting in the feeding of the panelists' master data into the database, sampling, invitation, data collection, and rewarding. Difficulties in extracting a common denominator arise from the offline or online implementation of all those steps combined with the possible usage of a variety of methods of data collection. Nonreactive observations of the surfing-behavior by means of client-logs, interviews in chat rooms, e-mail surveys, and WWW-fill-in forms are such example forms of online data collection. Again, we would like to suggest a negative definition. In our opinion, the term OP should not be used if study data are collected exclusively offline. One example is a WWW site linked up with a database that solely aims at recruiting panelists online but studies are carried out offline. One real-life example is the "Mystery Shopper"[4] scheme, which is a mere Web-based front-end of an otherwise offline panel.

The double-faced nature of Access Panels brings about more confusion of ideas with regard to the concepts "panel attrition" and "panel wave". The term panel attrition stems from the classical panel, and so it does not quite apply. In an OP, there are three possible types of drop-out. In individual one-time OP surveys, there can occur *OP survey nonresponse*, in the entire pool of participants permanent *OP attrition* and in longitudinal OP studies *OP wave attrition*. It rests with the individual OP administrator to decide after how many times of not responding to survey invitations a panelist is expelled from the panel. A less arbitrary point to determine the OP attrition is to eliminate nominal members on the occasion of prompting the panelists to update their profile.

Similarly, the term "panel wave" does not make sense in an Access Panel because it is unsuited to cross-sectional surveys.

To sum up, this paragraph illustrates the problems that go along with any attempt to recycle traditional terms. Because the concepts "panel attrition" and "panel wave" were developed for classical panels, they are at best meaningful for the longitudinal facet of an Access Panel.

Operating an OP at the same time both as a sampling source for various studies and as a classical panel can be methodologically compromising because uncontrollable panel bias might arise. In contrast to a classical panel where all the panelists are confronted with the same studies at the same frequency, this is mostly not the case in an OP. Online panelists have different survey histories and consequently do not take part in individual studies under equal conditions. To minimize cross-over, the same

---

[3]   Recently the term *online* has undergone a change of meaning. While it used to denote *being connected to a switched-on computer,* increasingly it is interpreted as *connected to or on the Internet.*

[4]   http://rampages.onramp.net/~focus/Shop_Info.html

panelists should not be sampled into both longitudinal and cross-sectional studies. In principle, however, the risk of carry-over effects also extends to successive one-time surveys.

By transferring the classical panel approach to the Internet, unique methodological particularities and numerous possibilities of how to run an OP on a practical level arise. The entire operation of a panel can be implemented on the Internet so that no offline contact between the panelists and the managers or researchers is necessary. Some of those implications and new questions shall be discussed briefly:

OP units can be individuals or households. In contrast to offline panels, an OP unit is comfortably identified by its e-mail address because it is faster and cheaper to invite sampled panelists by e-mail. Because everybody can get a vast number of free e-mail addresses, multiple registration of the same panelist as well as inaccessibility (because some e-mailboxes are not checked as regularly as conventional mailboxes) occur more often than in offline access panels.

The fieldwork phase in an OP survey is considerably shorter than usual. This asset, together with the economies when answering research questions, permit the frequency of surveys or panel waves to be substantially higher than in an offline panel. However, there is the need to find an optimum between, on one hand, participation fatigue and panel bias and, on the other hand, motivation and commitment (and profit).

Moreover, typical courses of panel careers of online panelists are largely unknown. How and for how long can panelists be bound? How is drop-out linked to characteristics of the panelists? What impact on survey drop-out or wave attrition does the lack of an interviewer have?

The Internet permits the utilization of innovative and easy-to-realize measures of panel maintenance such as newsletters, online games, and redeemable bonus-points. The effect of incentives on data quality and drop-out is chiefly unknown. There are, however, first indications that online survey drop-out can be reduced by material incentives (Frick, Bächtiger, & Reips, 1999; Knapp & Heidingsfelder, 1999). With regard to the rewarding of the panelists, an equilibrium needs to be found between ensuring their readiness to participate and discouraging incentive-hunters.

And finally, logging of page-contacts allows the researcher to monitor the participation process like never before.

3.3   How Does an Online Panel Work?

As can be seen in Figure 3.1, the OP circle starts with the potential panelists arriving at the OP Web site. Interested persons find their way to the site either by responding to measures of site-promotion such as submissions to search engines, banners and intercept technologies, links, viral marketing, mailing-lists or newsgroups, word-of-mouth, and referral schemes, or upon invitation by mail, e-mail, or phone. Panelists can also be recruited at the end of a one-time survey. According to Raulfs' (1998) and our own experience approximately 60% of survey respondents can be won over to a panel. Once on the Web site, potential panelists sign-up by filling out a registration form. In this questionnaire the panelists' profile data are gathered (e.g., socio-demographic and personal information) and fed into the linked-up database. When a sufficient number of panelists or a satisfactory number of particular target persons have enrolled, they can be sampled and subsequently invited to surveys. In order to keep nonresponse low, panelists normally are compensated for their participation. Possible incentives, which can also be used in combination, are direct payment, bonus-points, raffle tickets, options to donate the prizes, products, stock options, or nonmaterial inducements. The quality of OP data can be augmented by an array of measures such as time measurements on survey forms, regular updates of the profiles, following-up of unheeded invitations, consistency and reliability checks, reduction of OP attrition through measures of panel maintenance, and identity checks through offline contacts.

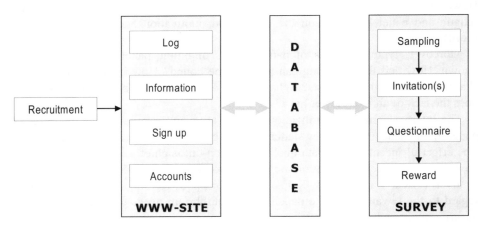

Figure 3.1: Model of an OP

3.4   Which IT-Infrastructure Is Needed to Operate a Typical Online Panel?

The backbone of an OP is a secured high performance Web-server with an OP Web site that is connected to a database. Typically, the Web site consists of the registration form, a possibility to contact the researchers or managers, and general pages that inform the visitor about the nature of the panel: how it works, who it runs, what the members can get for their participation, the panelists' rights and duties. The site can also accommodate password-protected personal areas where panelists are informed about open surveys, can update their profile data, and can inspect their account of amassed incentives and redeem them. The content of these personal areas is dynamically generated by automatically querying the database and displaying the contents of the corresponding cells. For more convenience, one requires an interface-tool that is coupled with the database. Ideally this tool enables the researcher, via a graphical interface, to draw random or quota samples from either the entire panel population, or from only a particular segment of the panel, which can be specified on the basis of the panelists' master data and histories. Then the tool automatically sends e-mail invitations to the sampled panelists and sets their survey-status in the database to "invited". Apart from mentioning the topic and the URL of the survey and what participants can earn, the invitation e-mail states the deadline for submission and approximately how long it takes to fill-in the survey. The panelists, then, can proceed to the survey-site and after a password-authentication the survey unfolds. Also, the interface-tool automatically administers the personal accounts of every panelist. Upon electronic submission of a completed survey the previous database-status "invited" is altered to "complete" and the panelist's account is credited with the prespecified compensation. In order to redeem the incentives, the panelist logs on to the personal area. Via a contact form the person can place an order, whereupon the incentives are paid off and the account is reset. The details of this process depend on the form of compensation used.

3.5   How Do Online Panels Compare to Other Methods of Online Data Collection?

Meanwhile the following insight has become commonplace: Because participants select themselves, WWW surveys are neither representative for the general population nor for the population of Internet users. This also applies to most of the current OP's. It is important to heed, however, that in general, online panelists select themselves for the panel in its entirety, but they do not choose themselves for individual surveys. For separate studies the OP is merely the sampling source from which probabilistic samples can be drawn. Consequently, self-selection takes effect only in the first (but most important) recruitment stage. Thus, undetectable confounds between the criteria of self-selection (e.g., Internet-usage, willingness to participate) and the research question can discredit study results. Strong sampling bias can be alleviated by using a multitude of online and offline recruitment techniques and locations. A validation of OP data through parallel representative offline surveys can unveil possible influences of the research medium and/or the sampling. If one were repeatedly to conduct expensive offline surveys alongside OP surveys, however, the sense of working with an OP would be undermined.

Self-selection is the most common but by no means the only possible course. If a universe is well defined and accessible, it can be made part of an OP, and therefore, be examined in this entirely. One example is a staff panel of a firm where all personnel have e-mail. Furthermore, switching media when recruiting panelists can be a way out of the representativeness problem. This way, the recruitment of participants happens by means of representative offline random samples (e.g., through CATI). All persons who have a PC and Internet access are eligible panel units. Such an OP can represent the community of Internet-users. Moreover, an offline recruited OP whose panelists are snail-mailed further access information is virtually free from duplicate registrations and inaccurate identity information (postal address, e-mail-address, and phone number). Another method of circumventing self-selection without a media-break is to send an invitation e-mail to randomly chosen Internet-users. One obstacle with this approach is the lack of a list of all Internet-users in analogy to a telephone directory in the offline world. Secondly and more important, sending unsolicited e-mails infringes the Netiquette. (At present calling people is not considered as unethical as sending spam-e-mails although a telephone call is more invasive.)

From an existing OP, regardless of whether it was recruited online or offline, probabilistic and nonprobabilistic samples can be drawn for separate surveys. In this connection, quota samples, in general, are not an adequate means to attain representativeness. A quota sample imitates the familiar distribution of characteristics within a desired universe. Face-to-face interviewers often arbitrarily interview persons according to their accessibility while fulfilling the set quota. In contrast to that, OP administrators, with the help of OP software, can choose panelists less-biased by subjective or availability factors. For the results from a quota sample to be generalizable at all, the criteria for the quota need to be relevant to the research question and be as exhaustive as possible. In order to fulfill the quota, reliable estimations about the universe's size and composition are required. Frequently, this information is not retrievable or up-to-date, and as a result, only obvious characteristics like demographics can be taken into account.

An ongoing challenge is making sure that a panel, once constructed, continues to accurately represent the reference population. This can be achieved by sample management, which has two components: ensuring ongoing co-operation from existing panelists through measures of panel maintenance, and bringing fresh people into the panel. In the first paragraph of this chapter we have seen that challenges of that kind are not unique to the online arena. However, because of the ongoing qualitative and quantitative changes of the Internet Community, it is especially costly to keep an OP up-to-date.

Thanks to the unstoppable spreading of the Internet not only OP's but also respondent-banks could sprout. As pointed out earlier, here respondents are not sampled but select themselves for all the individual surveys, too. Because respondent-banks share the same medium with OP's, as well as with one-time online surveys, they have a number of practical benefits in common. These include fast and cost effective turn-around of results, the opportunity to obtain large and heterogeneous samples, freedom from the constraints of testing people at a particular time and place, support of complicated routing patterns, diminished intrusiveness because respondents can self-schedule, real-time input-validation, broader stimuli potential through the integration of multimedia elements, standardization of experimenter effects, possibilities of conducting cross-cultural research without the expense of traveling, error reduction due to automated data handling, respondent monitoring through logfile analyses, and elimination of bias through randomized ordering of items and alternative answers (see Birnbaum, 2001).

3.6   What Extra-Advantages Do Online Panels Have?

OP's have numerous economic and methodological advantages over offline studies and over online studies where participants are recruited each time afresh. An OP affords great flexibility with regard to possible study designs. The whole range of both temporal observation plans (cross-sections and longitudinal studies) and designs for variance control (experimental and nonexperimental) can be realized. As described earlier, with OP's the representativity problem can at least be alleviated because panelists do not select themselves for individual surveys but for the panel in its entirety. Lacking generalizability can be avoided, altogether, through representative offline recruitment. Also, there are types of studies, which become smoothly realizable only with an OP because they demand special coordination and scheduling. One example is the evaluation of TV or radio shows. Panelists can be asked in advanced to watch a certain program and afterwards give their opinions.

The readiness to participate and, as a result, the response rate is usually higher than in free-standing WWW surveys. Moreover, the profiles and data gathered from earlier studies are known. Provided the OP is large enough, particular target samples (e.g., widows over 45 years of age) can be drawn without time- and money-consuming prescreening of large shares of the population. If need be, specific or low-incidence segments of the population can speedily be incorporated into the OP by means of (at times expensive) tailored recruitment campaigns. Because both the panelists' profile data and history are available, the items contained in a questionnaire can be limited to the truly pertinent ones. In contrast to free standing WWW questionnaires, the survey nonresponse rate can be calculated more accurately. It is known which persons with which profiles have failed to take part. This information allows a rough estimation of the sample bias. The occurrence of multiple participation is less likely in OP surveys than in one-time WWW surveys. Because an OP is operated on the (market) research with an OP is less expensive and faster. E-mails are cheaper and quicker to send than telephone calls or letters. The high degree of automation further reduces the operating costs. For instance, the sending of reminders to unheeded invitations or e-mails, which inquire whether a panelist is still interested to be in the OP, can be automatically scheduled. If an online gratification scheme is used, the crediting of a panelist's account happens immediately and automatically upon participation. Also, no labor is necessary for the allocation of incentives. Because researchers can fall back on a stock of potential respondents the time and expenses of recruitment are drastically reduced. Considering the rising participation fatigue of the Internet-population, it is more than likely that these economies are not neutralized by the newly arising costs due to panel maintenance.

3.7   Which Types of Online Panels Can Be Distinguished?

As pointed out in the second paragraph, the panel approach is compatible with different methods of data collection. The chosen design, method, and medium of data collection determine how OP's can be classified. First, there is the already mentioned discrimination between OP's and non OP's on two dimensions. According to the methodological panel definition, we distinguish OP's and respondent-banks. With regard to the medium of data collection, we distinguish offline panels versus online panels.

Once it is clear that one is dealing with an OP, further differentiation according to the used design is possible. On the temporal dimension, one can separate cross-sectional OP's from longitudinal OP's. According to the degree of variance control, it is possible to distinguish experimental from quasi-experimental panels. With regard to the applied method of data collection, multiple distinctions on manifold dimensions are possible. There can be OP's for more qualitative research versus OP's for rather quantitative research. In analogy to offline TV panels, there are nonreactive observation panels. Two examples are MediaMetrix[5] and NetValue[6]. The panelists' surfing behavior is constantly being monitored by means of consensually "bugged" clients or other software.

---

[5]   http://www.mmxi.com/
[6]   http://www.netvalue.com/

According to the medium of recruitment, OP's can be classified as offline re-cruited OP's versus online recruited OP's and therefore (but not necessarily) repre-sentative and nonrepresentative OP's. Another form of categorization takes the types of panelists into account. For instance, there are expert OP, staff OP, and consumer OP. Other classifications are possible according to the multifarious ways in which OP's can be implemented (e.g., used measures of panel maintenance, structure of the Web site, communication strategy).

3.8   What Is the Status Quo of Online Panel Research?

In order to get an overview of the state of research with OP's, we carried out a survey among OP operators in August and September 1999 (Göritz, Reinhold, & Batinic, 2000). The results of this survey elucidate how contemporary OP's are run on a prac-tical level and how they deal with different aspects of data quality. With the help of different search engines, we found 64 OP's that – at first sight – fulfilled the required criteria. That is, they did not seem to be pure respondent-banks and they did not ap-pear to exclusively gather study data offline. Our search was thorough but possibly not exhaustive. Also, our survey population is presumably biased towards English and German OP's because we made use of international and German search engines with English and German keywords.

Data were collected in two steps. First, we visited the OP sites and extracted as much information as possible on the variables in question. Next, we sent tailored e-mail questionnaires that contained questions we could not answer by visiting the sites as well as some open-ended items. When information from the OP sites differed from that of the mailing, we prioritized the questionnaire data. The overall response rate to the e-mail questionnaire was 39% (25 OP's) composed of 25% to the first mailing and 14% to a follow-up two weeks later. Two of the 64 OP sites contained invalid e-mail-addresses, so our questionnaires could not be delivered. The replies varied greatly in elaboration.

3.8.1   Description of the Panel Projects and Their Web sites

Reach: 34 of the sites indicate holding international panelists, 16 sites are bound to North America and 3 sites recruit exclusively Germans. We lack information from 11 sites.

Language: Eight sites are in German and the remaining 56 in English.

Age: 22 managers told us the year when they were founded. As visualized in Fig-ure 3.2, especially in 1999 OP's were sprouting. Because of the selection bias inher-ent in this study, this tendency is possibly undervalued. For us, it was more likely to come across older panels because they have more links pointing to them or have been indexed by robots with a higher probability.

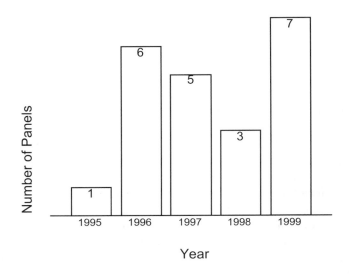

Figure 3.2: Year of foundation

Background: 56 OP's have a predominantly market research background and two have an academic background. Six sites could not be classified.

Demo-questionnaire: Nine operators offer their site visitors a test questionnaire prior to registration. The remaining 55 do not do so.

Personal areas: 26 sites comprise password-protected personal areas for their panelists. 27 do without this luxury. Of one site, we lack information.

Clientele: On 31 sites, potential panelists and customers are addressed simultaneously; whereas 33 panel sites exclusively concentrate on attracting and serving panelists.

Scope: 21 panels are dedicated to a particular topic (mostly IT or Internet related). The remaining panels are unrestricted in this sense.

Size: 24 OP's gave information about their number of panelists. As can be seen in Figure 3.3, the sizes ranged from 10 to 600.000 panelists. This heterogeneity partly is a result of the differing age of the panels. Some have been founded fairly recently and, therefore, are unlikely to be comprised of a great number of members. Moreover, it is questionable whether the more than 420.000 panelists in the three largest panels are active members. It is conceivable that those figures merely represent e-mail-addresses in a database.

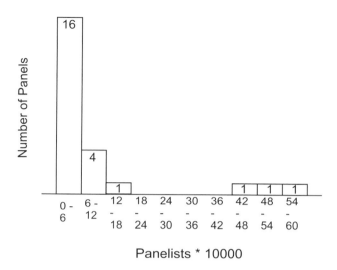

Figure 3.3: Number of panelists

Methods: In addition to quantitative online methods, 28 operators also use qualitative online methods for data collection such as online focus groups or interviews in chat rooms. 19 operators answered in the negative and 17 did not reply to this question.

Sign-up: Currently, with 54 sites, there is an accessible registration form; whereas with the remaining ten panels, there is no possibility to sign-up or the panel declares itself as being "full".

Recruitment: 11 managers indicated that they also recruit panelists offline. 42 solely recruit online and 11 did not answer.

Medium: All 51 panels from which we have information, gather data online (13 did not answer). Thus, our criteria for an online versus offline panel were met by all the sites. 21 operators apply offline methods in parallel such as telephone interviews, product evaluations, or focus groups whereas 30 panels exclusively use online methods.

Media break: 23 panels indicated that they are pure online panels where no medium other than the Internet is used. In contrast, 29 panels indicated sometimes leaving the Internet either for studies that involve offline contacts, for offline recruitment or offline identity checks via fax, telephone or snail mail. We do not have unequivocal information from the remaining 12 panels.

Test phase: Nine operators indicated to have had an elaborate test run or an experimental phase where different strategies were tried out. Five said they have not (yet) experimented with different ways to run the panel, 50 did not answer at all. Of the panels that tested different strategies, four operators stated that they were able to augment the survey response rate by increasing the compensation, whereas one panel said this tactic had no effect. One operator indicated that direct rewards work best. Another one remarked that the return rate drops markedly if more than the standard software is required for participation. One manager stated that the return rate can be augmented drastically by implementing additional raffles (e.g., PC's) from time to time. The methodological background of these narrative results is unknown.

Turn-round time: 23 administrators voiced the average duration of their fieldwork, which can be seen in Figure 3.4. The mean duration of data collection is nine days. We can see that results are obtained very quickly not only in theory but also in actuality.

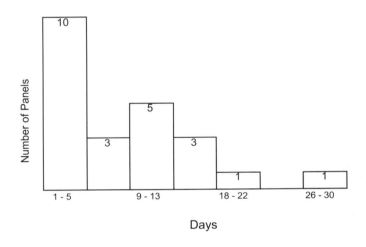

Figure 3.4: Days of fieldwork

3.8.2   Data Quality

Sampling: In eight panels respondents select themselves for individual surveys, and not only for the panel in its entirety. Because there was no sampling and subsequent inviting of panelists, our methodological criteria for an OP was violated. 44 sites do sample and invite their panelists to individual studies and from 12, we have no information.

Profiles: 53 panels gather profile data from their panelists at registration. Five stated that they do not collect any master data and from 6 panels, we do not know. Figure 3.5 depicts the number of profile items for the 53 panels. The median is 16 to 20 items. When we tried to submit an empty registration form we succeeded with eight panels but with the remaining 45, we were prompted to complete our entries (i.e., there is an automatic input validation).

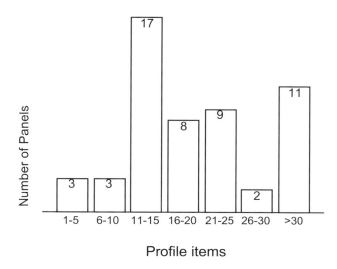

Figure 3.5: Number of profile items

Update of profiles: With 36 panels, the panelists' profiles are updated. Of these, 26 leave the frequency of this revision to the discretion of their panelists. Five administrators prompt their panelists to update their profiles once a year and another five sites prompt panelists every other year. Three administrators stated that there is no update taking place and 25 panels did not answer this question. This brings up the question of which criteria are used to expel merely nominal panel members from the database. Eight operators said they never exclude the data from the database, 43 did not answer this question and 11 stated that they do sweep the panel. Naturally, the researchers' criteria for excluding a panelist differ markedly. The following list includes exemplary answers: 1) after three or five times of not taking part in a survey, 2) multiple registrations of e-mail- or postal address, 3) invitation e-mail is not deliverable, 4) when panelists try to click through surveys, and 5) no response to e-mails which asks whether a person is still interested to be in the panel.

Postal address: To know the panelists' postal address is useful in many ways. Multiple registration is easier to detect because a panel unit is not merely identified by its comparatively variable e-mail-address. The scope of feasible studies is enlarged because one can make use of offline elements of data collection and panel maintenance (e.g., sending products for evaluation or giving material presents), which can also serve the subsidiary purpose of checking the panel unit and thereby promoting data quality. In our sample population, 40 sites ask for the postal and not only for the e-mail address of their participants, 11 sites do not collect the postal address and from the remaining 13 sites, we could not procure relevant information.

OP attrition: 15 administrators indicate an average survey response rate, which is depicted in Figure 3.6. The mean percentage of returned surveys is 53% with a minimum of 10% and a maximum of 75%. Also, 15 operators appraise the proportion of persons who only register and then do not take part in any study to which they are invited. The average of those estimates was 22% with a minimum of 2% and a maximum of 60%.

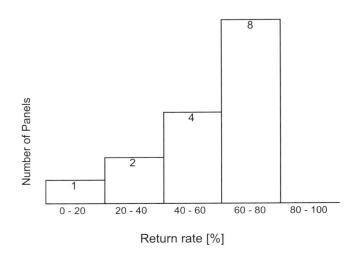

Figure 3.6: Return rate

Completeness: 15 administrators estimate the percentage of completed questions in their surveys. The mean is 84% with a minimum of 25% and a maximum of 100%.

Follow-ups: Twelve managers stated that they regularly e-mail follow-ups to unheeded invitations. Three of them estimated that 50% of the hitherto missing data could be gathered through this measure. Two panels gauge the success of such reminders to be 10% and one panel said 15%. Ten operators answered that they do not send reminders. 42 did not respond to this question.

Time measurements: Seven operators indicated carrying out time measurements on their surveys. Ten managers said "no" and from 47, we did not have information.

Individual measures: Ten operators answered an open-ended question that asked what other measures operators take to increase data quality. Some of the mentioned actions were: "reconfirmation of answers via telephone", "cross-referencing with the initial recruitment questionnaire", "design of questionnaire forms", "elimination of outliers on the basis of technical knowledge in the field", "pretests", and "technical support".

3.8.3   Panel Maintenance

Extrinsic motivation: 53 administrators compensate their panelists with material incentives of which 45 related that they rely on a variable gratification scheme and five on a unchanging one. Respondents from the variable group told us that the form and amount of compensation mainly depends on the customer, the budget, or the demands with regard to data quality. Four operators do not grant any material incentives and seven did not answer this question. Of the 53 panels which compensate panelists with material incentives, 33 reward directly either in cash or per check, ten rely on redeemable bonus-points, 26 stage sweepstakes, four offer the possibility of donating earned money, and 16 send presents (Audio-CD's, Internet access, software, T-shirts, gift certificates, or panelists can keep tested products). Multiple responses were possible because – as we have seen – the majority of panels gratify their panelists in a variable fashion. In addition to the regular compensation, with ten OP's panelists are entered into drawings or receive bonus points when signing-up. 25 panels said that they handle the allocation of incentives themselves whereas six panels said they rely upon cooperating firms or on a gratification scheme that involves an outsourcing of the distribution of material inducements (e.g., Amazon's electronic gift vouchers). 33 did not answer this question.

We also included a question for the granted amount of material gratification. Although managers were asked to estimate a per hour payment, 13 indicated a per survey payment. The mean amount of dollars per survey was 18, with a minimum of three and a maximum of 57. Since we have no information on how long it takes to fill out those surveys, however, this figure can only be of orientation value. Seven panels stated an average payment per hour of which the mean was $26 with a minimum of four and a maximum of 60. Five panels do not award direct payment but work with sweepstakes. They raffle off an average of $115 with a minimum of 50 and a maximum of 250 per survey.

Intrinsic motivation: More than half of the managers employ nonmaterial inducements in an attempt to evoke intrinsic motivation with their panelists: 11 sites promise fun, entertainment, or education, 22 assure that the panelists' opinion will make a change or shape the future, four sites mention that there is a benefit to academic research, five panels send newsletters, 21 operators communicate survey results at least sometimes, three send e-mails, and two panels feature a chat room.

3.8.4   Summary of the Survey

The heterogeneity of contemporary OP's reflect the pioneering spirit in this comparatively new arena. Current panels are trailblazers in finding out how to operate an OP effectively on a practical as well as on a methodological level. Undoubtedly, quality standards will develop with more experience in the field and a rising awareness of the technical and methodological potential inherent in the OP approach. Because of the small population and the porous data set from this survey among operators, any deductions that transcend a merely descriptive level (e.g., the relationship between survey-drop-out and amount and form of compensation) appear too speculative. As a consequence of the possible nonresponse bias many of the descriptive results of this survey are to be interpreted with caution. All in all, this survey gives a vital overview of the status quo of research involving OP's

3.9 Prospect

The research method OP combines the potential of panel designs with the benefits of the Internet as a platform for data collection. The Internet has now reached almost into one in three households in the Western world, and it continues to expand. The issues that we are facing today in terms of representativity of the online population can be viewed as transitory, in the same way that telephone interviewing was perceived in its initial stages. The lure of conducting comparatively inexpensive studies combined with a bundle of other advantages, as well as the whirled-up practical and methodological questions, should bring about a surge of systematic studies in the near future.

References

Birnbaum, M. H. (2001). *Introduction to behavioral research on the Internet*. Upper Saddle River, NJ: Prentice Hall.

Frick, A., Bächtiger, M. T., & Reips, U. (1999). *Financial incentives, personal information, and drop-out rate in online studies*. Paper presented on GOR '99. [Online]. Available: http://dgof.de/tband99/pdfs/a_h/frick.pdf.

Göritz, A. S., Reinhold, N., & Batinic, B. (2000). Marktforschung mit Online Panels: State of the Art. *Planung & Analyse, 3*, 62-67.

Hanefeld, U. (1987). *Das Sozio-ökonomische Panel: Grundlagen und Konzeption*. Frankfurt am Main, New York: Campus Verlag.

Knapp, F. & Heidingsfelder, M. (1999). *Drop-Out-Analyse: Wirkungen des Untersuchungsdesigns*. Paper presented on GOR '99. [Online]. Available: http://dgof.de/tband99/pdfs/i_p/knapp.pdf.

Laatz, W. (1993). *Empirische Methoden: ein Lehrbuch für Sozialwissenschaftler*. Frankfurt am Main: Deutsch.

Raulfs, A. (1998). Re: WWW Panel. *German Internet Research List gir-l*. [Online]. Available: http://infosoc.uni-koeln.de/archives/gir-l/msg00629.html.

Rendtel, U. (1990). Teilnahmebereitschaft in Panelstudien: Zwischen Beeinflussung, Vertrauen und Sozialer Selektion. *Kölner Zeitschrift für Soziologie und Sozialpsychologie, 42*, 280-299.

Rendtel, U. (1995). *Lebenslagen im Wandel: Panelausfälle und Panelrepräsentativität.* Frankfurt am Main, New York: Campus Verlag.

Rosnow, R. & Rosenthal, R. (1975). The volunteer subject revisited. *Australian Journal of Psychology, 28*, 97-108.

Roth, E. (Ed.). (1993). *Sozialwissenschaftliche Methoden: Lehr- und Handbuch für Forschung und Praxis.* München, Wien: Oldenbourg.

Tuma, N. B. & Hannan, M. T. (1984). *Social dynamics: models and methods.* Orlando: Academic Press.

4 Assessing Internet Questionnaires: The Online Pretest Lab

Lorenz Gräf

Questionnaires for the World Wide Web (WWW) are easy to plan and can be distributed over a large area. Carrying out surveys being that simple, one can easily forget that questionnaires are an artificial form of communication and crafting them is an art to be learned and mastered. The quality of online surveys has improved increasingly, yet mistakes that cause poor quality of data are still frequent. When analyzing mistakes, one must differentiate between mistakes made by beginners with little or no experience of survey techniques and mistakes caused by the translation of normal techniques to the new medium. Bearing in mind the fact that online surveys have only been possible since the middle of the nineties, it is clear why as yet no systematic knowledge of the possibilities of conducting WWW surveys exists. The University of Cologne has developed a virtual pretest studio to test and optimize WWW surveys before they are introduced into the field. On the basis of the experiences made there, this contribution will outline some of the more common mistakes and develop guidelines for valid online surveys. Furthermore, the online pretest studio will be introduced as a quality control device[1].

4.1 The Five Most Common Online Survey Errors

In our studies, it was possible to distinguish five groups of mistakes that can considerably impair data quality. Before specifying these problems, the demands of the "interview" communication form will be recapitulated (for a more detailed reference see Schnell, Hill, & Esser, 1995; Holm, 1975; Scheuch, 1972). Interviews depend on obtaining valid responses to the questions posed. There are four factors involved in interview communications: the interviewer, the respondent, the instrument, and the

[1] The Pretest Lab was devised in an extracurricular project at the University of Cologne, Germany. I would like to express my gratefulness to Christof Wolf, Beatrix Bernard, Andreas Kastner, Frank Messerschmidt, Kilian Teutsch, and Leonhardt Wohlschlager for their participation.

applied technology. Response distortions in online surveys are mostly attributed to errors caused by the tool or by the interviewee. They result from questions being posed incorrectly, from answers the interviewee cannot provide in the appropriate manner, and from interruptions. The interviewee should not choose the answer alternative that might most please the interviewer or those answers that correlate to the responses of coincidental third parties. He/she should not be allowed to give answers that are not subjectively correct, be it because of boredom, or to manipulate the results or to take short-cuts through the interview.

4.1.1 Technical Errors

Using the aid of search engines, it can be demonstrated clearly that surveys are being conducted in the WWW by numerous organizations or persons with little or no experience in conducting surveys on their own. For example, the Bavarian Home Office asks if citizens believe the elimination of border controls will weaken security. The Center for Development of Higher Education determines the acceptance of student fees. Wahlen.de is interested in online surfers' voting preferences. Sports pages often organize surveys among football fans, followers of TV shows, and cult figures. Since only a small amount of the surveys listed above are conducted by trained personnel, beginners' mistakes are often found in the questionnaires.

Data becomes void when the facts to be determined from the responses are not specified properly. Thematic and chronological references must be clear to all respondents. The next question, on voting preference does not meet this criterion: "If there were an election, who would you vote for?". The question may sound to the point, yet conceals some problems. Different interviewees might have different ideas about which election is meant (communal elections, senate elections, national elections, and European elections). How this question can be formulated properly is best demonstrated by the formulation used by the Elections Research Group: "If there were a national election [thematic reference] next Sunday [chronological reference], which party would you vote for with your second vote [vote definition][2]?" (Comments in square brackets, Lorenz Gräf).

A question should only contain one thematic reference. Multiple references make it difficult to discern which one respondents are expressing their opinion about. The next question highlights this problem: "How do you rate the police's [thematic reference No. 1] and the courts' [thematic reference No. 2] performance?" Often, expressions and phrases unknown to the respondents are used in questions. Example: "What do you expect from the introduction of ADSL?". Not all respondents are

---

[2] In Germany, voters have two votes: the first for specific persons, the second for a political party.

equally aware of the facts referred to in this question. The interviewee will either guess, randomly choose an answer, or discontinue the interview.

Further errors depend on answer categories. In closed questions, these have to meet the demands of classifications (completeness, exclusivity, and clearness). In particular, beginners tend to make the mistake of forgetting different answer possibilities, or they present overlapping categories. In a questionnaire on Internet usage patterns, the following possible answers were given to measure weekly usage: 0 to 2 hours, 2 to 5 hours, 5 to 10 hours, more than 10 hours. The classification is unclear at the borders between categories. Other mistakes are caused by a choice of unsuitable categories. For instance, in a survey on voting preferences, both CDU and CSU (joint parties in Germany) are offered as possible answers. In no election in Germany can the voter choose between CDU and CSU. Therefore, the results of this survey can only be interpreted as a statement for a fictitious country or for the hypothetical situation that a choice could be made between the two Christian parties.

Further mistakes made by beginners apply to the features of WWW formula entries. In pop-up menus, categories must be preselected, whereas radio buttons do not need to be. Hasty respondents are lured into accepting the preselected categories. The obtained results should be interpreted more as a reflection of the degree of laziness of that sample, rather than as a litmus test of the opinions of the survey participants.

4.1.2   The Questionnaire Is Too Long

The following mistakes are not only made by beginners. They mostly occur when survey techniques from other media are applied to the Internet without being adapted, and when the researchers have not learned how to adapt to the conditions of the medium when constructing questionnaires. We frequently receive questionnaires to assess from marketing departments of various companies. These questionnaires have been conceived as paper-and-pencil questionnaires and have then been pleasantly redesigned for the Internet [3]. Most of the questionnaires we received as drafts were too long. In mail surveys, clever layout often hides the length of the questionnaire. This is not possible with Internet questionnaires. The length of the questionnaire and the cancel ratio are dependent upon each other, and the answers are also more un-

---

[3]   Frequently, the assignment also states that the Internet questionnaire should equal the printed questionnaire. In doing so, one hopes to acquire comparative results. Since Internet surveys on a computer screen are filled in under conditions of a hypermedia computer environment, presentations have to be adapted to the screen. These adjustments refer less to the formulation of questions than to the screen layout (also advice on good WWW surveys further down in the text.).

reliable. As a rule of thumb, questionnaires with more than 15 to 25 questions are too long (see Bosnjak & Batinic, this volume) [4].

Questionnaire developers often compile several comparison processes into the same question, thereby distorting the actual length of the survey instrument. It has to be made clear that a question does not relate to the text unit preceded by the question number. Instead, each question relates to the requirement of expressing an opinion to a certain piece of information. In the following section, a segment of an Internet questionnaire is shown where 24 tasks to be fulfilled are displayed as one single question.

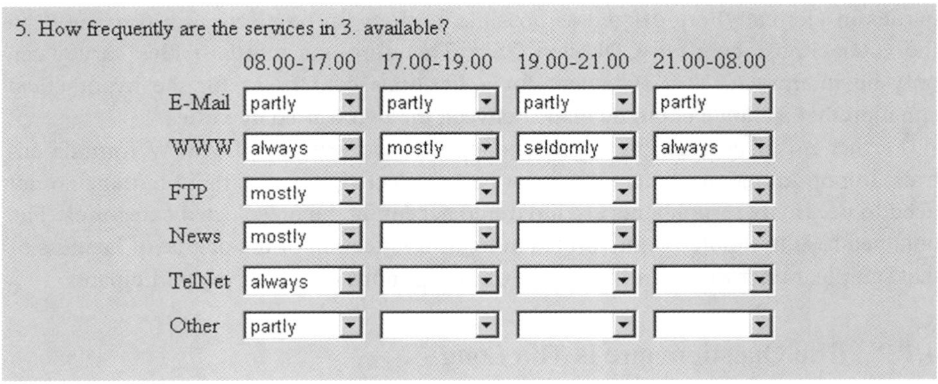

5. How frequently are the services in 3. available?				
	08.00-17.00	17.00-19.00	19.00-21.00	21.00-08.00
E-Mail	partly	partly	partly	partly
WWW	always	mostly	seldomly	always
FTP	mostly			
News	mostly			
TelNet	always			
Other	partly			

Figure 4.1: 24 Items concealed under one question number

In this screen-shot of the 24 inquiries shown in Figure 4.1, only 12 have been answered. In each cell, the respondent has to consider to what extent the selected services are accessible. She or he has to undertake temporal categorizations, which might not even correspond to his or her own habits and therefore demand several recalculations. The space-saving layout is deceptive with respect to the actual amount of information required. Many of the respondents will not be able to muster up the needed cognitive effort and will either refuse to answer the question or answer it unreliably. Since the survey is not being conducted by a federal statistics office, the painstaking precision of the survey is probably not necessary. Instead, it would have been ample to ask which of the services are not available or only available with difficulties. Furthermore, not all services must be included in the questionnaire. One can assume that the availability of TelNet and FTP do not differ from each other to large degree.

---

[4]   If the respondents are adequately prepared via a written letter, are interested in the topic, approve of the study's aims, and are open towards the survey's client, longer questionnaires can also be carried out.

In other cases, decisions the questionnaire designer could have made himself or herself are passed on to the respondent. If, for instance, a reader survey asks the readers of a magazine to rate articles in a recent (print) issue, the interviewee would be burdened unnecessarily with the cognitive effort. The respondent has to remember the article's name, and then fill in his evaluation. It would be more sensible if the articles – whose ratings are probably controversial in the editing office – were listed and then assessed. The acquired data would be more reliable, the editors could derive information on their own achievements and measure their internal ratings with the aid of readers' evaluations.

Some questionnaire designers are led astray by false notions of completeness. While possible answer categories in one question must meet the demands of answering a whole universe of possibilities, this does not apply to question items. The question depicted in the next screen-shot (Figure 4.2) actually consists of 21 questions. The interviewee must express his opinion to all 21 content items. It would be better if the client only named three to five categories he or she really wants to collect the opinions of the Web site's visitors on. If answers are demanded to too many questions, the likelihood of unreliable answers increases. A better way would be to test only those items the clients believe to be of importance. Contents rated equally by everybody do not need to be surveyed.

4.1.3   The Questionnaire Is Too Boring

Fun moments are of great importance when surfing and sifting through the WWW. Users will only stay on a certain Web site as long as it is interesting or appealing. This, of course, applies equally to questionnaires on the Internet. If the respondents are bored, they will not necessarily leave the questionnaire. However, they are more likely to be less concentrated, and will read question and answer categories more fleetingly, and consequently answer inaccurately. The questionnaire should be designed so as to give the user the impression of participating in an interesting conversation.

Questionnaires seem boring if they monotonously or uniformly ask for the same contents in a series of questions. Under these circumstances, producing an answer is no longer a challenge for the respondent. He or she already knows the answer, and is inactive during this section of the dialogue. If, however, interesting and apt questions are frequently posed, the respondent will feel intellectually challenged, and is content to impart his or her opinion on an exciting issue. It is unwise to repeatedly ask for an opinion on the same topic, even after other questions. The respondent will remember that this question was asked before, and is likely to consider the interviewer unintelligent, since the same opinion has been asked for twice.

	very interesting				very uninteresting
Products / solutions	☐	☐	☐	☐	☐
technical details	☐	☐	☐	☐	☐
Prices	☐	☐	☐	☐	☐
Contact addresses / distribution channels	☐	☐	☐	☐	☐
Company information	☐	☐	☐	☐	☐
Technology trends, trade news	☐	☐	☐	☐	☐
References	☐	☐	☐	☐	☐
Events (trade fairs, talks)	☐	☐	☐	☐	☐
Jobs	☐	☐	☐	☐	☐
Online magazines / online newspapers	☐	☐	☐	☐	☐
Technical articles, press releases	☐	☐	☐	☐	☐
Technical literature	☐	☐	☐	☐	☐
Glossary	☐	☐	☐	☐	☐
Contents	☐	☐	☐	☐	☐
Software downloads	☐	☐	☐	☐	☐
Guest books ("pin boards")	☐	☐	☐	☐	☐
Service point (maintenance, repairs)	☐	☐	☐	☐	☐
Coaching information (e.g. on PC courses)	☐	☐	☐	☐	☐
FAQ lists (lists with frequently asked questions)	☐	☐	☐	☐	☐
Freeware (e.g. screen savers, CD ROM)	☐	☐	☐	☐	☐
Price draws	☐	☐	☐	☐	☐

Figure 4.2: Too many item dimensions

The respondent can also easily become bored by long delays when filling in the questionnaire. This problem particularly affects survey programs that transmit one question at a time. The respondent expects a simple answer to be accepted equally quickly. A conversation partner who cannot grasp answers promptly is considered boring. The patience of the respondent is tested. The quality of his answers, however, is less dependent on potential bandwidth problems.

Questions that do not challenge the respondent can also lead to boredom (e.g., questions for obvious characteristics of the respondent). Any statistical particulars are of little interest to the respondent. The respondent gives a foreigner details, but does not receive new information in return. If such queries are too long-winded, or if they resemble pedantic inventory lists such as in Figure 4.1, the respondent quickly feels bothered, and cheated out of his or her time. Consequently, the interview is aborted.

4.1.4 Question Formulation or Presentation Is Not Adequately to the Medium

Users of the WWW treat text differently than readers of printed material. Documents are seldom read, instead they are "scanned". During this fleeting "passing over", only fragments of sentences are registered. The reader puts the registered text components together like a summary according to past experience and knowledge[5]. From findings made in usability research we now know that a user ignores all text elements considered to be unimportant, and in its place only takes notice of highlighted text passages (see Nielsen, 1997). In comparison to print media, the reading velocity of screen text is approximately 25% less. Nielsen deducts from this that the good WWW author should write 50% less. When applied to the questionnaire, these findings imply that question texts should be kept short and concise and should be presented clearly. Only a few facts should be mentioned in the question text. The following question formulated the topical reference very awkwardly: *"Which of the following topics would interest you, under consideration of the transmission medium, in the form of a complete course?"* This question demands a very attentive reader, and even then it is not quite clear in its intention. Rather, one should have asked which topics would be of interest to the respondent if offered as a course on the Internet.

Normally, it is correct to outline the topical reference, and to define the facts of the case precisely. In the following question, this was attempted in the case of costs for online access. *"The costs of Internet usage or an online service provider normally consist of a monthly basic charge for online services or for the service provider, and of an access rate for the Internet, as well as the telephone rates (not including monthly basic charges). How much do you pay for Internet access per month?"* Before the actual question is posed, the user is confronted with a mass of terms. The most important indication is hidden between the brackets. If one cannot assume that the whole population understands the same definition of a term, the premise of the question must be explained. However, this should be easy to understand and clear, so that all respondents are aware of the exact definition. One could have asked *"How much do you spend per month on Internet access and rates?"* With this formulation, the basic telephone charges are excluded.

The layout should be designed to simplify reading the text, and should ensure that the most important passages are in the respondent's view. In the case of wide screens, the text should not occupy all of the space, but should not be squeezed into small table columns (for further details on screen sizes, see below). The questionnaire's font should not be too small and the text corpus should be emphasized with prominent lettering.

---

[5] In order to describe such behaviour, cognitive psychology developed the concept of schemes or scripts. A summary of the scheme theory can be found in Schwarz (1985).

4.1.5   Matrix Questions in Table Form Are Unsuitable

From the results of our methodical research, items in matrix form, as they are often presented in written questionnaires, are unsuitable for online media. In this mode of presentation, many questions, which are all attributed to the same answer category, are positioned in a table (Figure 4.3). The question text is located in the far left-hand column of the table. The answer categories fill the columns to the right-hand edge of the screen. With tabular HyperText Markup Language (HTML) -tags, this type of presentation is easily implemented. However, what may seem practical for the HTML-designer, does not necessarily promote the understanding and correct answering of the question. This sort of layout causes incalculable effects. The respondents' answers are not exactly a result of their particular disposition, instead they are induced by the tool itself.

In methodology research, it has been discovered that respondents display a tendency to answer questions uniformly, because the cognitive effort is less than it would be if they always chose a new answer from the answer index. This effect already appears in interview questionnaires where the interviewer is in the position to correct replies. In the case of multiple choice questionnaires, the effect escalates. This effect is bound to turn up more frequently in WWW based surveys. Questionnaires on the WWW must be completed with the aid of a mouse and cursor. The cursor has to be positioned over the button and then depressed. The effort involved in positioning the cursor anew in each row is more costly than continuing in the same or neighboring column for each row. Furthermore, the eye occupies a certain position when looking at a screen. It is easier to view a printed page than a page displayed in a monitor. As a result of these structural circumstances, it can be concluded that it is easier for a respondent to choose only one column for the rest of his answers. The respondents find it difficult to move a mouse from left to right in order to express their opinion. In our questionnaire tests, respondents often admitted to having only answered along one column. This effect will occur more often, the less interested respondents are in the survey, the more tired or inattentive (bored) they already are, and the more difficult it is for them to find the right answer (the more unclear and unfitting the answer categories). Amongst highly motivated respondents who had a positive attitude towards the survey, were ready to divulge information, and were happy to spend time answering the survey, this type of effect was noted less frequently. Yet, in which survey can these conditions be observed?

The presentation of questions in a tabular form also poses a second problem. The association between question and answer items is decreased. When the respondent's eyes focus on the answer categories of the question, the actual reference is out of view and vice versa. The respondent might possibly forget the item about which she or he is expressing an opinion or forget the statements that evaluate the items.

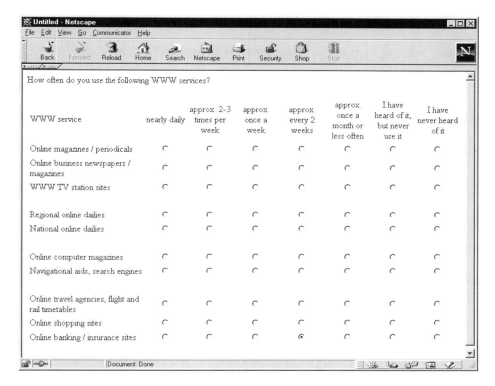

Figure 4.3: Danger of response bias in matrix questionnaires

With the aid of the depicted screen-shot in Figure 4.4, the problem can be demonstrated. When the respondent has to evaluate the third item *"TV stations', newspapers', and magazines' WWW services will become important sources of information for the European population"*, he is obliged to keep a note of the wording. In order to express his opinion, he orients himself in the same row to the right. He only finds circles here without any demarcation of the column position. Should he want to find out the meaning of the given position he must look at the column head. In order to select the radio button, he once again has to look down to focus on the correct row; an unnecessarily burdensome task. In his search for the correct category, the respondent's eyes might most likely come across yet another item. The reply to this question will be distorted by concurrent items. The reference point for a correct answer has disappeared. The received answers are inexact in their reflection of the respondent's opinions. The methodologically correct procedure would be to present each question individually to the respondent.

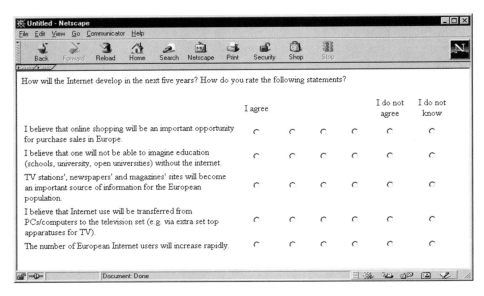

Figure 4.4: Connection between question and answer dimensions
dissipates in matrix questions

One possibility of reaching this ideal, without having to transmit each question individually, can be seen in Figure 4.5. Each question occupies one row.

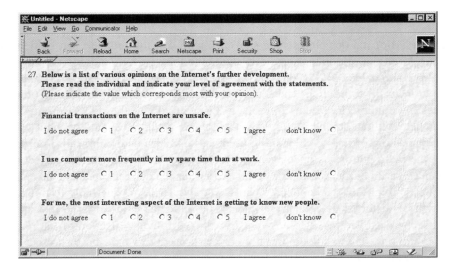

Figure 4.5: Layout recommendation for presenting item batteries
in a www survey avoiding the matrix format

Like this, the layout width can be defined so that only one or two eye movements are needed to register the question and answer dimensions. The answer categories are placed directly beneath the question. Each radio button is labeled clearly. The reference from question to answer category is retained.

4.2   Recommendations for Proper WWW Surveys

In the hypermedia Internet environment, the user follows the thread that captures his interest most strongly, and agrees most with his information preferences. Awareness is coupled with a state of forgetting oneself (flow) and playfulness (Hoffman & Novak, 1996; Csikzentmihaly, 1992). This state is brought about when the user: 1) perceives a certain amount of control over his interaction in the Internet environment; 2) focuses his thoughts on the interactive situation; and 3) finds the experience cognitively enjoying. This is achieved by an optimal mixture of curiosity, challenge, and aptitude. Without cognitive challenge at hand, boredom will set in easily. A questionnaire should be put together so as not to leave the respondent overtaxed or under challenged. Internet users' interest wanes (and simultaneously the quality of their answers) when they are not bound to a screen by forms of communication. Once suspense is declining, the respondents tend to answer the questions in such a way that they can complete the questionnaire in the shortest possible amount of time. That means that answers will possibly be answered incorrectly in order to short-cut answering the survey, or to choose those answers where one can expect little or no following inquiries.

To avoid such mistakes and to ensure the quality of the data, the following guidelines should be considered:

- Consider technical requirements.
- Formulate questions according to the rules of empirical social research.
- Establish credible communication with the respondent.
- Generate awareness and attention.
- Use eye-catching designs and implement usability criteria.
- Highlight central text passages.
- Avoid matrix questions.
- Keep questionnaires short.
- Employ filter questions.
- Carry out a pretest.

4.2.1 Consider Technical Requirements

HTML pages are visited by different people with different technological equipment. Some presentation techniques bear particular requirements on the client side. In surveys, none of the population should be excluded from the questionnaire because of technical problems. The technical requirements should bear the target group's minimal technical requirements in mind. This refers to file sizes and the amount of files to be transmitted, the use of graphics, and the use of advanced programming. Download time should be chosen so that interviewees with a slow modem connection can view the page in an adequate amount of time. If images need to be used, the files must be as small as possible, and should already be transferred with the first letter of correspondence or questions. Then the images need only be summoned from the browser's local cache folder for the following questions. Browser-specific HTML extensions should be avoided. Depending on the target group, neither Java nor JavaScript should be used. Focusing on a minimal standard for screen size allows respondents with smaller monitors to participate in the survey. In case some of the sample uses a text-based to obtain information from the WWW, the questionnaire should be conceived so that it can be completed without the use of a graphic browser.

4.2.2 Formulate Questions According to the Rules of Empirical Social Research

Social research has devised standards for the correct formulation of questionnaires. When compiling questionnaires with the intent of conducting serious surveys, these standards should be borne in mind (Dillman, 1978; Converse & Presser, 1988; Sudman & Bradburn, 1988; Schnell, Hill, & Esser, 1994; Schwarz, 1985). A summary of the most important tips can be found on german at http://infosoc.uni-koeln.de/www pretest/tips_zu_formulierungen.html. A questionnaire should be designed such that the questions are understood in the same way by all respondents. The questions should ideally be concise and formulated precisely. The question wording should not try respondents' abilities. The respondent should not be asked to answer questions on concepts unknown to him. One question should not contain too many concepts so that one part of the population will answer the first part, another part of the population the second part. In a closed question, the answer categories must be complete and should not overlap. Understandable notes should be given to aid answering the questions.

4.2.3   Establish Credible Communication with the Respondents

Internet users actively define their online behavior. This has to be considered when communicating with them. They wish to know precisely what to expect from a Web site and are not willing to be held up by complicated sentences, long connection rates, huge images, and graphics or Java applets. The aim of any survey should be communicated clearly. The questionnaire's layout should be designed according to the aim of the study. Similarly, the questions should correspond to the thematic reference. The users should not be forced to make alterations to their browser's preferences or should not, in any other way, feel subordinated. The introduction to the questionnaire must arouse the users' interest. The chosen layout should signal the survey's entertainment value. This is more important than offering incentives (see on undesired side-effects of prize draws, Gräf & Heidingsfelder, 1999). Communication with the user should be transparent throughout the interview. It should be clear to the user how many questions remain to be answered. The information concerning the duration should be honest, and multiple questions hidden in one question should not be counted as one single question.

4.2.4   Generate Awareness and Attention

Respondents who follow the questionnaire with interest and concentrate on answering the questions supply the preferred subjectively correct answers. Users who simultaneously send e-mails, look for information in a second browser window, or who follow their screen from the corner of their eyes provide fairly unreliable data. The questionnaire is to be devised to give the user the impression of participating in an interesting conversation. In an ideal situation, he or she will be under the impression that he or she is learning something by answering the questions. Boredom sets in when the questions are asked monotonously, when the user can anticipate the next question, when the topic is discussed for a time longer than the user wishes to dispense with, when the transmission of data and the loading time for the next pages take too long. The user is only attracted to the survey as long as the question-answer-situation is cognitively rewarding for him, and he enjoys filling in the answers.

4.2.5   Use Eye-Catching Design and Implement Usability Criteria

Design is one of the most important aids for the respondent when estimating the seriousness of the questionnaire's source. Usability research on the usability of Internet sites has shown that users have little or no understanding for bad design (Nielsen, 1997). Following Nielsen's findings, users do not appreciate having to scroll. They prefer seeing the information they need on the screen. Similarly, one must expect that users read texts comparatively fleetingly. They prefer grasping the central theme with less effort. If the questionnaire's layout does not correspond to this behavior then possibly opinions will be expressed on topics that were not even asked. In particular, frame technology must be avoided. Anything that requires extra effort on the part of the respondent diverts concentration from answering the questions. Scrolling must be reduced to a minimum, changing from one question to another should be facilitated via the implementation of a hyperlink. There should be a minimum of changes from keyboard entries to mouse entries. On the whole, maneuvering should be kept at the simplest level.

4.2.6   Highlight Central Text Passages

The questions should be clearly laid out for the user to see. The most important keywords should be easily visible. The answer items must be designed so that they can be referred to the proper questions. The references between question and corresponding answer must be maintained. The layout should not tempt the respondent to answer another category other than that corresponding to his own opinion. If possible, one page should be limited to one question. This principle of "one question, one page" is subject to bandwidth restrictions. Should there not be enough bandwidth available, one should try to direct the respondent to the comparison process, and not divert his attention with other cognitive processes.

4.2.7   Avoid Matrix Questions

No answering mistakes should be induced in the layout. Matrix questions in tabular form should be avoided since respondents might possibly choose those answers that are easiest to reach with the mouse, rather than those buttons that express their real opinion. Questions with similarly formed answer categories can facilitate answering, but must be clearly differentiated in order not to bore the respondent.

4.2.8   Keep Questionnaires Short

Many Internet users pay for online time and are quite aware of the running costs. Other users, however, who are not bound by costs only want to be briefly occupied with side activities, such as filling in questionnaires. These time restrictions must therefore be considered when planning a survey. One should not hold up respondents longer than necessary for the aims of the study. The questionnaire should only contain the most essential questions. Which topics come into consideration for the survey's aim, for the marketing decision or for other decisions must taken into account carefully for the Internet users. The questionnaire should only contain the most relevant questions. With reference to data quality, the old proverb "Less is more" also applies here. When counting the questions, one should consider that every comparison the respondent is asked to make is regarded as a question. In order not to jeopardize suspense and honest answers with it, no more than 25 opinions should be polled.

4.2.9   Employ Filter Questions

By using filter questions the quality of data can be increased, since wrong answers can be avoided. The hypertext-based medium of the WWW offers diverse possibilities. The survey dramaturgy can be specifically designed with one group of users in mind. Depending on whatever answer is given to certain key questions (filter questions), different questions can be posed next. The "conversation" remains interesting and exciting for the respondent. The respondent need not be held up with comparative analyses that do not apply to his case. The communication flow remains uninterrupted by superfluous information.

4.2.10 Perform a Pretest

Authors of questionnaires often have difficulties in recognizing the problems of a questionnaire. They are familiar with the contents and the question aims, and often overlook difficulties in comprehension. If the questionnaire is handed to people not involved in the development, weaknesses will quickly arise. With the help of the Internet, pretests can be carried out at relatively low cost. The test questionnaire can be sent to various members of the target group who have agreed to fill it in. The participants in the test should also be asked to answer questions on comprehension of the questionnaire. The questionnaire can also be tested by other experts. For this purpose, a posting can be sent, for instance, to the GIR-L Mailing list (German Internet Research-List, http://www.gor.de/). Particularly productive insights can be won through the use of a pretest lab, one type of which will be described in the following section.

4.3   The Pretest Lab

The demands to be met by skillful Internet surveys are high. They can hardly be fulfilled in everyday practice. In order to assist researchers, marketing experts, and private persons with the design of questionnaires suitable for the Internet, members of the University of Cologne founded a virtual pretest laboratory[6]. In the laboratory, WWW, and e-mail questionnaires are tested for correct formulation of questions, plausible question order and suitability for the medium. Furthermore, possible improvements are suggested and implemented. Testing, consulting, and client servicing all take place online. The advantages of the Internet are used to conduct pretests quickly and effectively.

Pretests are recommended in nearly every textbook on research methods. Nevertheless, they are hardly ever put into practice since they are considered exorbitant, and because questionnaire technicians often see themselves as experts who need little or no assistance. With the introduction of the Online Pretest Lab, any reservations against the execution of pretests are put to rest. Neither are surveys delayed, nor do test participants need to be found.

4.3.1   Theoretical Background of the Pretest Lab

For a long time, questionnaire development was considered an art form without any scientifically based construction guidelines. The evaluation of questionnaires was often seen as a question of style or taste. Based on systematic, methodic research, and cognitive psychological findings, a pretest science has evolved in the last few years. Research has been driven by academic research institutions in North America, the federal statistical offices of the Netherlands and Sweden, and by the ZUMA (The Center for survey research and methodology in Mannheim, Germany)[7]. In Sweden and Holland, pretest laboratories were founded with the purpose of thoroughly testing the federal statistical office's survey instruments, which had remained unchanged for decades (Bergmann, 1995; Akkerboom, Dehue, & Snijkers, 1996).

In these pretests, data on the answering process is polled systematically. Data is collected on how clear the formulations of the questions are, to what extent they support recall, how evaluation processes take place, and if the respondents are capable of transferring memorized information into the given answers. For this purpose, various techniques are employed (expert appraisal, focus groups, in-depth interviews, cognitive interviews, current or retrospective thinking-aloud, probing, confidence rating). In general, these pretests are quite costly. The compilation of data requires particularly skilled interviewers, the interviews are often recorded onto audio or video tape

---

[6]   Currently, the Cologne Pretest Lab Cologne is a Nonprofit Organization, open to anybody. The fees are levied according to the involvement of the particular member. Further information on the Pretest Lab can be found at: http://infosoc.uni-koeln.de/www pretest/.

[7]   An outline of the current status of pretest research can be found in Prüfer and Rexrodt (1996). The central theoretical ideas can be looked up in Sudman, Bradburn and Schwarz (1996).

and are subsequently analyzed thoroughly. This expenditure is justified in the case of fundamental research and for testing the federal offices' instruments, yet is unjustifiably large for most WWW surveys. By concentrating solely on the following methods, and by using the Internet thoroughly, this cost can be reduced to a minimum.

4.3.2   Methods Employed in the Online Pretest Lab

In the Online Pretest Lab, we apply techniques that are particularly productive without great cost. Experts trained in methodology evaluate the entered questionnaires, and in particular problem cases, we invite test persons to our PC lab to fill in online surveys, participate in a focus group, and discuss their opinions afterwards. This data is then supplemented with a special pretest survey in which members of the target population participate.

4.3.3   WebPEP: Webbased Pretest by Expert Panel

With the aid of the Internet, new possibilities of conducting an expert pretest with geographically distributed experts are easily accessible. A conceptual questionnaire is then posted on the Internet with certain marked points and is secured via a password. The URL is then sent digitally to select methodologically qualified persons. At the same time, information is given on the preferred evaluation. The experts evaluate the questionnaire from their desktop and fill in their comments in a prepared online form. A synopsis is then compiled from the comments and the mistakes are then classified. A coordinator processes the comments and compiles a problem file with data on error statistics.

For the implementation of expert pretests, we have created a special software environment called *WebPEP*. With this tool the experts can evaluate the questionnaire locally and send us back their comments. The answers are sorted according to the questions via a Common Gateway Interface (CGI) script. These are then classified via a WWW form according to an experimentally derived coding scheme. The script draws up a report of the mentioned errors. This report is used as the basis for the pretest account and for the compilation of suggestions for improvements.

With the expert test, the set of competent persons who can be approached for an evaluation of questionnaires is extended. Our expert pool comprises, for example, sociologists, market and media researchers, and methodology experts. Potential participants for questionnaire conferences are only a mouse click away. In contrast to a "real world" survey conference, experts do not have to all be present at the same time in the same place. Only a timeframe is set in which they should view and comment on the questionnaire. The temporal autonomy of each expert remains intact and transactional costs such as travel costs to survey meetings, accommodation, and other expenses do not apply. With this method, the Internet is employed as a fast and effective distribution medium.

4.3.4   Survey Usability Laboratory

Because of their expertise, experts recognize weak points in survey instruments. But because of their status as experts and their methodological knowledge, their comments on how "normal" respondents will complete a questionnaire are unreliable. In order to obtain information on real performance, the inclusion of test persons from the target population is absolutely necessary. Two methods are applicable. Respondents are asked about the process by which they produced answers (to the extent of their memory) via an online form. Behavior of which the respondents may not be aware is examined in a usability laboratory.

For the laboratory tests subjects are invited to a PC lab. There, they complete the questionnaire as if they were online. This allows us to collect data on screen technicalities of WWW questionnaires and to define the beneficial and hindering factors that are intrinsic to the medium. Furthermore, we can control and standardize the conditions of completion of the questionnaire. Following the completion of the questionnaire, the "guinea-pigs" discuss their experiences in a focus group.

4.3.5   WebPOP Web-Based Pretest by Online Population

Many of the techniques commonly conducted in laboratory pretests (Thinking Aloud, Paraphrasing, Probing by Interviewer) cannot be used in the WWW. In order to obtain the required meta-data on the answering process, we modify the questionnaire, and include extra questions for better understanding. This technique corresponds to the process of "Comprehension Probing" and "Confidence Rating" in personal interviews. In addition to the normal questions, the respondents are asked further questions associated with answering mechanisms. The extended questionnaire is then made available to a test sample from the target population and is evaluated in the same way as a "normal" survey. The execution potential, reliability, and usability of such a probing procedure has proved worthwhile in several projects.

4.4   The Advantage of Pretests

In view of the problems that surveys on the Internet can cause, and in light of the fact that many surveys are conducted by persons or institutions without the necessary methodological insight, we cannot overstress the importance of conducting pretests. By implementing pretests, questionnaires can be improved considerably. If one ensures that the guidelines mentioned above are adhered to, one will obtain more reliable data, and the clients will receive clearly contoured results, which can be put to use in finding solutions and decision-making. The respondents are more content, and are likely to participate in future polls.

References

Akkerboom, H. & Dehue, F. (1996). The dutch model of data collection for official surveys. *International Journal of Public Opinion Research, 9*, 126-145.

Akkerboom, H. (1996). Labor für die Entwicklung und den Test von Erhebungsinstrumenten In Statistisches Bundesamt (Ed.), *Pretest und Weiterentwicklung von Fragebogen*. Bd. 9 der Schriftenreihe Spektrum Bundesstatistik, (pp. 66-71). Stuttgart: Metzler-Poeschel.

Bergmann, L. R. (1995). Pretesting procedures at statistics Sweden's measurement, evaluation, and development laboratory. *Journal of Official Statistics, 11*, 309-323.

Dillman, D. (1978). *Mail and telephone surveys: The total design method*. New York: Wiley and Sons.

Converse, J. M. & Presser, S. (1986). *Survey questions – handcrafting the standardized questionnaire*. Beverly Hills: Sage.

Csikszentmihalyi, M. (1990). *Flow – the psychology of optimal experience*. New York: HarperCollins.

Forsyth, B. H., Lessler, J. T., & Hubbard, M. L. (1992). Cognitive evaluation of the questionnaire. In C. Turner, J. T. Lessler, & J. C. Gfroerer (Eds.), *Survey Measurement of Drug Use* (pp. 13-52). Rockville, Maryland: National Institute of Drug Abuse.

Franke, G. H. (1996). Effekte von Typographie und Itempositionierung in der Fragebogendiagnostik. *Zeitschrift für Differentielle und Diagnostische Psychologie, 17*, 187-200.

Gaiser, T. (1997). Conducting online focus groups: A methodological discussion. *Social Science Computer Review, 15*, 135.

Gräf, L. (1997). Pretest von WWW-Umfragen. In D. Janetzko, B. Batinic, D. Schoder, M. Mattinley-Scott, & G. Strube (Eds.), *CAW-97* (pp. 51-62). Freiburg i.Br.: IIG-Berichte.

Gräf, L. & Heidingsfelder, M. (1999). Bessere Datenqualität bei WWW-Umfragen durch das Rogator-Verfahren – Erfahrungen aus einem Methodenexperiment mit dem Internet-Rogator. In B. Batinic, L. Gräf, A. Werner, & W. Bandilla (Eds.), *Online Research* (pp. 112-126). Göttingen, Germany: Hogrefe.

Hoffman, D. & Novak, T. (1995). *Marketing in hypermedia computer-mediated environments: Conceptual foundations. Project 2000: Research program on marketing in computer-mediated environments, working paper No. 1*. [Online]. Available: http://www 2000.ogsm.vanderbilt.edu/paper_list.html.

Holm, K. (1975). *Die Befragung*. München: Francke.

Krueger, R. A. (1988). *Focus groups. A practical guide for applied research*. London: Sage.

Lessler, J. T. & Forsyth, B. H. (1996). A coding system for appraising questionnaires. In N. Schwarz & S. Sudman (Eds.), *Answering questions: methodology for determining cognitive and communicative processes in survey research*, (pp. 259-291). San Francisco: Jossey-Bass.

Nielsen, J. (1997). *Interface design for sun's www site*. [Online]. Available: http://www.sun.com/sun-on-net/uidesign/.

Nielsen, J. (1993). *Usability engineering*, Boston: Academic Press.

Novak, T. P. & Hoffman, D. L. (1997). *Measuring the flow experience among web users*. Paper presented at interval research corporation, July.

Presser, S. & Blair, J. (1994). Survey pretesting: Do different methods produce different results. In P. V. Marsden (Eds.), *Sociological methodology* (pp. 73-104). Oxford: Blackwell.

Prüfer, P. & Rexroth, M. (1996). Verfahren zur Evaluation von Survey-Fragen: Ein Überblick. *ZUMA-Nachrichten, 39*, 95-115.

Scheuch, E. K. & Rüschemeyer, D. (1972). Das Interview. Formen, Technik, Auswertung. In R. König (Ed.), *Praktische Sozialforschung I*. Köln: Kiepenheuer und Witsch.

Schnell, R., Hill, P., & Esser, E. (1995). *Methoden der empirischen Sozialforschung* (5. ed.). München: Oldenbourg.

Sudman, S. & Bradburn, N. (1988). *Asking questions. A practical guide to questionnaire design*. London: Sage.

Sudman, S., Bradburn, N., & Schwarz, N. (1996). *Thinking about answers. The application of cognitive process to survey methodology*. San Francisco: Jossey-Bass.

Schwarz, N. (1985). Theorien konzeptgesteuerter Informationsverarbeitung in der Sozialpschologie. In D. Frey & M. Irle (Eds.), *Theorien der Sozialpsychologie, Bd. III, Motivations- und Informationsverarbeitungstheorien* (pp. 269-291). Bern: Huber.

5 Context Effects in Web Surveys

Ulf-Dietrich Reips

5.1 Abstract

The quality of data collection on the Internet depends in part on potentially biasing surface characteristics of Web pages, such as pop-up menus. Also, answering behavior to survey questions is highly sensitive to cognitive contexts evoked by other survey questions. A Web experiment with two experimental phases is used to identify six potentially biasing factors. Manipulations of scale type, reading directionality, cursor entry position, question order, and – in contrast to findings from offline research – type of numerical labeling do not show effects. However, it is shown that it makes a difference whether survey questions are presented together on one Web page or separately on consecutive Web pages. Results are discussed with regard to general as well as online specific implications for the design of survey instruments and multiple response scales.

5.2 Introduction

The World Wide Web's (WWW) increasing popularity led to the beginning of this communication media's use as a data source for online research in various fields (Hewson, Laurent, & Vogel, 1996; Musch & Reips, 2000). Online data collection methods can be classified into three major subtypes: nonreactive data collection, Web experiments, and online surveys (Reips, 1997, this volume). Especially in online surveys the dependent measure often consists in the user's choice on a multiple response scale. Due to the analogy between online questioning and offline questioning it can be assumed that multiple response scales are prone to answering biases that have been discovered in the use of this measure in offline research (e.g., Schwarz & Hippler, 1994a, 1994b). Early investigations of computer-assisted surveying (e.g., Kiesler & Sproull, 1986) support this assumption. In a meta-analysis of 159 correlations from 29 studies on paper-and-pencil versus computerized test administration, Mead and Drasgow (1993) mostly found very high agreement.

Form and demand characteristics of response scales are dependent on the medium they are used in. The WWW offers a number of ways in constructing response scales. These scales may appear similar to those used in paper-and-pencil studies. On the other hand, scales may also look and function quite differently. Consider, for example, scales that take the form of "pop-up menus" on Web pages. At first glance, a pop-up menu looks like a piece of text within a rectangular shape (see Figure 5.1, top). This shape sometimes is in a different shade of gray or in a different color than the background of the Web page. Also, it might appear in a three-dimensional fashion. If the user clicks with her mouse cursor on the pop-up menu, then a scrollable menu appears (see Figure 5.1, bottom). With pop-up menus, before clicking on it, the user does not see the whole scale at once. Consequently, until clicking on it the user doesn't know how many items a scale contains. This is an obvious difference from scales administered in a paper-and-pencil format.

Figure 5.1: A pop-up menu in closed state (top)
and opened (bottom)

One goal of the present study is to find an answer to the question of whether such surface characteristics of WWW typical response scales may lead to biases in answering behavior.

In the literature certain answer-biasing influences are identified as independent of the research method that is used. For example, Schwarz and Hippler (1994a) were able to show that the cognitive context evoked by questions in a survey may influence the respondent's answering behavior in other questions. As a consequence, the present Web experiment aimed at replicating this and other effects including the influence of numeric labeling, question order, and scale polarity in questionnaires that were answered on the WWW.

5.2.1 Possible Biases Studied

The first question to be examined is one of *type of scale*. Are there differences in answering behavior depending on whether a scale is realized as a pop-up menu or as a button scale? Because in most Web browsers a pop-up menu closes as soon as the mouse arrow leaves the opened field, it can be assumed that choices are not equally easy to make. The user has to go back to the top and open the menu again, which may discourage her from choosing "strenuous" answers. Also, for some choices, hand movement is longer than for others. Therefore, answers on pop-up menus may differ systematically from answers on button scales.

A second issue to be looked at is *numerical labeling*. Different numerical labels of the same category on a scale may suggest different meanings even if the verbal labels at the end points are identical. For example, Schwarz & Hippler (1994a) found a more positive evaluation of politicians on eleven point scales in telephone interviews and mail surveys, if the numerical labels ranged from -5 to $+5$ instead of ranging from 0 to 10. Apparently, this is due to an attribution of a negative quality to numbers that carry a minus sign. Can this result be replicated in a Web experiment?

The third question to be answered involves the *natural reading direction* in western cultures. Does it matter whether the positive end of a scale is on the left or top versus the right or bottom?

Fourth, if the scale is in the form of a pop-up menu, then does it matter whether the *cursor entry and cursor entry label* are at the top of the scale or at the bottom of the scale?

Finally, later items in a survey may influence answering behavior in earlier items. Schwarz and Hippler (1994b) found such influences in mail surveys when compared to telephone interviews. In mail surveys, readers may read through the whole survey before answering the first question. They may go back to earlier questions and change their answers, or they may even choose to make one of the last items the first one they answer. This is not possible in telephone interviews. A comparable situation emerges in Web-based surveys, where survey items may either be placed on a single Web page or one by one on consecutive Web pages. If the hypothesis holds true that some questions will stimulate cognitive contexts that are capable of influencing answers to other questions then results in a single Web page condition should resemble those from a mail survey. The resulting pattern from a survey that is presented on multiple Web pages containing one item each should be similar to data from a telephone interview. In their study, Schwarz and Hippler (1994a, p.4) "asked respondents how much money they would be willing to donate to support the suffering citizens of Russia." The donation question was either immediately preceded or immediately followed by two questions about taxes, thereby evoking a cognitive spending context. As predicted, in the mail survey condition the amount indicated in the donation question was affected independent of whether the context questions preceded or followed the donation question. In the telephone interview, the answer to the donation question was only influenced by preceding questions.

Besides replication of Schwarz and Hippler's results using single versus multiple Web pages, the present Web experiment explores bidirectionality of context effects. While Schwarz and Hippler only looked at the effect a spending context may have on donations, it seems consequential to realize a design, which allows for evaluation of both directions a context influence could flow. The donation context may have influenced cognitions on spending as well. A second change is made in this study in regard to the focus of the spending question. While Schwarz and Hippler asked for the willingness to donate (i.e., an intended behavior), the present study asks for past donations (i.e., the memory of past behaviors).

5.3   Method

In order to explore whether several types of answering biases apply to online surveys, a Web experiment was conducted. As the name implies, Web experiments are experiments conducted on the WWW. They are relatively new in experimental research. The first Web experiments were conducted in 1995 (Musch & Reips, 2000). A typical Web experiment works as follows (see Figure 5.2, Reips, 1998, 2000b, this volume). At its core is a Web server computer program residing on a computer that is permanently connected to the Internet. Participants retrieve the experimental materials using Web browsers on their computers. The Web server serves the experimental materials, depending on the participants actions and small helper applications. These so-called CGIs (Common Gateway Interface script) can be used to perform a number of tasks, including randomized distribution of participants to experimental conditions (Kieley, 1996; Reips, 1996, 1998, 2000b). All page requests and form inputs made by participants are written to a logfile, which can then be analyzed. Figure 5.2 shows a schematic description of a Web experiment. Definitions, discussions, and descriptions of Web experiments can be found in Birnbaum (2000), Krantz, Ballard, and Scher (1997), and Reips (1995, 1998, 2000a, 2000b, this volume).

Krantz and Dalal (2000) have shown that most studies involving both WWW and laboratory samples show high agreement between data from both types of experiments. A recent survey showed a similar view is shared by most Web experimenters, who indicate a confidence in the ability of Web experiments to produce valid results (Musch & Reips, 1998).

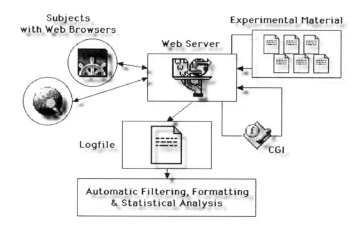

Figure 5.2: Schematic description of a web experiment
(from Reips, 1996)

The Web experiment was announced with a different entry page URL in the mailing list *gir-l (German Internet Research List)*, in order to check for a possible expert effect. As an incentive for participation and correct submission of their e-mail address, participants received a humorous story sent out by e-mail after completion of a series of experiments.

5.3.1   Participants

334 people started the experiment, as determined by distinct e-mail addresses and distinct computer addresses (IPs). 190 times the German entry page was used; 144 times the English entry page. Of the participants using the German language version, 41 were possible experts, as they used the URL announced in gir-l. Due to technical error (erroneous hyperlinking, leading to recurring pages), 24 data sets had to be discarded for the second experimental phase. 292 participants answered the demographical questionnaire at the end of the experiment (German: 158; English: 134), resulting in a drop out rate of 5.8%.

5.3.2   Procedure

Those people who followed the hyperlink from the Web Experimental Psychology Lab to the experiment were shown a Web page containing general instructions. This page informed about confidentiality of participation, asked for submission of the participant's e-mail address, and contained tests for pop-up menu compatibility and

JavaScript compatibility of the participant's Web browser. The Web experiment was built according to the "high hurdle technique" (Reips, this volume), which aims at reducing drop-out during the course of the Web experiment. After reading the general instructions page, participants clicked the "submit button" as an indication that they agreed to participate in the Web experiment. They then were randomly distributed to one of the 12 conditions of the first experimental phase (see Figure 5.3). These conditions were constructed according to a 2 (scale type) x 2 (numerical labeling) x 2 (reading directionality) design, with an additional dichotomous independent variable (cursor entry position) nested in the pop-up menu scale type.

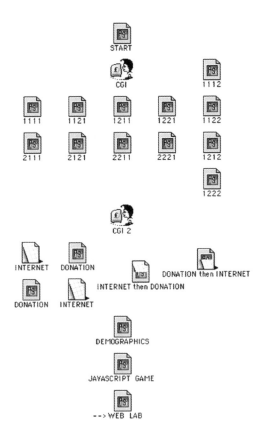

Figure 5.3: Experimental procedure: start, first experimental phase (12 conditions), second experimental phase (4 conditions), demographical questionnaire, JavaScript game. CGIs allow for randomized distribution of participants to conditions.

Each condition was realized on a single Web page containing the question "Overall, how satisfied are you with the quality of your connection to the Internet?" and the answering scale with the verbal end labels "not at all satisfied" and "very satisfied".

Pressing the "submit button" at the bottom of the Web page triggered random distribution via CGI to one of four conditions in the second experimental phase. These conditions resulted from administering presentation of the two spending context and donation context questions on one or two Web pages in both possible question orders. The questions were: "How many thousandth parts of your income would you pay for a good and reliable Internet connection?" and "On average, how many thousandth parts of your income did you give to the charities during the last two years?". Asking for fractions of income was a way to ensure an answer format that is largely independent of currency, socioeconomic class, and culture.

Following the second experimental phase participants were asked to answer three additional questions about their age, their sex, and their expert status regarding scientific online research. At the end participants had the opportunity to play a game on which no data were recorded. All other input made by the participants was written to a logfile residing on the Web server. The data in this logfile provided the basis for statistical analyses.

The Web experiment can be looked at on the WWW at the URL http://www.psych .unizh.ch/genpsy/Ulf/Lab/archive/89452Estart.html. (Offering the possibility of participation in the discussed experiment to you, the reader, is a general advantage of Web experiments, which may lead to an increased understanding of "Procedure" sections like this and make our science's research much more transparent. For a discussion see Reips, 1997, 2000a.)

5.4   Results

To check whether experts for online research show a different performance than non-experts two t tests were computed. An alpha level of .05 was used for all statistical tests. There were no significant differences, neither on the satisfaction question in the first experimental phase, $t(323) = .56$, $p = .58$, nor on the difference in income allocation for a donation and an Internet connection, $t(243) = .30$, $p = .77$. Thus, it was concluded that meta-knowledge about online research had no biasing influence on answering behavior in this Web experiment. Consequently, the data of both groups were pooled for the following analyses.

5.4.1   Experimental Phase 1

A 2 (language) x 2 (scale type) x 2 (numerical labeling) x 2 (reading directionality) ANOVA revealed a significant main effect for language $F(1, 309) = 6.68$, $MSE = 5.42$, as well as a significant interaction between language and reading directionality, $F(1, 309) = 6.93$, which carried over to a three-way interaction with numerical labeling and the four-way interaction, $Fs(1, 309) = 6.25$ and 3.92, respectively, $p < .05$. Also, there was no significant effect for cursor entry position, $t(164) = .59$, $p = .55$. Figure 5.4 shows the mean results acquired during this experimental phase.

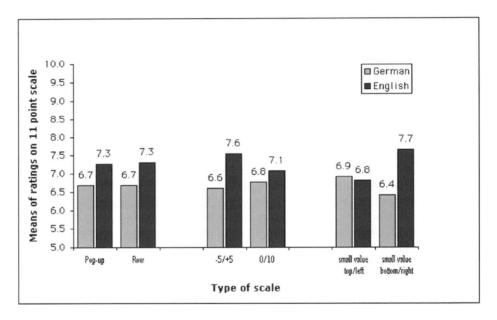

Figure 5.4: Mean ratings during first experimental phase for satisfaction with Internet connection

5.4.2   Experimental Phase 2

A 2 (question separation) x 2 (question order) ANOVA revealed a significant main effect for question separation on the difference in income allocation for a donation and an Internet connection, $F(1, 229) = 8.62$, $p = .004$. There was no significant main effect for question order, and no significant interaction, $Fs(1, 229) = .01$ and $.81$, respectively. For the means see Figure 5.5.

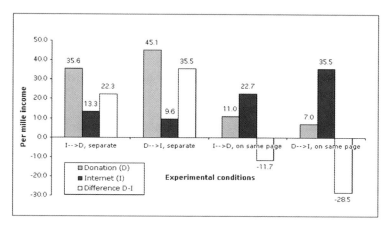

Figure 5.5: Mean reported donations, intended expenses for
Internet connection, and differences between both figures, in
thousandth of income

5.4.3 Demographical Data

60.1% (161) of those participants who answered the question for sex indicated that
they are male, 39.9% (107) checked the mark for "female". Distribution of stated age
is shown in Figure 5.6. Out of 267 participants who answered the "insider" question
34.1% (91) stated that they considered themselves to be an "insider".

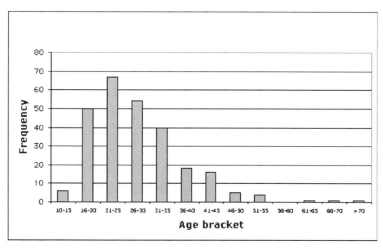

Figure 5.6: Distribution of stated age

5.5   Discussion

Pending replication of the present results it can be cautiously concluded that:

- Whether multiple questions are asked on the same or on different Web pages can lead to different answers. This seems to be due to varying cognitive contexts evoked by the questions themselves.
- This context effect is not only present for intended actions (e.g., how much money to donate, see Schwarz & Hippler, 1994a), but extends to statements about past behaviors (e.g., how much money one has donated). These results support the assumption that such statements about past behaviors might be based on an estimate of how one would behave in the present.
- Surface characteristics of Web questionnaires like pop-up menus versus button scales and numerical labeling don't seem to have an influence on answering behavior of Web participants.
- The difference found in the first experimental phase between language versions of the experiment might be due to real speed differences in Internet connection. The average speed of Internet connections is higher in English language societies than in German language societies. Other possible explanatory candidates for this difference are subtle semantic variations in meanings of terms, or cultural differences, such as a potential tendency towards more pronounced statements in the U.S.A. For evaluations of people, such as evaluations of politicians in Schwarz and Hippler (1994b), one might be able to replicate their findings on the effect of numerical labeling, since such evaluations are less factual.

Going further than Schwarz and Hippler (1994a), the design of the present study allows for the cautious proposal of a hypothetical "total context model." In other words, the total amount of expenditure behavior, no matter whether intended or remembered, is a salient cognitive barrier, which cannot easily be penetrated by context effects. This total amount is then distributed according to a function determined by the relative strength of cognitive contexts involved, and the possibility to show and/or change answering behavior.

A general conclusion that can be drawn is that WWW specific surface characteristics of surveys such as pop-up menus do not seem to make a difference. It remains open to further clarification whether the quality of online data collection is generally prone to similar effects as offline data collection, or whether there are medium specific biases. The primary practical WWW specific implication for the design of survey instruments is that one should not assume that it does not matter whether survey questions are asked together on a single Web page or separated with a Web page for each question.

References

Birnbaum, M. H. (Ed.). (2000). *Psychological experiments on the Internet*. San Diego, CA: Academic Press.

Hewson, C. M., Laurent, D., & Vogel, C. M. (1996). Proper methodologies for psychological and sociological studies conducted via the Internet. *Behavior Research Methods, Instruments, & Computers, 28*, 186-191.

Kieley, J. M. (1996). CGI scripts: Gateways to world wide web power. *Behavior Research Methods, Instruments, & Computers, 28*, 165-169.

Kiesler, S. & Sproull, L. S. (1986). Response effects in the electronic survey. *Public Opinion Quarterly, 50*, 402-413.

Krantz, J. H., Ballard, J., & Scher, J. (1997). Comparing the results of laboratory and world wide web samples on the determinants of female attractiveness. *Behavior Research Methods, Instruments, & Computers, 29*, 264-269.

Krantz, J. H. & Dalal, R. (2000). Validity of web-based psychological research. In M. H. Birnbaum (Ed.), *Psychological experiments on the Internet* (pp. 35-60). San Diego, CA: Academic Press.

Mead, A. D. & Drasgow, F. (1993). Equivalence of computerized and paper-and-pencil cognitive ability tests: A meta-analysis. *Psychological Bulletin, 114*, 449-458.

Musch, J. & Reips, U.-D. (2000). A brief history of web experimenting. In M. H. Birnbaum (Ed.), *Psychological experiments on the Internet* (pp. 61-85). San Diego, CA: Academic Press.

Reips, U.-D. (1995). *The web experiment method*. [Online]. Available: http://www.genpsy.unizh.ch/Ulf/Lab/WWWExpMethod.html.

Reips, U.-D. (1996, October). *Experimenting in the world wide web*. Paper presented at the 1996 society for computers in psychology conference, Chicago. [Online]. Available: http://www.psych.unizh.ch/genpsy/reips/slides/scipchicago96.html.

Reips, U.-D. (1997). Forschen im Jahr 2007: Integration von Web-Experimentieren, Online-Publizieren und Multimedia-Kommunikation [Science in the year 2007: Integration of Web experimenting, online publishing, and multimedia communication]. In D. Janetzko, B. Batinic, D. Schoder, M. Mattingley-Scott, & G. Strube (Eds.), *CAW-97: Cognition & Web*. Freiburg: IIG-Berichte.

Reips, U.-D. (1998). Web-Experiment [Web experiment]. In F. Dorsch, H. Häcker, & K.-H. Stapf (Eds.), *Psychologisches Wörterbuch, 13* [psychological dictionary]. Bern: Huber.

Reips, U.-D. (2000a). The web experiment method: Advantages, disadvantages, and solutions. In M. H. Birnbaum (Ed.), *Psychological experiments on the Internet* (pp. 89-114). San Diego, CA: Academic Press.

Reips, U.-D. (2000b). Das psychologische Experimentieren im Internet [Psychological experimenting on the Internet]. In B. Batinic (Ed.), *Internet für Psychologen* (2nd ed.) (pp. 319-343) [Internet for psychologists]. Göttingen, Germany: Hogrefe.

Schwarz, N. & Hippler, H. (1994a). Subsequent questions may influence answers to preceding questions in mail surveys. *ZUMA-Arbeitsberichte, 7*.

Schwarz, N. & Hippler, H. (1994b). The numeric values of rating scales: A comparison of their impact in mail surveys and telephone interviews. *ZUMA-Arbeitsberichte, 8*.

6 Understanding the Willingness to Participate in Online Surveys – The Case of E-Mail Questionnaires

Michael Bosnjak & Bernad Batinic

Why some people participate in surveys, and others do not is one major focus of interest for survey researchers. Hereby, the academic attention has been devoted to characteristics on the part of the respondents' actual situation when confronted with a request to participate (e.g., Esser, 1986; Goyder, 1987) as well as to those on the side of the survey instruments and procedures (e.g., Dillman 1978, 2000).

Relevant works on the question, which motives cause people to participate in *Internet-based* surveys as a relatively new form of data collection (see Batinic & Bosnjak, 2000), have to our knowledge not yet been published. Based on the assumption that similar reasons to those of "classical" surveys (e.g., by telephone, postal, and personal interviews) also determine the intention to participate in Internet-based surveys, we refer to Porst and von Briel (1995), whose theoretical considerations are based on the works of Esser (1973, 1986). According to Porst and von Briel (1995), the following three main aspects have been found to determine the willingness to participate in "classical" surveys:

- *Altruistic reasons.* These are present if persons participate in a survey because of a "moral obligation" and motives to help. Surveys are mostly perceived as important for "society", "politics" or the "well being" of a society.
- *Survey-related reasons* indicate situational and/or contextual factors, which are directly connected to the specific survey situation. These reasons comprise the perceived seriousness of the survey, the interest and/or curiosity in a specific topic etc.
- Porst and von Briel (1995) speak of *personal reasons* if the willingness to participate in a particular survey is essentially determined by dispositional factors (e.g., an interest in self-knowledge or perhaps a professional interest like learning effects for social sciences students).

On the basis of this categorization, we examined (1) to what extent this taxonomy can be replicated empirically in a qualitative investigation for the case of e-mail surveys, and (2) which relative significance the motives elicited might have for respondents in a subsequent intercultural investigation conducted via the World Wide Web (WWW) and e-mail.

With regard to the progress of research on characteristics of the survey situation (context factors) which influence the willingness to participate in e-mail-based surveys, Tuten (1997) argues that in particular the interest in the topic formulated in the e-mail's header as well as the familiarity with the sender represent crucial factors for an e-mail to be opened at all. Parallels can be drawn to the opening and reading of sales letters.

Following these findings, we also examined (3) which sort of information in advance increases the subjective likelihood of participation and (4) how much time people would employ for responding to an e-mail based questionnaire.

Finally, we will report our findings of a further study, which deals with the survey-related factor "purpose of the survey". In particular, we follow up the question whether scientific surveys are "more accepted" than business surveys.

The results presented in this contribution are based on data collected in spring 1996 within the context of a series of intercultural online surveys. Altogether 357 people were interviewed, whereby survey methods (WWW and e-mail questionnaires) and language versions (German and English) varied. In one of the questionnaires on the "acceptance of e-mail surveys," whose results serve as the basis for this contribution, the respondents were asked to imagine an e-mail questionnaire being sent to them unsolicited. A detailed description of the series of investigations can be found in Bosnjak (1997).

6.1   Determinants of the Willingness to Participate in Online Surveys: Motives and Information Provided in Advance

With the help of a qualitative investigation with open-ended response formats, we elicited motives effective for participation willingness, as well as survey-related information that could increase the individual's likelihood to participate in Online Investigations via e-mail. In this (preliminary) study, 25 participants responded to the questionnaire published within the CompuServe online service in one of the Internet-related discussion forums "Germany online", "German Internet forum", and "PC-Online".

Although of a relatively small sample size, the results indicate that the extracted motives-for-participation suggested by Porst and von Briel (1995) could be replicated. "Material incentives" acted as an additional motive (see Table 6.1).

Table 6.1: Items on the participation motive and on advance information relevant to participation

Question aspects	Extracted statements / items (classification of the reasons for participation according to Porst & von Briel 1995, in parentheses)	Exemplary answers
Motive for participation	Material incentive	"…of course a financial compensation should be offered."
	Curiosity (survey related reasons)	"My interest in the subject would be important."
	Self-knowledge (personal reasons)	"I'd like to know where I stand with my opinion compared to other participants."
	Contribution to research (altruistic reasons)	"...I am (almost) always willing to contribute for research."
Advance information relevant to participation	Information on the exact aims of the investigation	"Information on the purpose and the exact aims of the study would be very important for my decision."
	Information on access to the e-mail address	"... I also would like to find out where they got my e-mail address."
	Feedback on the results	"... if all it means is work I would not participate. If I were to be supplied with the results, perhaps yes."
	Complete anonymity of the answers	"…participation in the survey should always be voluntary and anonymous."
	Personal appeal of the researcher	"…I would consider a polite and a personal tone important."

The respondents stated that the following survey-related information given in advance would affect their willingness to participate: (1) information about the exact aims of the investigation, (2) information on access to the e-mail address, (3) the guarantee of receiving feedback of the results, (4) complete anonymity of the answers, as well as (5) the presence of a personal appeal to participate.

In the following main investigation conducted via the Web and e-mail, each separately in English and German (2 x 2 Design), the extracted items of both question aspects in Table 6.1 were ordered randomly in separate item blocks. These were then to be classified by a group of 357 participants on the basis of seven point rating scales according to their subjective significance for participation in a scientific survey sent out by e-mail (on a scale from "completely unimportant" to "very important").

On the basis of the data on the individual items, separate ranking rows were formed for the motives relevant for participation and for information in advance; besides a ranking row for all respondents, a further row for each of the two language versions (German and English) was formed to determine intercultural differences.

The ranking row specified in Table 6.2 resulted from participation relevant motives. "Curiosity" was named as the most important motivational factor, followed by "contribution to research", the appeal of "self-knowledge", and last "material incentives"; no intercultural differences were observed in the ranking.

Table 6.2: Ranking row of motives related to participation

Specified items: Motives relevant to participation	Ranking of all participants (Mean rank according to Friedman-Test in parentheses; n = 357)
Curiosity	1 (3.22)
Contribution to research	2 (3.02)
Self-knowledge	3 (2.25)
Material incentives	4 (1.51)

Among the provided items testing the individual's importance-judgments on the aspect information provided in advance relevant to the willingness for participation, "information on access to the e-mail address" was most important to the respondents, followed by a guarantee of "feedback about the results", subsequently "information on the exact aims of the investigation", followed by measures to ensure "the complete anonymity" of the answers, and as the relatively most unimportant component: "the personal request by the researcher" (see Table 6.3).

With regards to differences between the two language versions, the explicit guarantee of feedback was rated slightly higher than for "information on access to the e-mail address" by the German participants in comparison to the English language-version participants.

The ratings provided by the participants indicate that essentially nonmaterialistic reasons determine the participation willingness for the case of e-mail surveys. Survey related reasons occupy the first position ("curiosity"), followed by altruistic reasons ("contribution to research"), and personal reasons ("self realization"). Such self estimates do not necessarily have to agree with actual behavior in a specific survey situation. Nevertheless, the results reported here are relevant in three ways: a) they offer a first orientation for survey organizers, b) help to clarify how intentions towards survey participation are formed respectively grounded, and c) they can be consulted as a starting point for an experimental investigation which explicitly includes behavioral criteria.

Table 6.3: Ranking row of advance information relevant to participation

Specified items: advance information relevant for participation	Ranking of all participants (Mean rank according to Friedman-Test in parentheses; n = 170)	Rankings for english language questionnaires (Mean rank according to Friedman-Test in parentheses; n = 170)	Rankings for german language questionnaires (Mean rank according to Friedman-Test in parentheses; n = 187)
Information on access to e-mail address	1 (3.48)	1 (3.45)	2 (3.51)
Feedback on the results	2 (3.44)	2 (3.33)	1 (3.54)
Information on the exact aims of the study	3 (3.29)	3 (3.07)	3 (3.49)
Complete anonymity of the answers	4 (2.86)	4 (3.03)	4 (2.72)
Researcher's personal appeal	5 (1.92)	5 (2.12)	5 (1.74)

In particular, the answers on the preferred type of information in advance could also be interesting for applied survey research. Information about the exact aims of the investigation was of less importance to the respondents than information on access to the personal e-mail addresses or the offer of a report of the findings. We were surprised by the relatively small significance attached to anonymity, because especially with e-mail surveys, collecting further information based on the participant's return address is a relatively simple procedure (e.g., with the help of search machines on the Internet). Only two of the 357 participants took advantage of an anonymization procedure offered by us in this investigation.

6.2 Amount of Time Provided Voluntarily

So far, little is known about how much time potential participants are willing to spend on a scientific online survey *without* receiving material compensation. Answers to this question could provide first indications on what can be considered a reasonable length for consequent Internet-based investigations.

Asked for the *amount of time spent voluntarily* for scientific questionnaire surveys conducted via e-mail, the proportional answer distribution displayed in Figure 6.1 resulted for all respondents.

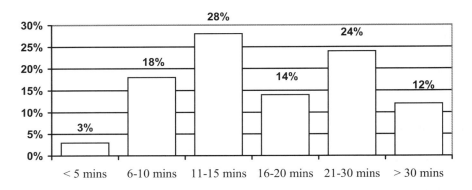

Figure 6.1: Amount of time provided voluntarily for scientific e-mail surveys in minutes (in % with n = 357)

If the sample is divided into two equally large groups, the category limits lie between the response categories 11-15 minutes and 16-20 minutes. People who, according to their own statements, would allow for more than 30 minutes (12%) were given the opportunity to specify their statements on the basis of a text-field entry. In this group, 60% replied with one hour, 17% two hours; in 3% of the cases the maximum, voluntarily provided amount of time amounted to two and a half hours.

With regards to the dimensions "language version" and "survey mode", Table 6.4 demonstrates that the respondents to the English language questionnaires selected the two upper categories more frequently (31.2% 21-30 minutes, 14.7% over 30 minutes) than the German language questionnaire participants (17.6% 21-30 minutes, 10.2% over 30 minutes).

The collected statements suggest that the respondents did not answer in line with the slogan "the shorter, the better". The majority (79% of the respondents) would have raised at least 10 minutes' time for participation. A reason for this could be that the topic of the survey is considered less important in the case of very short surveys. Participating in insignificant surveys, however, contradicts a set of participatory motives.

Table 6.4: Amount of time provided voluntarily for scientific e-mail questionnaires in dependence of language version

	Language version			
	English		German	
	Count	%	Count	%
Less than 5 minutes	3	1.8%	8	4.3%
6-10 minutes	21	12.4%	44	23.5%
11-15 minutes	41	24.1%	59	31.6%
16-20 minutes	27	15.9%	24	12.8%
21-30 minutes	53	31.2%	33	17.6%
More than 30 minutes	25	14.7%	19	10.2%
Total	170	100.0%	187	100.0%

6.3 Differences in the Acceptance Between Scientific vs. Business Surveys

Whether online investigations are more accepted for scientific than for business purposes is important for future online surveys. If one considers the rapid progress of the
Internet's commercialization coupled with many firms wish to collect data on (potential) users of their services for business-related objectives, the question arises
whether "the image" of Internet-based business surveys differs from that of scientific
surveys. The concept of "acceptance" can be defined as the connotative meaning of
attitude objects, – in this case the e-mail questionnaire sent to a potential participant
– and can be operationalized in the form of polarity profiles respectively semantic
differentials. The semantic differential concept was developed by Osgood, Suci, and
Tannenbaum (1957) in order to measure the connotative meaning of a word and/or a
concept. Subjects are requested not to describe a word and/or a concept in a rational
sense, instead they should associate spontaneously. In order to facilitate a comparison
over different concepts, the respondents are given a standardized list of bipolar adjective-pairs (e.g., good-bad, interesting-uninteresting, etc.), which represent the terminal points on a seven-point scale. The respondents have to classify a given concept
on these scales with the use of markings. According to Osgood, Suci, and
Tannenbaum (1957), as well as Hofstaetter (1957, 1977) the pairs of characteristics
are not independent of each other. The variety of usable adjective-pairs can be traced
to the following three dimensions (so-called EPA model): evaluation, activity, and
potency. In order to estimate the acceptance of two attitude objects, the evaluative
dimension is of particular interest.

Table 6.5: Adjective-pairs of the questionnaire used with the corresponding
semantic dimensions according to Osgood et al. (1957)

Semantic dimension	Opposite pairs of the questionnaire
Evaluation	Good/bad
	Positive/negative
	Interesting/uninteresting
	Pleasant/unpleasant
Activity	Attractive/unattractive
	Arousing/soothing
	Active/passive
	Tense/relaxed
Potency	Transparent/obscure
	Reserved/obtrusive
	Controllable/uncontrollable
	Strong/weak

The item pool used (see Table 6.5) is based on suggestions made by Osgood, Suci, and Tannenbaum (1957) as well as Hofstaetter (1957, 1977). Some items were replaced with more appropriate pairs of opposites. For our successive presentation, only the results the set of items belonging to the evaluative dimension will be analyzed.

In all four evaluative pairs of adjectives, significant differences could be observed which accounts for differences in meanings. With reference to the direction of the respective deviations from the averages it is evident that e-mail questionnaire surveys, conducted for scientific purposes, are (in comparison to business surveys) statistically highly significantly:

- classified as "better" ($M_{sci} = 1.12$, $M_{bus} = -0.75$; $t = -18.92$, $df = 357$, $p < .01$),
- evaluated "more positively" ($M_{sci} = 1.01$, $M_{bus} = -0.87$; $t = -18.04$, df = 356, $p < .01$),
- considered "more interesting" ($M_{sci} = 1.36$, $M_{bus} = -0.32$; $t = -14.73$, $df = 355$, $p < .01$), and
- "more pleasant" ($M_{sci} = 0.78$, $M_{bus} = -0.91$; $t = -16.21$, $df = 356$, $p < .01$).

With the aid of a two-factorial ANOVA (factor 1: language version; factor 2: surveys mode) we examined whether statistically significant main and interaction effects in each of the cases for business and scientific e-mail surveys could be observed.

In the following section, the statistically important main effects will be summarized; Tables 6.6 and 6.7 describe the exact averages and test statistics (F-values, degrees of freedom, levels of significance, and explained variance).

- Main effects – language version: business surveys reveal significantly smaller negative values for the English-language investigation over all four evaluative pairs of opposites. Scientific surveys are only rated more highly by participants of the English language questionnaires than those in the German sample for the opposites pair good-bad.
- Main effects – investigation procedures: business surveys were classified as being significantly (1) worse, and (2) more negative by WWW participants than by the e-mail participants. Scientific surveys, on the other hand, were rated "more interesting" by the WWW participants than by the e-mail participants.
- Interaction effects – language version * investigation procedures: no statistically significant interaction effects were observed.

Table 6.6: Descriptive and test statistics for the main effect "language versions"

Language version		English (n = 169)	German (n = 183)	Test statistics for the main effect "language versions"
Attitude object	Opposite pairs (negative area in parentheses)	Means and (standard errors)		
Business surveys	good	-0.23	-1.22	$F(1, 350) = 34.35, p <$
	(bad)	(.12)	(.12)	.01; $Eta^2 = .09$
	Positive	-0.39	-1.3	$F(1, 350) = 29.88, p <$
	(negative)	(.12)	(.12)	.01; $Eta^2 = .08$
	Interesting	0.18	-0.76	$F(1, 350) = 24.51, p <$
	(uninteresting)	(.14)	(.13)	.01; $Eta^2 = .07$
	Pleasant	-0.24	-1.53	$F(1, 350) = 64.19, p <$
	(unpleasant)	(.12)	(.11)	.01; $Eta^2 = .16$
Scientific surveys	good	1.30	0.95	$F(1, 350) = 5.62, p < .01;$
	(bad)	(.11)	(.10)	$Eta^2 = .02$

The respondents' statements lead us to assume that the willingness to participate in scientific Internet surveys is clearly higher than with business surveys. However, slight intercultural differences and variations dependent on the mode of data collection can also be observed. The participants of the English language questionnaire have a smaller negative attitude towards answering business surveys. Participants who we reached via the WWW showed more of a negative attitude towards business surveys.

Table 6.7: Descriptives and test statistics for the main effect
mode of administration

Mode of administration		WWW (n = 179)	e-mail (n = 173)	Test statistics for the main effect "investigation procedure"
Attitude object	opposite pairs (negative area in parentheses)	Means and (standard errors)		
Business surveys	Good (bad)	-0.92 (.12)	-0.53 (.12)	$F(1, 350) = 5.26, p <$ .05; Eta^2 = .02
	Positive (negative)	-1.02 (.12)	-0.66 (.12)	$F(1, 350) = 4.60, p <$ .05; Eta^2 = .01
Scientific surveys	Interesting (uninteresting)	1.55 (.11)	1.16 (.10)	$F(1, 350) = 6.74, p <$ .05; Eta^2 = .02

6.4   Summary and Outlook

In this contribution, we presented results from an investigation conducted in Spring 1996 via the WWW and e-mail in two different language versions. The questions addressed referred to selected, influential determinants of the willingness to participate in Internet-based surveys conducted via e-mail. The following partial questions represented the focus of attention:

Which motives influence the willingness to participate in e-mail surveys? What sort of information in advance can (from the point of view of the interviewees) increase their willingness to participate? It was shown that curiosity as well as a general willingness to contribute to research represented substantial factors relevant to participation, and were clearly regarded as more important than material incentives. Also, the promise in advance of receiving a feedback of the results represents an important determinant for the intention to participate in e-mail surveys.

How much time is applied voluntarily for participation in an Internet-based questionnaire investigation? The judgments provided indicate that the subjects do not adhere to the slogan "the shorter the better". Instead, the majority (79% of respondents) are prepared to spend at least 10 minutes.

Are scientific surveys "more accepted" than business surveys? Our results indicate that scientific surveys are generally considered significantly "more interesting", "pleasant", "better", and more "positive" than e-mail surveys for business purposes. This suggests that scientific online surveys are more accepted than those for business purposes.

The findings presented here are based on statements made by participants. Predictions of actual behavioral patterns can only be made under reservation. In future, a more theoretically grounded and experimentally substantiated procedure would be required (see e.g., Reips, in this volume), where (1) motivational conditions could be induced (see Tuten, Bosnjak, & Bandilla, 1998), and where (2) advance information on the survey, and (3) the necessary duration of participation could be varied. Furthermore, the question arises about which connections exist between motives for participation and the quality of data obtained in a survey (e.g., "falsification tendencies", and/or answering tendencies in the broader sense). Under these circumstances, it is perhaps conceivable that the "material incentive" motive may encourage potential participants to provide some sort of answers, but that consequently the questionnaires are only filled in superficially respectively with less cognitive effort compared to conditions with intrinsic motivators.

References

Batinic, B. & Bosnjak, M. (2000). Psychologische Fragebogenuntersuchungen im Internet. In B. Batinic (Ed.), *Internet für Psychologen* (2nd ed.) (pp. 287-317) [Internet for psychologists]. Göttingen: Hogrefe.

Bosnjak, M. (1997). *Internetbasierte, computervermittelte psychologische Fragebogenuntersuchungen*. Mainz: Gardez.

Dillman, D. A. (1978). *Mail and telephone surveys: The total design method*. New York: Wiley.

Dillman, D. A. (2000). *Mail and Internet surveys: The tailored design method*. New York: Wiley.

Esser, H. (1973). Kooperation und Verweigerung beim Interview. In E. Erbslöh, H. Esser, W. Raschka, & D. Schöne (Eds.), *Studien zum Interview*. Meisenheim am Glan: Hain.

Esser, H. (1986). Über die Teilnahme bei Befragungen. *ZUMA Nachrichten, 18*, 38-47.

Goyder, J. (1987). *The silent minority: Nonrespondents on sample surveys*. Cambridge: Polity Press.

Hofstätter, P. R. (1957). *Psychologie*. Frankfurt a.M.: Fischer.

Hofstätter, P. R. (1977). *Persönlichkeitsforschung*. Stuttgart: Kröner.

Hofstätter, P. R. & Lübbert, H. (1994). Die Untersuchung von Stereotypen mit Hilfe des Polaritätsprofils. *Zeitschrift für Markt-, Meinungs- und Zukunftsforschung, 37, 7571-7581*.

Osgood, C. E., Suci, G. J., & Tannenbaum, P. H. (1957). *The measurement of meaning*. Urbana: University of Illinois Press.

Porst, R. & von Briel, C. (1995). Wären Sie vielleicht bereit, sich gegebenenfalls noch einmal befragen zu lassen? Oder: Gründe für die Teilnahme an Panelbefragungen. *ZUMA Arbeitsberichte, 4*, 1-17.

Tuten, T. L. (1997). Getting a foot in the electronic door: Understanding why people read or delete electronic mail. *ZUMA Arbeitsbericht, 8*, 1-26.

Tuten, T. L., Bosnjak, M., & Bandilla, W. (1998). *An elaboration likelihood approach to understanding response rates in web-based surveys: A proposal.* [Online]. Available: http://www.or.zuma-mannheim.de/tuten/webnet98_ proposal/.

7 Generalizability Issues in Internet-Based Survey Research: Implications for the Internet Addiction Controversy

Viktor Brenner

Psychology researchers are increasingly recognizing the potential value of the Internet as a research tool. Ranging from surveys to real-time experiments in learning and cognition, the amount of psychological research being conducted online is increasing. Clearinghouses, such as those maintained by the American Psychological Society (http://psych.hanover.edu/APS/exponnet.html) or the Internet Psychology Lab (http://www.psych.unizh.ch/genpsy/Ulf/Lab/WebExpPsyLab.html) maintain links to multiple ongoing studies and make it easier for potential participants to take part in online research. Internet-based research is attractive because it is relatively inexpensive, allows for rapid collection, provides access to large potential subject pools of unmatched diversity, and may even reduce the effect of social desirability on sensitive data (Kiesler, Walsh, & Sproull, 1992). However, data quantity is not a substitute for data quality, and in Internet-based research a key data quality question pertains to the generalizability of results.

Generalizability, also known as external validity (Kazdin, 1998), is the general term for the extent to which the conclusions drawn from a specific study with a specific sample are also true of some larger population. If one cannot generalize conclusions beyond the specific sample from which they were drawn, what is left is in essence a series of case studies. Case studies provide interesting examples of things that happen to some people, but specific cases may or may not have any implications for the rest of the world. Thus, establishing the limits of generalizability in Internet-based research is a primary concern: without this data, it is impossible to know how to interpret the findings of research conducted via the Internet. However, research evaluating the generalizability of Internet surveys is all but nonexistent at present.

This chapter will examine the issue of generalizability as it relates in particular to Internet survey research. Existing evidence regarding the limits of generalizability in Internet surveys will be examined. Generalizability questions and issues of classification will then be applied to the question of whether using the Internet is addicting (pathological Internet use), a controversial area of research that has historically been highly dependent on Internet survey methodology.

7.1   Generalizability Theory

The term generalizability stems from the generalizability theory (Cronbach, Gleser, Nanda, & Rajaratnam, 1972) of measurement. Generalizability theory is an extension of classical testing theory, which can be summed up by the equation

$$X = T + e$$

where X represents a measured or observed score, T represents true or actual score, and e represents error. In this model all measured scores are made up of a true score (the individual's actual amount of the construct of interest) and error (everything else that affects an observed score) in unknown proportion. To the extent that errors of measurement are random (unsystematic error), they are normally distributed and therefore tend to sum to zero. As a result, the observed score is the best estimate of the true score for each individual.

This model has guided psychological measurement and test development since its inception and also underlies classical conceptualizations of reliability and validity. However, it relies on an assumption that because errors sum to zero their effect on a specific case will be negligible and the true score will fall within the limits defined by the standard error of measurement. Generalizability theory expands on classical testing theory by focusing on the fact that measurement error is not a single entity but rather is an almost infinite set of error terms that capture the cumulative effects of error variance caused by all of the particulars of a measurement situation. Rather than be satisfied with assumptions about errors summing to zero when they are uncorrelated with the true score – which is probably never true in the absolute sense – generalizability theory attempts to measure the influence of the various sources of error on scores. In this way, cases where measurement errors are more or less likely to occur can be identified. When conducted in the research context, this quantification of error allows one to determine in what populations an experimental finding is likely to be reproduced by virtue of the presence or absence of significant sources of error variance. For instance, if persons of different genders respond differently to a sexual behavior questionnaire, the results of a survey whose respondents are primarily male is unlikely to provide an accurate picture of female behavior. In this situation, the results are said to not generalize to females because they were based primarily on males. Thus, generalizability is an empirical issue, determined by the amount of variance in responses caused by confounding factors such as gender. When the effects of these sources of error have not been determined, the mere existence of factors that may plausibly lead to differential results between various populations calls generalizability into question. These factors are referred to as threats to generalizability.

When threats to generalizability exist, the issue of sample representativeness becomes important. If a factor is known to affect a certain type of measurement, then the degree to which those results can be generalized to a larger population corresponds to the degree to which the sample mirrors the population on that factor. Thus, if age or marital status affects generalizability, then in order for the results to generalize to the whole population, the composition of the sample must closely correspond to that of the population of interest in age and marital status. If some age groups are over-represented, the sample is said to be biased and it becomes increasingly questionable to apply the research findings to other groups. However, a biased (nonrepresentative) sample does not automatically produce an incorrect estimate of a population parameter; this only occurs when significant error variance is introduced into the measurement of the attribute of interest. If the variable that has not been representatively sampled does not correlate with attributes being studied, there can still be generalization. However, it becomes crucial to empirically demonstrate that differences on those factors do not affect the results in question.

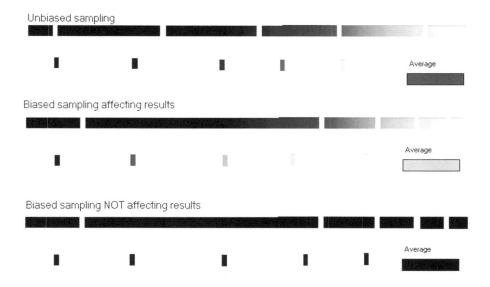

Figure 7.1: Graphical representation of the relationship between
sampling bias and generalizability of results

Even so, there is no substitute for unbiased sampling: even if a source of bias can be shown to not directly affect a specific measurement, that source of bias will correlate with other, unmeasured sources of bias that may. The issue of alternate explanations of the data cannot ever be completely resolved when biased sampling exists. Empirical demonstration of equivalence between groups, however, provides a basis for making a claim of generalizability.

As a hypothetical example, consider a study of chat room and auction Web site usage. Imagine further that self-reported time spent in a chat room may be relatively similar across people of different ethnicity and gender, but may be highly dependent on age and marital status. If the sample in this particular study over-samples young, single persons, it would be likely to result in misleading assessments of attitudes towards self-disclosure in chat rooms. On the other hand, if use of online auction Web sites is about the same regardless of age or marital status, it becomes plausible that this sample's attitudes towards electronic commerce might be an accurate representation of the entire population. Nevertheless, because both age and attitudes towards electronic commerce might be correlated with an unmeasured factor such as risk-taking behavior, generalizability is still less uncertain than if the sample were representative.

Figure 7.1 demonstrates graphically this relationship between biased sampling and generalizability. The black-to-white color spectra represent any more or less normally distributed population characteristic, from height to neuroticism. From each population a sample of five individuals has been selected, with the average of that sample shown in the lower right-hand corner of each spectrum. In the first case, we see that the sample is unbiased, in that all areas of the population distribution (the color spectrum) are about equally likely to be included in the sample. When we average of the colors in the sample, we see that this average closely approximates the central tendency (median color) of the population. In the second example, this same population is sampled in a biased fashion; lighter tones are more likely to be included than darker ones. As a result, the average color of the sample is considerably lighter than the actual central tendency of the population. Finally, the third example shows the same biased sampling of the population. However, because there is no color variance, the sample average corresponds to the population central tendency. Thus, although the latter two examples both involve biased sampling, only the second case results in biased estimates of the central tendency of the population.

This fact that biased samples do not automatically result in biased or erroneous results explains why it is that surveys in particular need to be concerned with generalizability issues. If a study measures a behavior – a perception or cognition experiment for example – that all people can be reasonably expected to perform in the same way, the fact that a biased sample is used to study that behavior is not problematic. For example, college student/Introductory Psychology samples have long been used, particularly in social psychology research, to represent the behavior of all individuals. This generalization is defensible so long as it is reasonable to assume that every person's responses to things like social cues and group dynamics are similar. In fact, a recent study (McGraw, Tew, & Williams, 2001) has replicated the results of several cognitive or social psychological experiments using an online administration, thus demonstrating equivalence of method and by extension generalizability. With surveys, however, the purpose is not to measure individual behavior in a specific, predefined situation but rather to report on their behavior in situations other than the experiment itself. There is no longer any corresponding expectation that the behavior of these individuals is equivalent, and thus generalizability questions are much more important. For this reason, this chapter focuses specifically on generalizability as it pertains to Internet surveys.

Generalizability then is a matter of degree; all results can be generalized to some populations (the "universe of generalization"; Shavelson, Webb, & Rowley, 1989) on the basis of being representative of those populations or differing from the sample only in elements that do not introduce error into measurement. The greatest advance of generalizability theory is that the limits of generalization can thus be empirically quantified. Unfortunately, the process is cumbersome and seldom actually done. When the limits of generalizability have not been firmly established, the question of generalizing from a set of results becomes an argument: is it reasonable and convincing that the specific result is an accurate representation of the entire target population? Or are there plausible alternate explanations of the present results that cast doubt on the generalizability of the results?

7.1.1   Sources of Bias in Internet Surveys

When considering to what extent Internet surveys are generalizable, it becomes clear that there are an almost overwhelming number of threats to generalizability. As shown in Table 7.1, there are numerous sources of potential bias that may be involved in a given online survey. Further, the presence or absence of these threats to generalizability vary by specifics of a given survey such as who the population of interest is, how the data is gathered, and how it is being measured.

Table 7.1: Potential sources of bias in Internet surveys

Source of bias	Generalizability questions	Hypothetical example of how this bias could affect results
Internet users vs. nonusers	Are users representative of the general population in demographics, attitudes, behavior, etc.	Internet users may be better educated, highly middle class, and more liberal
Web surveys vs. e-mail surveys	Do persons who respond to e-mail surveys differ from those who respond to web surveys	Web survey responders may spend more time surfing, e-mail survey responders may have less negative attitudes towards junk mail
Volunteers vs. non-volunteers	Do persons that volunteer to participate differ from those who do not?	Volunteers may be more altruistic or have more free time
Specific types of users: Web vs. Internet Relay Chat (IRC) vs. e-mail, etc	Are frequent/primary web-users representative of the population of Internet users? (for web-based surveys)	Web users may be less socially involved and more likely to be compulsive shoppers
Frequent vs. infrequent users	Since web-based research is likely to oversample heavier users, are they representative of all users? Is either more representative of the general population?	Frequent users may be younger and more socially isolated than infrequent users
Work vs. entertainment users	Are persons who use the web for work undersampled? How might this affect generalizability?	Inclusion of information technology professionals may result in underestimations of the threshold of excessive use
Talkers vs. lurkers	A special case of volunteer vs. nonvolunteer in online research; do people who participate frequently online differ from those who seldom or never participate	Lurkers may be more paranoid and less self-disclosing, talkers may be more histrionic
Website preferences	How do the differences between people who read various web sites – which affects the probability of inclusion – affect generalizability	MSNBC users may be more informed, vote more, and be higher SES than Ebay users

The biggest leap in generalization would be to generalize from the results of an online survey to the general population. In this enterprise, numerous factors that distinguish Internet users from nonusers introduce threats to generalizability. For instance, Internet users tend to be more educated and have higher income (Hoffman & Novak, 1998b). They also are disproportionately white: except at the highest income levels, whites are much more likely to use the Internet than minority group members of equivalent education and income (Hoffman & Novak, 1998a), a disparity known as the "racial-digital divide" (Jackson, 1999). From the standpoint of generalizability, the existence of differences in education, income, and ethnicity – among the demographic factors that frequently moderate other variable relationships – make it hard to justify generalizing from Internet samples to the general population[1]. Perhaps as a result, few have attempted to support a generalization to the general population from an Internet survey.

One common application of Internet surveys is the measurement of Internet behavior itself. This is intuitively reasonable in that the population that can be surveyed via the Internet is the population of interest. Surveys of Internet users have generally followed either of two methods: e-mail surveying and World Wide Web (WWW) surveying. Common e-mail methodology involves identifying e-mail addresses through sources such as the Usenet newsgroups system. The alternative would be to identify users through ownership of an Internet access account; in practice, this information is generally protected by privacy policies on the part of Internet Service Providers (ISPs), whether commercial, corporate, or educational. While e-mail selection enjoys the advantages of experimenter control over subject inclusion, there are several major problems with this method. Potential sources of bias stem from over-representation of users of the Usenet (and frequent posters in particular) and only having access to individuals who choose to make their Internet presence public. There are also ethical issues; sending unsolicited e-mail invitations to participate in a survey are generally unwelcome and frequently result in very hostile responses from potential respondents (Witmer, Colman, & Katzman, 1999; Tse, 1998; Frye, 1999). In Internet parlance, this practice is termed "spamming" and is regarded with the same animosity as unsolicited telephone sales calls. It is ethically questionable to cause emotional upset in potential subjects in this way, while those who actually do respond are likely to be biased towards persons with less unfavorable attitudes to-

---

[1] The racial-digital divide is an area of controversy in its own right; some social commentators have predicted the development of a meritocracy whereby Internet users have greater access to the wealth and benefits of society while minority groups would be consigned to lower social and economic standing by their failure to capitalize on digital opportunities. In this context, it is interesting that the racial-digital divide is most pronounced among current students, who have equality of access to the Internet through their schools but do not equally utilize their access.

ward "spam". As a result of these problems with e-mail surveys, Web-based surveys are preferable.

While WWW surveys do not generally evoke the hostility of e-mail surveys/spam, major generalizability issues remain. Many WWW-based surveys are self-selected anonymous surveys, which introduces the same general biases generally associated with volunteer versus randomly selected samples (Buchanan & Smith, 1999). Although it is possible to have a WWW-based survey that is not self-selected, other means of subject recruitment require either a variation of the e-mail technique described above or else a method of capturing user identities through observation of Web behavior. Both methods introduce difficult ethical questions related to individual expectations of privacy and control over access to their e-mail addresses.

Regardless of whether e-mail or WWW-based, surveys will tend to over-represent users who frequently utilize the Internet medium that is used to identify participants. If a user spends more time using Usenet, Internet Relay Chat (IRC), or a Multiple User Dungeon/Domain (MUD) instead of the WWW, they become increasingly less likely to be part of a Web survey, thus introducing generalizability questions. Over-lapping with preferred usage as a source of bias is amount of usage as a source of bias. Current methods of identifying potential participants rely on Internet usage behavior to identify potential subjects and thus over-select persons who use the computer more frequently. Amount of usage in and of itself is probably not as good a predictor of participation as the amount of recreational (versus business-related) usage. If the population of interest is really Internet users, those who use the Internet primarily for job-related activities are not only likely to be difficult to locate, they may be physically insulated from being contacted for such nonbusiness purposes as surveys by technological firewalls in computer systems and company policies of usage, introducing another source of bias. Finally, amount of usage is likely to be confounded by the amount of direct participation in the Internet for predicting likelihood of participation. The phenomenon of "lurking" is well known in Internet terminology; users who sit back and observe Internet discussions (listservs, IRC, MUD, etc) but seldom if ever participate. Such users can be expected to be both considerably different in many ways than more active participants and less likely to participate in a survey, producing generalizability problems.

Just as the specific method used to identify participants (including self-selection) introduces sources of bias, the *location* used to identify participants also introduces bias. If one wishes to recruit participants using the Usenet news hierarchies, a good deal of thought should be put into whether to include users of the alt.sex and alt.binaries.pictures newsgroups in the potential subject pool. For self-selected WWW-based surveys, the equivalent issue is deciding where to advertise/link the survey site. The major search engines are an obvious place to establish links with a survey site, but they are numerous and personal experience has shown that they are not equally fast in establishing links. Furthermore, difference in user characteristics and in the likelihood of the survey being returned to users as highly relevant to specific search terms will vary; using search engines is unlikely to produce even sampling. Thus, secondary links are common; however, the specific sites to which surveys are linked themselves introduce potential sources of bias. Two of the largest Internet-based surveys have been primarily linked to the home pages of major news providers such as MSNBC (Cooper, Scherer, Boies, & Gordon, 1999) and ABC (Greenfield, 1999). These surveys produced very large responses, but the quantity of data they produced may lead to a sense of false security surrounding their external validity. Clearly, a person who regularly – or ever, for that matter – checks news Web sites can be conceivably different from someone whose primary Web use involves Internet auction houses such as Ebay. Such variances constitute serious threats to generalizability.

7.1.2   Internet Generalizability Data

Clearly, there are many sources of bias involved in almost any methodology for conducting Internet surveys. However, it is still true that bias does not automatically negate generalizability if the dimensions along which sampling is not representative do not affect the outcome domain. Given that a number of Internet surveys have been conducted, what do their results suggest about the magnitude of the problem caused by sampling bias? The data that address this question exist in two types: studies that directly compare results across methods and estimates of population parameters across studies.

Direct comparison data is gathered when researchers collect the same manner of data using both an online and an offline (generally face-to-face) method. While direct comparison data tends to be favorable towards the quality and comparability of data collected online, they tend to differ in significant ways from the standard Internet survey situation. Kobak, Taylor, Dottl, Greist, Jefferson, Burroughs, Katzelnick, & Mandell (1997) reported that psychiatric diagnoses made using the Structured Clinical Interview for DSM-IV (SCID-IV) were generally comparable to those gathered by the PRIME-MD computer-administered questionnaire, with an overall kappa agreement with the SCID-IV of .67. However, the PRIME-MD system was designed and tested for use on a free-standing computer within a medical office setting. Similarly, when an office-based computerized gynecological questionnaire was compared with the same questionnaire administered face-to-face, counterbalanced for order of administration, kappa agreement of responses was at least .75 for nine of eleven questions, and a median kappa of .85 (Hasley, 1995). While encouraging, these studies were not Internet-based, and it is not known if the same results would be found if the comparison were with an online questionnaire.

Table 7.2: Variability of gender estimates among
pathological Internet use surveys

Source	N	Male ratio
Young (1996)[a]	396	40%
Thompson (1996)[a]	104	75%
Egger (1996)[a]	450	84%
Brenner (1997a)	563	73%
Brenner (1997b)	1844	64%
Morahan-Martin & Schumacher (1997)	277	54%
Scherer & Bost (1997)	531	46%
Cooper, Scherer, Boies, & Gordon (1999)	9177	86%
(MSNBC sexuality study)		
Greenfield (1999a)	18,000+	84%

Buchanan and Smith (1999) administered Gangestad and Snyder's (1995) self-monitoring questionnaire as a WWW survey advertised in several psychology-related newsgroups and in paper-and-pencil format to college students. They found equivalent factorial structures between the two sets of data, and were generally optimistic about the future of personality assessment on the Internet. However, these results demonstrate the construct validity of the instrument and to some degree internal validity (Kazdin, 1998). Since no claim is made or tested that the distribution of results observed in these samples is representative of a larger population, generalizability is not actually addressed at all.

Thus, while the direct-comparison research appears favorable towards online research, it has not yet directly addressed questions of generalizability. Thus it is necessary to look at indirect evidence for generalizability. The most readily available evidence comes from comparisons of demographic and other sample parameters drawn from across multiple studies. To the extent that different studies attempt to sample the same population of interest – usually Internet users in general – then there should be consistency between demographic parameters. Inconsistency is most likely to be caused by method variance as was described in the previous section. Thus, the consistency in estimates of stable demographic parameters provides a good estimate of the representativeness of Internet survey sampling.

Unfortunately there is a great deal of inconsistency in the demographic characteristics of samples recruited by various Internet studies. Table 7.2 shows the variability present between surveys related to pathological Internet use in the simplest and least ambiguous of demographic variables, gender. If the survey sample is representative of the population of Internet users, as intended, then to the extent that the male-to-female ratio of users is unchanged each of the male-female ratios reported represent independent estimates of the same parameter. It is thus discouraging to see that estimates of the male-female ratio range from 40% to 86%. Brenner (1999), utilizing the first eight studies listed in Table 7.2 used the chi-square statistic to determine that the variance in the binomial parameter estimate of gender was *89 times* greater than expected by chance (M. B. Miller, personal communication, August 17, 1999). In light of the rapid changes that take place in the cyberworld, it is entirely plausible that the male-to-female ratio of Internet users changed over the time period reflected by these studies. As a result, the assumption that these are all independent estimates of the same stable population parameter is almost certainly false. However, it stretches the limits of plausibility to argue that this variance in gender ratio can be accounted for entirely by changes in the actual Internet population – especially since the general sense is that the male-to-female ratio has decreased, whereas the highest ratios are found in the most recent studies. Thus, it seems clear that the results of these surveys are affected by at least one significant source of bias, and the value of their results as an indicator of population behavior is uncertain.

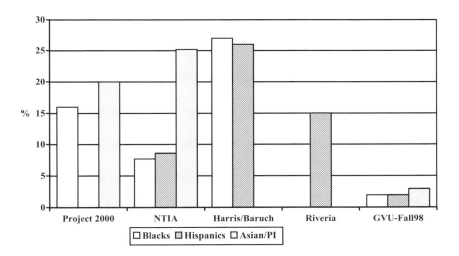

Figure 7.2: Disparities among surveys: race/ethnicity online, U.S.-1998 (reproduced with permission from Jackson, 1999)

The differences between Brenner 1997a and 1997b provide a good illustration of why the differences in gender estimates are almost certainly due to methodological factors as sources of bias. Brenner (1997a) was an interim report based on data gathered during the first three months of the self-selected WWW-based *Internet usage survey* that ran from February 1996 to May 1997; Brenner (1997b) was the final data from the entire survey and included the data from the first report. In order for the gender ratio to decrease 10% (73% to 64%) in the second year of the survey, the male-female ratio or respondents had to change from almost 3 to 1 male at the beginning to very close to 50-50 at the end. Perhaps this corresponds to a massive influx of female Internet users in the latter part of 1996; more likely, it reflects a greater visibility the survey enjoyed in its latter stages. The survey was never advertised on the Usenet, it was only linked to major search engines. However, during 1996 many major American news sources reported on the Interim findings of the survey and included the URL for others to participate. Thus, method variance is clearly a plausible and sufficient accounting of the apparent influx of females in the survey over time.

This variability is not limited to gender ratios and not limited to the pathological Internet use literature. Jackson (1999) reports similar disparity in data describing size and ethnicity of cyberspace. Survey-based estimates of the total number of Internet users (not all of which were online) range from a low of approximately 40 million to a high of almost 110 million, or a range up to three times larger than the parameter estimate itself. Even more striking is the variation in estimates of the number of minority Internet users (Figure 7.2). Depending on which survey is consulted, the percent of ethnic minorities using the Internet ranges from 10% to 50%, with no agreement as to which ethnic minorities are most prevalent. Bandilla (this volume) has shown that Internet surveys systematically under-represent new Internet users as well. Thus, variability appears to be the norm when comparing Internet surveys samples.

To date, there has been one direct comparison of the demographic characteristics of a self-selected Internet survey sample (n = 72) and a college student sample (n = 56). Smith and Leigh (1997) found that while the two samples differed in age (95% of the college student sample was under 30, compared with 65% of the Internet sample) and gender ratio (Internet sample, 74% male; college student sample, 80% female) they did not differ significantly in sexual orientation, marital status, ethnicity, education, and religiosity. Further, comparing the results of a series of questions regarding sexual fantasies with those of an earlier, paper-and-pencil study found no significant differences. However this may be misleading for two significant reasons. First, when comparing results with the previous study – which was also conducted using college students – the Internet sample was apparently combined with the college student sample. Second, the value of a null finding in comparison to another college student sample, themselves generally acknowledged to be nonrepresentative, is open to debate. Thus, current data strongly suggest that Internet surveys are highly susceptible to method variance and sampling bias, casting serious doubts on their generalizability.

7.1.3   Bias, Disinhibition, and Generalizability

Given that Internet surveys are likely to produce biased, nonrepresentative samples, it must be empirically demonstrated that equivalent results are produced using different survey methods in order to make a case for generalizability, as McGraw et al. (2001)

have with for social and cognitive psychology experiments. Since the conceptual basis for such generalization is that the attribute being measured does not vary between the (biased) sample and the population of interest, this equivalence is subject-specific; that is, it must be separately established for every content domain that is being measured. In other words, unless previous research has shown that online and offline samples produce the same results in the content domain being studied, direct empirical evidence must be supplied to support any claim of generalizability.

One issue that comes into play when considering the equivalence of Internet survey results with other samples is the phenomenon of disinhibition (Joinson, 1999). Most frequently seen in the phenomon of "flaming", disinhibition refers to online social behavior where conventional norms of behavior and concerns about social presentation and judgement are greatly reduced or absent. It is theorized that because social cues are less salient online, they have less inhibitory effect on behavior. If so, then it can be expected that responses to online surveys will be disinhibited as well. Thus, some studies that have compared technology-assisted versus face-to-face or paper-and-pencil surveying have found that the former are more likely to endorse sensitive or nonsocially-desirable behavior. A major study of adolescent behavior found that respondents were more likely to admit a history of male homosexual encounters, IV drug use, and sexual contact with IV drug users (Turner, Rogers, Lindberg, Pleck, & Sonenstein, 1998) when using a computer to respond to audio-taped questions as compared to more traditional survey methods. Similarly, in Hasley's (1995) comparison of gynecological histories, women were more likely to admit not exercising or giving themselves breast exams on the computer. While this is sometimes interpreted that the Internet provides better data quality with sensitive topics, without a gold standard of comparison to say whether face-to-face or online surveys provide more accurate estimates of reality, it really only means that endorsement probability is higher. It is equally plausible that respondents utilize a lower threshold of endorsement online when addressing the same question; clinicians may recognize a parallel in the MMPI-2 F scale. Clients who are not taking the test with the motivation and mental set that is expected become more likely to endorse the low-frequency items that comprise the F-scale and thus may produce invalid results. Disinhibition does not mean that results are invalid, but it suggests that in endorsing items participants don't necessarily have in mind the same construct that the item is intended to measure. As an example, if an adolescent has had sex with someone who they know to have become an IV drug user later after their relationship ended, what is the correct response to Turner et al.'s (1998) question about having unprotected sex with an IV drug user? In cases such as this, factors such as social desirability and response styles may explain differential endorsement rates as much as the underlying construct.

In sum, generalizability cannot be assumed when using Internet survey methodology. The available data suggest that large variance exists between surveys based on methodological differences that produce nonrepresentative samples. This does not automatically mean that these results cannot be generalized, but it does mean that generalizability must be first established by demonstrating equivalent results across different survey methodologies. This is of course seldom practiced, because the advantages of Internet research in time, cost, etc. are lost when a parallel, traditional survey must also be conducted. The current state, then, of Internet surveying is that many are conducted, but their value in indeterminable because the limits of generalizability have not been established in that domain. The Internet continues to be a promising avenue for research; however, this initial research must focus more on the method itself than on any specific content area.

7.1.4   The Case of Pathological Internet Use

As an example of the generalizability implications of Internet surveys, the preceding analysis will now be applied to the question of whether use of the Internet can result in an addiction. The term pathological Internet use has recently emerged as the preferred term for describing this potential disorder with the DSM-IV category pathological gambling frequently being cited as its prototype. Internet surveying in this population makes intuitive sense because Internet users are the defined population of interest, and the relatively low base rate of Internet use in the general population reduces the yield available using more traditional survey methods. As a result, almost all of the research in this area has used Internet surveying as a method.

As was shown in Table 7.2, pathological Internet use surveys have generally had large samples, but the variance in gender ratios in the various samples suggests varying degrees of bias present in all of them. As a result, it becomes impossible to generalize beyond the individual samples involved. Thus, the fact that Greenfield (1999a, 1999b) reports that 6% of respondents to his survey met his criteria for "compulsive Internet use" should not be taken to mean that 6% of all Internet users are addicted. On the other hand, the fact that any respondents met such criteria suggests that at least some individuals perceive themselves to have a problem with the Internet.

In essence, the existence of individual users meeting a set of criteria represents a set of case studies. In this case, such surveys demonstrate that individuals exist who describe themselves as having experiences similar to those found in other addictive disorders. Whether or not this is equivalent to being addicted is another matter entirely. Griffiths (1998) makes the philosophical statement that if one can find an individual who meets the criteria for a given disorder, that disorder must exist. This is debatable, not only because of issues of data reliability, but also because one can create any manner of definition of any kind of syndrome one wants, and it is likely that one can find someone who fits that definition. Whether or not there is any external validity to that definition is another question. One could elect to define Internet Dependence as anyone who spends more than 40 hours per week connected to the Internet; anyone who runs e-mail in the background of their PC all day is now by definition disordered. In no way has the pathological Internet use literature been irresponsible in this way; however, there is little agreement about what signs should be indicators of the disorder (if it exists). Griffiths (1998) chose to define Internet Addiction based on theoretical criteria for behavioral addictions, as did Brenner (1997) in reference to the work of Peele (1985); Young (1996) adapted DSM-IV substance dependence criteria, and Greenfield (1999) used the criteria for pathological gambling. Such inconsistency in definition makes it impossible to directly compare the results of these various studies; at the same time, it is entirely understandable given the lack of any gold standard of comparison.

The current situation in regards to pathological Internet use is a prototypical bootstraps problem (Cronbach & Meehl, 1955). In short, the bootstraps problem is that in the absence of any independent method of measuring or classifying individuals in relations to a disorder, there is no way to validate a measure of that disorder except in reference to other measures of that disorder. Once a system of classification exists, it provides a reference for the classification to be refined; thus, once a reliable method of measurement exists the definition of the disorder can be "pulled up by the bootstraps" in relation to this measurement. There is, however, no easy way to gain a standard of measurement/classification when none is present; measurement can only be related to other attempts to measure the same thing, in a circular fashion, without any way to demonstrate any construct validity in any of the measures.

There is one specific situation in which the bootstraps problem can be definitively resolved: a taxonic situation. A taxonic situation exists when a general population is in reality comprised of two qualitatively different subpopulations – in this case, addicted versus nonaddicted. In a taxonic situation, when measures that differentiate between the two taxa are given members of the population, a specific pattern of correlations occurs: there will be negligible correlation between measures within each taxon but a moderate correlation if members of the two taxa are mixed. This occurs because the members of one taxon will necessarily tend to score higher on all measures that differentiate taxa than the members of the other taxon. Thus, if pathological Internet users exist, we would expect that they would spent more time online, and spend less time sleeping, and have received more work reprimands than nonaddicts. However, within the group of pathological users there might be little correlation between these measures. These specific mathematical properties of taxonic situations result in specific mathematical properties within data sets that can be detected using the method(s) of coherent cut kinetics (Meehl, 1994). Coherent cut kinetics are a set of methods for mathematically analyzing the properties of data collected on a large population and determining whether the characteristic properties of taxonicity are present. The super bootstraps theorem (Meehl, 1965) proved that the existence of these properties (1) proves underlying taxonicity in the data set, (2) can be used to estimate the relative size of each taxon, and (3) can be used to generate an optimum cutoff score on each measure of the taxa that will maximize the percent of correct classifications made. Thus, if one has a moderately valid way to differentiate between taxa, this can be converted into a gold standard or comparison that did not exist previously.

Unfortunately, Internet usage-related consequences are not taxonic. Brenner (1997) applied MAXCOV-HITMAX, the most commonly used method of coherent cut kinetics, to data gathered from the Internet usage survey, and failed to find the characteristic signatures of taxonicity. Although the data utilized for this analysis were biased in many of the ways described previously, this bias would serve to lead to incorrect estimates of the relative size of each taxon but should not affect the ability to identify taxonicity in the first place. Therefore, if a pathological Internet use disorder exists, it does not represent a qualitative distinction from other Internet users.

Although Internet usage fails the test of taxonicity, it must be noted that taxonicity is not a requirement for a valid clinical syndrome. Taxonic distribution is a *sufficient* but not a *necessary* element in a valid clinical syndrome. The DSM-IV contains examples of generally accepted clinical syndromes that are taxonic (schizophrenia) and that are not taxonic, but rather represent a continuum from normal to pathological (depression). In fact, the lack of a direct correspondence between taxonicity and our classification of disorders has led to a continuing dialogue about what are the defining features of things that we call disordered (Wakefield, 1999; Lilienfeld & Marion, 1999). However, the absence of any external markers to validate or invalidate the concept of pathological Internet use means that the literature continues to rely heavily on correlations to itself and surveys of users of unknown generalizability. Clearly, individuals exist whose quality of life has deteriorated as a result of their use of the Internet, but this does not mean that the Internet is a thing that is inherently addictive and/or dangerous (Grohol, 1998).

As with most new phenomena, most of the first psychological research on Internet usage has been inspired by clinical contact with these unfortunate individuals; as time passes, we gain a broader perspective on the Internet phenomenon and our views of its threat potential may change. Already, several commentators have noted that it is a general social response to react to new technologies with fears of their potential danger (Stern, 1999; Gackenbach, 1998). Historical investigations have shown that similar fears were expressed by contemporaries with the advent of radio, telephones, and television. Our reaction to the addictive potential of the Internet may be yet another manifestation of a general human response to new technology. Perhaps the greatest influx of perspective has come from a recent work by Joseph Walther (1999) on the hypothetical and absurd Communication Addiction Disorder, a disorder of excessive talking (talkaholism) that causes harmful interference with one's online communications. Using existing literature, he was able to show (1) a sizable percentage of talkers could be classified as abnormally communicative, (2) relationships between talking and academic outcomes, (3) the existence of tolerance and withdrawal in talking behavior, and (4) evidence for Griffiths' (1998) criteria for addiction. This work provides a lesson in perspective on how easy it is to over-interpret theoretical classifications and interpretation of outlying and thus "deviant" responses on questionnaires.

7.2   Conclusions

Generalizability, then, is not a fixed quality but rather a matter of the degree to which findings are also true of a general population of interest. The Internet provides many new and exciting opportunities for research that will undoubtedly be expanded and developed in the coming years; however, at this point the limits of generalizability in Internet research are unknown. Internet surveys need to be particularly aware of this problem because they are more reliant on generalizations based on sample representativeness than other types of Internet research. Not only are there many plausible threats to external validity present in Internet survey methodology, many of which are likely to be specific to the content and location of a specific survey, but indirect evidence of the variation in what should be relatively stable parameters seems to show that these factors have exerted a sizable effect on existing surveys.

Fortunately, generalizability is an empirical issue. Comparisons can be made between samples and between subject areas to determine the amount of influence these factors have on research findings and will allow one to determine the extent of generalizability. This research seems to be priority one in this area, for without it one does not know how to evaluate the results of Internet surveys, regardless of content area.

The area of pathological Internet use is an area that requires special scrutiny because of its historical dependence on Internet survey methodology. There are substantial questions of data quality and generalizability as well as inconsistency of definition. Some recent work suggests that fear of new technology may be one of important psychological phenomenon at work, and societal responses to previous technologies provide intriguing parallels. However, there are some ways in which the Internet is decidedly different from media that have existed before. One way is in its interactivity; while the telephone is interactive, it requires you to know the party to whom you are communicating, while the Internet provides forums for mass broadcasting and for meeting new people. The Internet is also, at least at present, relatively seamless; whereas watching television provides markers of the passage of time in the form of commercials every 15 minutes (in the U.S.) and changing of programs every 30-120 minutes, the Internet moves from one page to another on command and thus it may be easier to loose track of time online; as advertising increasingly works its way onto the Internet, this may change. Finally, the Internet allows the user to choose the content of the medium, while other media such as radio and television do not provide this choice. In light of this, it may well be that the "danger" of the Internet is in its provision of large-scale access to other individuals who share one's inherent interests, be it bull terriers, needlepoint, or bondage and discipline. The opening up of these avenues of communication and reinforcement may challenge many individuals' abilities to balance the various aspects of their lives; this would seem to be a far cry from calling the Internet "addictive". Indeed, Davis (2001) has suggested that pathological Internet use can follow two patterns, a general pattern consistent with most model of addiction and a specific pattern whereby the Internet acts as the medium of delivery of some other content that is the actual addictive "hook". The latter conceptualization may well provide a more cogent framework for future work in this area.

The prevalence of Internet surveys is likely to continue to grow; students are frequently among those most interested in the new medium and can be expected to continue to develop the medium. As such, it is particularly important to research the medium for its own sake *now*, defining the limits of generalizability in order to determine the value of Internet surveys, before it becomes commonplace to see broad statements of human behavior being made on the basis of sensational results with uncertain generalizability.

References

American Psychiatric Association. (1994). *Diagnostic and statistical manual of mental disorders* (4th ed.). Washington, DC: Author.

Brenner, V. (1997a). Psychology of computer use: XLVII. Parameters of Internet use, abuse, and addiction: The first 90 days of the Internet usage survey. *Psychological Reports, 80*, 879-882.

Brenner, V. (1997b). Update on the Internet usage survey. In J. M. Morahan-Martin (Chair), *Can Internet usage be pathological?* Symposium presented at the American Psychological Association convention, Chicago.

Brenner, V. (1999). Generalizability in Internet-based (survey) research. In B. L. Gordon (Chair), *New findings on effects of Internet use*, symposium presented at the American Psychological Association convention, Boston.

Buchanan, T. & Smith, J. L. (1999). Using the Internet for psychological research: Personality testing on the world wide web. *British Journal of Psychology, 90*, 125-144.

Cooper, A., Scherer, C. R., Boies, S. C., & Gordon, B. L. (1999). Sexuality on the Internet: From sexual exploration to pathological expression. *Professional Psychology: Research and Practice, 30*, 33.

Cronbach, L. J., Gleser, G. C., Nanda, H., & Rajaratnam, N. (1972). *The dependability of behavioral measurements: Theory of generalizability of scores and profiles*. New York: Wiley.

Cronbach, L. J. & Meehl, P. E. (1955). Construct validity in psychological tests. *Psychological Bulletin, 52*, 281-302.

Davis, R. A. (2001). A cognitive-behavioral model of pathological Internet use. *Computers in Human Behavior, 17, 187-195.*

Frye, N. E. (1999). Internet demographics and participant recruitment. In N. E. Frye (Chair), *Conducting research vie the Internet*, symposium presented at the 1999 American Psychological Convention, Boston.

Gackenbach, J. (Ed.). (1998). *Psychology and the Internet: Intrapersonal, interpersonal, and transpersonal implications*. San Diego: Academic Press.

Gangestad, S. W. & Snyder, M. (1985). "To carve nature at its joints": On the existence of discrete classes in personality. *Psychological Review, 92*, 317-349.

Greenfield, D. N. (1999a). The nature of Internet addiction: Psychological factors in compulsive Internet use. In B. L. Gordon (Chair), *New findings on effects of Internet use*, symposium presented at the American Psychological Association convention, Boston.

Greenfield, D. N. (1999b). *Virtual addiction: Help for netheads, cyberfreaks, and those who love them.* Oakland, CA: New Harbinger.

Griffiths, M. (1998). Internet addiction: Does it really exist? In J. Gackenbach (Ed.), *Psychology and the Internet: Intrapersonal, interpersonal, and transpersonal implications*. San Diego: Academic Press.

Grohol. J. M. (1998). Future clinical directions: professional development, pathology, and psychotherapy online. In J. Gackenbach (Ed.), *Psychology and the Internet: Intrapersonal, interpersonal, and transpersonal implications*. San Diego: Academic Press.

Hasley, S. (1995). A comparison of computer-based and personal interviews for the gynecologic history update. *Obstetrics & Gynecology, 85*, 494-498.

Hoffman, D. L. & Novak, T. P. (1998a). Bridging the racial divide on the Internet. *Science, 280*, 390-391.

Hoffman, D. L. & Novak, T. P. (1998b). *Bridging the digital divide: The impact of race on computer access and Internet use.* [Online]. Available: http://www2000.ogsm.vanderbilt.edu/paper_list.html.

Jackson, L. A. (1999). Who's on the Internet? Making sense of Internet demographic surveys. In N. E. Frye (Chair), *Conducting research vie the Internet*, symposium presented at the 1999 American Psychological Convention, Boston.

Joinson, A. (1998). Causes and implications of disinhibited behavior on the Internet. In J. Gackenbach (Ed.), *Psychology and the Internet: Intrapersonal, interpersonal, and transpersonal implications*. San Diego: Academic Press.

Kazdin, A. E. (1998). *Research design in clinical psychology* (3rd Ed). Needham Heights, MA: Allyn & Bacon.

Kiesler, S., Walsh, J., & Sproull, L. (1992). Network based electronic field research. In J. Edwards & F. Bryan (Eds.), *Methodological issues in applied psychology* (pp. 239-268), New York: Plenum.

Kobak, K. A., Taylor, L. vH., Dottl, S. L., Greist, J. H., Jefferson, J. W., Burroughs, D., Katzelnick, & Mandell, M. (1997a). Computerized screening for psychiatric disorders in an outpatient community mental health clinic. *Psychiatric Services, 48,* 1048-1057.

Lilienfeld, S. O. & Marion, L. (1999). Essentialism revisitied: Evolutionary theory and the concept of mental disorder. *Journal of Abnormal Psychology, 108,* 400-411.

Meehl, P. E. (1965). *Detecting latent clinincaltaxa by fallible quantitative indicators lacking an accepted criterion* (Rep Pr-65-2). Minneapolis: University of Minnesota, Reports from the Research Laboratories of the Department of Psychiatry.

Meehl, P. E. (1994). Bootstraps taxometrics: Solving the classification problem in psychopathology. *American Psychologist, 50,* 266-275.

Morahan, M. & Schumacker (1997). Incidence and correlates of pathological Internet use. In J. M. Morahan-Martin (Chair), *Can Internet usage be pathological?,* symposium presented at the American Psychological Association convention, Chicago.

McGraw, K. O., Tew, M. D., & Williams, J. E. (2001). The integrity of web-delivered experiments: Can you trust the data? *Psychological Science, 11,* 502-510.

Peele, S. (1985). *The meaning of addiction: Compulsive experience and its interpretation.* Lexington, MA: Lexington Books.

Scherer, K. & Bost, J. (1997). Internet use patterns: Is there Internet dependency on campus? In J. M. Morahan-Martin (Chair), *Can Internet usage be pathological?,* symposium presented at the American Psychological Association convention, Chicago, Illinois.

Shavelson, R. J., Webb, N. M., & Rowley, G. L. (1989). Generalizability theory. *American Psychologist, 44,* 922-932.

Smith, M. A. & Leigh, B. (1997). Virtual subjects: Using the Internet as an alternative source of subjects and research environment. *Behavior Research Methods, Instruments, & Computers, 29,* 496-505.

Stern, S. E. (1999). Addiction to technologies: A social psychological perspective of Internet addiction. In J. M. Morahan-Martin (Chair), *Internet addiction – supporting evidence, alternative explanations, and limitations of research*, symposium presented at the APA Convention, Boston.

Turner, C. F., Ku, L., Rogers, S. M., Lindberg, L. D., Pleck, J. H., & Sonenstein, F. L. (1998). Adolescent sexual behavior, drug use, and violence: Increased reporting with computer survey technology. *Science, 280,* 867-873.

Tse, A. C. (1998). Comparing the response rate, response speed, and response quality of two methods of sending questionnaires: E-mail vs. mail. *Journal of the Marketing Research Society, 40,* 353-361.

Wakefield, J. C. (1999). Evolutionary versus protope analyses of the concept of disorder. *Journal of Abnormal Psychology, 108,* 374-399.

Walther, J. P. (1999). Communication addiction disorder: Concern over media, behavior, and effects. In J. M. Morahan-Martin (Chair), *Internet addiction – supporting evidence, alternative explanations, and limitations of research*, symposium presented at the APA Convention, Boston, MA. [Online]. Available: http://www.rpi.edu/~walthj/docs/cad.html.

Witmer, D. F., Colman, R. W., & Katzman, S. L. (1999). From paper-and-pencil to screen-and-keyboard: Toward a methodology for survey research on the Internet. In S. G. Jones, (Ed.), *Doing Internet research: Critical issues and methods for examining the Net* (pp. 145-161). Thousand Oaks, CA: Sage.

Young, K. (1996). *Internet addiction: The emergence of a new clinical disorder.* Unpublished manuscript cited in Griffiths, 1998.

8 Personality Assessment via Internet: Comparing Online and Paper-and-Pencil Questionnaires

Guido Hertel, Sonja Naumann, Udo Konradt, & Bernad Batinic

The history of personality assessment is also a history of the development of different methodological tools and their implications for the reliability of measurement. In ancient times, these assessment tools were rather simple (and sometimes odd) deriving stable personality traits from visible indicators such as body stature, physiognomy, or scull size. However, with the introduction of psychoanalysis in the beginning of this century scholars attempted to "go behind" the visible surface of a person exploring unconscious motives and personality patterns by the analysis of dreams and projective tests. Although providing interesting insights, these attempts were often struggling with a low degree of consistency between researchers that led to problems of validity, and thus usability (e.g., Guilford, 1959).

Today, the most popular tools for personality assessment are questionnaires. With the first versions developed in the beginning of this century, personality questionnaires became increasingly popular in the Forties and Fifties. This popularity was largely due to their economy and standardized structure that enabled reliable and valid measurements. These questionnaires were usually administered as paper-and-pencil versions that were easily duplicated but required coding procedures. Since the Seventies, however, these procedures have been further simplified by computer-based administrations of the questionnaires. Computerization not only increased the economy of personality testing, but also provided additional opportunities for refinement due to the "memory" of computers, such as random item orders or adaptive testing (Burke, 1993). With the beginning of the new millennium, it seems as if we are again opening a new chapter of personal assessment by exploring chances and challenges of applying personality measures via the Internet.

In this chapter, we will discuss advantages and disadvantages of personality assessment via the Internet and provide empirical evidence on the feasibility and reliability of such a procedure. The exploration of personality assessment via the Internet is not only relevant for psychological research (e.g., online surveys or experiments such as those reported in this volume; Birnbaum, 1999), but has also major implications for applied fields such as personnel selection, placement, and development. After briefly reviewing the literature on computer supported and Internet-based personality assessment, we present an empirical study exploring the feasibility of online personality assessment. We compare reliability and validity indicators of these online personality measures with a parallel paper-and-pencil application. A discussion of the results and suggestions for future opportunities of Internet-based assessment concludes this chapter.

8.1   Computer-Based Personality Testing

The general idea behind computerized personality testing is quite simple: Instead of completing questionnaires in a paper-and-pencil form, participants type their answers directly into a computer. Anyone who has coded questionnaire data can imagine how enthusiastically scholars reacted to this idea. Indeed, computerized testing can be quite convenient, cost-effective, and environmentally friendly (i.e., it saves a lot of paper). The only precondition is that appropriate computer equipment is available.

Apart from these economic and ecological issues, computerized questionnaires have a number of additional advantages. As already mentioned, computers have the capability of handling much larger item-pools than what is usually printed on paper-and-pencil versions, and can draw random samples from these item pools. Thereby, one can control different artifacts such as order or context effects, and handle issues of test-material protection. Moreover, computer-based administration facilitates adaptive testing, assigning questionnaire items based on earlier answers of a participant. Although this procedure is still discussed controversially (e.g., Overton, Harms, Taylor, & Zickar, 1997), it can enable more refined measurement without using a larger number of items (e.g., Burke, 1993; Mead & Drasgow, 1993; Wainer, 1990).

Another advantage of computerized testing is that the answer behavior of participants can be explored unobtrusively by measuring decision times and answer correction online. Such data provide additional insight into the reliability of personality scales (Maschke, 1989). Moreover, computerized tests might increase a sense of anonymity because participants only hit keys on a keyboard (or touch the screen) instead of writing answers in their personal handwriting. Some authors have reported that participants respond more honestly to sensitive personal questions in computer questionnaires (Evan & Miller, 1969; O'Brain & Dugdale, 1978) and admit to engaging in more socially undesirable behaviors (e.g., Carr, Gosh, & Ancil, 1983). However, more recent research found little differences in honesty of participants' answers between computerized and paper-and-pencil testing (Martin & Nago, 1989; Lautenschlager & Flaherty, 1990; see Burke 1993 for a review). More research is desirable, particularly with nonstudent samples, to conclusively answer these questions.

Comparing computerized and conventional paper-and-pencil tests according to other aspects of reliability and validity also revealed only small differences between the two procedures (see Burke, 1993; Mead & Drasgow, 1993, for reviews). The only notable exception are speed-related tests. It seems that computer-keyboards enable participants to respond faster than paper-and-pencil questionnaires, which leads to changes of performance norms particularly in aptitude testing (Burke, 1993). On the other hand, inappropriate hardware and software design can sometimes produce difficulties in computerized testing, thereby decreasing average speed compared to conventional paper-and-pencil tests. However, because personality tests are mostly non-speeded, we do not further discuss these aspects.

Taken together, computerized personality tests have a number of benefits over paper-and-pencil versions without a notable decrease in psychometric properties (Barrett, Alexander, Doverspike, Cellar, & Thomas, 1992; Burke, 1993). In addition to the already mentioned issues, computer tests seem to be well accepted by participants (Burke, Normand, & Raju, 1987) and can provide fast and accurate interpretations given the appropriate equipment is available (Farrell, 1989). Combining these advantages of computerized tests with the increasing options of the fastly growing Internet leads to a number of interesting opportunities for social sciences as well as for applied issues. Before we provide a sample study of such assessments, we will briefly discuss some special issues of Internet-based personality assessment.

8.2   Internet-Based Personality Assessment

Internet-based assessment is a new but promising and growing field. Although there is already some research available that compares Internet-based questionnaires with more traditional methods such as paper-and-pencil tests (see Rietz & Wahl, in this volume; Smith, 1999; Stanton, 1998; Wilhelm, 1999), systematic research on personality measures is still lacking (see Buchanan & Smith, 1999, for a notable exception). However, it seems reasonable that the positive résumé of computerized personality assessment at local computer stations can be transferred to computerized assessment via Internet because administration and answering mode are very similar.

Moreover, Internet-based assessments imply a number of additional advantages. Recruiting participants via Internet give access to a large number of participants even with special characteristics. Expenses for conducting these assessments are very low, because laboratory space, time, and materials can be minimized, and data acquisition and analyses run automatically. Also, advertising for studies might be simpler and more convenient via Internet, as well as less expensive (see Batinic & Bosnjak, 2000 in this volume). Moreover, (perceived) anonymity might be higher in Internet-based questionnaires because there is no face-to-face contact with any researcher or a research location. Studies on flaming (Kiesler, Siegel, & McGuire, 1984) suggest that persons surfing on the Internet often experience a lack of social control that might lead to even less inhibitions to answer personal sensitive questions or admit socially undesirable behavior as in other computerized test settings.

However, these possible advantages also imply higher risks for Internet-based compared to traditional tests. The broader range of potential participants that are contacted worldwide via Internet reduces researchers' control of the subject sample. Although there are means to address certain subject groups (e.g., by specific advertisements and/or passwords via e-mail), Internet samples are often more heterogeneous (in geographical location, cultural background, etc.) than traditional questionnaire samples. On the other hand, although the number of Internet users is growing rapidly, they are still not representative in sex, age, occupations, education, geographical, or cultural background for the main population (Stanton, 1998).

Moreover, the advantages of (perceived) anonymity in Internet questionnaires can lead to lower data reliability particularly when participants are not highly motivated, or enjoy playing with different identities. Data reliability can also be reduced by participants' lack of confidence in computer use, by the usability of the human-computer interface, and by environmental factors like heat, noise, mood state, fatigue, or drug consumption that are not under the researchers' control (Stanton, 1998). Although techniques available to check for such biases, it is still an empirical question whether questionnaire data, and particularly personality data, of participants recruited via the Internet are as reliable and consistent as data collected with traditional measures.

In order to explore the quality of Internet-based personality assessment, we conducted a feasibility study comparing personality questionnaires administered via Internet and via paper-and-pencil. The personality scales we used were chosen based on their relevance for communication processes since the study was part of a larger study on preferences of communication media (Naumann, Hertel, Konradt, & Batinic, 1999). However, the chosen personality concepts (the "Big Five inventory," Self-Monitoring, and social anxiety scales) are among the most popular personality concepts and are relevant for many other domains in research as well as applied psychology (e.g., personnel selection).

The first main question of our study was whether personality tests via the Internet would be accepted by Internet users. While some evidence suggests that Internet questionnaires and experiments are generally accepted, little is know about the reaction to personality scales. Traditional personality questionnaires are usually poorly accepted (Schuler, 1993) which may be due to the low transparency of items, criteria, and conclusions. This might be particularly valid for the Internet where the absence of a researcher might additionally increase distrust and skepticism. Therefore, we were interested whether persons were willing at all to complete such an instrument on the Internet.

The second leading question was whether personality data collected via the Internet are as reliable and valid as data collected with paper-and-pencil questionnaires.

Answering this question entails a number of methodological problems. Although it seems desirable to compare different questionnaire modes using the same people, this is difficult to realize. Many personality scales do not have parallel versions. Moreover, recruiting people for face-to-face test sessions and then asking them to participate in an Internet questionnaire might produce a sample that is not representative for people who are only recruited via Internet. On the other hand, contacting participants first via Internet and later asking them to complete an additional paper-and-pencil questionnaire might raise problems of confidentiality (see Buchanan & Smith, 1999, for similar arguments).

As a consequence, we compared the two questionnaire modes by analyzing the internal consistencies of the used personality data (i.e., scale reliability and factorial structure) for both the Internet and the paper-and-pencil questionnaire. As an additional reliability measure, we compared the number of missing values in both versions. Moreover, as external consistency criteria, we investigated the construct validity of the used scales by correlating them with other personality scales and with behavioral measures. If participants on the Internet showed lower motivation or dishonesty as in traditional measures, internal as well as external consistency of the Internet scales should be lower as in the paper-and-pencil questionnaire. Moreover, the number of missing values should be higher in the Internet application. On the other hand, if the consistency scores turn out to be comparable between the two questionnaire modes, we would have evidence that Internet personality assessments are as reliable and valid as traditional measurements. Below, we describe the procedure and main results of our study.

8.3   Questionnaire Study

8.3.1   Participants

Two-hundred-and-fifty persons participated in the study, 136 via Internet and 112 answering the paper-and-pencil questionnaire. Participants of the paper-and-pencil sample were recruited by the second author at the campus of the University of Kiel. Accordingly, most of them (97%) were students enrolled for subjects such as math and natural sciences (26%), economics (23%), psychology (21%), law (8%), and medicine (6%). In the Internet sample, 56% were students but from different (German) universities (no study subjects were recorded in this sample). Of the remaining participants, 31% were full-time employees, 9% worked part-time, and 4% were unemployed. Related to the differences in occupational background, the age average in the Internet sample was slightly but significantly higher (M = 29.7) than the average for the paper-and-pencil sample (M = 24.1; $t(246)$ = 5.86; p < 0.001).

Interestingly, there were nearly equal numbers of females and males in the Internet sample (43% females, 57% males). Given that there are still more male than female Internet users (Stanton, 1998), this might be an indication that women have higher interests in questionnaires on topics related to psychology and communication (see also Buchanan & Smith, 1999). In the paper-and-pencil sample, males somewhat dominated the sample (64% males, 36% females), presumably due to the general distribution of females and males at the University of Kiel and the sex of the recruiting person.

8.3.2   Procedure

The Internet version was developed using the WWW questionnaire generating tool (Batinic, Puhle, & Moser, 1999). The questionnaire was advertised at different locations on the Internet, such as mailing lists, some Web sites, and the psychology homepage of the University of Kiel.

As an incentive, a lottery was conducted at the end of the study with a potential prize of about $55. To protect confidentiality, participants in the paper-and-pencil sample wrote their name and phone number on a form separate from the questionnaire. In the Internet sample, a separate form was attached at the bottom of each questionnaire where participants could enter their e-mail address. This form was sent separately to the research team. Of course, people in both samples could decide to participate without revealing any personal information (7% in the Internet and 16% in the paper-and-pencil version chose this option).

In order to ensure that people only participated once in the Internet study, we compared the Internet Protocol (IP) addresses of those questionnaires we received. This is a rather conservative procedure because it results in the exclusion of people who participate using the same computer (e.g., in a university computer lab). However, in the current sample no double entries occurred. Moreover, we also controlled e-mail addresses for double entries because theoretically a person could participate more than once using different computers (with different IP addresses). However, again no double entry was observed. In the paper-and-pencil sample, the participants were recruited by the same experimenter and could only participate if they had not already participated in the Internet version. Moreover, after completing the paper-and-pencil questionnaire, participants were asked not to participate in the Internet version.

8.3.3   Material

Since the study was part of a larger questionnaire study (Naumann et al., 1999), participants received in addition to demographic and personality items also questions on their current usage and preferences of different communication media (i.e., phone, e-mail, face-to-face interaction). Thus, the average time needed for the questionnaires was about 10 minutes for the Internet version and about 30 minutes for the paper-and-pencil version. However, due to space restrictions we only describe material here that is relevant for the comparison of the personality measures.

In the beginning, participants in both the Internet and the paper-and-pencil version received a short introduction explaining that the study sought to explore individuals' use of communication media. Demographic data were collected such as age, sex, education, and employment situation. Then, participants indicated their average use of different communication media on 5-point scales. Next, the three personality measures, the "Big Five" personality inventory, the self-monitoring scale, and social anxiety scales, were applied. Each personality measure is described below.

"Big Five" inventory. This general personality inventory was developed by Costa and McCrae (1985; McCrae & Costa, 1987). It comprises one of the best validated and accepted taxonomies today. The first factor is called *neuroticism* and can be described by terms such as worrying, insecure, self-conscious, and temperamental. The second factor, *extraversion,* is defined by terms like sociable, fun-loving, affectionate, friendly, and talkative. These two factors are often related to negative and positive affectivity, respectively. The third factor is *openness to experience* and can be described by attributes like original, imaginative, broad interests, and daring. The fourth factor, *agreeableness,* is best defined by its negative pole, containing terms like mistrustful, skeptical, callous, unsympathetic, uncooperative, stubborn and rude. Finally, the fifth factor, *conscientiousness,* is described by attributes such as dutiful, scrupulous, and moralistic (see McCrae & Costa, 1987, for a more detailed description of the five factors).

The factorial structure of these scales has been replicated in studies using self-ratings as well as ratings by spouses or peers (McCrae & Costa, 1987). Although the origins of the five factors as well as their exact interpretations are still under discussion, the general structure seems to be quite robust. Moreover, scoring of the items is balanced to control for acquiescence, and social desirability appeared not to bias the scores (McCrae & Costa, 1983, 1987). We translated the original scales into German following Borkenau and Ostendorf (1993). Each of the five subscales contained 12 items that were answered on 5-point scales.

Self-monitoring. The general idea of this concept, first developed by Snyder (1974), is that persons differ in the degree to which they adapt their social behavior to situational norms, expectations, and requirements. People high in Self-Monitoring try to observe and regulate expressive behaviors and self-representation, whereas low self-monitors behave according to their personal feelings and beliefs, independently of demands of the current situation. Like the Big Five, the Self-Monitoring scale is a often-used personality scale in psychological research (Buchanan & Smith, 1999). Moreover, Self-Monitoring seems to be an important aspect for understanding the preferences for different communication media.

Although Snyder (1974) described Self-Monitoring as a one-dimensional concept, later research with English as well as German versions of the scale revealed different and independent subscales of the original questionnaire (e.g., Buchanan & Smith, 1999; Miller & Thayer, 1989; Nowack & Kammer, 1987). We applied two German subscales "social skills" and "inconsistency" developed by Nowack and Kammer (1987; see also Mielke & Kilian, 1990). Each of the subscales contained nine items originally answered on 7-point scales. The *social skills* scale measures perceived social and acting abilities. People scoring high on this scale are extroverted, friendly, helpful, and sympathetic. The *inconsistency* scale measures perceived inconsistency between current expressions and behaviors on the one hand and feelings, attitudes, and thoughts of a person on the other hand. People scoring high on this scale are sensitive for social cues and tend to adapt their social behavior to situational demands, even if this is in conflict with their personal values and beliefs. Both subscales have satisfying reliability and validity scores and correlate slightly negatively with each other (Mielke & Kilian, 1990, Nowak & Kammer, 1987; see also Moser, Diemand, & Schuler, 1996; Nowack, 1994).

Social anxiety. Finally, we applied the social anxiety subscale (12 items) of the self-consciousness scale developed by Fenigstein, Scheier, and Buss (1975). We used the German adaptation of the scale by Merz (1986).

Together, we applied eight different subscales belonging to three popular personality concepts that cover a broad range of important personality aspects, and have major impact for psychology research and applied issues. Earlier research has demonstrated that all of these concepts have sound psychometric properties and robust dimensional structure. In the paper-and-pencil versions, we applied the complete scales, resulting in a total of 90 items. These items were arranged in an alternating order such that subscale items were detached from each other. All personality items had the same 5-point answer scale (strong agreement – strong disagreement).

For the Internet version, each of the subscales was shortened based on scale reliability scores of earlier validations (Borkenau & Ostendorf, 1993; Merz, 1986; Mielke & Kilian, 1990). This was done because, according to our experiences, participation rate in Internet questionnaires decreases when the survey takes more than 15 minutes to complete. The Big Five inventory was reduced to three items per subscale based on an assumption that this construct is robust enough to still provide reliable data. The subscales of the remaining concepts were reduced to five items per subscale. For each of the eight subscales, we chose the items with the highest scale-reliability scores.

Of course we are aware that reducing well-developed subscales may decrease psychometric properties and bias scale norm comparisons. However, because the purpose of our study was mainly correlational and we derived our scale items from relatively robust concepts, we felt that these risks were appropriate in exchange for a higher participation rate. Moreover, by comparing short and long versions of the paper-and-pencil subscales we could directly estimate changes in the internal consistency due to the scale length.

8.4 Results

Feasibility. During five weeks data collection time, 136 persons from various regions of Germany participated in the Internet study. Given that we only advertised the study in a few Internet locations (no mailing lists or psychology-related newsgroups as in Buchanan & Smith, 1999; no direct e-mail advertisement as in Stanton, 1998), that the questionnaire was relatively long, and that participants were restricted to German speaking persons, we consider the number of participants quite satisfying. Also, we did not receive any critical e-mails from Internet users, which also suggests that the questionnaire was well accepted. Analyzing the participation rate over time, we found the usual peak in the first days of the posting, followed by a continuous decrease of participants later.

As another indicator of acceptance and/or motivation of participants, we compared the number of missing values in both questionnaires. One could argue that higher variability in motivation and thoroughness of Internet users might lead to more missing values in the Internet version. However, a study by Stanton (1998) comparing Internet and paper-and-pencil applications of a survey on perceived organizational fairness showed even fewer missing values in the Internet (about 3.0%) compared to a paper-and-pencil version (5.7%). In our study, very few data were missing in both the Internet ($M = 0.4\%$) and the paper-and-pencil questionnaire (M = 0.3%) with no significant differences between the version, $t < 1$. Thus, both paper-and-pencil and Internet data showed similarly high quality in completeness of answer behavior.

Scale reliability. Coefficient alphas were determined for each of the eight scales separately for the Internet and the paper-and-pencil questionnaire. In order to explore effects of different scale-lengths, we also computed alphas for the paper-and-pencil questionnaire including only items that were also used in the Internet questionnaire. The results are shown in Table 8.1. As can be seen, the consistency scores of the paper-and-pencil questionnaire based on the complete subscales were satisfying (most alphas > 0.70). Only the score of the inconsistency subscale was rather low (0.58). However, excluding two items with very low item-scale correlations increased the alpha of this scale to 0.71.

The reliability scores of the Internet questionnaire were generally lower, which is not surprising given the smaller number of items in each subscale. However, as Table 8.1 shows, the alpha scores were still in an acceptable range (mostly above 0.70). Only the extraversion subscale showed lower reliability in this sample (alpha = 0.59). Moreover, comparing the Internet scales with scales in the paper-and-pencil sample that consist of the same items as the Internet version demonstrated that the Internet scales were at least as reliable as the (shortened) paper-and-pencil version. In most cases, alphas of the Internet scales were equal or higher than alphas of the paper-and-pencil scales. Thus, the decrease in reliability of the Internet scales compared to the full paper-and-pencil scales did not exceed effects that can be explained with the reduced item number. In other words, Internet application of the personality scales did not generally reduce the reliability of the scales.

Table 8.1: Scale reliabilities (alpha) for the Internet and
the paper/pencil sample

	P/P sample	P/P sample '	Internet sample
Big five			
Neuroticism	0.86	0.57	0.71
Extroversion	0.79	0.62	0.59
Openess for Experience	0.74	0.58	0.68
Agreeableness	0.77	0.64	0.70
Conscientiousness	0.86	0.74	0.72
Self-monitoring			
Social skills	0.72	0.64	0.72
Inconsistency	0.58	0.65	0.80
Social anxiety	0.84	0.82	0.80

Note: P/P Sample' indicates the analysis of the p/p questionnaire data including only the three or five items each scale that were used in the Internet sample.

Factor structure. As a further comparison of the internal consistency of the two questionnaire versions, we tested whether the factorial structures of the Big Five and the Self-Monitoring concept could be replicated in the different questionnaire data. Analyses for the two personality concepts were computed separately because some of the subscales of the Big Five inventory and the Self-Monitoring scales are intercorrelated (e.g., Miller & Thayer, 1989; Moser et al., 1996).

Factor analyses (varimax) on the paper-and-pencil subscales of the *Big Five inventory* replicated the five factor model relatively well. Eigenvalues of the first five components in the rotated solution were 7.1, 6.1, 5.3, 3.4, and 3.1, with the remaining scores below 2.2. The five components explained about 42% variance. Inspection of the component matrix revealed that most subscales items had the highest factor loadings on the identical component (see Table 8.2). Only one item of the openness subscales had higher loadings on a different component.

Computing the same analysis in the paper-and-pencil sample including only items that were also used in the Internet sample showed a clearer picture (which is not surprising given that items for the Internet subscales were selected according to their item-scale correlations). This time the Big Five structure was nicely replicated, with only five components having eigenvalues higher than 1.0. The respective scores were 2.6, 2.1, 2.0, 1.3, and 1.2. Together, these components accounted for about 62% variance. Inspection of the factor loadings showed that this time all subscale items had their highest loadings on identical components (see Table 8.2).

Analyzing data from the Internet questionnaire revealed a pattern very similar to the latter results. The five factor structure was well replicated in the analysis, revealing five components with eigenvalues above 1.0. The respective scores were 3.0, 2.2, 2.0, 1.4, and 1.1, with the remaining scores below 0.8. Together, these five factors accounted for 66% of variance. Factor loadings of the subscale items again showed a clear structure (see Table 8.2).

Table 8.2: Factor loadings of items in the Internet and paper/pencil sample

	P/P sample	P/P sample '	Internet sample
Big five			
Neuroticism	0.51-0.67	0.63-0.73	0.69-0.88
Extroversion	0.32-0.66	0.59-0.88	0.51-0.83
Openess for exp.	0.00-0.66	0.70-0.72	0.73-0.80
Agreeableness	0.27-0.74	0.69-0.81	0.75-0.81
Conscientiousness	0.54-0.77	0.76-0.83	0.72-0.84
Self-monitoring			
Social skills	0.07-0.73	0. 21-0.77	0.61-0.72
Inconsistency	0.06-0.72	0. 38-0.79	0.61-0.84

Note: P/P Sample' indicates the analysis of the paper/pencil questionnaire data including only the items that were also used in the Internet sample.

We then analyzed the structure of the two *Self-Monitoring subscales* in a similar way. (We did not include social anxiety items in this analysis because items of this scale might overlap with aspects of Self-Monitoring such as social skills.) The analysis of the paper-and-pencil questionnaire replicated the two-factorial structure. Although the factor analysis (varimax) revealed 4 components with eigenvalues higher than 1.0, the inspection of the scree plot suggested a clear difference between the first two (eigenvalues = 3.4 and 2.5) and the second two components (eigenvalues = 1.5 and 1.4). Reducing the analysis to the two strongest components (accounting for about

33% variance) revealed factor loadings mostly consistent with the subscale pattern. Only two items in each scale had higher loadings on the opposite component than the other subscale items (see Table 8.2 for the range of factor loadings).

Analyzing the reduced scales in the paper-and-pencil questionnaire revealed a similar picture. Again four components showed eigenvalues higher than 1.0 with a clear drop between the second and the third component in the scree plot (eigenvalues = 2.6, 1.8, 1.2, and 1.2). Reducing the number of components to two (accounting for about 44% variance) this time revealed only factor loadings consistent with the subscales of the items (see Table 8.2).

The data from the Internet version showed the clearest replication of the expected two-factorial structure. In this analysis only two components had eigenvalues higher than 1.0 (3.2 and 2.3), accounting for about 55% variance. The factor loadings of the items were all above 0.60 and consistent with the expected subscale pattern (see Table 8.2).

Like the results with regard to the Big Five subscales, these data demonstrated that the internal consistency of the Internet questionnaire data was (at least) as good as that of the paper-and-pencil version. The factorial structures of both the Big Five and the Self-Monitoring concept had been clearly replicated. Although having slightly lower scale reliabilities, shortening the subscales did not affect the structure of the main concepts in the Internet version. Although these results have to be interpreted carefully, they show that shortening robust personality scales according to item-scale correlation scores can be a considerable compromise between reliability issues and issues of processing time in research on the Internet.

Construct validity. Besides testing the internal consistency of subscales, our study allowed some explorations of the construct validity of the measured personality concepts in both the Internet and the paper-and-pencil sample. First, we could compare the inter-correlations between the eight measured personality subscales in both data samples. (In the following analyses, subscale scores only include items used in both the Internet and the paper-and-pencil questionnaire. However, results using the complete scales would be very similar because the shortened and the complete subscales were highly correlated in the paper-and-pencil sample, all $r > 0.80$.) As documented in Table 8.3, this comparison showed high correspondence between the two questionnaire modes as illustrated in the level and direction of the correlation scores. Only two out of 12 significant correlation scores in the paper-and-pencil version did not match similar significant correlation scores in the Internet version. However, those cases were rather of marginal theoretical impact for the included scales (agreeableness x social anxiety; conscientiousness x social skills). Correlation patterns that have been theoretically justified and empirically documented in earlier research, such as between neuroticism and extraversion (McRae & Costa, 1987), neuroticism and inconsistency (Moser et al., 1996), or social anxiety and social skills (Merz, 1986) were well replicated in our data, particularly in the Internet sample.

As a second comparison of construct validity indicators between the Internet and paper-and-pencil data, we explored the correlations between personality scores and behavior-related data. As mentioned in the beginning, the current study was part of a larger investigation on use and preferences of communication media. Although the complete results of this research will be reported elsewhere (Naumann et al., 1999), we used some of the preference ratings as external criteria for a comparison of construct validity indicators between Internet and paper-and-pencil questionnaire data. If the personality scales in both questionnaire modes measured the same constructs, we not only should expect similar intercorrelations between the personality concepts but also with behavior-related data such as use or preferences for communication media given certain communication goals.

Perhaps the communication goal that is most sensible for personality dispositions is managing personal conflicts with another person. In our study, participants were asked to indicate how much they preferred different communication media (phone, letter/Fax, e-mail, face-to-face interaction, etc.) when they had a communication goal of managing a personal conflict. Due to restricted space, we only report the correlations between personality subscales and preference ratings for face-to-face interaction. (However, the correlation scores for the remaining ratings were also very similar in the two questionnaire samples.)

Generally, we would expect that persons high in neuroticism, inconsistency, and social anxiety would rather avoid direct face-to-face interaction in conflicts. On the other hand, people high in extraversion and perceived social skills should prefer face-to-face interaction compared to other communication means. This is exactly what the data showed (see Table 8.4). Moreover, although the results were somewhat clearer in the Internet sample, the direction of the correlations was similar in both questionnaire versions. Thus, the intercorrelation of the personality scores and the correlations between personality scores and (selected) behavioral data suggest no differences in construct validity between Internet and paper-and-pencil versions of our questionnaire.

Table 8.3: Correlation scores between personality subscales in the Internet and paper/pencil questionnaire

	Neuroticism	Extrovers.	Openness	Agreeableness	Conscient.	Social skills	Inconsist.	Social anxiety
Neuroticism		-0.38**					0.49**	0.46**
Extroversion	-0.30**					0.47**	-0.27**	-0.33**
Openness for exp.						0.18*		
Agreeableness			0.33**				-0.36**	n.s.
Conscientiousness						n.s.		
Social skills	0.29**	0.27**			-0.20*			-0.51**
Inconsistency		-0.21*		-0.27**				0.33**
Social anxiety	0.46**	-0.26**		0.28**		-0.45**	0.29**	

Notes: Correlation scores of the p/p sample are printed in the lower left half of the table, correlation scores of the Internet sample in the upper right half. ** indicate scores with $p < 0.001$, * indicate scores with $p < 0.05$. Nonsignificant correlation scores are indicated by n.s. only if there was a significant score in the other sample.

Table 8.4: Correlations between personality subscales and media preferences

	P/P Sample	Internet Sample
Neuroticism	-0.10	-0.27*
Extroversion	0.18[+]	0.26*
Social Skills	0.15	0.23*
Inconsistency	-0.20*	-0.31*
Social anxiety	-0.17[+]	-0.37*

Note: * indicates scores with $p < 0.05$, [+] indicates scores with $p < 0.10$. Correlations scores of the remaining personality subsscales (openness, agreeableness, and conscientiousness) were nonsignificant, all $/r/ < 0.10$.

Differences between the Internet and the paper-and-pencil sample. After demonstrating satisfactory internal and external consistency of the personality measures, we compared the Internet and the paper-and-pencil sample with respect to differences in personality profiles. According to popular stereotyping, one could argue that persons surfing the Internet are rather shy, inhibited, and prefer interacting with their social environment via computer rather than via direct contact. Thus, one could suppose that Internet users are rather low in extraversion and perceived social skills, and rather high in social anxiety, inconsistency, and neuroticism. On the other hand, one could also argue that Internet users are relatively high on openness for experience because they explore new forms of information and communication technology.

However, participants in our study did not differ significantly in any of the measured personality aspects. The only marginal differences indicated slightly higher perceived social skills for participants of the paper-and-pencil sample, $t(238) = 1.86, p < 0.07$, and slightly higher conscientiousness values for participants of the Internet sample, $t(243) = 1.76, p < 0.08$. These tendencies are certainly not strong enough to justify any of the above sketched hypotheses. Instead, the data showed that although participants in the Internet and paper-and-pencil sample were quite heterogeneous in age, place of residence, and occupational background, they were still quite similar in their personality profile. Thus, these data suggested no systematic biases of Internet samples compared to traditional paper-and-pencil subject samples.

8.5   Discussion

The topic of this chapter was to explore advantages and disadvantages of personality assessment via Internet and providing empirical evidence on feasibility, reliability, and validity of such a procedure. Our study has shown quite promising results for Internet assessments.

Acceptance by Internet users was generally good. We received no complaints or criticisms during or after our study. The number of participants was satisfying given that personality scales usually have rather poor acceptance (e.g., Schuler, 1993), that we advertised at only a few (nonpsychology related) Internet sites, and that our questionnaire was relatively long (74 items total). Of course, some incentive has to be given to participate. In our case, we offered small monetary prizes instead of feedback on the questionnaire (e.g., Buchanan & Smith, 1999) because we wanted to prevent the potential for personality issues to become too salient. The high number of e-mail addresses that participants sent with the answered questionnaire suggested that these incentives and its provision were also well accepted. Moreover, this kind of incentive presumably contributed to the extremely low number of missing values in both questionnaire versions because participants were instructed that only completely filled questionnaires would be participating in the final lottery.

Besides the good acceptance of the Internet questionnaire, indicators of internal consistency showed satisfying reliability of the applied personality measures. Although we used only shortened personality subscales in the Internet, the scale reliabilities were mostly above 0.70 and the factorial structures of the administered personality concepts were well replicated. Moreover, the consistency scores of the Internet questionnaire were at least as good as in the parallel paper-and-pencil short-version of the scales.

Finally, the exploration of validity issues also suggested no quality difference between Internet and paper-and-pencil data. The inter-correlation patterns between personality subscales as well as the correlation patterns between personality data and behavior ratings were very similar in the Internet and the paper-and-pencil data, suggesting that the applied personality scales measured similar constructs. Moreover, comparison of the two participant samples revealed no major differences on personality aspects, suggesting that participants who were recruited via Internet and participants recruited via personal contact do not differ in their personality profiles.

Together, our results extend the already existing positive evidence of the psychometric quality of Internet surveys and ability tests (Rietz & Wahl, 2000, this volume; Stanton, 1998; Wilhelm, 1999) demonstrating that personality assessment via Internet is a viable alternative to traditional forms of data collection and measurement. This result could have major implications for psychology research as well as for applied issues such as personnel selection.

8.6   Outlook and Further Research

Of course, the presented research is only a starting point for the exploration of personality assessment via Internet. Along with similar results from Buchanan and

Smith (1999), we have explored only a limited number of personality scales. Other personality measures might not be as simply transferred to Internet applications. Moreover, more research is necessary to specifically address issues of honesty and social desirability in Internet questionnaires. Although the lack of consistency differences between our two questionnaire data implicitly suggest no greater vulnerability of Internet data, it is desirable to know if there are factors that may increase or decrease such biases (e.g., differences in participants' motivation). This is particularly relevant from an applied perspective; consider, for instance, the Web-based selection of job candidates where incentives for social desirability effects are very high. Methodological designs for those studies can be adopted from related research on reliability with traditional personality measures (repeated measurement, cross-validation designs, etc.), since the main problem of credibility is similar for most (reactive) measures (see Paulhus, 1986, for an overview).

Another important issue for further research is to explore extensions of the methodological range of Internet assessment. The research reported so far was restricted to adaptations of questionnaires that are usually administered as paper-and-pencil versions. However, the technical opportunities of computer-based assessment via Internet include also computerized-adaptive tests, interactive exercises, online interviews, and virtual role-plays. These tools can extend and enrich traditional assessment measures, as well as provide additional process measures such as response latencies. For example, we currently validate such a Web-based assessment tool for call-center agents that includes personality scales, a speed test, and audio-taped scenarios for situational tests.

We do not argue that Internet-based assessment will completely replace traditional paper-and-pencil or computer-based testing. Too many problems related to conducting objective personality assessments via the Internet are still unsolved – and perhaps can not be solved at all. One example is the protection of developed scales and instruments against unauthorized usage and publication. We certainly do not want a situation where the "right" answers to personality items are published in books, or in the Internet itself. Thus, personality scales must be protected somehow. The legal situation today is still unclear.

However, Web-based personality testing is an interesting complement of traditional tests that enables easy and fast test administrations relevant in many cases (e.g., during the development and refinement of new scales, or for inexpensive pre-selections of candidates in personnel selection campaigns). Although a number of problems of data reliability were discussed in the beginning, the analyses of our study revealed no major restrictions in psychometric properties or validity issues (see also Buchanan & Smith, 1999), so that further administration of this new tool for personality assessment can be recommended.

References

Batinic, B. & Bosnjak, M. (2000). Fragebogenuntersuchungen im Internet [Surveys on the Internet]. In B. Batinic (Ed.), *Internet für Psychologen* (2nd ed.) [Internet for psychologists] (pp. 287-317). Göttingen: Hogrefe.

Birnbaum, M. H. (1999). *Psychological experiments on the Internet.* San Diego: Academic Press.

Borkenau, P. & Ostendorf, F. (1993). *NEO-Fünf-Faktoren Inventar (NEO-FFI) nach Costa und McCrae* [NEO-five-factor inventory following Costa and McCrae]. Göttingen: Hogrefe.

Buchanan, T. & Smith, J. L. (1999). Using the Internet for psychological research: Personality testing on the world wide web. *British Journal of Psychology, 90,* 125-144.

Burke, M. J. (1993). Computerized psychological testing: Impacts on measuring predictor constructs and future behavior. In N. Schmitt & WC Borman (Eds.), *Personnel selection in organizations* (pp. 203-239). San Francisco, CA: Jossey-Bass.

Feningstein, A., Scheier, M. F., & Buss, A. H. (1975). Public and private self-consciousness: Assessment and theory. *Journal of Consulting and Clinical Psychology, 43,* 522-527.

Guilford, J. P. (1959). *Personality.* New York: McGraw-Hill.

Kiesler, S., Siegel, J., & McGuire, T. W. (1984). Social psychological aspects of computer-mediated communication. *American Psychologist, 39,* 1123-1134.

Maddux, C. D. & Johnson, L. (1998). Computer-assisted assessment. In V. H. Booney (Ed.), *Psychological assessment of children* (pp. 87-105). New York: Wiley.

Maschke, P. (1989). Die Bearbeitungszeit von Persönlichkeitsfragebögen in der Eignungsauswahl: Ein Indikator für Verfälschung? [Processing times of personality questionnaires in assessments: Indicator for distortion?]. *Zeitschrift für Differentielle und Diagnostische Psychologie, 10,* 121-127.

McCrae, R. R. & Costa, P. T. (1987). Validation of the five-factor model of personality across instruments and observers. *Journal of Personality and Social Psychology, 52,* 81-90.

Mead, A. D. & Drasgow, F. (1993). Equivalence of computerized and paper-and-pencil cognitive ability tests: A meta-analysis. *Psychological Bulletin, 114,* 449-458.

Merz, J. (1986). SAF: Fragebogen zur Messung von dispositioneller Selbstaufmerksamkeit [SAF: Questionnaire for measuring dispositional self-consciousness]. *Diagnostica, 32,* 142-152.

Mielke, R. & Kilian, R. (1990). Wenn Teilskalen sich nicht zu dem ergänzen, was die Gesamtskala erfassen soll: Untersuchungen zum Self-Monitoring-Konzept [If subscales do not go together as the concept demands it. Empirical studies of the Self-Monitoring-concept]. *Zeitschrift für Sozialpsychologie, 21,* 126-135.

Miller, M. L. & Thayer, J. F. (1989). On the existence of discrete classes in personality: Is self-monitoring the correct joint to carve? *Journal of Personality and Social Psychology, 57,* 143-155.

Moser, K., Diemand, A., & Schuler, H. (1996). Inkonsistenz und soziale Fertigkeiten als zwei Komponenten von Self-Monitoring [Inconsistency and social skills as two components of self-monitoring]. *Diagnostica, 42,* 268-283.

Naumann, S., Hertel, G., Konradt, U., & Batinic, B. (1999). Effects of personality traits on preferences for communication media. Unpublished raw data.

Nowack, W. (1994). Self-monitoring and social skills. *European Review of Applied Psychology, 44*, 299-304.

Nowack, W. & Kammer, D. (1987). Self-presentation: Social skills and inconsistency as independent facets of self-monitoring. *European Journal of Personality, 1*, 61-77.

Overton, R. C., Harms, H. J., Taylor, L. R., & Zickar, M. J. (1997). Adapting to adapting testing. *Personnel Psychology, 50*, 171-185.

Paulhus, D. L. (1986). Self-deception and impression management in test responses. In A. Angleitner & J. S. Wiggens (Eds.), *Personality assessment via questionnaire* (pp. 143-165). New York: Springer.

Schuler, H. (1993). Social validity of selection situations: A concept and some empirical results. In H. Schuler, J. L. Farr, & M. Smith (Eds.), *Personnel selection and assessment. Individual and organizational perspectives* (pp. 11-26). Hillsdale, N.J.: Erlbaum.

Smith, M. A. & Leigh, B. (1997). Virtual subjects: Using the Internet as an alternative source of subjects and research environment. *Behavior Research Methods, Instruments, and Computers, 29*, 496-505.

Wainer, H. (1990). *Computerized adaptive testing: A primer*. Hillsdale, New Jersey.

Wilhelm, O. (2000). *Psychologie des schlussfolgernden Denkens: Differentialpsychologische Prüfung von Strukturüberlegungen* [Psychology of Reasoning: Testing of Structural Theories]. Hamburg: Dr Kovac.

Wilhelm, O. (1999). *Ability and achievement testing on the world wide web*. Paper presented at the German Online Research (GOR '99), Erlangen.

9 Comparison of Psychologists' Self Image and Their Image in the Internet and in Print

Ira Rietz & Svenja Wahl

In the last few years, interest in the image of psychology and its representatives has increased (Baumann, 1995; Utecht, 1990). The relevance of maintaining a positive, or near-to-reality, image has also been widely recognized by psychologists themselves. The BDP publication "Psychologists in the public eye" (1996), released by the association on the occasion of its fiftieth anniversary, can be applied as an example of internal discussion of this topic. In the German-speaking community, even Spada (1997), Bausch (1996), and Lindner (1996) have dealt with the situation and its developments.

Critical debate on the image of psychology has a long tradition (see among others Fürntratt & Gutsche, 1969; Thumin & Zebelmann, 1967; Vontobel & Ries, 1969). There is a consensus that the image of psychology and its representatives is afflicted with problems in public discourse. According to Benjamin (1986), the image of psychology is composed of the subject's popularity, as well as knowledge of the subject matter. Perrig-Chiello and Perrig (1992) as well as Wood, Jones, and Benjamin (1986) proved that there is insufficient knowledge of psychological subject matter and its fields of activity. Frohburg (1995), Laux (1977) and Richter (1996) confirmed the profession's bad reputation, in particular in comparison to medical occupational groups. Against this background, a study was conducted on the image of psychology, whereby the content emphasis lay on the comparison of the image and self-image of psychologists.

Due to advanced technology, further possibilities of data acquisition, besides classic paper-pencil questionnaires, are at our disposal, specifically, online surveys on the Internet. The question still remains to which extent data culled online is comparable to data collected in traditional methods. From an economic point of view, an attractive possibility for gathering data is presented. On the basis of the submitted question, a comparison of different methods of data acquisition was conducted in the study presented here. For this purpose, in addition to the classic paper-pencil questionnaire, the data acquisition instrument was also adapted to an HyperText Markup Language (HTML) questionnaire to be answered online via the World Wide Web (WWW).

9.1   Possibilities and Limits of Data Acquisition on the Internet

According to Wallbott (2000; see also Hahn & Günther, 2000), the Internet, as a new medium for communication and information, offers promising possibilities in particular for psychologists. Due to the increasing spread and use of Internet access, precisely aimed self and external portrayals can be constructed to reach many potential users economically. The medium, therefore, offers new chances for image building. The Web sites of the Organization of German Psychologists (http://www.bdp-verband.org/), as well as the German Society for Psychology (http://www.dgps.de/) can be mentioned as examples in this context. On their own homepages, most university institutes also offer detailed information on psychology (e.g., timetables, publication lists, psychological articles, and research findings) both for interested laymen and for experts (see also Krueger, Ott, & Funke, 2000). This kind of external portrayal is both relevant from an internal scientific and from an audience perspective, since an impression of what psychologists actually do has not yet been adapted to reality. Trapp, Hammond, and Bray (1996) point out the possibilities for use of the Internet for cooperating with and supporting colleagues, as well as for communicating amongst experts. The additional possibilities of using the Internet as a consultation and therapy tool need only be mentioned briefly here (see Wallbott, 2000).

A further type of application on the Internet is in the field of teaching. The Internet can be used as an educational training medium to reach a large number of geographically separated students simultaneously (see Wallbott, 2000). In particular for psychology, with its rising numbers of students, this can be of an advantage (Bausch, 1996). Recently, the increasing frequency of lectures held in a virtual environment (e.g., Heidbrink, 2000; Nistor & Mandl, 1995) clearly illustrates that this advantage is already being applied to common practice.

By far, one of the most interesting possibilities displayed by the Internet for psychologists lies in the various uses as a research medium for psychological experiments and surveys. Above all, in the field social psychology and media psychology interesting research issues can be tested. A further emphasis is put on studies of communication habits and processes (computer-mediated communication (CMC) vs. face-to-face (f2f) communication). Although the possibilities of the Internet are not necessarily limited in their field of research to questionnaire surveys and opinion polls, these do tend to dominate the field thus far.

Naming critical issues in administration of psychological experiments and questionnaires, Hewson, Laurent, and Vogel (1996) mention anonymous answers to questionnaires. The respondents must rest assured that their identity remains unknown to the experimenter. This is of particular relevance, since Esposito, Agard, and Rosnow (1984; see also Kury, 1994) managed to illustrate that guaranteeing anonymity reduces both the effects of social desirability and experimenter effects, as well as various other response tendencies. A specific advantage on the Internet is the ease with which a large number of test persons can be reached in the shortest possible time (see Batinic & Bosnjak, 2000; Wallbott, 2000).

Apart from promising possibilities and the obvious advantages of the new medium, some other problematic aspects need also be considered. One main facet is often the lack of or difficulty in controlling test subjects, as well as the ability to control the spread of the instrument (see Batinic & Bosnjak, 2000; Reips, 2000). How reliable are entries in a questionnaire? How can sample distortions be avoided or controlled? Does the Internet surfer stereotype of a shy and socially disturbed male who spends most of his evenings in front of a computer screen apply?

As Döring states (1995, p.327), the typical Internet user is "between 20 and 30 years old, male, academically trained, works in a full-time job in the field of information technology, is a student or active in research. He lives in North America, Europe, Japan or Australia" (see also Bandilla, in this volume). The rising ratio of women points out the problem of sample theory, that the group of female Internet users is a dynamically sampled population (Batinic & Bosnjak, 2000). In this context, the multi-level selection processes, which occur until completion of a questionnaire or participation in an experiment, pose a disadvantage that has, until now, not been solved satisfyingly (Reips, 2000). Though, Krebs (1995) points out that such self-selection processes do not only arise in Internet-based surveys.

9.2   Findings

Vis-à-vis the equivalence of different data acquisition methods, numerous findings already exists based on different contexts. Reuband and Blasius (1996) examined to what extent response patterns vary with the type of data acquisition (f2f versus postal versus telephone surveys). The effect assumed by them, that a tendency for social desirability increases with the intensity of personal contact, could not be confirmed according to their results (see also Esposito, Agard, & Rosnow, 1984; Kury, 1994).

Studies on the representativeness of samples in connection with the use of different survey methods were conducted by Bogner (1996), and by Swoboda, Muhlberger, Weitkunat, and Schneeweiss (1997). In a comparison between telephone, computer-mediated, and Internet surveys, Bogner (1996) rates the results as a clear confirmation of a lack of representativeness in online surveys. The possibility of reaching specific target groups, however, is considered an advantage (see also Reips, 2000). In a comparison between e-mail and online surveys, Swoboda et al. (1997) also come to the conclusion that Internet surveys are not able to supply representative data on total populations.

Mehta and Sivadas (1995) compared response rates in a postal and an e-mail survey. According to their results, dispatching the questionnaire via e-mail ensures more manageability than the postal method. The authors assume that most users with a mailbox will check these regularly. Besides, access to the personal mailbox is password protected. In Mehta and Sivadas' (1995) study, more than half of the completed e-mail questionnaires were sent back within the first two to three days. In the post office group, it took 3 weeks to receive approximately half of the completed responses. Only a few significant differences were apparent between response rates and the rate of unanswered questionnaires; except that the open questions answered by the e-mail contacts were answered more at length. The authors came to the conclusion that e-mail surveys are clearly quicker and cheaper, yet cannot be employed as an exclusive method due to the population's reduced access possibilities.

Only recently has the Internet come to be considered as a medium for conducting experiments in psychology; this requires assessment. In this context Krantz, Ballard, and Scher (1997) carried out a comparison between WWW and laboratory experiments on the determinants of female attraction. Despite differences in the experimental procedures, which resulted as a necessary consequence of the W3-approach, the W3 and laboratory data proved comparable. However, the authors noted that the data they culled was extremely durable, and that the treatment conditions differed from each other considerably. According to Krantz et al.'s opinion (1997), studies based on more subtle material are less promising. Also, the potential for influencing subjective cognition or affective conditions, as well as the test subjects' attitudes needs to be reviewed extremely critically.

On the whole, the findings presented are still vague with regard to some points, indicating a need for more research, in particular into the use of online surveys.

9.3   Question

In order to attain more confirmation for the hitherto discussed comparability of paper-pencil versus Web data, this study conducted a comparison between the two different data acquisition methods. Content wise, the survey can be integrated into the previously mentioned problem of psychology's image. In line with Hofstaetter (1965), a questionnaire was conceived to compare the image nonpsychologists have of psychologists with the psychologists' self-image and their presumed image.

Hofstaetter (1965), Vontobel and Ries (1969), Koeske, Koeske, and Mallinger's (1993) studies, and the results of a pilot study (Rietz & Wahl, 1997) suggest that the psychologists' self-image is more positive than their actual image. The presumed image, however, is usually more negative than the actual image people have. The results of the studies mentioned here are based on paper-pencil questionnaires such that the validity of these hypotheses will also have to be examined for data acquired on the net.

9.4   Development of the Research Instrument

The research instrument developed for this purpose was called "Questionnaire for the Evaluation of Psychology" (Q-E-P). Besides Hofstaetter's twelve original items, the design included 36 new items. The questionnaire brings up common beliefs about the psychologist's occupation (e.g., "At a first glance, psychologists can detect whether somebody is disturbed or normal", "Psychologists often take cover behind incomprehensible scientific language", or "Because of personal difficulties, more and more people decide to study psychology"). The items were rated on a five-point scale between "I agree" and "I do not agree".

The 48 items were specified with three different sets of instructions. The nonpsychologists had to crisscross how they rated psychology and its representatives (image). The demographic data requested was gender, age, and occupation. The number of contacts to psychologists in their occupation and in their private lives was also asked.

The psychologists had to answer two parts. One part consisted of finding out their self-image. In the other part, the presumed image was requested by completing the questionnaire in the manner a nonpsychologist might. In this subsample, the demographic data culled was age, gender, graduation year, as well as the vocational field of activity.

9.5   Implementation

Consistent with the aimed methodical comparison, the Q-E-P data was raised in two different manners. On the one hand, the Q-E-P was distributed in the traditional print mode. In the other instance, the questionnaire was converted to HTML and uploaded on the WWW. The survey was planned and conducted according to the recommendations laid down by Hewson et al. (1996), Batinic and Bosnjak (2000), and Reips (2000).

On the basis of the sample theory considerations stated previously, the composition of a representative sample on the Internet is difficult because of the dynamic character of the population, among other things. Distribution of the questionnaire is also difficult to carry out. Self-selection processes are, as previously mentioned, measurable in the case of both acquisition methods. These fundamental factors need to be considered later when discussing the results.

The WWW data acquisition was conducted as follows. In order to reach the sub-sample of psychologists on the WWW, a short call for participation was published according to random principles in the appropriate newsgroups and in selected mailing lists relevant to psychology. Apart from this method, a list of psychologists with e-mail addresses was compiled from various psychology-related address listings on the Internet (e.g., http://www.psychologie.de/). Every third psychologist on this list received a short e-mail with the request to take part in the survey. To point out the questionnaire to nonpsychologists on the WWW, the following URL http://www.unibw-hamburg.de/PWEB/psypae/ver.html was entered in all German-language search engines. However, since this required active participation by potential participants, another method was needed to refer Internet users to the survey. In the German-language domains (i.e., Germany, Austria, and Switzerland), an extensive list of e-mail addresses was generated by randomly combining the first three letters of the surname in address search engines. Every third person on this list received an e-mail with reference to the survey, and a request for participation.

The paper-pencil sample was recruited from several different sources. The subsample of nonpsychologists was partly compiled from students of the University of the German Federal Armed Forces (N = 133; nonpsychology students). The other test subjects (N = 36) were asked to participate using the snowball system. The psychologists who were to fill out the paper-pencil version of the questionnaire were contacted by writing down and addressing every third name in the "Psychology" section of the Hamburg Yellow Pages. Some psychologists participated in the study after responding to calls in the scientific publication *Report Psychologie,* the publication of the Professional Association of German Psychologists. Further details on the composition of the subsamples can be found in Table 9.1.

Table 9.1: Description of the psychological subsamples

Psychologists (Paper-pencil version) N = 45	Psychologists (WWW Version) N = 105
33.3% men; 66.7% women	52.4% men; 47.6% women
Age: 28 to 71 years	Age: 18 to 64 years
($M = 43.89$; $SD = 10.03$)	($M = 29.53$; $SD = 6.87$)
Nonpsychologists (Paper-pencil version) N = 169	Nonpsychologists (WWW Version) N = 262
88.2% men; 11.2% women	64.9% men; 35.1% women
Age: 18 to 66 years ($M = 23.97$; $SD = 6.76$)	Age: 15 to 56 years ($M = 26.95$; $SD = 7.43$)
Private acquaintance with psychologists: 45.3%	Private acquaintance with psychologists: 67.1%
no private contact: 54.7%	no private contact: 32.9%
Professional contact with psychologists: 74.9%	Professional contact with psychologists: 53.3%
no professional contact: 25.1%	no professional contact: 46.7%

The average age of the psychologists who completed the print-version Q-E-P was 44 years old. In the WWW sample, the average age was considerably younger at 30 years. In the subsample of nonpsychologists who answered the paper-pencil version, the average age was approximately 24 years; the average age of the nonpsychologists in the WWW subsample was similar at scarcely 27 years. The high portion of women is noteworthy in the two WWW samples. In the case of the psychologists' subsample, this may be to due to the high ratio of women in the occupation (Lindner, 1996; Spada, 1997). With regard to the fields of activity, distribution is varied in the paper-pencil and WWW psychologist samples. The evidently lower ratio of clinical psychologists in the WWW sample can probably be attributed to the fact that only very few therapeutic clinics or hospitals have access to the Internet. The data was culled in the period between January and October 1997.

9.6   Results

Only 32 items, which could clearly be assigned to a positive or negative estimate of psychology, were considered in the evaluation. Those items were all polarized in the same direction. Low values can always be interpreted as a positive opinion on psychology, high values as a negative opinion.

9.6.1   Comparison of the Two Data Acquisition Methods in the Three Perspectives: Self-image, Presumed Image, and Actual Image

In the presentation of the results, the differences between the two data acquisition variants are viewed first. For this purpose, three separate comparisons were carried out: (1) the self-image of the psychologists in the WWW and print versions, (2) the presumed image of psychologists in the WWW and print versions, and (3) the actual image described by the nonpsychologists in both samples.

In each case, t-tests were computed between two of the three perspectives, since a bi-factorial analysis of variance with the independent variables Version (paper-pencil vs. WWW) and Image (self-image, image, presumed image) could not be conducted due to the partial dependence of the samples. The mean value comparisons resulted in the values presented in Table 9.2.

The manner of differentiation between the self-image of the psychologists in the print version and the WWW sample was of interest for the method comparison. In the 32 items, significant differences between the paper-pencil and the WWW psychologists sample were noted in ten items. Of particular relevance is the fact that in eight of ten significant items, the self-image of the psychologists fared better in the print version than in the WWW sample. In the majority of items, no differences resulted from the comparison of method.

Table 9.2: Ratio of significant items in the comparison between paper-pencil and www sample (self-image, PI: presumed image, I: image)

Level of significance	Self-image: Print version – WWW	PI: Print version – WWW	I: Print version – WWW
$ </ = .001$	2	1	4
$ </ = .01$	2	2	2
$ </ = .05$	6	6	5
$ > .001$ (n.s.)	22	23	21

The results were similar in the comparison of presumed images in the subpartial samples of the psychologists. Differences between the presumed image were only noted in 9 of the 32 significant items. Similar to the self-image comparison, the comparison of presumed image illustrated that the evaluation usually turned out better in the paper-pencil version (in seven of nine items) than in the WWW sample. However, no predominantly significant differences could be determined between the two data acquisition variants.

Similar to the two previous comparisons, in the review of image, differences only resulted in a third of the significant average values. Of the 32 items, 11 differed significantly in their print and WWW version responses.

In sum, there are no fundamental differences between the results in the WWW and paper-pencil samples. Despite the different survey methods, the results are comparatively equal. In the case of the few significant items answered differently, it could be proven that both in the case of the self-image and the presumed image, the estimates of the psychologists who had to complete the paper-pencil versions were clearly more positive than the opinions in the WWW sample. In the comparison of image in both data acquisition variants, no uniform tendency could be confirmed.

9.6.2 Comparison of Perspective Between WWW and Paper-Pencil Samples

In the first part of the presentation of the results, the differences in perspective were reviewed in each case between the paper-pencil and WWW sample. It was demonstrated that one could arrive at quite comparable results in both data acquisition procedures.

A further aspect of the comparison of the two data acquisition methods concerns the correlation *between* the perspectives (i.e., the self-image, the presumed image, and the actual image). In the second part of the presentation of the results, the accent is on whether the respective relationships of the paper-pencil data can be found in analogy in the data raised on the WWW.

Respectively, the average value differences of two of the three perspectives were examined vis-à-vis significance with t-tests for independent samples (self-image vs. image; presumed image vs. image), or for dependent samples (self-image vs. presumed image). For the comparison of method, these were calculated separately for the paper-pencil and WWW samples respectively. This allowed for a control of whether the relationship between the three perspectives occurs comparably in the paper-pencil and WWW samples.

Paper-pencil samples

In the following section, the results of the perspective comparisons in the subsamples that completed the paper-pencil version will be presented first. Table 9.3 gives an overview of the findings.

To begin with, the self-image of the psychologists is to be contrasted with the image of the nonpsychologists. Of the 32 items, 26 differences proved significant. In line with the findings presented in the relevant literature, self-image is predominantly and significantly more positive (23 items) than external opinion.

Table 9.3: Ratio of significant items in the perspective comparisons
in the paper-pencil version (self-image, PI: presumed image, I: image)

Level of significance	Self-image: Print version – WWW	PI: Print version – WWW	I: Print version – WWW
$</ = .001$	16	23	28
$</ = .01$	6	1	2
$</ = .05$	4	3	1
$> .001$ (n.s.)	6	5	1

In the comparison between presumed image and actual image, 27 items were answered significantly differently. The largest difference was noted in item 9 ("Because of personal difficulties, more and more people decide to study psychology"). Psychologists assumed receiving significantly more approving answers to this item from nonpsychologists than these actually gave. In 26 of the 27 significant items, the direction of the average value differences turned out as expected (i.e., the presumed opinion is more negative than the actual opinion). Moreover, the psychologists' self-image is compared to their presumed image. One can assume that the presumed image will turn out worse than the self-image. Of the 32 items, 31 were answered significantly differently. With the exception of two instances, the self-image is substantially more positive than the presumed image. A diagram of the average value progression of the three perspectives is shown in Figure 9.1.

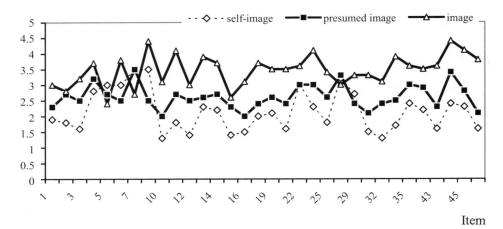

Figure 9.1: Self-image, presumed image, and image in the paper-
pencil version

WWW samples

Following on from the reviews of the relationships in the paper-pencil version, the
following section will deal with the results of the WWW samples (see Table 9.4).

In the WWW samples, 23 significant differences arose between self-image and the
actual image. In 20 cases, the self-image is clearly more positive than the actual image. The tendency confirmed in the paper-pencil version can therefore also be confirmed for the WWW version. This could be rated as a further indication of the comparability of the survey methods.

Table 9.4: Ratio of significant items in the perspective comparisons in the
WWW sample (self-image, PI: presumed image, I: image)

Level of significance	Self-image: Print version – WWW	PI: Print version – WWW	I: Print version – WWW
$\leq$ = .001	18	32	32
$\leq$ = .01	4	0	0
$\leq$ = .05	1	0	0
> .001 (n.s.)	9	0	0

In the comparison of the actual image described by the nonpsychologists between the
image presumed by psychologists, highly significant differences were noted in all
items. Except for a few exceptions, the mean value differences correspond to the
forecasted trajectory (i.e., the presumed image is evidently worse than the actual im-

age). The evaluations of item 10 differed strongest along this trajectory ("Psychology is a science to be taken seriously"). Finally, the psychologists' self-assessment is compared to their actual estimate. One can assume that the presumed image is worse than the self-image. In the WWW sample, all of the 32 mean value differences proved to be highly significant; 28 out of 32 items were in the predicted direction. A diagram of the average value progression of the three perspectives for the WWW version is shown in Figure 9.2. The self-image and the actual image of the psychologists run almost parallel in the WWW sample, and can be characterized as predominantly positive. The presumed image is presented as undoubtedly worse. To sum up, the findings demonstrate that the progression of the average values is very similar, regardless of the method of data acquisition (paper-pencil vs. WWW).

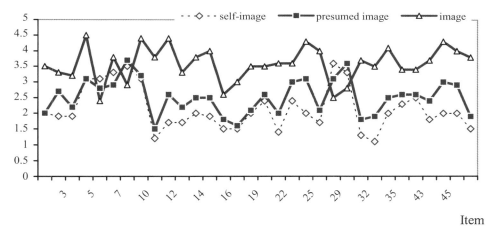

Figure 9.2: Self-image, presumed image, and image in the
WWW sample

9.7   Conclusion

The evaluation of the results of this study was conducted on the level of the single items. The development of rating scales is still pending. In a first analysis of the item intercorrelations, an interpretable data structure was only discernible in the case of the psychologists' self-image. A review of the correlations for the presumed and actual images did not result in any meaningful interpretations of the item intercorrelations. From a content perspective, the findings can be interpreted in such a way that psychologists have quite a differentiated self-image with a definable range of topics. Nonpsychologists seem to possess less of a differentiated image of psychology and its representatives. This is also in line with the initially discussed findings in the relevant literature. The correlation samples documented in the self-image will, in the course of further research, require factor-analytical confirmation.

In the first step, the two survey methods were compared with regard to the responses in the print and WWW version within one perspective. To a large extent, no significant differences were noted in the responses. Only in a scarce third were the answers significantly different. The answers in the print version tended to be more positive than those in the WWW version. This tendency could be proven both in the case of self-image and presumed image. A possible interpretation of these findings could be found in results on social desirability. It was stated that with increasing anonymity, the tendency towards the social desirability of answers decreases (see Kury, 1994; Sassenberg & Kreutz, in this volume). Despite some differences in the responses to the items, the data can in summary be interpreted in such a way that comparability of the results generally seems to be given.

With reference to the age and gender distribution in the samples completing the WWW version, there was considerable conformity with references to the literature (see Batinic & Bosnjak, 2000; Döring, 1995). Due to the mentioned sample theory considerations, it can be assumed that the problem of sample representativeness must nevertheless remain unsettled. In the present state of research on Internet use, a final estimation of the representativeness of data raised in the Internet cannot yet be completed.

With regard to the psychologists' sample, the different composition relevant to fields of activity was considerable. A mean value comparison, however, failed to result in any significant differences in the item responses between psychologists working in clinics and those involved in research. Consequently, a partition of the sample into further subsamples was avoided.

In the second step, the method comparison was expanded to accommodate relationships between the perspectives (i.e., the self-image, presumed image, and actual image). The relationship between the three perspectives is uniform in the print version and the WWW version. If one were to compile a ranking, the self-image of the psychologists would on average come first, then the actual image, followed by the presumed image some distance apart. Psychologists may not be as highly rated by nonpsychologists as they rate themselves, yet the presumed estimate is not as bad as they assume. This result was proven regardless of the applied survey method. The findings of both analysis steps in the study presented here suggest that Internet-collected data are comparable to paper-pencil data.

The results of the completed survey should be discussed critically with regard to the possibilities of using the Internet for psychological surveys. Given that data collected on the Internet is comparable to data culled from traditional methods, the advantages of using the Internet as a survey medium are evident. In the future, cultural comparison studies will be conducted more easily due to the potential of the medium. Despite this theoretically positive assessment, many questions remain unanswered. In the case of psychological surveys on the Internet, nonrespondents continue to pose a problem. This also needs to be qualified by mentioning that the distribution of Internet access cannot, particularly in Germany, be described as widespread. With the number of Internet users growing at a daily rate, the development is on the right track, however.

In the future, the multimedia possibilities of the Internet should also be used more extensively to accommodate for conducting proper psychological experiments, in addition to conducting surveys, so far prevalent in this field. In this context, the experiment conducted by Krantz et al. (1997) can be referred to as a good example.

References

Batinic, B. & Bosnjak, M. (2000). Fragebogenuntersuchungen im Internet. In B. Batinic (Ed.), *Internet für Psychologen* (2nd ed.) (pp. 287-317) [Internet for psychologists]. Göttingen: Hogrefe.

Baumann, U. (1995). Bericht zur Lage der deutschsprachigen Psychologie 1994 – Fakten und Perspektiven. *Psychologische Rundschau, 46*, 3-17.

Bausch, M. (1996). *Arbeitsmarkt-Infomrationen 1996 für Psychologinnen und Psychologen.* [Online]. Available: http://www.psychologie.uni-bonn.de/zav/zav_96.htm.

Benjamin, L. T. Jr. (1986). Why don´t they understand us? A history of psychology´s public image. *American Psychologist, 41*, 941-946.

Berufsverband Deutscher Psychologen und Psychologinnen (Ed.). (1996). *Die Psychologen im Spiegel der Öffentlichkeit. Meinungen prominenter und anderer Zeitgenossen zu einem Berufsstand. 50 Jahre BDP.* Bonn: Deutscher Psychologen Verlag.

Bogner, W. (1996). Die Validität von Online Befragungen. *Planung und Analysen, 6*, 9-12.

Döring, N. (1995). Internet: Bildungsreise auf der Infobahn. In L. J. Issing & P. Klimsa (Eds.), *Informationen und Lernen mit Multimedia* (pp. 305-336). Weinheim: Psychologie Verlags Union.

Esposito, J., Agard, E., & Rosnow, R. (1984). Can confidentiality of data pay off? *Personality and Individual Differences, 5*, 477-480.

Frohburg, I. (1995). Zum Ansehen der Psychotherapeuten: Wie man über uns denkt und was man von uns hält. *GwG-Zeitschrift, 100*, 12-18.

Fürntratt, E. & Gutsche, H.-J. (1969). Untersuchungen zum Image der Psychologie in Deutschland. I. Stellung der wissenschaftlichen Psychologie zu anderen Fachgebieten in der Vorstellung von Oberschülern. *Psychologische Beiträge, 11*, 368-389.

Hahn, A. & Günther, A. (2000). Psychologie im Internet: Bestandsaufnahme und Entwicklungstendenzen. In B. Batinic (Ed.), *Internet für Psychologen* (2nd ed.) (pp. 125-191) [Internet for psychologists]. Göttingen: Hogrefe.

Heidbrink, H. (2000). Ein virtuelles Methodenseminar an der FernUniversität. In B. Batinic (Ed.), *Internet für Psychologen* (2nd ed.) (pp. 479-507) [Internet for psychologists]. Göttingen: Hogrefe.

Hewson, C. M., Laurent, D., & Vogel, C. M. (1996). Proper methodologies for psychological and sociological studies conducted via the Internet. *Behavior Research Methods, Instruments, and Computers, 28*, 186-191.

Hofstaetter, P. R. (1965). Was man von Psychologen erwartet. In F. P. Hardesty & K. Eyferth (Eds.), *Forderungen an die Psychologie* (pp. 252-270). Bern: Huber.

Koeske, G. F., Koeske, R. D., & Mallinger, J. (1993). Perceptions of professional competence: Cross-disciplinary ratings of psychologists, social workers, and psychiatrists. *American Journal of Orthopsychiatry, 63*, 45-54.

Krantz, J. H., Ballard, J., & Scher, J. (1997). Comparing the results of laboratory and world wide web samples on the determinants of female attractiveness. *Behavior Research Methods, Instruments, and Computers, 29*, 264-269.

Krebs, D. (1995). Selbstselektion: Demographisches oder attitudinales Problem. *ZA-Information, 36*, 114-125.

Krueger, T., Ott, R., & Funke, J. (2000). Das WWW als Medium der Außendarstellung. In B. Batinic (Ed.), *Internet für Psychologen* (2nd ed.) (pp. 241-259) [Internet for psychologists]. Göttingen: Hogrefe.

Kury, H. (1994). Zum Einfluß der Art der Datenerhebung auf die Ergebnisse von Umfragen. *Monatszeitschrift für Kriminologie und Strafrechtsreform, 77*, 22-33.

Laux, G. (1977). Über die Einstellung der Bevölkerung zum Psychiater und zum Psychotherapeuten. *Nervenarzt, 48*, 331-334.

Lindner, I. (1996). *Studienführer Psychologie* (3. ed.). München: Lexika.

Mehta, R. & Sivadas, E. (1995). Comparing response rates and response content in mail versus electronic mail surveys. *Journal of the Market Research Society, 37*, 492-493.

Nistor, N. & Mandl, H. (1995). *Lernen in Computer-Netzwerken. Erfahrungen mit einem virtuellen Seminar. Forschungsbericht 64.* München: Ludwig-Maximilians-Universität.

Perrig-Chiello, P. & Perrig, W. (1992). Psychologie – besser oder schlechter als ihr Ruf? Überlegungen zu einer Meinungsumfrage. *Psychoscope, 13*, 6-8.

Reips, U.-D. (2000). Das psychologische Experimentieren im Internet. In B. Batinic (Ed.), *Internet für Psychologen* (2nd ed.) (pp. 319-343) [Internet for psychologists]. Göttingen: Hogrefe.

Reuband, K.-H. & Blasius, J. (1996). Ausschöfungsquoten und Antwortmuster in einer Großstadt-Studie. *Kölner Zeitschrift für Soziologie und Sozialpsychologie, 48*, 296-318.

Richter, B. (1996). Das Image der Psychotherapie. *Psychotherapie-Forum, 4*, 6-9.

Rietz, I. & Wahl, S. (1997). Welches Image hat die Psychologie und der Beruf des Psychologen in der Öffentlichkeit: Ergebnisse einer Befragung. In G. Richardt, G. Krampen, & H. Zayer (Eds.), *Gesellschaft im Wandel. Beiträge zur Angewandten Psychologie. 4. Deutscher Psychologentag des Berufsverbandes Deutscher Psychologinnen und Psychologen.* Bonn: Deutscher Psychologen Verlag.

Spada, H. (1997). Lage und Entwicklung der Psychologie in Deutschland, Österreich und der Schweiz. *Psychologische Rundschau, 48*, 1-15.

Swoboda, W. J., Muhlberger, N., Weitkunat, R., & Schneeweiss, S. (1997). Internet surveys by direct mailing: An innovative way of collecting data. *Social Science Computer Review, 15,* 242-255.

Thumin, F. J. & Zebelmann, G. (1967). Psychology versus psychiatry: A study of public image. *American Psychologist, 22,* 282-286.

Trapp, A., Hammond, N., & Bray, D. (1996). Internet and the support of psychology education. *Behavior Research Methods, Instruments, and Computers, 28,* 174-176.

Utecht, T. (1990). Psychologe/Psychologien: Entwicklungen auf dem Arbeitsmarkt in den 80er Jahren. *Informationen für die Beratungs- und Vermittlungsdienste der Bundesanstalt für Arbeit,* 275-277.

Vontobel, J. & Ries, M.-L. (1969). Das Bild des Psychologen in der Öffentlichkeit und die Vermutungen der Psychologen darüber. *Schweizerische Zeitschrift für Psychologie, 28,* 111-134.

Wallbott, H. (2000). Warum ist das Internet wichtig für die Psychologie? In B. Batinic (Ed.), *Internet für Psychologen* (2nd ed.) (pp. 1-5) [Internet for psychologists]. Göttingen: Hogrefe.

Wood, W., Jones, M., & Benjamin, L. T. (1986). Surveying psychology's public image. *American Psychologist, 41,* 947-953.

10 Ability and Achievement Testing on the World Wide Web

Oliver Wilhelm & Patrick E. McKnight

The increasing use of Internet-based measurement necessitates understanding the strengths and limitations for using methods that eliminate direct contact to test-takers and experimental control. Experimental control problems may be reduced substantially by manipulations nested in the design of the measure but these problems are not eliminated. In contrast, the validity of the tests remains unknown in this medium. Performance measures may be more suitable for Internet distribution than other measures since the goals of the assessment are familiar to the test-taker. In addition, the stimuli presented in the measure are focused on eliciting a maximal effort to assess achievement or capability. What remains uncertain is whether the test-taker's estimated ability corresponds to a reasonable estimate of her ability. The first step, however, is to assess the psychometric properties of Internet-based tests to assess, at a minimum, the reliability of the measure. In an effort to explore the psychometric properties of Internet-based tests, data from more than 2,500 subjects who took either an ability test on deductive reasoning or an achievement test of business administration knowledge were analyzed. Analysis of the data supports the assumption that testing using the Internet can yield valid and useful information.

10.1 Paper-Pencil vs. Computerized Testing

When computers were first used for measuring psychometric traits, they served primarily to apply formerly impossible variants of adaptive and tailored testing (Lord, 1979) and to identify formerly unknown abilities and their incremental validity and utility (Cory, 1977; Cory, Rimland, & Bryson, 1977). The possibility of carrying out psychometric testing using computers offered several new perspectives to measure human performance or personality dispositions that in turn facilitated and accelerated the development of adaptive and tailored testing. The high degree of test economy in all stages of testing (instructions, test presentation, and data analysis) (Klinck, 1998) combined with the possibility of gaining additional information (e.g., through the registration of latencies (Neubauer, Urban, & Malle, 1991), represent substantial advantage over ordinary paper-and-pencil testing. Such advantages should be considered when planning to construct a new measurement instrument. Additionally, adjusting difficulty level of items according to the information gained during a test session reduces needed testing time without sacrificing reliability or validity of the instrument, and avoids effects that may result from fatigue and boredom (Wainer, 1990). Furthermore, there are hints that the computer presentation of a test might be associated with a higher degree of objectivity (Maiwald & Conrad, 1993) potentially associated with higher honesty and self-revelation (Buchanan & Smith, 1999), however these gains in objectivity are not necessarily evident with computer-based testing. Finally computer assisted testing additionally permits the use of iterative item generation technologies, time parameterized testing, and latent factor-centered design (Kyllonen, 1997).

One drawback is that computer assisted testing requires substantial technical resources and the access to the tests is usually restricted to keyboard entry. It is also important to note that some aspects of human performance simply cannot be measured by keyboard entry alone (e.g., visual spatial performance as measured by block design). Aside from possible benefits and necessities related to the selection of a test medium, changes in the psychological characteristics of measurement instruments must be investigated to make sure that the validity of a measurement instrument is not threatened.

For survey questionnaires or personality tests, changes in the psychometric properties that are associated with changes in the testing medium may be mere artifacts. Changes in the psychometric properties for performance tests could be caused by distinct demands of the testing medium. If participants are asked to show "typical behaviors" then changes in the testing medium should have little effect. Alternatively, if participants are asked to show "maximal effort" in different testing environments then the medium may have an influence. For example, in the mapping sentence of Radex theories of human intelligence structure (Guttman, 1965; Jäger, Süß, & Beauducel, 1997), not only the nature of the testing material (e.g., verbal, number, figural material) or the required intellectual operation (reasoning, creativity, memory or mental speed), but also the mode of answer production (paper-and-pencil, computer keyboard) of the test media, can be viewed as causing part of the observable individual differences.

One factor that could influence the psychometric properties of ability and achievement tests is the general degree of familiarity of the subjects with the medium "computer", which might be a source of individual differences affecting the test results. Moreover, the requirements of certain tasks seem to depend on and, thus, change in different experimental settings, resulting in different skill demands (e.g., motor or perceptual). This aspect seems to apply to the problems of presenting speeded ability tests on a computer in particular. Previous research has shown that the medium of presentation greatly affects the reliability of the test results. This raises the question of validity of the test results in the different application modalities (Mead & Drasgow, 1993). In the present discussion, we will not be concerned with speed tests or speeded tests. The effects of speededness itself on the validity of reasoning tests (Wilhelm & Schulze, 2000) combined with difficulties of reliably restricting time limits in Internet administered tests led us to administer only unspeeded tests. A test is considered unspeeded if under unlimited time, performance does not change compared to performance under time constraints. But computer illiteracy could still threaten the validity of tests if cognitive resources are devoted to tasks other than the ones that should be measured. If a participant is preoccupied with handling an input device or with navigating through the displayed document, then less time and fewer processing resources are available to solve the tasks making up the test.

There can be little doubt that the overall level of computer literacy in the population raises with the widespread professional and private use of computers. People seeking psychological tests on the Internet probably have enough computer literacy to be unaffected by the change in the medium. There is, however, no direct empirical test of this claim. An empirical test of this hypothesis is exacerbated by the fact that the causal direction could be in the opposite direction (i.e., subjects higher in achievement or ability are higher in computer literacy). Probably a mutual influence of computer literacy and ability/achievement is most plausible. The test materials that were used in the studies described later were kept simple in order to hold demands on technical equipment and navigation through the documents as low as possible. Nevertheless, it cannot be excluded that computer literacy is causing part of the internal consistency of any given test administered computer assisted.

10.2 Controlled vs. Uncontrolled Computerized Testing

Involved cognitive processes in ability and achievement testing *can* be altered with changing media, however, the experimental control *is* altered with changing administration method. Internet-based ability and achievement testing differs from ordinary computer assisted testing in that the experimental control is very low. Hence, there are two general sources of distinctiveness between ordinary computerized and Internet-based testing: the lack of person mediated communication and the reduction in experimental control. The introduction of Internet-based testing could facilitate and improve several aspects of usual psychometric testing as well as ordinary experimenting (Reips, 1999). For example, access to a larger and more diverse community of research participants could be gained (Buchanan & Smith, 1999; Reips, 1999). Costs and resource consumption per study could be reduced. The power of experiments can be raised dramatically by including more subjects such that research otherwise not realizable can be carried out, and subsamples of hard to access subjects could participate in the research (Reips, 1999).

However using Web-based performance testing raises several severe questions concerning the validity of measurement instruments. Due to the essentially uncontrolled testing situation it is usually unknown if subjects understand the instructions they were given or if they follow the instructions with respect to the use of auxiliary means. In addition, total testing time allowed is difficult to assess. Finally, it is usually unknown why participants are motivated to take part in a study, how motivated participants are and how physically fit they are (e.g., if they participate relaxed and awake or stressed, tired, and drunk). On the other hand we ought to recognize that those questions are not easily answered with laboratory research. If we claim, for example, that participants take part in laboratory research for course credit, does this result in the elimination of motivational and effort differences between participants? It is unlikely that these manipulations alone produce the uniformity that most researchers assume. In laboratory settings, researchers observe participants' effort, concentration, attention, and compliance with the demands of the task. Most researchers assume that they can differentiate or, at a minimum, distinguish subjects who stand out on any of the relevant aforementioned factors.

It remains unclear how Internet-based test administration or research influences motivation and, as a result, outcomes in general, ability and achievement tests in particular. Motivation to participate in Web-based testing is likely to be higher overall, because participants are self-selected and motivated in their pursuit to test themselves, and their efforts often have some cost – usually associated with using the Internet. Since subjects participating in Internet administered tests invest time, money, and effort in completing the tests, we assume motivation to participate on those tests to be fairly high. In addition, it is likely, that a substantial proportion of users just quickly peruse the test to gain some knowledge of the test or fail to respond to items once they find out that the test is harder and more frustrating than expected.

The questions regarding Internet-based ability testing are addressed in the forthcoming discussion. Results from the analyses are expected to support the contention that Internet-based ability test administration ought to have negligible impact on psychometric properties and ability estimates for subjects ought to be generalizable across test administration procedures.

10.3 Method

All subjects in the presented data were self-selected. The results they achieved had no real consequences. It is this fact and the properties of the data that make us think that people did not cheat. They simply had no reason to do so. Conversely the feedback participants received was said to contain only useful information if the persons followed the instructions. If the results had implications for participants (i.e., educational exams or personnel selection tests) then severe efforts to escape experimental control would have to be assumed to be maximal. The testing environment was assumed to elicit "maximal behavior" in answering questions without violating rules given in the instructions. In the context of strong outcome implications, subjects would be expected to maximize their success by using any auxiliary means available. The auxiliary means can consist of taking notes (primarily for ability tests) and consulting for example technical documents (primarily for achievement tests). Since the subject's "maximal behavior" is assumed and subjects were contributing voluntarily with specific instructions to not use any auxiliary means, outcomes were assumed to be representative of the subject's ability.

In this paper, two Web-based experiments will be described. The relationship between Web-based tests and ordinary paper-and-pencil tests for both ability and achievement tests have been described in detail elsewhere (see Wilhelm, Witthöft, & Größler, 1999). Here the focus will be on Internet data primarily, with only brief discussions of paper-and-pencil data of the same measurement instruments.

The adaptation of the tests for use via World Wide Web (WWW) was done with the primary aim to keep the similarity between both test versions as high as possible and to keep the demands on browsers and the quality of the network connection as low as possible as a secondary aim. The test consists of one HyperText Markup Language (HTML) -page including the instruction and the item material. The items are answered using a multiple choice type with the number of alternatives ranging from three to five. The two tests can be found at:

- www.psychologie.uni-mannheim.de/psycho2/forsch/wmc/tests/removed_tests/wwt.htm
- www.psychologie.uni-mannheim.de/psycho2/forsch/wmc/tests/removed_tests/dt.htm

Before the tests being described and analyzed here were accessible via WWW, the URL of the virtual test laboratory was submitted to several search engines and Web catalogs. No such marketing has been done for the specific tests analyzed here and no tracking of users has been done in order to keep the promised confidentiality at a maximum[1]. Subjects received an individual feedback letter per e-mail that contained their score, the position relative to other WWW participants, and instruction on how to interpret the scores, and a warning against over interpreting any result.

10.4 Study 1

10.4.1 Purpose

It is widely acknowledged that reasoning is the core construct of human intelligence (Marshalek, Lohman, & Snow, 1983). Deductive and inductive reasoning can be found in any major theory of intelligence structure and in any major intelligence structure test (Carroll, 1993; Jäger, 1984; Jäger, Süß, & Beauducel, 1997). Nevertheless there are only a few distinct deductive reasoning tests in German language (Wilhelm, 2000). Additionally the available tests are biased with respect to their content. Inductive reasoning tasks are associated with figural content and deductive reasoning tasks are associated with verbal and numerical content. Mediated through this confound, deductive reasoning might be more associated with crystallized intelligence and inductive reasoning more associated with fluid intelligence (Amthauer, Brocke, Liepmann, & Beauducel, 1999). Removing this confound indeed reveals *one* major reasoning factor (Wilhelm & Schulze, 2000). Beyond the lack of deductive reasoning tests in general, the available tests usually are *not* constructed on the theoretical basis of process theories from cognitive psychology. So the major purpose of study one is to collect a large data set on newly developed tests of deductive reasoning that were constructed on the basis of the mental model theory of deductive reasoning.

---

[1]   We checked for the effect of strictness of inclusion criteria elsewhere (Wilhelm, Witthöft, McKnight, & Größler, 1999) and found little to no effect. It is essential to bear in mind, that the incentives for participation have a big effect on the number of subjects participating more than once (Frick, Bächtiger, & Reips, 1999). Some incentives may actually increase the likelihood of duplicate subject entries, however, efforts were taken to eliminate these incentives so as to decrease duplicate entries thus increasing the proportion of subjects who complete the measure for intrinsic reasons. We assume that responses from subjects who only gain intrinsic rewards are more likely to give their best effort and provide the most valid performance data.

10.4.2 Instruments

In this study, two deductive reasoning tests were adapted for Internet administration. Both of the reasoning tests have been used in several studies as paper-and-pencil versions (Wilhelm & Conrad, 1998; Wilhelm, 2000). The test formats were identical to those used by Wilhelm and Schulze (2000). In addition, longer forms of both tests have been adapted for Internet administration – results of those adaptations are reported elsewhere (Wilhelm, Witthöft, & Größler, 1999).

The reasoning test is a composite of 18 propositional reasoning items and 12 syllogistic reasoning items (see Table 10.1 for sample items). In the syllogistic test, items are about properties of certain elements. In the propositional test, items are about actions of a fictive machine. The construction of both parts of the deductive reasoning test is based on the theory of mental models (Johnson-Laird & Byrne, 1991) (for a detailed test description and results, see Wilhelm & Conrad, 1998 and Wilhelm, 2000).

It is an essential property of those tests to be constructed on the basis of a well-tested theory from cognitive psychology. This starting point allows reflection about the detailed form of the items and to compare expected with observed difficulties, because the ongoing cognitive activities are focused and can be matched with the theoretically desired reasoning processes. Deductive reasoning tasks can take a variety of forms. Reasoning problems can be either concrete or abstract. Abstract problems unnecessarily interfere with the construction of mental models. Hence only concrete forms are to be considered possible. Reasoning problems that are contrary to prior knowledge require inhibitory abilities during model construction and manipulation and, hence, "pollute" the measurement of the cognitive processes of interest. Finally reasoning problems framed in a way that is compatible with prior knowledge can be either factually identical with previously stored information or can be possible forms of such knowledge. The former instantiation usually prevents reasoning processes from being carried out and, hence, the latter is chosen as the best possible form of reasoning problems. All reasoning items used in this study have this form.

Besides the mental model theory of deductive reasoning several other theories explaining either performance on deductive reasoning tasks or the occurring errors exist. Amongst those theories are so-called rule theories (e.g., Rips, 1994) or dual process theories, which usually distinguish phases of reasoning processes, a heuristic and an analytic one (Evans, 1989; Stanovich & West, 2000). The theory of mental models is theoretically the most elaborate system to explain deductive reasoning and it is empirically the most rigorously tested and confirmed theory of deductive reasoning.

In short the mental model theory assumes that deductive reasoning is based on the manipulation of mental models (DeSoto, London, & Handel, 1965) and can be described as taking place in three phases (Johnson-Laird & Byrne, 1991, 1993). In phase one, ordinary text comprehension is required to understand the premises; verbal ability and prior knowledge come into play here. The result of phase one is an internal model of what was described. In the second phase, a parsimonious description of the model is constructed. The description of the model should include semantic content that was not apparent or explicit in the premises. If this goal cannot be reached then the conclusion process is interrupted without valid conclusion as output. In the third phase, the essential deductive work is carried out. Subjects try to reject the conclusion they derived in phase two by carrying out a search for counter examples. This search is guided by no general algorithm or strategy and is usually terminated, when the capacity limitations of working memory are reached. If no model can be constructed that is compatible with the premises but incompatible with the preliminary drawn conclusion, the conclusion is necessarily true. If a counterexample is found the search for one restarts in phase two. The higher the number of mental models compatible with the premises of an item, the higher the load on working memory. The higher the load on working memory, the higher the proportion of errors because the required processes can no longer be carried out by the temporarily exhausted limited capacity working memory system.

The theory of mental models was successfully applied to propositional (Johnson-Laird, Byrne, & Schaecken, 1992, 1994), spatial relational (Ehrlich & Johnson-Laird, 1982; Byrne & Johnson-Laird, 1989), temporal (Schaecken, Johnson-Laird, & d'Ydewalle, 1995), syllogistic (Johnson-Laird & Bara; 1984), multiple quantified (Johnson-Laird & Tabossi, 1989) and meta-deductive reasoning (Johnson-Laird & Byrne, 1991).

Table 10.1: Sample tasks for the propositional and syllogistic reasoning tests

Test	Propositional reasoning	Syllogistic reasoning
Question	If the lever moves and the valve closes, then the interrupter is switched. The lever moves. The valve closes.	No expensive car is fast. Some expensive cars are not white.
Answers	1. The interrupter is switched. 2. The interrupter is not switched. 3. None of the two above is necessarily true. 4. Omitted	1. Some white cars are not fast. 2. Some fast cars are not white. 3. Some white cars are fast. 4. No white car is fast. 5. All fast cars are white. 6. Omitted

Subjects were instructed to carefully read the instructions. The instructions had a general part (welcoming subjects, instructions to not use any auxiliary means in order to receive useful feedback, instructions on how to proceed) and a special part, explaining the meaning of logical connectives used in the items and discussing a sample item. After completing all the items of the propositional test, subjects were asked how long it took them to complete the items, if they tried to solve the reasoning problems with a verbal or spatial strategy (see Ford, 1995 for a discussion of both reasoning styles), and approximately how many questions they thought they solved correctly. The same questions were asked after completing the syllogistic test. Before submitting their data, participants were additionally asked to indicate their sex, age, profession, the highest completed education level and the number of years of schooling.

10.4.3 Subjects

A total of 2,182 subjects were included in the analysis. Observations were excluded if there existed more than one missing answer in the reasoning items and more than one submission from a single e-mail address (exceptions were allowed only where explicit redundant addresses were explained by the test-taker). The relaxed inclusion criteria seemed sufficient since the completion of the test requires considerable time and effort. However, there are no guarantees that the compromise between noise in the data and use of the available data is optimal with this strategy. Future investigations will include the systematic variation of inclusion criteria and its influence on ability and achievement data. The distribution of age ($M = 26.4$ years, $SD = 7.9$), and occupation resembles those found in other samples (see Figure 10.1 and 10.2).

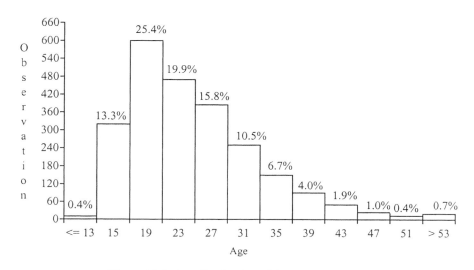

Figure 10.1: Age distribution of the www sample

Of 2,036 persons indicating their sex, 62% were male. The mean number of years of education was 14.5 with a standard deviation of 3.7 years.

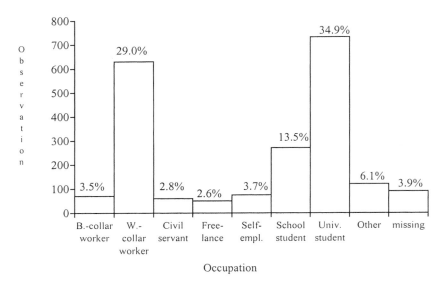

Figure 10.2: Occupations in the www sample

The completed education levels of the sample are shown in Table 10.2.

Table 10.2: Completed education levels in the www sample

Education levels	Percent
Primary	8.0%
Secondary	16.4%
High school grad.	34.5%
Stage studies	10.7%
Graduation	19.0%
Promotion	2.5%
missing	8.7%

Since the syllogistic as well as the propositional reasoning test were administered unspeeded, no fixed time limits were applied. Instead subjects were asked to indicate how long they worked on each of the two tests (Figure 10.3). Participants worked for 12.5 minutes on the propositional test ($SD = 6.0$) and for 12.7 minutes on the syllogistic test ($SD = 6.4$). The time demands on both tests correlate with .62. The correlation with the scores on both tests is very low (.03 for the propositional test and .12 for the syllogistic test).

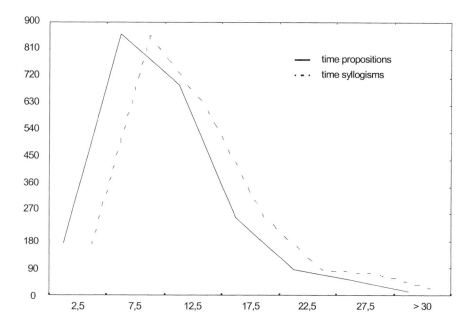

Figure 10.3: Time demands for the syllogistic and propositional
reasoning test

10.4.4 Results

In Table 10.3, item statistics for the total test are given. The mean difficulty of .6 is in
the range of optimal difficulty and part whole corrected item-total correlations with a
mean of .42 as well as the mean of .58 of the normed slopes of the item characteristic
curves of a two parameter IRT model are good values. The mean communality of .24
the items yield in a one-factor principal component factor analysis is satisfying for
binary items.

Table 10.3: Item statistics for the deductive reasoning test

Item	M	r_{it}[1]	com[2]	slope[3]	Item	M	r_{it}	com	slope
01	.87	.38	.20	.72	16	.37	.47	.26	.58
02	.69	.37	.18	.48	17	.48	.39	.18	.48
03	.78	.45	.26	.65	18	.41	.57	.39	.79
04	.74	.49	.31	.68	19	.48	.41	.20	.48
05	.88	.44	.25	.77	20	.37	.55	.36	.74
06	.75	.42	.23	.57	21	.50	.46	.27	.61
07	.82	.44	.26	.68	22	.75	.34	.16	.54
08	.40	.41	.21	.49	23	.65	.36	.17	.42
09	.40	.53	.34	.64	24	.92	.20	.05	.39
10	.57	.47	.28	.56	25	.61	.51	.32	.68
11	.64	.45	.26	.54	26	.86	.35	.17	.55
12	.67	.44	.24	.58	27	.86	.44	.25	.76
13	.44	.44	.25	.58	28	.55	.31	.12	.38
14	.47	.49	.29	.65	29	.66	.51	.32	.72
15	.39	.47	.25	.58	30	.47	.56	.37	.73

[1] r_{it} = part whole corrected item test correlation,
[2] com = correlation with first unrotated factor of a principal component solution,
[3] slope = on unity normed slope of item characteristic curve for a 2 parameter IRT model

At the time of writing this paper, both reasoning tests have been used only with school and university students. Implicitly it is assumed that the tests measure reasoning ability in other age, education, and occupation groups too. In Table 10.4 means, standard deviations, and alphas for both parts of the reasoning tests can be compared across occupational groups together with the correlation of both test parts. In accordance with the assumptions, workers have the lowest mean on both test parts – probably due to poorer education opportunities for those participants. Amongst all other occupational groups there are only small differences, except for the students, who outperform all other groups on both tests. Participants with missing data on the occupational question performed the poorest and had the largest dispersions on both test parts. Consequently, significantly higher alphas (Feld, 1969) and a strong correlation of both test parts can be found. Apart from the group of workers, occupation seems to have a negligibly small influence on the correlation of both test parts.

Table 10.4: Means, dispersions, Cronbach's alpha, and correlations for different professions

Group	Syllogisms			Propositions			r syll/prop
	M	SD	alpha	M	SD	alpha	
Worker	.56	.27	.83	.41	.18	.68	.36
Employee	.69	.24	.78	.56	.24	.85	.60
Officer	.69	.24	.79	.54	.24	.85	.62
Freelancer	.71	.22	.75	.54	.17	.65	.58
Entrepreneur	.71	.21	.73	.54	.22	.81	.67
Pupils	.64	.22	.73	.54	.23	.82	.57
Students	.75	.21	.76	.65	.23	.84	.57
Other	.66	.24	.77	.52	.23	.83	.50
Missing	.37	.36	.94	.37	.25	.86	.72
All subjects	.64	.25	.81	.54	.24	.85	.61

The validity of both tests can be tested if groups with different educational background are compared. Although an increase in mean performance with increasing education can be expected, the alphas and intercorrelation of both test parts should remain unaffected (except for statistical artifacts like ceiling and floor effects). Indeed there is a substantial mean effect of up to one standard deviation. After high school graduation there are scarcely any mean differences between groups. The correlation of both tests seems to be unaffected by educational background. The correlation is substantially lowered only for persons with completed primary school. This effect could be due to a floor effect on the propositional test or to distinct strategies for deductive reasoning (e.g., to not search for counterexamples)[2].

Table 10.5 includes the descriptive statistics of a study with 294 high school students. The education those subjects reported was comparable to the subject's summarized under the label secondary school. At least two things are apparent from comparing the values of the paper-and-pencil subjects to those of the WWW samples. First the performance in the paper-and-pencil sample is comparable in magnitude to the performance of the WWW subsample with primary school education only. This finding may reflect differences in motivation to participate as well as self-selection issues. When calibrating the samples for education, the WWW sample outperforms the paper-and-pencil sample by about half a standard deviation unit in the syllogistic test and about a third of a standard deviation unit in the propositional test. Restriction of range phenomena may be evident in the paper-and-pencil sample. Although it is additionally or alternatively possible that the WWW sample range is artificially en-

---

[2]   A similar effect can be found for paper-and-pencil data of the syllogistic test (Wilhelm & Conrad, 1998). There, subjects of below average intelligence had zero correlations between multi-model-syllogisms and intelligence.

hanced, we assume the restriction in range in the paper-and-pencil sample to be more influential. Consequently, in the paper-and-pencil sample, the alphas and the inter-correlation of the tests are underestimations of the true values. It is important to note that a direct comparison of paper-and-pencil and WWW performance is not easy to accomplish. Differences in the maximal behavior observed could be attributed to several factors and indeed those factors (most prominently amongst them the motivation to participate, self selection, issues of experimental control, and may be effects of the medium itself) could be considered to influence performance simultaneously. It then is a much harder job to ensure equivalence of tests of maximal behavior than it is to ensure this psychometric quality for tests of typical performance. This assumption should hold at least for situations in which no cheating on the measures of typical behavior is to be expected.

Table 10.5: Means, dispersions, Cronbach's alpha, and correlations for different education levels

| Group | Syllogisms | | | Propositions | | | r |
	M	SD	alpha	M	SD	alpha	syll/prop
Primary school	.55	.23	.72	.42	.20	.76	.38
Secondary school	.62	.24	.76	.48	.19	.73	.54
High school graduation	.73	.22	.75	.60	.23	.84	.58
Stage studies	.77	.21	.76	.67	.24	.85	.59
Graduation	.78	.21	.77	.65	.23	.84	.53
Promotion	.76	.25	.83	.72	.25	.88	.60
Missing	.48	.31	.88	.42	.24	.83	.63
Paper pencil	.51	.21	.71	.45	.16	.61	.30
All www subjects	.64	.25	.81	.54	.24	.85	.61

The mental model theory of deductive reasoning does explain how deductions are carried out with a great variety of materials. The theory is neutral with respect to the "mental code" that is used in performing deductions. There are stable individual differences in the strategies people use when answering deductive reasoning problems. This is not only apparent in the ways used to teach logic, for example set theory (Quine, 1969), Euler circles or the truth table approach, but also in empirical research (Sternberg, 1980; Ford, 1995).

At the end of both of the tests, participants were asked independently whether they derived their conclusions using a verbal or figural strategy (items used a five-point Likert scale anchored by "not at all" and "always"). For brevity we collapse the results across the two tests after aggregating the verbal and figural questions by subtracting the latter from the former. The two questions were negatively correlated for both tests (indicating that whether one or the other strategy was applied but not both). Across the tests the verbal questions and the figural questions were correlated with .59 and .66 respectively. The results appear to sufficiently support the aggregation of the two difference scores (their intercorrelation is .61) into one strategy variable. The relationship of the combined strategy items with reasoning performance is shown in Figure 10.4.

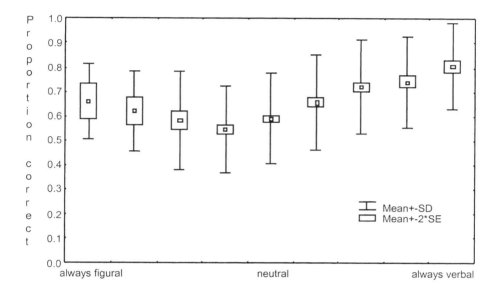

Figure 10.4: Verbal and figural strategies and
reasoning performance

The correlation of the strategy variable with the reasoning score of both tests is .35. As can be seen from Figure 10.4 there are nonlinear trends in the relationship between both variables. The beta weights are .26 for the strategy variable and .16 for the quadratic trend. Obviously the lack of strategy application has the worst effect on reasoning performance, while figural as well as verbal strategies seem to be helpful, with stronger effects observable for the verbal strategy[3]. Although there are more refined methods to measure strategy application (Leutner & Plass, 1998), the present effect is of substantial size and in need of further explanation.

Self-estimation of performance (i.e., questions answered correctly) was used as a variable to predict reasoning performance. Subjects estimated the number of questions they answered correct independently for both tests. The correlation of both estimates is .61, an estimate large enough to support the aggregation of both variables therefore increasing construct reliability (Wittmann, 1988). The zero order correlation of the overall score and the combined self-ratings is .56[4].

Two variables that should reflect effort of participants were the required times for the syllogistic and propositional test (see Figure 10.3 for the distribution of required times). The required time for both tests correlates .62 with each other. Again a correlation of this magnitude justifies aggregation to required total time. There is only a small positive correlation with required time and total score of .10. Additionally this correlation vanishes when times below 10 minutes for the total test are excluded from the analysis ($r = .05$). First this result should be considered as a reflection of the absence of speedness effects. In addition, very brief periods of test taking are associated with lower scores. Apparently a small proportion of test takers were perusing the tests without real engagement.

In a multiple regression with total score as dependent variable and age, years of education, performance self estimate, strategy, and required time as predictors, 41% of the total variance of the reasoning test is explained (complete case sample size for this analysis is 1,642). Although the direction of explanation in this analysis should not be viewed as expressing a direction of causality, the analysis shows substantial systematic variance that could not easily be explained as artifact.

The test administration of a deductive reasoning test as an instantiation of an ability test using the Internet seems to produce valid and useful data. The scores are reli-

---

[3] Some caution is indicated with respect to this interpretation. A zero difference between both strategy variables can indicate the absence of strategy use as well as the overuse of strategies (e.g., trying to apply both sorts of strategies to each problem). Focusing on people with −1, 0 or 1 values on the difference variable, the correlation between performance and the sum of the four strategy application items is -.15. Improved techniques for the analysis of the problem apparent here can be found in Breckler (1994).

[4] The correlation of .56 should be viewed with caution. On the one hand, participants can be assumed to have some insight into how good they performed on a reasoning test. However, on the other hand the high correlation can equally reflect the motivation participants invested in answering the questions. Then the correlation would only reflect that participants realistically expect little engagement to result in low scores. If this is true, little engagement should be associated with little time efforts. However the self-estimation score and the required time correlate only with .06 with each other.

able and the intercorrelation among test scores and between test scores and biographical variables follow the assumptions. To test this claim, the size of the correlations between both test parts was checked for differences between the Internet data and a paper-and-pencil study (Wilhelm & Schulze, 2000). The correlations between both test parts ($r = 0.61$ for the Internet sample and $r = 0.29$ for the paper-and-pencil sample) are significantly different (Fischer's $Z = 8.835$, $p < 0.001$). We tried to enhance comparability of the two samples by computing a restriction of range correction for the correlation in the paper-and-pencil sample (Gulliksen, 1987). The corrected correlation is $r = 0.54$, and is not significantly different from the correlation in the WWW sample (Fischer's $Z = 1.43$, $p = 0.15$). The result confirms the notion that the differences in correlations between the two media could be attributed to sample characteristics (e.g., restriction of range). A more direct test of equivalence would however include subjects that were parallel on different biographical background variables considered to influence test performance.

10.4.5 Discussion

One of the most essential questions that was asked with the emergence of computerized testing is on the equivalence between computerized and paper-and-pencil test administration. The same question is relevant regarding the setting of the testing environment. The difference between computerized and paper-pencil testing methods lies probably not in the involved abilities (e.g., handling the computer) but in the mediation of communication by a person and the behavioral control of subjects.

The lack of person mediated communication could be one factor introducing distinct abilities in distinct testing methods. Usually the instructions on reasoning tests are a sensitive topic. Altering them, abbreviating them, or removing sample items from them can easily alter the psychometric properties of a test. In the deductive reasoning tests applied in this study, the instructions were very sensitive. They contain phrases like:

> If in the premises a sentence like "If the chain moves, the pedal is pressed" occurs, this does not mean that a pressed pedal necessarily occurs with a moving chain.

> If in the premises a sentence like "The chain moves or the pedal is pressed" occurs, this does mean that the machine is carrying out at least one of the two activities, it can carry out both activities however.

Subjects failing to carefully read or understand the instructions have a severe disadvantage. That a substantial proportion of participants did not carefully read the instructions was apparent, for example, in participants complaining that the use of the term "or" has not been made unequivocally. While in ordinary testing situations it can be ensured that all subjects understand the instructions (everyone can answer the sample item, everyone pays attention to the instructions, no one asks about the meaning of instructions when giving extensive opportunity to do so), WWW test administration does not afford this opportunity.

There are several reasons that could account for different mixtures of abilities required in the two administration methods. The Internet administration could call for other motor abilities or procedural computer knowledge. Ordinary test administrations could favor persons with higher test taking skills. The Internet method could attract participants that attack the reasoning problems in another way. The proportion of subjects using auxiliary methods or answering in a random fashion could be higher for Internet administered tests. The different biographical, geographical, and motivational background of samples available in laboratory research and accessible via Internet could account for possible differences. These and other reasons could be responsible for violations of psychometric equivalence (Steyer & Eid, 1993).

In study one, very highly educated subjects, all of them self selected, participated. Compared to school or university students that participate at best with mediocre motivation, a substantial performance difference is to be expected. Additionally, restriction and enhancement of range could alter the internal structure and the relation with external criteria. All of those effects can be considered violations of equivalence, although the deviations of equivalence can possibly all be explained by differences in the samples.

As a final aspect of testing the validity of the reasoning data, we compare the data gained via Internet administration with data collected by paper-and-pencil testing with a focus on the answer patterns participants produce in both methods. Within ability and achievement tests, it is usually assumed that one latent factor or a mixture of latent factors constant across items is responsible for the answers produced by participants. The probabilistic relation between an answer on an item and the person parameter is best expressed in item characteristic curves frequently used in item response theory. The Rasch model is one specific model that assumes that all item characteristic curves have the same shape. If the Rasch model holds, then specific objective comparisons are possible (regardless of the items used the same person parameters emerge and vice versa (see Irtel, 1995, for specific objectivity in other IRT models). One method to test whether the Rasch model holds in a given data set is to estimate the item parameters with different subsets of participants. In the current context, the administration method could be used to divide the sample in two subsamples. If the parameter estimates deviate, then two possible latent classes can be distinguished. Alternatively, there are IRT models that search for maximally different answer patterns and create inductively gained latent classes (Rost, 1990; von Davier & Rost, 1995). If the administration methods have only a small or zero effect on how answers are produced and if the differences in sample characteristics are not responsible for heterogeneity of answer vectors, then membership to latent groups is not correlated with administration method.

In Table 10.6, the likelihood and the values of penalty functions for the ordinary Rasch model (1 class) and the mixture distribution Rasch model can be found. The 2-class solution fits the data better than the one class solution on all indexes and the likelihood ratio test in the last column supports this conclusion.

Table 10.6: Likelihood and penalty functions for the rasch and mixed rasch models

	1 class	2 classes	
- 2 log likelihood	32906.62	32015.84	Diff log likel.: 890
AIC	32968.61	32141.84	Diff df: 32
BIC	33123.2	32455.99	$p < 0.0001$
CAIC	33154.2	32518.99	

The class membership variable and the administration method are practically unrelated ($r = .04$). It seems reasonable to conclude that the administration method has no substantial influence on the answer patterns participants generated under different administration methods in these ability tests.

10.5 Study 2

10.5.1 Purpose

Despite the enormous significance of having economics and business administration knowledge in a great variety of jobs, there are no widely used or well known tests to measure such knowledge in German language. One available general business administration test (Krumm & Seidel, 1970) is rather outdated. However, recently a German adaptation of an American economics test (Soper & Walstad, 1987) was published (Beck & Krumm, 1999). Unfortunately, the economics test is not suitable for general business acumen. Both tests are on a difficulty level that maximizes discrimination between persons of an intermediate ability and not amongst the most able subjects. One of the major aims of this study is to evaluate a test that is able to discriminate among highly and very highly capable subjects.

The general business administration knowledge test used in study 2 was previously used in several studies in complex problem solving (Größler, 1998, 1999; Wittmann & Süß, 1999). In those studies, only students of general business administration were included in an effort to keep the level of expertise among the subjects at the upper level. However the reliability and validity in those studies was low. To exclude that restriction of range phenomena or artificial homogenizing of subjects is responsible for these results, it was decided to use the test with experts who have a more diverse biographical background.

10.5.2 Instruments

In order to keep the heterogeneity of the content area of the test at a maximum, the area of general business administration was preclassified into nine content areas:

- general management,
- cost accounting,
- financial accounting,
- production management,
- finance,
- strategic management,
- marketing,
- commercial law, and
- taxation

This preclassification matches well with the way general business administration is taught in Germany. Since we included only 20 questions in the first version of the test, it could not be expected to find empirical associations between the content areas. The preclassification drawn here does not necessarily imply an association between the included areas. The purpose of not strictly applying facetted preclassification of items is more to ensure heterogeneity of items and broadness and completeness of operationalization (Blumberg, 1981; Edmundson, Koch, & Silverman, 1993; Klauer, 1984; Shye, 1988). For the domain of general business administration, we would expect either a strong general factor or a structure similar to the above mentioned nine areas[5], which will probably show considerable mutual dependencies. Due to the lack of sufficient numbers of items for all scales, no confirmatory models can be computed for the version of the general business test applied in this study.

Only a right/wrong answer format was used for the questions of the business administration test. The default value for all items was "omitted". Omitted questions

---

[5]   Possibly some of the scales would need a more fine-grained distinction (for example, production management into production theory and production planning) or could be merged on a higher level (for example, cost accounting and financial accounting to accountancy). Additionally it cannot be excluded that some of the items are misclassified in an empirical sense. However, none of the experts involved in constructing the test expressed doubts with respect to the classification of items or the lack of scales (Wilhelm, Witthöft, McKnight, & Größler, 1999).

are coded as wrong in all analysis. Since there are only 20 questions, a score of 10 is expected based upon chance or guessing. Hence it should not be expected that the test shows excellent psychometric properties. It is more appropriate to consider the test to be under construction and a precursor of a further developed measure of business administration competence.

Table 10.7: Sample questions and answer format for the tests

Test	Management knowledge test
Question	The contribution margin is calculated as revenues minus variable costs.
Answers	1. right / 2. wrong / 3. omitted

Before starting to work on the test items, subjects were asked to complete several questions related to their education in business administration. Participants were asked detailed questions about the area and duration of business administration education and were given an opportunity to give additional details about their education in open formatted questions.

After the educational section, participants were asked personal questions about business administration. Those questions were:

- Do you make your tax declaration yourself?
- Do you have additional pension funds?
- Do you take care of accumulation of capital?
- Do you read the "Handelsblatt", "Capital", "Managermagazin", "Wirtschafts-woche" or the "Financial times" regularly, sometimes, or never?
- Are you self-employed?
- What is your yearly income?

In addition to these validity-related questions, subjects were asked upon completion to estimate the number of questions answered correctly, education duration, highest completed education level, profession, age, and sex.

10.5.3 Subjects

A total of 615 subjects took the general business administration test via Internet. The mean age of participants was 26.8 years with a standard deviation of 7.9 years and 65% of the subjects were male. The mean duration of education was 15.5 years ($SD = 6.5$). The distribution of profession and education mimics the one described for the deductive reasoning test.

It is plausible to assume that the effects of self-selection – although present in the data on the reasoning test – are stronger in the business administration test. This should be the case because it is easier for subjects to realize whether the available knowledge matches the demands. Hence it was expected that participants with a background in business administration would take the test. Table 10.8 shows the educational background of the participants with a special focus on education that could be relevant for performance in a business administration test.

Table 10.8: Educational background of participants

Education	Proportion
Business administration	35.3
Economics	8.3
Information sciences	6.0
Business administration engineering	4.0
Business administration teacher	1.6
Other business related university education	4.8
Business high school	9.8
Trading school	7.1
Occupational training	11.9
Other business related education	5.8

10.5.4 Results

The mean number of correct solutions is 11.55 with a standard deviation of 2.87. This implies that 35.8% of all subjects are below the guessing probability. However this fact alone does not imply that those subjects have been guessing. We will return to that point later and try to clarify it by more analysis.

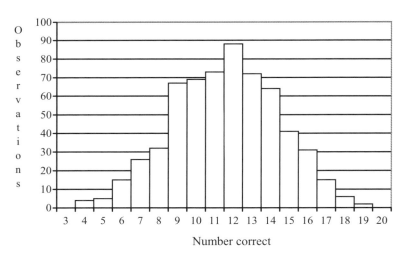

Figure 10.5: Distribution of raw scores

In Table 10.9, basic psychometric statistics for the test are shown. All discrimination indexes are substantially smaller than the values found for the reasoning test. Some items show mean difficulties below the guessing probability. In contrast, all discrimination indexes have positive values for all items.

Table 10.9: Item statistics for the business administration test

Item	M	r_{it}[1]	com[2]	slope[3]	Item	M	r_{it}	com	slope
01	.71	.20	.11	.30	16	.49	.22	.20	.40
02	.58	.18	.16	.33	17	.61	.01	.01	.10
03	.45	.15	.11	.29	18	.64	.05	.01	.15
04	.82	.14	.14	.37	19	.38	.11	.03	.20
05	.75	.02	.00	.15	20	.29	.14	.13	.32
06	.76	.19	.13	.35	21	.50	.27	.27	.48
07	.64	.24	.19	.39	22	.61	.11	.02	.17
08	.70	.08	.03	.19	23	.58	.09	.03	.18
09	.30	.11	.02	.18	24	.52	.32	.36	.57
10	.73	.09	.04	.22	25	.48	.21	.12	.32

[1] r_{it} = part whole corrected item test correlation,
[2] com = correlation with first unrotated factor of a principal component solution,
[3] slope = on unity normed slope of item characteristic curve for a 2 parameter IRT model

If a group of participants were guessing, their likelihood of guessing ought to be positively related to item difficulty. To test this assumption, items were classified as difficult if the item mean was below .6 and not difficult if greater than .6. It should be expected that the first group of items shows lower item total correlations, smaller communalities, smaller slopes of the item characteristic curves, smaller average inter-item correlations and a smaller alpha. However the opposite is true. The hard items perform better on all psychometric criteria – a result that can not occur if the data are noisy and random.

Table 10.10: Psychometric properties of hard and easy items

	Hard items ($p < .6$)	Easy items ($p > .6$)
Sum	4.2	6.3
Average item-test correlation	.16	.10
Average communality	.13	.06
Average ICC slope	.30	.22
Average inter-item correlation	.07	.03
Cronbach's alpha	.44	.23

The conclusion that no more guessing occurs on the hard items is supported by the uniformity in the guessing parameters of a three-parameter IRT model.

The validation strategy for the business administration test was somewhat different from the procedure adapted for the reasoning test. Although there are data supporting the validity of the test (Größler, 1998, 1999), none of the procedures applied
in the previous work (e.g., complex problem solving scenarios) could be applied via
Internet. As an alternative, the authors attempted to measure the biographical background of the participants as a proxy for learning opportunities in business administration and personal interest in that area.

Subjects were asked about their personal and educational background in business
administration. The questions asked in both areas were aggregated into compound
values that were then used to explain business knowledge. For example, the business
journals that participants read were weakly correlated to performance in the test (Figure 10.6).

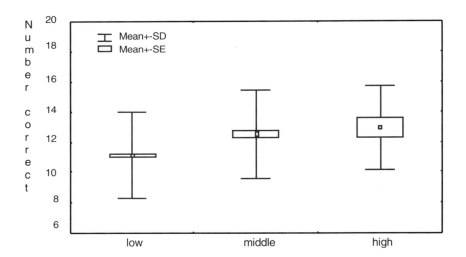

Figure 10.6: Reading of business journals and test performance
number correct

In a multiple regression, business administration performance was regressed on an
aggregate of the personal biographical questions, a compound of the education related questions, and the duration of education of the participants. The three variables
explain only nine percent of the total variance of the business knowledge test. The
beta weights are .26 for the business education variable, .14 for the duration of education variable and, not significant, .05 for the personal biographical variables. There
are two plausible causes for this poor proportion of explanation. First the biographical questions did not measure what they were supposed to measure and second the

business administration test is not reliable and valid enough in its current form. Although only a small proportion of variance was accounted for, it could still be all the available variance. However the partial correlation between the items with odd and even numbers after controlling for business education, personal occupation with business, and years of education is .288. Compared to the correlation of .335 that can be found between odd and even items, this decrease is not substantial.

Similar to the ability test from study one, it is possible that, although the results reported so far are similar to the results found for the paper-and-pencil version, the answer patterns are associated with administration method. To compare the two methods in a mixture rasch model, the data of 83 students of business administration were added to the database and the one and two classes solution were computed for the total sample.

Only two of the four indexes favor the two class solution. The likelihood ratio test in the last column of Table 10.11 supports the two classes solution however. Accepting the two classes solution to test for an association of administration method and class membership reveals a correlation of .02. Similar to the deductive reasoning test, the inductively gained class membership parameters show no association with administration method.

Table 10.11: Likelihood and penalty functions for the rasch and mixed rasch models

	1 class	2 classes	
- 2 log likelihood	9017.68	8935.71	Diff log likel.: 82
AIC	9059.68	9021.71	Diff *df*: 22
BIC	9141.35	9188.94	$p < 0.0001$
CAIC	9162.35	9231.94	

10.5.5 Discussion

To partially validate the test results of the two knowledge tests, we aggregated the biographical questions and computed the correlation with the test score. The resulting correlations are small ($r = 0.227$ for the Internet sample and $r = 0.234$ for the paper-pencil sample[6]) and not significantly different (Fischer Z = 0.058, $p = 0.95$). The size of the correlations is, in part, a function of the reliability. Consequently the low validity of the economics knowledge test could be a result of a lack of reliability. Irrespective of the method applied, it was not possible to show convincing psychometric properties for the business administration test. On a correlational level the results for

---

[6] Since the standard deviations of the variables are not substantially different no restriction of range correction has been applied.

the Internet administrated business administration are as disappointing as the results for the paper-and-pencil version.

The lack of validity may only be a consequence of poor reliability. As a consequence of the poor results, several steps are planned. First, the number of items will be increased to form a larger pool of items to gain better estimates of reliability. Second, we expect to utilize a real parallel test calibrated on expert-rated estimated difficulties and domains of business administration knowledge. Third, cultural differences will be investigated by using versions in English language. Finally, the authors aim to systematically revise the answer format to assess if the method of test construction accounts for the poor test psychometric properties. We are optimistic that those interventions will increase the reliability of the tests and provide us with more useful information about the properties of the measure. If, however, the causes for psychometric problems lie on another level those interventions will be useless. One option that cannot be excluded finally is that the test measures are reliable and valid but only for a small area of ability and this cannot distinguish amongst participants. There are currently no data available to evaluate this alternative explanation.

10.6 General Discussion

The purpose of these studies was the feasibility and utility of administering and analyzing ability and achievement tests on the Internet. Regardless of these aims, mean performance differences between samples were evident – owing mostly to the differences in education and relevant knowledge. Given the large Internet samples, post hoc calibration with data from other sources (e.g., paper-and-pencil data) for demographic variables considered relevant might yield further insights in the similarities and differences associated with different testing methods. The main interest was to show that data from ability and achievement tests applied via Internet can be reliable and valid and mimic those collected with ordinary methods. Aside from the psychometric methods applied in this study, multiple group analysis in structural equation modeling is another perspective that may show promise. Since the answer format seems to be responsible at least for some of the psychometric problems, other methods will be tested (e.g., letting participants express their confidence in their answers for each item and weighing the responses accordingly). To capitalize on the advantages of Internet-based research, the focus of future work will include cultural and language related differences by offering tests in German and English language.

The use of ability and achievement tests via Internet can be seen in several pragmatic aspects. First, it is easy to find subjects with a broad or very narrow range in biographical background. Second, in research with low expected effect sizes, the large WWW samples can substantially increase power above a critical level (power >

.80). Third, pretests with new measurement instruments are easily carried out for measure development. Finally, replication of research findings based on paper-and-pencil tests could be accomplished as was demonstrated in these two studies.

Future research can focus effects of media on performance through experimental manipulations. In addition, research on this topic could investigate the psychological consequences resulting from the variation of the test medium in order to isolate the factors that are responsible for varying performances (e.g., paper might represent a more effective external memory and could lead to a relief in working memory load).

References

Amthauer, R., Brocke, B., Liepmann, D., & Beauducel, A. (1999). *Intelligenz-Struktur-Test 2000* [Intelligence-Structure-Test 2000]. Göttingen: Hogrefe.

Beck, K. & Krumm, V. (1999). *Wirtschaftskundlicher Bildungs-Test (WBT)* [Economics Education Test]. Göttingen: Hogrefe.

Blumberg, P. (1981). A practical methodology for developing content parallel multiple choice tests. *Journal of Experimental Education, 50,* 56-63.

Breckler, S. J. (1994). A comparison of numerical indexes for measuring attitude ambivalence. *Educational and Psychological Measurement, 54,* 350-365.

Buchanan, T. & Smith, J. L. (1999). Using the Internet for psychological research: Personality testing on the world wide web. *British Journal of Psychology, 90,* 125-144.

Byrne, R. M. J. & Johnson-Laird, P. N. (1989). Spatial reasoning. *Journal of Memory and Language, 28,* 564-575.

Cory, C. H. (1977). Relative utility of computerized versus paper-and-pencil tests for predicting job performance. *Applied Psychological Measurement, 1,* 551-564.

Cory, C. H., Rimland, B., & Bryson, R. A. (1977). Using computerized tests to measure new dimensions of abilities: An exploratory study. *Applied Psychological Measurement, 1,* 101-110.

DeSoto, L. B., London, M., & Handel, L. S. (1965). Social reasoning and spatial paralogic. *Journal of Personality and Social Psychology, 2,* 513-521.

Edmundson, E. W., Koch, W. R., & Silverman, S. (1993). A facet analysis approach to content and construct validity. *Educational and Psychological Measurement, 53,* 351-368.

Ehrlich, K. & Johnson-Laird, P. N. (1982). Spatial description and referential continuity. *Journal of Verbal Learning and Verbal Behavior, 21,* 296-306.

Evans, J. St. B. (1989). *Bias in human reasoning: Causes and consequences.* Hove, UK: Lawrence Erlbaum Associates.

Feld, L. S. (1969). A test of the hypothesis that cronbach's alpha or Kruder-Richardson coefficient twenty is the same for two tests. *Psychometrika, 34,* 363-373.

Ford, M. (1995). Two modes of mental representation and problem solution in syllogistic reasoning. *Cognition, 51,* 1-71.

Frick, A., Bächtiger, M. T., & Reips, U.-D. (1999). Financial incentives, personal information, and drop-out rate in online studies. In U.-D. Reips, B. Batinic, W. Bandilla, M. Bosnjak, L. Gräf, K. Moser, & A. Werner (Eds.), *Current Internet science – trends, techniques, results. Aktuelle Online-Forschung – Trends, Techniken, Ergebnisse.* [Online]. Available: http://dgof.de/tband99/

Gulliksen, H. (1987). *Theory of mental tests.* Hove, UK: Lawrence Erlbaum Associates.

Größler, A. (1998). Structural transparency as an element of business simulators. In System Dynamics Society (Ed.), *Proceedings of the sixteenth international conference of the system dynamics society* [CD-ROM Proceedings]. Québec, Canada.

Größler, A. (1999). The influence of decision time on performance in use of a business simulator. In R. Y. Cavana et al. (Eds.), *Systems thinking for the next millenium – The proceedings of the 17th international conference of the system dynamics society* [CD-ROM Proceedings]. Wellington, New Zealand.

Guttman, L. (1965). A faceted definition of intelligence. *Scripta Hierosoluminata, 14,* 166-181.

Hewson, C. M., Laurent, D., & Vogel, C. M. (1996). Proper methodologies for psychological and sociological studies conducted via the Internet. *Behavior Research Methods, Instruments, & Computers, 28,* 186-191.

Irtel, H. (1995). An extension of the concept of specific objectivity. *Psychometrika, 60,* 115-118.

Jäger, A. O., Süß, H.-M., & Beauducel, A. (1997). *Berliner-Intelligenz-Struktur Test: BIS-Test, Form 4* [Berlin-intelligence-structure-test: BIS-test form 4]. Göttingen: Hogrefe.

Johnson-Laird, P. N. & Bara, B. (1984). Syllogistic inference. *Cognition, 16,* 1-61.

Johnson-Laird, P. N. & Byrne, R. M. J. (1991). *Deduction.* Hove, UK: Lawrence Erlbaum Associates.

Johnson-Laird, P. N. & Byrne, R. M. J. (1993). Précis of deduction. *Behavioral and Brain Sciences, 16,* 323-333.

Johnson-Laird, P. N., Byrne, R. M. J., & Schaecken, W. (1992). Propositional reasoning by model. *Psychological Review, 99,* 418-439.

Johnson-Laird, P. N., Byrne, R. M. J., & Schaecken, W. (1994). Why models rather than rules give a better account of propositional reasoning: A reply to Bonatti and to O'Brien, Braine, and Yang. *Psychological Review, 101,* 734-739.

Johnson-Laird, P. N. & Tabossi, P. (1989). Reasoning by model: The case of multiple quantification. *Psychological Review, 96,* 658-673.

Klauer, K. J. (1984). Kontentvalidität [Content validity]. *Diagnostica, 30,* 1-23.

Klinck, D. (1998). Papier-Bleistift- versus computerunterstützte Administration kognitiver Fähigkeitstests: Eine Studie zur Äquivalenzfrage [Paper-pencil vs. computerized administration of cognitive ability test: A study on the equivalence question]. *Diagnostica, 44,* 61-70.

Krumm, V. & Seidel, G. (1970). *Wirtschaftslehretest BWL* [Business administration test]. Weinheim: Beltz.

Kyllonen, P. C. (1997). Smart testing. In R. F. Dillon (Ed.), *Handbook on testing* (pp. 347-368). Westport, CT: Greenwood Press.

Leutner, D. & Plass, J. L. (1998). Measuring learning styles with questionnaires versus direct observation of preferential choice behavior in authentic learning situations: The visualizer/verbalizer behavior observation scale (VV-BOS). *Computers in Human Behavior, 14*, 543-557.

Lord, F. M. (1979). Some item analysis and test theory for a system of computer-assisted test construction for individualized instruction. *Applied Psychological Measurement, 1*, 447-455.

Maiwald, J. & Conrad, W. (1993). Entwicklung und Evaluation des MTP-C: Mannheimer Test zur Erfassung des physikalisch-technischen Problemlösens als Computerversion [Development and evaluation of the MTP-C: Mannheim test to measure physical-technical problem solving abilities computer assisted]. *Diagnostica, 39*, 352-367.

Marshalek, B., Lohman, D. F., & Snow, R. E. (1983). The complexity continuum in the radex and hierarchical models of intelligence. *Intelligence, 7*, 107-127.

Mead, A. D. & Drasgow, F. (1993). Equivalence of computerized and paper-and-pencil cognitive ability tests: A meta-analysis. *Psychological Bulletin, 114*, 449-458.

Neubauer, A. C., Urban, E., & Malle, B. F. (1991). Raven´s advanced progressive matrix: Computerunterstützte Präsentation versus Standardvorgabe [Raven's advanced progressive matrix: computer assisted versus standardized presentation]. *Diagnostica, 37*, 204-212.

Quine, W. V. (1969). *Set theory and its logic.* Cambridge: Belknap Press of Harvard University Press.

Reips, U.-D. (1999). The web experiment method: Advantages, disadvantages, and solutions. In M. H. Birnbaum (Ed.), *Psychology experiments on the Internet.* San Diego, CA: Academic Press.

Rips, L. J. (1994). *The psychology of proof: Deductive reasoning in human thinking.* Cambridge, MA: MIT Press.

Rost, J. (1990). Rasch models in latent classes: An integration of two approaches to item analysis. *Applied Psychological Measurement, 14*, 271-282.

Schaecken, W., Johnson-Laird, P. N., & d'Ydewalle, G. (1996). Mental models and temporal reasoning. *Cognition, 60*, 205-234.

Shye, S. (1988). Modern facet theory: Content design and measurement in behavioral research. *European Journal of Psychological Assessment. 14*, 160-171.

Soper, J. C. & Walstad, W. B. (1987). *Test of economic literacy: Examiners manual* (2nd ed.). New York: Joint Council on Economic Education.

Stanovich, K. E. & West, R. F. (2000). Individual differences in reasoning: Implications for the rationality debate? *Behavioral and Brain Sciences, 23*, 645-665.

Stanton, J. M. (1998). An empirical assessment of data collection using the Internet. *Personnel Psychology, 51*, 709-725.

Sternberg, R. J. (1980). Representation and process in linear syllogistic reasoning. *Journal of Experimental Psychology: General, 109*, 119-159.

Steyer, R. & Eid, M. (1993). *Messen und Testen* [Measuring and testing]. Berlin: Springer.

Von Davier, M. V. & Rost, J. (1995). *WINMIRA: A program system for analysis with the rasch model, with the latent class analysis and with the mixed rasch model.* Kiel: Institute for Science Education (IPN).

Wainer, H. (1990). *Computerized adaptive testing: a primer.* Hillsdale, NJ: Erlbaum.

Wilhelm, O. & Conrad, W. (1998). Entwicklung und Erprobung von Tests zur Erfassung des logischen Denkens [Development and evaluation of deductive reasoning tests]. *Diagnostica, 44,* 71-83.

Wilhelm, O. & Schulze, R. (2000). *Timed and untimed reasoning ability: Evidence for substantial differences.* Unpublished manuscript, University Mannheim.

Wilhelm, O., Witthöft, M., & Größler, A. (1999). Comparisons of paper-and-pencil and Internet administrated ability and achievement tests. In P. Marquet, S. Mathey, A. Jaillet, & E. Nissen (Eds.), *Proceedings of IN-TELE 98* (439-449). Berlin: Peter Lang.

Wilhelm, O., Witthöft, M., McKnight, P., & Größler, A. (1999). On the psychometric quality of new ability tests administered using the WWW. In U.-D. Reips, B. Batinic, W. Bandilla, M. Bosnjak, L. Gräf, K. Moser, & A. Werner (Eds.), *Current Internet Science – Trends, Techniques, Results. Aktuelle Online Forschung – Trends, Techniken, Ergebnisse.* [Online]. Available: http://dgof.de/tband99/.

Wittmann, W. W. (1988). Multivariate reliability theory. Principles of symmetry and successful validation strategies. In R. B. Cattell & J. R. Nesselroade (Eds.), *Handbook of multivariate experimental psychology* (pp. 505-560). New York: Plenum.

Wittmann, W. W. & Süß, H.-M. (1999). Investigating the paths between working memory, intelligence, knowledge, and complex problem-solving performances via Brunswik symmetry. In P. L. Ackerman, P. C. Kyllonen, & R. D. Roberts (Eds.), *Learning and individual differences. Process, trait and content determinants* (pp. 77-108). Washington DC.: APA Books.

11 Psychological Experimenting on the World Wide Web: Investigating Content Effects in Syllogistic Reasoning[1]

Jochen Musch & Karl Christoph Klauer

11.1 Introduction

The implementation and results of World Wide Web (WWW) experiments on belief bias in syllogistic reasoning are reported here. Closely parallel data were obtained both in traditional laboratory experiments and on the Web, providing strong support for the validity of WWW research. Owing to the large sample sizes, the Web experiments helped to estimate solution percentages and model parameters with greatly enhanced accuracy as compared to the laboratory and made it possible to precisely assess the relative merits of competing accounts of belief bias. It is concluded that the Internet is a useful and promising new research tool for the study of human deductive reasoning.

Traditional syllogisms were first devised by Aristotle, and for centuries, philosophers believed them to be the basis of all rational thought. The following is an illustrative example of a valid Aristotelian syllogism:

Premise 1:   All violin players are musicians.
Premise 2:   No musicians are rude people.
Conclusion: Therefore, no violin players are rude people.

There are four different figures in which the premises and the conclusion in an Aristotelian syllogism can be arranged:

	Figure 1	Figure 2	Figure 3	Figure 4
Premise 1	C-B	C-B	B-C	B-C
Premise 2	B-A	A-B	B-A	A-B
Conclusion	A-C	A-C	A-C	A-C

---

[1]   This chapter describes in part data that are reported in the manuscript "On belief bias in syllogistic reasoning" (Klauer, Musch, & Naumer, 2000).

The two premises and the conclusion can each contain four different quantifiers (All, None, Some, Some-not). Thus, altogether there are 4 x 4 x 4 x 4 = 256 different syllogisms. Reversing the order of premises (which is irrelevant from the point of view of a logician, but not from that of a psychologist) doubles the number of syllogisms and hence, 512 possible syllogisms (48 of which are valid) can be distinguished (Evans, Newstead, & Byrne, 1993).

When psychologists began to investigate how naive reasoners deal with syllogistic reasoning tasks, they soon found that the content of a given conclusion influences whether a syllogism like the above is considered valid (Evans et al., 1993). Specifically, conclusions are accepted more readily when reasoners find them believable than if they disbelieve them, irrespective of their actual logical validity (e.g., Wilkins, 1928). This bias facilitates the logical response when logic and belief agree, that is, if the conclusion is believable and the syllogism valid or if the conclusion is unbelievable and the syllogism invalid; it opposes the logically correct response when logic and belief are in conflict.

Early demonstrations of this so-called *belief bias* often focused on its social psychological implications. For example, Henle and Michael (1956) presented syllogisms like the following:

Premise 1: All Russians are Bolsheviks.
Premise 2: Some Bolsheviks regiment people.

There is no valid conclusion to this syllogism, but those subjects with an anti-Russian attitude were more inclined to endorse the invalid conclusion that "All Russians regiment people" than subjects with a neutral attitude towards Russians (the authors were unable to obtain a pro-Russian group large enough for statistical treatment in the Cold War climate of the 1950s). Belief bias can thus be described as an irrational tendency to maintain one's beliefs, manifested by a facilitation in the drawing of inferences congruent with those beliefs, and by an inhibition of inferences contrary to them. Although belief bias is thought to operate in many fields, from deductive reasoning to interpersonal communication, the majority of experimental studies of this phenomenon have investigated belief bias in syllogistic reasoning (Evans et al., 1993).

A robust finding that soon emerged and that any theory of belief bias must explain is an interesting interaction between logical validity and believability such that the effects of believability are more marked on invalid conclusions. This interaction between logic and belief is illustrated in Figure 11.1 which presents data from Experiment 1 by Evans, Barston, & Pollard (1983). It can be seen that the effects of belief are numerically stronger on invalid syllogisms than on valid ones. Equivalently, the effects of logic are more pronounced for unbelievable conclusions than for believable ones.

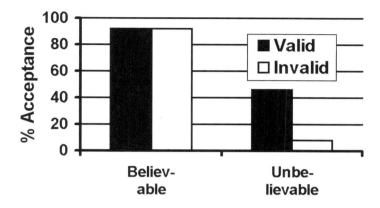

Figure 11.1: Percentage frequency of decisions to accept conclusions in exp. 1 by Evans et al. (1983)

11.1.1 Theoretical Explanations

Several explanations of belief bias have been proposed to account for the above basic as well as additional findings. In accordance with the information-processing metaphor of human cognition, an important question has been at which stage of information processing the bias arises: during input, processing, or output. First, a belief could distort the interpretation and representation of the premises. Second, it could directly influence the reasoning process. Finally, belief could bias the response stage, in which the result of the reasoning process is mapped onto an observable response.

The *selective scrutiny model* (Evans et al., 1983; Evans, 1989) assumes that the effects of belief occur prior to any logical reasoning. Reasoners begin by evaluating the believability of the conclusion. A believable conclusion is accepted, whereas an unbelievable conclusion instigates a logical analysis as to whether or not the conclusion is necessitated by the premises. Thus, logic should have an effect on syllogisms with unbelievable conclusions, but not on those with believable conclusions.

A competing *account by mental models* (Oakhill, Johnson-Laird, & Garnham, 1989; Newstead, Pollards, Evans, & Allen, 1992) places the cause of the effect into the reasoning stage. The account is similar to the selective scrutiny model in that it is assumed that there is less logical analysis when the conclusion is believable than when it is unbelievable. However, in either case, reasoners initially construct one model of the premises and test whether the conclusion is consistent with that model or not. An inconsistent conclusion is then correctly rejected and a consistent one is accepted, if it is believable. Unbelievable consistent conclusions on the other hand trigger the search for alternative models and counterexamples that characterizes the mental-model account of human reasoning (Johnson-Laird & Bara, 1984). Thus, for one-model problems, it is predicted that there is no interaction of logic and belief because the one model that is always assumed to be constructed is sufficient for determining the correct response. However, according to the mental model account, logic should have a greater effect on syllogisms with unbelievable conclusions than on those with believable conclusions in the case of indeterminately invalid multiple-model syllogisms. In this case, more than one model must be constructed for a logically correct decision, and the likelihood of detecting a second model that refutes the conclusion is greater when a search for counterexamples is triggered by an unbelievable conclusion (Newstead et al., 1992). According to the mental model account, an interaction of logic and belief is therefore predicted for indeterminately invalid multiple-model problems, but not for one-model syllogisms (Evans, Newstead, Allen, & Pollard, 1994). It is less clear what, if anything, follows for the reasoning parameters of valid multiple-model syllogisms (Klauer, Musch, & Naumer, 2000).

Finally, the *misinterpreted necessity model* (Evans et al., 1983; Evans, 1989) attributes the bias to the response stage. The model distinguishes between indeterminately invalid and determinately invalid syllogisms. For indeterminately invalid syllogisms, the conclusion is neither falsified, nor determined by the premises. An example is the following: "All A are B. All B are C. Therefore, Some C are not A". If the premises falsify the conclusion, as in "All A are B. All B are C. Therefore, Some A are not C", the syllogism is termed determinately invalid. The misinterpreted necessity model postulates that participants fail to understand properly what it means to say that a conclusion does not follow from the premises. In particular, reasoners are at a loss when the conclusion is possible, but not necessitated by the premises, that is when the syllogism is indeterminately invalid. In this case, their decisions are assumed to be based on believability.

The misinterpreted necessity model is a response stage account of belief bias, because believability of conclusions does not affect the reasoning stage. Only if the reasoning process does not arrive at a definite response, believability is used as a nonlogical cue in selecting a plausible response. According to the misinterpreted necessity model, the reasoning process results in this state of uncertainty for indeterminately invalid syllogisms, but is able to discriminate the logical status of valid as well as determinately invalid syllogisms correctly. However, certain valid and determinately invalid syllogisms are quite difficult (Johnson-Laird & Bara, 1984), suggesting that a definite and confident response may not always be arrived at in evaluating these syllogisms. It is therefore plausible to assume that the state of uncertainty and the ensueing vulnerability to believability cues sometimes also arises in the case of valid and determinately invalid syllogisms, if less often than for indeterminately invalid syllogisms. A modified model of this kind is in fact entertained by Evans and Pollard (1990) as well as by Newstead et al. (1992).

All of the above explanations have some problems in accounting for the data. For example, the mental-model account as well as the account by misinterpreted necessity must both be supplemented by response bias mechanisms, sometimes specified as conclusion filtering (Oakhill et al., 1989), to explain the fact that belief bias is also found for one-model problems as well as for valid syllogisms, respectively (the modified misinterpreted necessity model, however, handles belief bias for valid syllogisms without further modifications). The selective scrutiny model fails to explain why there are often effects of logic even for believable conclusions. Detailed discussions of these theories and their respective empirical support are found in Evans et al. (1993; see Chapter 8, this volume), Newstead et al. (1992), Newstead and Evans (1993), and Oakhill and Garnham (1993) among others.

11.1.2 Response Bias

It is plausible to assume that whenever reasoners fail to deduce a definite and confident response but are nevertheless being forced to answer, they are likely to select a response option on the basis of nonlogical extraneous factors such as believability (Evans & Pollard, 1990; Markovits & Nantel, 1989; Polk & Newell, 1995), atmosphere, perceived base rate of valid syllogisms (of which we take advantage in the present experiments) or whatever other peripheral cue seems helpful in making a plausible guess at the correct response. But is there any evidence for an independent impact of belief on the reasoning stage over and above the response stage? There are indeed results that indicate that the size of belief bias interacts with logical factors such as the validity of the syllogism, and whether or not the syllogism is a multiple-model or a one-model syllogism (Newstead et al., 1992; Oakhill et al., 1989). In particular, Newstead et al. (1992; see also Evans et al., 1994) consistently observed the interaction of logic and belief exemplified in Figure 11.1 for multiple-model syllogisms, but not for one-model syllogisms.

As explained by Newstead et al. (1992), most of their findings are consistent with the (modified) misinterpreted necessity model, however, which is a pure response stage model. As elaborated below, only one finding could not be reconciled with the misinterpreted necessity model, namely that an interaction was not found when indeterminately invalid and valid one-model syllogisms were used (Newstead et al., 1992, Exp. 3). This finding is a null finding, however, and Gilinsky and Judd (1994) used exactly the same kinds of syllogisms in a much larger study which yielded strong evidence for the existence of the interaction in question.

11.1.3 The Basic Model

We started our research by formulating a simple, explicit model of how reasoning processes and response bias interact. The model is a simple threshold model of the kind that has been successfully applied to the study of reasoning processes by Evans (1977), Krauth (1982), and Klauer and Oberauer (1995). It is a member of the class of multinomial models that has recently seen a growing range of successful applications in cognitive psychology (e.g., Klauer & Wegener, 1998)[2]. Despite its simplicity, the model is sufficiently general to serve as a framework in which the different substantive models can be compared with respect to their relative success in accounting for the data.

The model assumes that there is a reasoning stage and a response stage. The reasoning stage outputs either the correct decision about the logical status of the syllogism with a certain probability r or, with probability $1 - r$, a state of uncertainty is entered. The response stage simply selects the correct response in the first case. If a state of uncertainty is reached, response bias comes into play. With a certain probability a, the response "valid" is selected in this case, and with probability $1 - a$, the response "invalid" is selected. Thus, the model has two qualitatively different parameters. The parameter r refers to the probability with which the correct decision is determined in the reasoning stage. We assumed the parameter r to vary not only as a function of the logical status of the syllogism but also as a function of the believability of the conclusion, thereby accommodating those accounts of belief bias which assume that belief has an impact on the reasoning process itself. The parameter a is a response bias parameter which is assumed to vary as a function of peripheral cues to logical validity such as the perceived base rate of valid syllogisms. We also assumed that the parameter a can vary as a function of believability, thereby modeling response-bias based belief bias.

In the experiments conducted to test our model we intended first of all to realize a rich enough data base that would allow us to estimate all parameters of our model and to test hypotheses about them. To this end, we directly manipulated response bias and collected conclusion-acceptance data from three groups. In each group, the same syllogisms were presented. The groups differed, however, in terms of the perceived

---

[2] Batchelder and Riefer (1999) discuss the estimation and testing techniques needed and review substantive applications. Computer software for estimating parameters and testing the models is available via Internet (http://xhuoffice.psyc.memphis.edu/gpt/index.htm) from Xiangen Hu. There are two programs available: an older DOS version called MBT and a Windows95/NT version called GPT (Hu, 1997).

base rates of valid syllogisms[3]. This was done by telling reasoners that the syllogisms they would see were randomly sampled from a large pool of syllogisms that contained either a low, medium, or high percentage of valid syllogisms. We expected this base rate manipulation to affect response bias: the tendency to accept the syllogism in a state of uncertainty (when its actual validity cannot be determined for certain) should increase with the instructed base rate. In fitting our model, we therefore used different response bias parameters for each group. As an additional refinement, we employed a multiplicative decomposition of the response bias parameters into separate factors for the group and for the believability of the conclusions:

$$a_{xy} = \alpha_x \, \beta_y$$

where x = (low, medium, large), and y = (believable, unbelievable). This multiplicative decomposition allows to absorb the base-rate manipulation in just one set of parameters, the α-parameters, and to assess the impact of belief on the response stage separately from the impact of base rate. If $\beta_b > \beta_u$, belief bias is exhibited by the response stage.

11.2 Study 1: A Laboratory Experiment with One-Model Valid and Indeterminately Invalid Syllogisms

Based on an extensive literature review and meta-analysis (see Klauer, Musch, & Naumer, 2000, for a more detailed report), we decided to begin our experimental work with the one-model valid and indeterminately invalid syllogisms employed by Gilinsky and Judd (1994) and Newstead et al. (1992).

The following syllogism exemplifies the kind of syllogism that was used in Study 1 (and also later in Study 2).

All fish are quadronates.
All quadronates are trout.
Therefore, all fish are trout.

The syllogism is valid and its conclusion unbelievable. The two premises can be integrated into only one mental model according to the mental-model theory. If the conclusion is reversed ("All trout are fish"), the syllogism becomes invalid. It is indeterminately invalid, because it is possible to construct situations in which both the premises and the conclusion are true; consider, for example, a situation in which the

---

[3] Note that although the believability of the conclusion is likely to affect response bias, manipulating belief is not the desired response-bias manipulation, because it may have an effect on the reasoning stage.

only fish are trout. Table 11.1 gives examples for the six cases spanned by the logical status of the syllogism and the believability of the conclusion (believable, unbelievable, neutral).

Table 11.1: Examples of one-model syllogisms used in studies 1 and 2

| | Syllogisms | |
Conclusion	Valid	Invalid
Believable	All trout are acquerites. All acquerites are fish. All trout are fish.	All plants are pherimers. All pherimers are grasses. All grasses are plants.
Neutral	All stoics are emerunes. All emerunes are sophists. All stoics are sophists.	All vegetarians are beriates. All beriates are Tibetan monks. All Tibetan monks are vegetarians.
Unbelievable	All electric appliances are quadronates. All quadronates are video recorders. All electric appliances are video recorders.	All tables are shalleres. All shalleres are pieces of furniture. All pieces of furniture are tables.

In a traditional laboratory experiment, we collected the responses of 72 University of Bonn students (24 in each base-rate group). Each participant evaluated twelve syllogisms, two from each cell of a design spanned by logical status (valid versus invalid) and belief (believable, unbelievable, neutral conclusion). Figure 11.2 shows the relative acceptance frequencies as a function of the presumed base-rate of valid syllogisms and the validity and believability of conclusions.

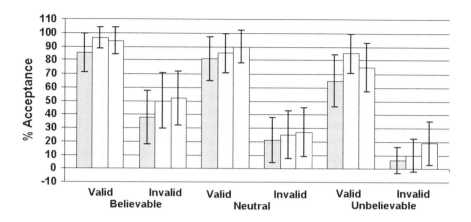

Figure 11.2: Percentage frequencies of decisions (and their 95% confidence intervals) to accept conclusions in study 1

When the model was fitted to the data from Figure 11.2, the goodness-of-fit statistic for the baseline model indicated a very good fit of the model. Thus, it is possible to describe the data by means of a model that assumes equal reasoning stage parameters across groups and maps all differences between groups on the response bias parameters α_x , x = (low, medium, high).

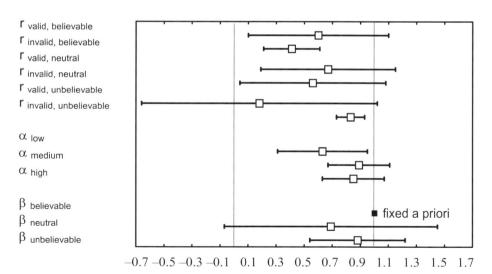

Figure 11.3: Parameter estimates and their 95% confidence intervals in study 1

In Figure 11.3, the maximum-likelihood estimates of the model parameters are given. Tests of the model parameters (see Klauer, Musch, & Naumer, 2000, for more details) were not very informative because of the large standard errors of estimates. The base-rate manipulation was only partly successful, $\alpha_{low} < \alpha_{medium}$, but $\alpha_{medium} = \alpha_{high}$. There were significant differences between the r parameters, but the small sample size did not allow to determine whether these differences were due to an interaction of logic and belief, or to main effects of either factor. Thus, the full promise of the present approach could not be realized. To obtain further progress, we felt it was necessary to repeat Study 1 (possibly excluding the syllogisms with neutral conclusions) using a very large sample of participants. No such sample was, however, available to us in our local department. It was this dilemma that led us to decide to conduct Study 2 on the WWW.

11.2.1 Experimenting on the WWW

The growth of electronic communication networks and in particular the Internet has, in recent years, been phenomenal. The latest and most influential part of the Internet, a global hypertext system called the WWW, was born in the early 1990s at the European Laboratory for Particle Physics (CERN; see Musch, 2000, for a history of the development of the Internet over the past 30 years). In recent years, the imagination of a growing number of psychologists has been caught by an unforeseen opportunity the WWW presents: A new environment in which to do research. Drawing on so-called forms (fill-out forms first introduced in version 2.0 of the HyperText Markup Language, HTML), the WWW first offered the possibility to conduct psychological research independent of any geographical constraints. At this point in time, the majority of Internet-mediated studies appear to be questionnaire based, with surveys of various sorts being the most common (Batinic, 1997; Batinic, Werner, Gräf, & Bandilla, 1999). However, the number of researchers conducting experimental research on the Web is constantly rising (Musch & Reips, 2000; Reips, 2000a). As its paramount advantage, the Internet allows to conduct experiments with participants from all over the world rather than with the usual student sample from the local university. It thus has the potential to serve as an alternative or supplemental source of subjects and research environment for traditional psychological investigations (Buchanan & Smith, 1999; Reips, 1999, 2000a, 2000b; Smith & Leigh, 1997; Wilhelm & McKnight, Chapter 10, this volume).

11.2.2 Advantages of Web experiments

Using the Internet to conduct research offers several advantages over traditional research practices (see Reips, 2000a, for a summary). The potential to obtain very large sample sizes with relatively little time and effort is generally considered the most important benefit of Web experimenting. In many laboratory studies the number of participants is too small and hence, the power of such studies is often low (Erdfelder, Faul, & Buchner, 1996). This contrasts sharply with the large average number of 427 participants in the 26 Web studies reviewed by Musch and Reips (2000). Other oft-quoted benefits are the high speed with which Web experimenting is possible, and the low cost of conducting studies on the Web. The latter are due to considerable savings of lab space, experimenters, equipment, and administration (Buchanan & Smith, 1999; Schmidt, 1997; Smith & Leigh, 1997). Web experiments can be run around the clock and even allow for simultaneous access by a large number of participants. Consequently, there are no scheduling problems, and institutional regulations as well as the need for funding lose their confining impact on research. Once an experiment is set up, everything is done automatically and with little need to intervene. This allows to collect large data sets which are required in many research contexts, as for example in randomized response surveys (Bröder & Musch, 2000; Musch, Bröder, & Klauer, 2001).

While Web experiments dispose of the need to physically collect data, as well as the need to transcribe paper-and-pencil data, they also solve the problem of missing data. Respondents often overlook a particular question or skip a question with the intent to return (but forget to; Schmidt, 1997). Incomplete data can also arise from respondents who do not wish to supply an answer for personal reasons or from disinterested people who do not intend to contribute complete data. Using a Common Gateway Interface (CGI) script, it can be ensured that Web experiment participants answer all questions by acknowledging incomplete submissions with an error message (Schmidt, 1997).

The overwhelming majority of traditional psychology experiments make no effort whatsoever to ensure that the samples used are representative of the larger population being studied. On grounds of this custom, the external validity of traditional laboratory studies can be questioned (Sears, 1986). In fact, it has been criticized that psychology has become the study of the behavior of the suburban White American college sophomore (Reips, 2000a). While in hypothetico-deductive research it might not really matter who the participants are (Bredenkamp, 1996), if psychological research is to be generalized to the general population, it is a problem that more than 80% of all psychological studies are conducted with students as participants, while only about 3% of the general population are students (Reips, 2000a). As a result, psychological theories may often be too narrow in scope (Reips & Bächtiger, 1999). An additional cause for concern is that psychology students who most commonly participate in university research usually do so for course credit. They may therefore be less-than-eager participants. People who – out of interest or curiosity – seek out and choose to participate in Web experiments are probably more motivated participants

(Reips, 2000a). The typical Internet sample also has a much broader age distribution and includes participants from much more diverse professions than does the typical student sample, thereby increasing the external validity of findings (Smith & Leigh, 1997).

Of course, the common concern about the unrepresentativeness of university student samples is not really overcome in Web research because Internet samples are hardly representative of the general population. For example, Web samples are usually biased toward young males of above-average socio-economic and educational status (Krantz & Dalal, 2000; Schmidt, 1997). However, participants recruited via the Web vary to a much greater degree than those typically recruited by traditional means in terms of age, language, and culture, as well as the construct one is attempting to measure (Buchanan & Smith, 1999). It can also be expected that the heterogeneity of Internet users will further increase and approach that of the general population as more and more people get online (although the problems of nonprobabilistic sampling and self-selection will continue to preclude true representativeness). At any rate, even present Web samples are certainly less biased than traditional samples, and allow to compare the results of the typical university population of late adolescents to that of a more geographically dispersed population of computer-literate individuals varying widely in age. Within this target population, Web experiments allow to conveniently determine which person variables are important for the outcome of an experiment. This feature of Web studies may finally turn out to be the most useful (Krantz & Dalal, 2000).

11.2.3 Disadvantages of Web experiments

Along with the obvious benefits of WWW research, there also come some definite threats to its internal validity (Hewson, Laurent, & Vogel, 1996; Johnson-Laird & Savary, 1998; Krantz, Ballard, & Scher, 1997; Schmidt, 1997; Smith & Leigh, 1997; Wilhelm & McKnight, Chapter 10, this volume). Perhaps most importantly, the Web researcher has no control whatsoever over the conditions under which participants complete his or her experiment. Unknown and uncontrollabe factors such as noise, distraction by environmental stimuli, physical and psychological distance between participants and the experimenter, participant's mood, fatigue, and motivation may increase unexplained variance in the dependent variables (Schmidt, 1997; Smith & Leigh, 1997). Moreover, there is no guarantee that participants working on a given task will not consult other people, draw diagrams, look up answers in text books, and so forth even if instructed not do to so (Johnson-Laird & Savary, 1998). Although, to some extent, this is also a problem in conventional experimentation (especially when group testing is involved), the cited problems were the biggest concern of Web experimenters participating in a recent survey of Musch and Reips (2000). Of course, one might suspect that such circumstances introduce numerous unknown confounding variables which might have the effect of increasing noise in the data and reducing the proportion of variance in dependent variables accounted for by the manipulation of independent variables. However, one may also consider noise of this kind to be a source of variance which actually increases the generalizability of results. This is because in traditional research, any result may be due to specifics of the laboratory environment, whereas in Web experiments, external validity is enhanced by the diversity of settings under which participation takes place (Reips, 2000a).

The most serious problem resulting from the lack of control over the testing situation relates to potential manipulations of the data. Difficulties may arise from people trying to foil the experiment. A particular danger for Web experiments lies in the possibility of multiple participation (Smith & Leigh, 1997). Participants may – accidentally or in attempt to foil the experiment – submit their responses more than once, possibly by varying their answers to see how their final scores are affected (Schmidt, 1997). In fact, we observed such behavior that cannot be prevented by current browser software repeatedly in the logfiles of the experiments reported below. Several participants mailed us that they did so to check, after receiving the first performance feedback, which answers were wrong and what changes would lead to an enhanced performance. Fortunately, several techniques exist to deal with this problem (Buchanan & Smith, 1999; Reips, 2000a, 2000b; Schmidt, 1997; Smith & Leigh, 1997) and are in fact used by most researchers conducting Web experiments (Musch & Reips, 2000). Most of these techniques try to uniquely identify each participant, and to filter out all suspicious submissions. This can be done by examining a variety of aspects of the data provided by the participants, such as e-mail and (much less easy to fake) Internet Protocol (IP) addresses.

11.2.4 The validity of Web experiments

While the relative importance of the various advantages and disadvantages associated with Web experimenting will continue to be a matter of debate, the most important issue undoubtedly is the question of the validity of Web experiments. As with any technological innovation, Web experimenting needs to be assessed with respect to whether its results are useful and valid. One plausible approach is to conduct the same experiment both in the laboratory under well-controlled conditions and over the Web. If the same psychological variables are driving the results of both data sets, the trends in the data should be very similar, leading to highly convergent results. Several studies have been conducted that allow a cautious and preliminary answer to the validity question. Krantz and Dalal (2000) review these studies and report that across a wide range of designs and variables, there is remarkable congruence between laboratory and Web-based results. Similarly, in a recent survey of Musch and Reips (2000), almost all Web experimenters observed complete or good agreement between their Web and lab data. There was not a single experiment for which a strong divergence between the two methods of data collection was reported. This comparability was found despite the great potential for variations in experimental environment and equipment and also occurred despite the small differences in the experimental procedures that are a necessary consequence of the use of the WWW. For example, in Krantz, Ballard, and Scher (1997), results indicated that the Web and laboratory data on judgments of female attractiveness (as a function of weight, hip to waist proportion, bust size and buttock size) could essentially replace each other. Although replications and extensions of this finding are certainly needed, the consistent correspondence hitherto observed between Web and lab data is astounding (Birnbaum, 1999; Krantz, Ballard, & Scher, 1997; Krantz, 1998; Senior, Phillips, Barnes, & David, 1999). We therefore decided to conduct Study 2 on the Web.

11.3 Study 2: A Web Experiment with One-Model Valid and Indeterminately invalid Syllogisms

The main goal of Study 2 was to validate the frequency data obtained in Study 2 using the data from a larger sample of Web participants. At the same time, on the basis of this larger sample, we hoped to be able to realize the potential of the present approach more fully. The same syllogisms as in Study 1 were used, excluding for the sake of brevity the ones with neutral conclusions.

11.3.1 Web Experiment Method

Procedure. The experiment closely followed the design and procedures of Study 1. In particular, there were three groups that differed in terms of the instructed base rates of valid syllogisms. The experiment was realized on an IBM-compatible PC that was connected to the Internet as a so-called WWW server. A JAVA (Gosling & McGilton, 1995) program running on that computer randomly assigned participants to the base-rate groups, outputted the appropriate hypertext markup language (HTML) pages with instructions and problems, and handled the data supplied by participants using the common gateway interface (CGI; Kieley, 1996).

The experiment consisted of a start page, an experimental page, and a feedback page. The experiment was offered in a German and an English version that were reached by different links. From the start page of each version, it was possible to reach the start page of the other version directly. The start page informed participants that after a short introduction they would have the opportunity to respond to eight problems. Participants were also told that at the end of the tests, they were to receive feedback on their results, and that among all participants who answered all the questions (independent of score) lots would be drawn for three prizes ($50, $30, and $10, or alternatively € 50, € 25, and € 10). Contact details and affiliation of the experimenters were given, as was an option to give feedback via e-mail. For each participant who decided to proceed, the JAVA program constructed and presented an experimental page. In particular, the program randomly assigned the participant to one of the three base-rate groups and constructed appropriate instructions. The experimental page comprised the instructions, the syllogisms, and a biographical questionnaire.

The instructions were the same as in Study 1 with the exception that the paragraph manipulating the base rate was presented in larger font size than the rest of the instructions. This was done because the results of a small pilot study indicated that when base-rate instructions were written in normal font, they had smaller effects on acceptance rates, probably because they were more easily overlooked by less careful readers. Participants were asked not to turn back and forth between problems once they had started and not to make notes or draw diagrams.

The experimental page then continued with the eight syllogisms, which were constructed as in Study 1, but did not comprise the four syllogisms with neutral conclusions. Thus, there were two syllogisms from each cell of the table spanned by logical validity (valid versus invalid) and belief (believable versus unbelievable conclusion). The order in which the eight syllogisms appeared on the experimental page was newly randomized for each participant using the JAVA program installed on the Web server. Participants responded to each problem by clicking one of two buttons labeled "correct" and "false".

The experimental page continued with a short biographical questionnaire. Among other questions, participants were asked if they considered themselves logic experts because of their education or occupation. This was done because we anticipated that individuals with a background in formal logic would constitute an important portion of the participants, and we wanted to identify these individuals. We also asked participants to specify their e-mail address if they wanted to participate in the lottery. Finally, at the end of the experimental page, we asked participants to check one of the following response boxes:

I answered all the questions carefully and submit the data for the first time now. I want to participate in the lottery [default option versus:]

I just want to see the results by way of trial without taking part seriously. If you do not take part seriously when submitting the data for the first time, you cannot take part in the lottery, however! Please choose this option a) if you are not taking part for the first time, b) if you have not dealt thoroughly with all questions, c) if you already know the solutions, or d) if for some reason you think that your data are not suitable for interpretation in a scientific study on human reasoning.

At the bottom of the experimental page, participants were asked to submit their responses by clicking a button labeled "I am finished. Submit!" if they were certain that they had responded to all the problems and biographical questions. The JAVA program then checked whether all questions had been responded to and reminded participants of missing answers. If answers were missing, participants were asked to complete their responses and to resubmit the experimental page. A missing data problem could thus not arise. We feel that the possibility of an automatic check for incomplete data is an important advantage of Web experiments over traditional paper-and-pencil procedures.

Next, the JAVA program constructed a feedback page based on participants' responses. It provided feedback on the participant's performance, along with guidelines on how to interpret it. In particular, participants were told their number correct score and the average number correct of the 72 University of Bonn students of Study 1. All experimental manipulations and the purpose of the study were explained, including a full citation of Evans et al. (1993) for anyone interested in finding out more. Participants were explained the phenomenon of belief bias and the design of the experiment. Furthermore, it was explained that we were interested in the effect of the instructed base rate on reasoning to see how it would interact with belief bias, and participants were informed about the three different base-rate groups realized in the experiment. Finally, they saw their response frequencies for the two problems of each cell of the data table in the format of Table 11.1 along with the logically correct frequencies. The feedback page concluded with the e-mail addresses of the experimenters, who were available for additional questions[4], and a list of links to other online studies and related Web sites.

Participants. To recruit a large number of people to complete the experiment, we publicized our study both online and via more traditional media. First, we submitted the site's WWW information to the most popular WWW database search engines after including the meta-tags "logic, quiz, puzzle, think, experiment" into our Web pages. Second, we posted a short announcement of the experiment to various usenet newsgroups related to the topic of our study (e.g., alt.human-brain, alt.usenet.surveys,

---

[4]   We received well over one hundred e-mails during the course of our experiments. Many participants argued over the correctness of some of their responses, thereby giving us valuable feedback on possible program errors (fortunately, there were none). Several participants asked for more extensive feedback on some aspect of his or her performance. We also received many favourable and encouraging mails stating that the experiment was a very stimulating and interesting one. No complaints concerning the little element of deception about the ostensible base-rate of true syllogisms were filed.

rec.puzzles, sci.psychology.misc, de.alt.umfragen, de.sci.psychologie, z-netz.alt.kno-belecke). Third, we posted our experiment on the American Psychological Society's list of experiments maintained by John Krantz (1998), in Ulf Reips' (1995) laboratory for psychological Web experiments, and on several other Web pages containing links to online studies and experiments, quiz contests, sweepstakes, and giveaways. The experiment was described as a short logic test with individualized feedback and the possibility to win attractive money prizes[5], conducted by the department of Social and Personality Psychology of the University Bonn for scientific purposes. To arouse curiosity and to get on the top of the alphabetically ordered lists, we entitled our experiment *"Are you a logical thinker?"*.

While all of the described activities were very successful in attracting participants, we also made a disappointing experience when we tried to attract participants by giving a radio interview. This attempt was a complete failure as indicated by the server logfiles for the time shortly after the interview. It seems that very few radio listeners have access to the Web (or are willing to write up a Web address for later use), and that the Internet itself is much better suited to recruit participants for a Web experiment.

Data analysis. When data collection was complete, we used very conservative selection criteria based on a host of self-reported and objective indices to screen out suspicious data sets prior to analysis. We felt this was necessary because as indicated by a large number of feedback mails we received during data collection, our syllogisms were highly involving and interesting to many participants, giving them a strong incentive to repeatedly submit different solutions in an attempt to identify possible errors. The following criteria had to be satisfied for a submission to be included in the data analysis: No submission had been received from the same Internet protocol (IP) address and/or, if provided, e-mail address. Throughout the entire series of experiments reported here, a cumulative record was kept of the IP-addresses and e-mail addresses of submissions to screen out any participant who might already have participated in the current or a previous experiment in the series. Deleting all subsequent submissions from a given IP address is a very conservative procedure because a heavily used machine in a computer laboratory may be used by many individuals, and several computers with different users are frequently connected to the same IP address (e.g., via proxies, firewalls, and dial-in providers allocating their pool of IP addresses dynamically). Although some of the discarded submissions may therefore in fact have been valid, we decided rather to err on the side of caution.

---

[5]   In a recent survey among web researchers, Musch and Reips (2000) found a trend for a higher number of participants per week when some form of financial incentive (individual payments or lottery prizes) was offered (49 versus 37 participants per week based on small samples of 13 and 7 web experiments, respectively).

Other criteria were that the participant stated that he or she had responded to all questions carefully and submitted data for the first time, that English (or German in the German version) was his or her native language, and that a minimum of 3 and a maximum of 30 minutes had passed between calling up the start page and submitting the final data.

Table 11.2: Number of submissions and frequencies of successive exclusions

	Study 2		Study 4	
Number of submissions	6212		7442	
Criterion	Excluded	Remaining	Excluded	Remaining
Technical failures	119	6093	13	7429
Repeated IP or e-mail address	2463	3630	3670	3759
Nonserious submission	349	3281	449	3310
Nonnative speaker	1015	2266	798	2512
Response outside temporal window	130	*2136*	123	*2389*

While the experiment was online, the number of submissions satisfying the above criteria was checked in regular intervals, and the experiment was finished after more than 2000 submissions had been received after about three months (this rate accelerated in later experiments, when a number of links had been set up that pointed to our Web laboratory). In Table 11.2, the numbers of submissions that were excluded due to the different criteria are presented along with the demographics of the final sample, for the present Study 2 as well as for Study 4 that will be described in more detail below.

11.3.2 Participants' Demographics

In the present as well as in all other Web experiments reported below, the proportion of female participants was higher in the English version (58%) than in the German version of the experiment (28%), suggesting that women form a larger percentage of Web users in English-speaking countries. This confirms similar observations by Reips (1996; see also Krantz & Dalal, 2000). The gender by language version pattern is also in line with the surveys conducted by the Georgia Institute of Technology's Graphics, Visualization, and Usability (GVU, 1998) Center's semi-annual general survey of Web users, which shows more gender equality in the United States than in Europe. It probably reflects a general trend of gender distribution in the two populations: In the USA, more people have access to the Web and therefore, gender distribution more closely reflects the 50% base rate in the general population. In Germany, surfing on the Web obviously still is a predominantly male endeavor, although the number of female surfers is rising.

An interesting difference between language versions arised with respect to the distribution of knowledge of language. In the German version, 92% of participants indicated to be native speakers of German. Another 5% said their German was fluent, and 3% said it was pretty good. In the English version, only 72% of participants were native speakers of English. 12% of participants said they were fluent English speakers, and 12% said their English was pretty good. There were another 3% who said it was not very good, and 1% who said it was poor. Obviously, more nonnative speakers take part if an experiment is offered in English as compared to German. Therefore, Web experimenters should ask for their participants' language proficiency when they conduct Web studies in English, at least if a very good knowledge of English is essential for interpreting the data. As already noted earlier, we decided to include only native speakers in our analyses because of the relatively subtle linguistic manipulations we employed (nonnative speakers were in fact somewhat less influenced by the base-rate manipulation).

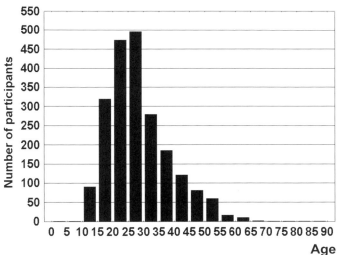

Figure 11.4: Age distribution of Web participants

Previous studies have shown that the average age of respondents to Web studies lies between 25 and 35 years, with typical standard deviations of about 10 (Buchanan & Smith, 1999). This was confirmed by our present sample with a mean age of 29 years (median: 27 years) and a standard deviation of 10 years. Because no study has reported the exact age distribution of Web participants (Krantz & Dalal, 2000), the respective distribution is depicted in Figure 11.4 for Study 2 (the distribution was

almost exactly the same in subsequent Web experiments). This age distribution suggests that Internet samples cover a much broader range of age brackets than traditional samples, a fact that is likely to increase the external validity of Web studies
(Reips, 1996).

As can be seen in Figure 11.5, the Web sample was also characterized by a much
larger variety of professions than is typical of university laboratory research.

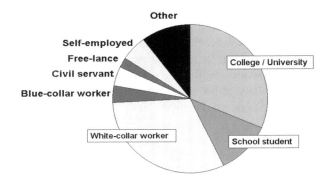

Figure 11.5: Occupations of Web participants

Figure 11.6 shows the significant differences in the average number of correctly
solved syllogisms between members of different occupations.

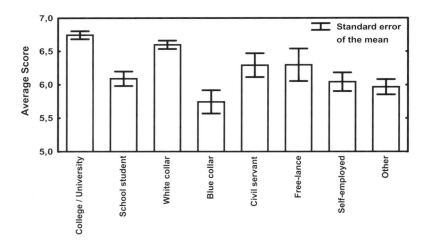

Figure 11.6: Total score of participants with different occupations

Table 11.3 gives the field of academic studies for the student participants. As can be seen, students from a wide variety of disciplines participated.

Table 11.3: Field of academic studies (%)

	Study 2	Study 4
No college/university studies	23	24
Pedagogic	2	1
Humanities and arts	9	10
History	1	1
Computer science	11	10
Law	3	3
Mathematics	4	4
Medicine	4	3
(Natural) science	12	11
Philosophy	1	1
Social science	7	8
Sports	0	0
Language	2	2
Theology	0	0
Economy and management	10	8
Other	12	13

None of the psychology participants in our laboratory had received formal training in logic. In the Web, a majority of participants (60% in the present and an approximately equal number in the subsequent experiments) indicated to have received some formal training in logic. Probably this was partly due to self-selection because the study was announced as a study in logic. We used formal knowledge of logic as an additional independent variable in the analysis of the Web experiments and conducted separate analyses for the participants who described themselves as particularly familiar with formal logic and formal thinking problems (N = 1290), henceforth referred to as logic experts, and for the more naive reasoners (N = 846).

The relative frequencies with which naive reasoners accepted conclusions are shown in Figure 11.7 separately for each base-rate group. Although in Study 1, students with no background in formal logic had been excluded, the data of logic experts (who in fact comprised the majority of Web participants and achieved a significantly higher total score than the naive reasoners, $M = 6.7$ versus $M = 6.1$, $p < .0001$), were also analyzed. The data of the logic experts are shown in Figure 11.8.

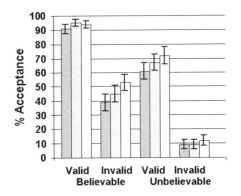

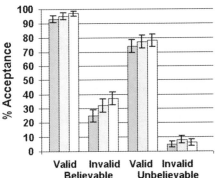

Figure 11.7: Percentage frequencies of decisions of naïve reasoners (and their 95% confidence intervals) to accept conclusions in study 2

Figure 11.8: Percentage frequencies of decisions of logic experts (and their 95% confidence intervals) to accept conclusions in study 2

Since there is as yet not much experience with this methodology, an important first step was to validate the Web data by means of the laboratory data obtained in Study 1. A log-likelihood ratio test compared the laboratory data from Figure 11.2 (excluding syllogisms with neutral conclusions) with the naive reasoners' Web data as shown in Figure 11.7. The nonsignificant test statistic for equality of the twelve relative frequencies confirmed that both data sets were in close agreement. Thus, although the naive Web sample differed from the traditional sample in a number of ways, these differences had little, if any, effects on the results. This agreement does not simply reflect a lack of test power caused by the relatively small size of the laboratory sample: the same test comparing the laboratory data and the Web data for logic experts revealed highly significant differences between the two data sets, even though both are grossly similar in the general pattern of the effects of belief, logical validity, and base rate. In this sense, there is both convergent as well as discriminant validity for the Web data (Campbell & Fiske, 1959). This result suggests that Internet subjects can be used as a valid subject population in the study of syllogistic reasoning.

11.3.3 Model-Based Analyses for Naive Reasoners

The multinomial model was fit to the data from the naive reasoners. Although conventional levels of significance are not reasonable in situations like the present in which there is a power $(1-\beta)$ of .99 to detect even tiny ($W = .05$; Cohen, 1988) departures from the null hypothesis, the goodness of fit of the model was surprisingly good, and the data did not lead to a rejection of the model at the 5% significance level. Figure 11.9 shows the parameter estimates and their standard errors. As expected, the parameters for the effects of the base-rate instruction now increased monotonically with the instructed base rate due to the larger sample size, $\alpha_{low} < \alpha_{medium} < \alpha_{high}$. As in Study 1, there was no evidence for a belief bias at the level of the response stage, $\beta_b = \beta_u$. Owing to the larger sample size, the results showed that the r parameters are much larger in the two cases where logic and belief agree than in the two cases where they disagree. As can be seen in Figure 11.10, the logic experts achieve much higher r parameters than the naive reasoners when logic and belief disagree. However, it was possible to use the same parameters for the impact of base rate and belief bias at the response stage in both groups when different reasoning stage parameters were admitted. Thus, naive reasoners and logic experts differed in the reasoning stage, but not in the response stage. Once an expert did not arrive at a correct solution with certainty in the reasoning phase, he or she was subject to the same biases at the response stage as were more naive reasoners.

Taken together, Study 2 was successful in replicating all central aspects of Study 1. Conducting the study on the WWW gave interesting insights into the similarities and differences between naive and expert syllogistic reasoning and helped considerably to expand traditional laboratory research on belief bias. The much larger sample of Web participants resulted in much more reliable estimates of solution percentages and as a result, much better estimates of the model parameters. Hypothesis tests were consequently more informative.

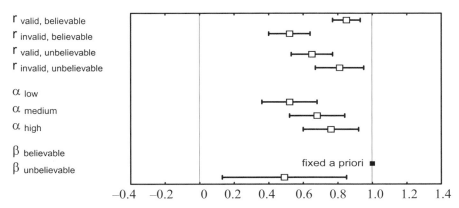

Figure 11.9: Parameter estimates and their 95% confidence intervals for naive reasoners in study 2

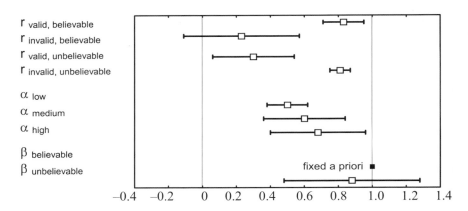

Figure 11.10: The same data for logic experts

Neither the account by misinterpreted necessity, nor the account by mental models was consistent with the pattern of reasoning stage parameters. Rather, an interesting interaction of belief and logic emerged at the level of these parameters: Reasoning easiness was quite high when logic and belief agreed, that is when the syllogism was valid and the conclusion believable or when the syllogism was invalid and the conclusion unbelievable, and was low when logic and belief disagreed.

11.4 Study 3: A Laboratory Experiment with Three-Model Valid and Indeterminately Invalid Syllogisms

Studies 3 and 4 extended the previous findings with a new kind of syllogism and for the sake of brevity, are only briefly described here (see Klauer, Musch, & Naumer, 2000, for a more detailed report). Study 3 was a laboratory experiment and used the three-model valid and indeterminately invalid syllogisms that were most frequently used in previous studies on belief bias (e.g., Evans et al., 1994; Newstead et al., 1992). Participants were 60 University of Bonn students (20 in each base-rate group) from different faculties who had not participated in Study 1.

Again, the multinomial model fitted the data well. The base-rate groups differed significantly in their overall tendency to accept conclusions, and there was little evidence for belief bias in the response stage. However, the large standard errors of estimates of the reasoning stage parameters again precluded any strong conclusions with regard to the competing theories of belief bias. The problem of too low power was to be ameliorated by Study 4, which tried to repeat Study 3 with a much larger sample of participants and was therefore conducted again as a Web experiment.

Table 11.4. Examples of three-model syllogisms used in studies 3 and 4

| | Syllogisms | |
Conclusion	Valid	Invalid
Believable	Some musical instruments lie on the stage. No violins lie on the stage. Some musical instruments are not violins.	Some skyscrapers stand at the harbor basin. No buildings stand at the harbor basin. Some buildings are not skyscrapers.
Neutral	Some species of monkeys are in the cage. No pheromone-producing animals are in the cage. Some species of monkeys are not pheromone-producing animals.	Some fungi are in the test tube. No spongiforms are in the test tube. Some spongiforms are not fungi.
Unbelievable	Some liquors are part of the merchandise. No drinks are part of the merchandise. Some liquors are not drinks.	Some tools lie on the table. No screwdrivers lie on the table. Some screwdrivers are not tools.

11.5 Study 4: A Web Experiment with Three-Model Valid and Indeterminately Invalid Syllogisms

Study 4 used the same syllogisms as Study 3 with the exception of the ones with neutral conclusions. The total number of Web participants (after screening out suspicious data sets) was 2,389. Separate analyses were conducted for the logic experts (N = 1,350) and the naive reasoners (N = 1,039). In both cases, the multinomial model achieved a good fit to the data in spite of the high test power for detecting even small deviations from the model that is implied by the large sample size.

When the Web data for naive reasoners were compared to the data from laboratory Study 3, close agreement was obtained between the two data sets. Unlike in Study 2, the laboratory data was also consistent with the logic experts' data, possibly because the differences in performance between naive reasoners and logic experts were not as pronounced in this study as in Study 2.

On the basis of the larger sample of participants, it was possible to obtain more accurate estimates of the model parameters and higher statistical test power for testing the crucial hypotheses of theoretical interest. As in Study 2, neither the account by misinterpreted necessity, nor the account by mental models was entirely consistent with the pattern of reasoning stage parameters. Naive reasoners were most proficient at discriminating the logical status of invalid syllogisms with unbelievable conclusions, whereas the remaining three r parameters could be set equal. For logic experts, the reasoning stage parameters were higher than those of the naive reasoners, but their profile depended upon logical status and believability in a similar manner.

11.6 Summary

A series of laboratory and Web experiments was conducted to test competing theories of belief bias. Because there is as yet limited experience with Web data, each WWW study was accompanied by a parallel laboratory study, and the Web data were formally validated against the laboratory data by means of χ^2 tests of the equality of the acceptance rates. In addition, very conservative screening criteria and consequent and extensive randomization were used to control for the methodological problems such as multiple submission that have the potential to compromise Web data. High agreement between the Web data and the laboratory data was demonstrated in each case, suggesting that careful Web studies have the potential to become a useful tool in the study of reasoning (see also Johnson-Laird & Savary, 1998). The Web experiments also provided a means to address the common concern about the unrepresentativeness of university student samples. It was both interesting and reassuring that the results of lab and (naive) Web participants were found to be comparable with respect to all main findings. The Web experiments helped to estimate solution percentages and model parameters with greatly enhanced accuracy as compared to laboratory experiments, and thus made it possible to precisely assess the relative merits of competing accounts of belief bias.

The results show for the first time that syllogism-evaluation data are affected by the perceived base rate of valid syllogisms. The effect extended relatively uniformly over the different kinds of syllogisms employed, and both naive reasoners and logic experts did not differ qualitatively in their reaction to the base-rate manipulation, although they differed markedly in reasoning capability. The multinomial model provided formal statements of these observations by successfully relegating the effects of the base-rate manipulation to the response stage. Findings and analyses supported the assumption that perceived base rate does not affect the reasoning stage, but acts on the response stage through uncertainty-based response bias.

Based on the findings of the two laboratory and the two Web experiments, we developed a new theory of belief bias within the general mental-model framework (Johnson-Laird & Bara, 1984). This new theory, which is described in detail in Klauer, Musch, & Naumer (2000), was built around three central ideas: First, in the syllogism-evaluation task participants attempt to construct models not only of the premises, but they attempt to integrate the premises and the conclusion (or its logical opposite) into a coherent semantic model. Second, unbelievable, but not believable, conclusions often trigger what we called, following Klayman and Ha (1987), negative tests of the validity of the syllogism. Negative tests consist of the attempt to integrate the logical negation of the conclusion, rather than the conclusion itself, with the premises into a coherent semantical representation. Third, premises which imply strong conflicts with prior knowledge are difficult to integrate into a coherent semantic model. Taken together, the new theory's assumptions can account for all findings reported in this chapter and in the belief bias literature.

It is important to note that it were the Web experiments and not the laboratory studies that led to the development of the new theory of belief bias, which stood the test in additional laboratory and Web experiments (Klauer, Musch, & Naumer, 2000). There is no doubt that a much larger amount of time and money would have been needed to achieve the empirical and theoretical progress obtained on the basis of the present Web experiments if data collection would have been restricted to the laboratory. Of course, this is is not to say that the Internet in itself is a better research environment than its conventional equivalent, only that the much larger samples associated with Web experimenting can be essential in some experimental paradigms. It will also require many more studies to truly determine what type of research can validly be conducted on the Internet. For example, several features of the present research may have contributed to its success. First, the presentation of syllogisms over the Web can be done with even the most simple ASCII characters and does therefore not depend on the participants' type of display, computer, operating system, and browser. Research on syllogisms does not require the use of graphics, sounds, and fine-grained response time measurements all of which can be used in Web experiments in principle, although with more potential problems (e.g., because of differences in sound and video cards; Krantz, Ballard, & Scher, 1997; Smith & Leigh, 1997; Welch & Krantz, 1996). Moreover, our manipulations were very powerful. In particular, the effects of validity and believability were quite strong. Studies employing more subtle manipulations may not run as successfully on the WWW (however, there was no problem with the more fine-grained base-rate manipulation in the present study). We also did not attempt to alter the participant's emotional state or attitudes, and it remains to be tested whether such manipulations can be successfully conducted in Web studies. Other examples of experiments that may be difficult or impossible to realize on the Internet include experiments requiring face-to-face interactions between the experimenter and the subject, longitudinal studies, or research that requires the exchange of physical items (Smith & Leigh, 1997). In many areas of research where such limitations do not play a role or can be overcome, online data collection is rapidly increasing (Musch & Reips, 2000; Wilhelm, Witthöft, & Grössler, 1999). We would not be surprised if within the next few years, a fair proportion of psychological studies will be conducted on the Web.

In view of this development, it is interesting to note that the number of Web experiments that have found their way into scientific journals is still low (but see Birnbaum, 1999; Hänze, Hildebrandt, & Meyer, 1998; Klauer, Musch, & Naumer, 2000; Krantz, Ballard, & Scher, 1997; Schmalhofer, Elst, Aschoff, Bärenfänger, & Bourne, 1999; Welch & Krantz, 1996). Of course, one reason for this is that the first Web experiments started only in recent years. It remains to be seen whether the editors and reviewers of traditional journals will accept the growing number of papers reporting data from Web experiments. We believe that the Internet offers great potential for psychological research, but in exploiting this potential, care must be taken that Web experimenting does not fall into disrepute. The evidence presented here supports the notion that Web experiments on syllogistic reasoning are a real possibility. As with all computerized testing, however, the question of whether a Web experiment can be considered equivalent to its traditional laboratory antecedent must be answered individually for each paradigm and experiment.

11.7 Outlook

The present experiments concentrated on one particular content effect within the domain of syllogistic reasoning, namely, belief bias. However, there is also a long research tradition with content-neutral syllogisms that also investigates the determinants of conclusion acceptance. Conversion and atmosphere bias are just two of the theories that have been proposed to account for the results obtained with such content-neutral syllogisms (Evans et al., 1993). Because an extremely large number of participants is necessary to obtain enough data to assess the relative merits of the proposed theories in accounting for the solution frequencies of the total set of all 512 possible syllogisms, most previous studies on syllogistic reasoning had to be and have been conducted on only a small subset of the total number of syllogisms. Very large-scale studies involving all possible syllogisms are highly desirable, however, because they allow for a simultaneous check of all existing competing theories of syllogistic reasoning within a single homogeneous sample of participants. The encouraging and promising experiences with the present set of experiments led us to decide to tackle this task, and a study designed to determine the difficulties of all possible 512 syllogisms is currently on the Web.

References

Batchelder, W. H. & Riefer, D. M. (1999). Theoretical and empirical review of multinomial processing tree modeling. *Psychonomic Bulletin & Review, 6,* 57-86.

Batinic, B. (1997). How to make an Internet based survey? In W. Bandilla & F. Faulbaum (Eds.), *SoftStat '97 – Advances in Statistical Software 6* (pp. 125-132). Stuttgart: Lucius & Lucius.

Batinic, B., Gräf, L., Werner, A., & Bandilla, W. (Eds.). (1999). *Online Research.* Göttingen, Germany: Hogrefe.

Birnbaum, M. H. (1999). Testing critical properties of decision making on the Internet. *Psychological Science, 10,* 399-407.

Bredenkamp, J. (1996). Grundlagen experimenteller Methoden [Foundations of experimental methods]. In E. Erdfelder, R. Mausfeld, T. Meiser, & G. Rudinger (Eds.), *Handbuch Quantitative Methoden* [Handbook of quantitative methods] (pp. 37-46). Weinheim, Germany: Psychologie Verlags Union.

Bröder, A. & Musch, J. (2000). *Detecting cheating and testing psychological assumptions in the randomized response technique.* Unpublished manuscript, University of Bonn.

Buchanan, T. & Smith, J. L. (1999). Using the Internet for psychological research: Personality testing on the world wide web. *British Journal of Psychology, 90,* 125-144.

Campbell, D. T. & Fiske, D. W. (1959). Convergent and discriminant validation by the multitrait-multimethod matrix. *Psychological Bulletin, 56,* 81-105.

Cohen, J. (1988). *Statistical power analysis for the behavioral sciences* (2nd ed.). Hillsdale, NJ: Erlbaum.

Erdfelder, E., Faul, F., & Buchner, A. (1996). GPOWER: A general power analysis program. *Behavior Research Methods, Instruments, and Computers, 28,* 1-11.

Evans, J. St. B. T. (1977). Toward a statistical theory of reasoning. *Quarterly Journal of Experimental Psychology, 29,* 621-635.

Evans, J. St. B. T. (1989). *Bias in human reasoning: Causes and consequences.* Hillsdale, NJ: Erlbaum.

Evans, J. St. B. T., Barston, J. L., & Pollard, P. (1983). On the conflict between logic and belief in syllogistic reasoning. *Memory and Cognition, 11,* 295-306.

Evans, J. St. B. T., Newstead, S. E., Allen, J. L., & Pollard, P. (1994). Debiasing by instruction: The case of belief bias. *European Journal of Cognitive Psychology, 6,* 263-285.

Evans, J. St. B. T., Newstead, S. E., & Byrne, R. M. J. (1993). *Human reasoning.* Hillsdale, NJ: Erlbaum.

Evans, J. St. B. T. & Pollard, P. (1990). Belief bias and problem complexity in deductive reasoning. In J. P. Cavernie, J. M. Fabre, & M. Gonzalez (Eds.), *Cognitive biases* (pp. 131-154). North-Holland: Elsevier.

Gilinsky, A. S. & Judd, B. B. (1994). Working memory and bias in reasoning across the life span. *Psychology and Aging, 9,* 356-371.

Gosling, J. & McGilton, H. (1995). *The JAVA language environment: A white paper. Sun* Microsystems. [Online]. Available: http://java.sun.com/whitePaper/java-whitepaper-1.html.

GVU Graphics, Visualization, & Usability Center (1998). *GVU's www user surveys.* [Online]. Available: http://www.cc.gatech.edu/gvu/user_surveys/.

Hänze, M., Hildebrandt, M., & Meyer, H. A. (1998). Feldexperimente im WWW: Zur Verhaltenswirksamkeit des „mere-exposure"-Effekts bei der Informationssuche [Field experiments in the world wide web: Effectiveness of the „mere exposure" effect on information seeking]. *Psychologische Beiträge, 40,* 363-372.

Henle, M. & Michael, M. (1956). The influence of attitudes on syllogistic reasoning. *Journal of Social Psychology, 44,* 115-127.

Hewson, C. M., Laurent, D., & Vogel, C. M. (1996). Proper methodologies for psychological and sociological studies conducted via the Internet. *Behavioral Research Methods, Instruments, and Computers, 28,* 186-191.

Hu, X. (1997). *GPT.EXE: Software for general processing tree models.* [Online]. Available: http://141.225.14.108/gptgateway.htm.

Johnson-Laird, P. N. & Bara, B. G. (1984). Syllogistic inference. *Cognition, 16,* 1-61.

Johnson-Laird, P. N. & Savary, F. (1998). *Ilusory inferences: A novel class of erroneous deductions.* Unpublished manuscript, Princeton University, New Jersey.

Kieley, J. M. (1996). CGI scripts: Gateways to world wide web power. *Behavior Research Methods, Instruments, and Computers, 28,* 165-169.

Klauer, K. C., Musch, J., & Naumer, B. (2000). On belief bias in syllogistic reasoning. *Psychological Review, 107,* 852-884.

Klauer, K. C. & Oberauer, K. (1995). Testing the mental model theory of propositional reasoning. *Quarterly Journal of Experimental Psychology, 48A,* 671-687.

Klauer, K. C. & Wegener, I. (1998). Unraveling social categorization in the "Who said what?"-paradigm. *Journal of Personality and Social Psychology, 75,* 1155-1178.

Klayman, J. & Ha, Y.-W. (1987). Confirmation, disconfirmation, and information in hypothesis testing. *Psychological Review, 94,* 211-228.

Krantz, J. H. (1998). *Psychological research on the net.* [Online]. Available: http://psych. hanover.edu/APS/exponnet.html.

Krantz, J. H., Ballard, J., & Scher, J. (1997). Comparing the results of laboratory and world wide web samples on the determinants of female attractiveness. *Behavioral Research Methods, Instruments, and Computers, 29,* 264-269.

Krantz, J. H. & Dalal, R. (2000). Validity of web-based psychological research. In M. H. Birnbaum (Ed.), *Psychological experiments on the Internet.* San Diego: Academic Press.

Krauth, J. (1982). Formulation and experimental verification of models in propositional reasoning. *Quarterly Journal of Experimental Psychology, 34,* 285-298.

Markovits, H. & Nantel, G. (1989). The belief-bias effect in the production and evaluation of logical conclusions. *Memory and Cognition, 17,* 11-17.

Musch, J. (2000). Die Geschichte des Netzes: ein historischer Abriß [The net's history: a synopsis]. In B. Batinic (Ed.), *Internet für Psychologen* (2nd ed.) (pp. 15-37) [Internet for psychologists]. Göttingen, Germany: Hogrefe.

Musch, J., Bröder, A., & Klauer, K. C. (2001). Improving survey research on the world wide web using the randomized response technique. In U.-D. Reips & M. Bosnjak (Eds.), *Dimensions of Internet science.* Lengerich: Pabst Science Publishers.

Musch, J. & Reips, U.-D. (2000). A brief history of web experimenting. In M. H. Birnbaum (Ed.), *Psychological experiments on the Internet* (pp. 61-85). San Diego: Academic Press.

Newstead, S. E. & Evans, J. St. B. T. (1993). Mental models as an explanation of belief bias effects in syllogistic reasoning. *Cognition, 46,* 93-97.

Newstead, S. E., Pollard, P., Evans, J. St. B. T., & Allen, J. L. (1992). The source of belief bias effects in syllogistic reasoning. *Cognition, 45,* 257-284.

Oakhill, J. & Garnham, A. (1993). On theories of belief bias in syllogistic reasoning. *Cognition, 46,* 87-92.

Oakhill, J., Johnson-Laird, P. N., & Garnham, A. (1989). Believability and syllogistic reasoning. *Cognition, 31,* 117-140.

Polk, T. A. & Newell, A. (1995). Deduction as verbal reasoning. *Psychological Review, 102,* 533-566.

Reips, U.-D. (1995). *The web's experimental psychology lab.* [Online]. Available: http://www.psych.unizh.ch/genpsy/Ulf/Lab/WebExpPsyLab.html.

Reips, U.-D. (1996). *Experimenting in the world wide web.* Paper presented at the 26th Annual Meeting of the Society for Computers in Psychology, Chicago, IL.

Reips, U.-D. (1999). Theorie und Techniken des Web-Experimentierens [Theory and techniques of web experimenting]. In B. Batinic, L. Gräf, A. Werner, & W. Bandilla (Eds.), *Online Research* (pp. 277-295). Göttingen, Germany: Hogrefe.

Reips, U.-D. (2000a). The web experiment method: Advantages, disadvantages, and solutions. In M. H. Birnbaum (Ed.), *Psychological experiments on the Internet* (pp. 89-114). San Diego: Academic Press.

Reips, U.-D. (2000b). Das psychologische Experimentieren im Internet [Psychological experimenting on the Internet]. In B. Batinic (Ed.), *Internet für Psychologen* (2nd ed.) (pp. 319-343) [Internet for psychologists]. Göttingen, Germany: Hogrefe.

Reips, U.-D. & Bächtiger, M.-T. (1999). *Are all flies drosophilae? Participant selection bias in psychological research.* Manuscript in preparation.

Schmalhofer, F., Elst, L., Aschoff, R., Bärenfänger, O., & Bourne, L. (1999). Mentale Modelle sozialer Interaktionen: Wie Texte über Sozialbetrügereien verstanden werden [Mental models of social interactions: How readers comprehend texts about cheating behaviors]. *Zeitschrift für Experimentelle Psychologie, 46,* 204-216.

Schmidt, W. (1997). World wide web survey research: Benefits, potential problems, and solutions. *Behavior Research Methods, Instruments, and Computers, 29,* 274-279.

Sears, D. O. (1986). College sophomores in the laboratory: Influences of a narrow data base on social psychology's view of human nature. *Journal of Personality and Social Psychology, 51,* 515-530.

Senior, C., Phillips, M. L., Barnes, J., & David, A. S. (1999). An investigation in the perception of dominance from schematic faces: A study using the world wide web. *Behavior Research Methods, Instruments, and Computers, 31,* 341-346.

Smith, M. & Leigh, B. (1997). Virtual subjects: Using the Internet as an alternative source of subjects and research environment. *Behavior Research Methods, Instruments, and Computers, 29,* 496-505.

Thompson, V. A. (1996). Reasoning from false premises: The role of soundness in making logical deductions. *Canadian Journal of Experimental Psychology, 50,* 315-319.

Welch, N. & Krantz, J. (1996). The world wide web as a medium for psychoacoustical demonstrations and experiments: Experience and results. *Behavior Research Methods, Instruments, and Computers, 28,* 192-196.

Wilhelm, O., Witthöft, M., & Grössler, A. (1999). Comparisons of paper-and-pencil and Internet administrated ability and achievement tests. In P. Marquet, A. Jaillet, & E. Nissen (Eds.), *Proceedings of IN-TELE 98* (pp. 439-449). Berlin: Peter Lang.

Wilkins, M. C. (1928). The effect of changed material on the ability to do formal syllogistic reasoning. *Archives of Psychology, 102,* 1-83.

12 Online Research and Anonymity

Kai Sassenberg & Stefan Kreutz

In the last few years, the World Wide Web (WWW) has gained increasing recognition as a marketing forum. The growth has not reached its limit yet. German multimedia agencies report an increase in sales of 93% from 1998 to 1999 (w&v, 2000). In the field of opinion research, the WWW is also gaining more importance. Batinic and Bosnjak (2000, see also Bandilla, this volume; Tuten, Urban, & Bosnjak, this volume) discuss in depth the advantages and drawbacks of conducting questionnaire surveys on the Internet. To a greater extent, however, questions significant to the use of the Internet remain unclear. Assessments of Web advertising effects in comparison to conventional advertising effects, or which aspects must be considered when planning Web questionnaires are both examples of such questions. Central to both of these areas of application on the WWW are phenomena, which, above all, are the focus of social psychological examination.

Advertising measures on the WWW are aimed at changing attitudes,

- When planning Web questionnaires, social desirability (i.e., response behavior oriented towards the interviewer's expectations) must be avoided in order to obtain the survey participants' genuine attitudes.
- Attitude changes and socially suitable answering behavior are forms of social influence that, in the case of the WWW, cannot be directly attributed to contacts between humans. Instead, these are caused by computer based forms of communication.

This chapter will present theories and laboratory findings on social influence exerted by computer-mediated communication (CMC) in comparison to direct communication situations. Furthermore, these will be discussed with reference to their applicability for creating marketing measures and questionnaires on the WWW. First, a concise overview of the theories on social influence in comparison between CMC and face-to-face (f2f) communication will be given. Then, with the introduction of the SIDE (Social Identity DEindividuation)-Model (Spears & Lea, 1994), a particularly reliable approach for this context will be singled out. Following the explanation of the model, two studies will be presented. The first study deals with a laboratory experiment conducted according to the previously common paradigm. The second study was staged in the form of a WWW experiment that, because of its procedure, resembles WWW marketing measures. Finally, we will conclude with a discussion of the model and the findings with reference to effects for designing marketing measures and questionnaires on the WWW.

12.1 Theories of Social Influence in a Media Comparison

In the first models discussing the comparison of social influence in different media, the degree of social presence (i.e., the possibility of acoustic, visual or physical contact with one's communication partner) was considered central to the theory. Based on the *British Post Office*, and on their *social presence model*, Short's project group described social presence as a cause of social influence (Short, Williams, & Christie, 1976). Therefore, the larger the presence, the stronger the mutual influence would be on attitudes and behavior.

In his *cuelessness model,* Rutter (1987) postulated the reverse association, since findings indicated that mutual social influence decreased with increasing social presence. Rutter assumed that with the number of social indication stimuli a medium can convey, the task orientation of the discussion will increase, whereby social orientation would decrease. Due to the resulting greater information density in communication, social influence would increase in concurrence with diminishing social influence. A general trend towards lesser socially oriented contents in CMC compared to f2f could, however, not be substantiated in the studies (Finholt & Sproull, 1990; Walther, 1992, 1995).

Consequently, on the basis of these findings, a model of social influence was derived which would not include all possible media, as was the case with previously described approaches, but would instead contemplate the specifics of CMC. Upon this presupposition, the *reduced social cues* approach (RSC) was formulated (Kiesler, Siegel, & McGuire, 1984; Kiesler & Sproull, 1992). Derived from the two previously described models, RSC's central assumption states that, in contrast to f2f communication, less information is given on social context in CMC. The communication situation is therefore considered less as social interaction. Beyond these assumptions, a psychological stimulus mechanism (and not only the medium's characteristics or a person's behavior) is also described by the RSC approach as barely social – in contrast to the models presented beforehand. The authors assume that, due to the reduction in social indication stimuli, social norms are considered less because the communication partners consider themselves to be distanced from one another and, in extreme cases, believe they are unknown to their communication opposite. This condition provokes a reduction in attention to the impression caused by other people and, hence, antinormative and unregulated behavior. On the whole, their behavior becomes more extreme, more impulsive, and less oriented towards social behavioral norms. This extreme and deregulated behavior should incur greater social influence in CMC than in f2f communication since a greater amount of and more radical contents and opinions are expressed and exchanged (Kiesler et al., 1984). The advance in explaining differing social influences of f2f and CMC with RSC still remains unclear since the psychological stimulus mechanism was hitherto an empirically unsubstantiated hypothesis.

The investigation of RSC followed in a series of studies that compared the social influence of groups communicating via f2f with that of groups discussing via chats or e-mail. The findings did not confirm the expectations in all of the studies. Although in one section of the studies, greater social influence was noted in groups that were communicating via computers than in those where communication was based on f2f communication (Siegel, Dubrosky, Kiesler, & McGuire, 1986; Kiesler et al., 1984), another series of studies revealed that a lesser degree of social influence occurred in CMC groups than in f2f groups (e.g., McGuire, Kiesler, & Siegel, 1987).

12.2 The SIDE Model

These findings renewed doubts concerning the mediator stimulus mechanism between social stimulus indications and social influence (Spears & Lea, 1992). Furthermore, the findings on the reduced social cues approach indicate that an additional influential variable must exist that, to some extent, even reverses the effect of the medium. The SIDE model (Spears & Lea, 1994) introduces an alternative explanatory mechanism, as well as an additional influential variable in order to be able to integrate the available findings. In the meantime, a whole row of findings has become obtainable that confirm the previous model (Postmes & Spears, 1998, in press; Postmes, Spears, & Lea, 1998, 1999; Reicher & Levine, 1994a, 1994b; Reicher, Levine, & Gordijn, 1998; Spears, Lea, & Lee, 1990).

The SIDE Model examines two influential variables varying between CMC and f2f communication, whose occurrence, however, is not restricted to the media comparison. On the one hand, this is referred to as the person's knowledge of her/his communication partner, from now on referred to as *anonymity*. Alternately, as with the RSC, the subjective possibility of allocating action to oneself is important. This is referred to as *identifiability* in the following section, according to the SIDE model. This distinction is to be illustrated with an example: if a person builds a homepage on the WWW she or he knows that she or he is identifiable to the visitors of the homepage, depending on if personal information can be found on the site. However, the readers remain anonymous to the author. Vice versa, the visitor of such a homepage knows she or he is not recognizable to the author. The author, however, is not anonymous for the reader.

In the context of the SIDE model, the objectively describable level of anonymity or identifiability is not decisive, as opposed to the person's perception. With reference to identifiability, this must, in particular, be taken into account, since a person's behavior does not differ between situations where she or he is unobserved, and situations where she or he is observed yet unaware of the fact. The knowledge of identifiability is relevant for social influence.

The SIDE model consists of two aspects, both concerned with the effect of one of the two central variables on social influence: *the cognitive aspect,* which explains the consequences of anonymity for social influence, and *the strategic aspect,* which explains the effect of identifiability on social influence.

12.2.1 The Cognitive Aspect of the SIDE Model

The cognitive aspect of the SIDE model is based on the self-categorization theory (Turner, Hogg, Oakes, Reicher, & Wetherell, 1987). The theory states that, depending upon their situation and contextual circumstances, people either see themselves more as a member of a group, or as a distinct individual. In the case of salient *social identity* (i.e., predominantly considering oneself a member of a group), a person's behavior and attitudes are oriented towards those norms and stereotypes associated with group affiliation. For example, in the instance of a conflict of resources between different offices in a company, the employees of the respective offices will predominantly consider themselves as members of their group, or office. The social identity of an employee of the office comes to the fore. Going into action on behalf of the office corresponds to the stereotyped behavioral norm. In another context (e.g., labor disputes), another form of group affiliation is of importance and decisive for actions.

In the case of a salient *personal identity*, if the person predominantly sees her/himself as an individual, behavior and attitude are to a large extent adjusted to individual needs. This is the case, for example, in a competitive situation between two people.

Following the cognitive aspect of the SIDE model, anonymity effects social influence differently according to the salient personal or social identity underlying the respective situation (see Figure 12.1). In general, the SIDE model states that with increasing anonymity, less information is available on the communication partners. This results in a stronger attachment to rules of behavior (identification) associated with personal or social identity. For people whose focus of attention is aimed at social identity, this is put down to their scarce knowledge of the group members, and the group's homogeneity resulting from it (Spears & Lea, 1994). As findings on the self-categorization theory demonstrate, the subjective homogeneity of a group facilitates an affiliation with the group (Wilder, 1990). Because of a lack of knowledge of other group members, people with a more salient personal identity do not possess knowledge of the common characteristics necessary for a reduction in focus on personal identity, and a stronger orientation towards social identity. Without such information, no information is available which could initiate perception and salience of a common group affiliation.

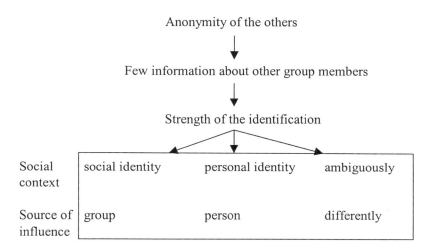

Figure 12.1: The cognitive aspect of the SIDE model

In summary, the cognitive aspect of the SIDE model states that, in the case of salient social identity related to context, there is a stronger focus on a corresponding group's behavior norms with increasing anonymity. In the case of a more salient personal identity, the focus on individual needs increases with increasing anonymity.

12.2.2 The Strategic Aspect of the SIDE Model

The strategic aspect of the SIDE model (Figure 12.2) focuses more on other people's expectations, and is less concerned with how one sees oneself (Spears & Lea, 1994). For others, the ability to identify a person leads to an evaluation of their own behavior against the background of expectations of one's opposite. This effect is fortified if the identifiable person has sanctions to fear from his observers. Identifiability brings about a focus on the observer's behavior norms. These observers can either be one's own group members or members of a different group (Reicher, Spears, & Postmes, 1995).

If a scientist builds a personal homepage with links to her institute's homepage, she is aware of the fact that she is identifiable as page administrator to members of her own institute, as well as members of other institutes. Consequently, when selecting the homepage's information and page design, she will not want to breach either her own institute's colleagues' or other institute's norms.

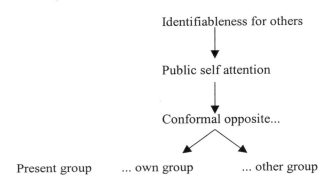

Figure 12.2: The strategic aspect of the SIDE model

All things considered, the SIDE model, therefore, comes to conclusions on the two aspects of people's perception. These two aspects play a large role in CMC. On the one hand, the cognitive aspect focuses on the possibility of perceiving other people. The strategic aspect, on the other hand, gives the impression that there is a possibility that one might be perceived or identified.

12.2.3 Previous Procedure for Examining the SIDE Model

From an empirical perspective, the strategic aspect of the SIDE model can be considered well corroborated (Reicher et al., 1995). In the meantime, the cognitive aspect of the SIDE model has also been examined likewise in a series of studies (Postmes & Spears, in press; Sassenberg & Boos, 1997; Spears, Lea, & Lee, 1990; Taylor & McDonald, 1996; Walther, 1997), yet the paradigmatic procedure of examination seems doubtful. As an example, the investigation, which followed the usual paradigm, will be introduced. The analysis here is only a summary; a more detailed description of the survey procedure and the results can be found in Sassenberg and Boos (1997).

An experiment was conducted according to the paradigm of group polarization. 69 student test subjects were asked to indicate their opinion on an issue on a rating scale before and after a discussion. The discussions took place in groups of three. The test subjects were asked to what extent a medicine too expensive for them would have to have healing chances in order for them to steal it for their partner on the verge of death (analogous to Kohlberg's Heinz dilemma, see Hinter, 1987). They were to make their decision on a scale of one (minimum healing chance) to 100% (sure recovery). A decision for sure recovery indicates an orientation towards valid law. A decision for minimum healing chances indicates an orientation towards the needs of the partner, or one's own needs. According to instructions, the salience of the social identity of the discussion group, or the salience of the personal identity of each individual, was ensured prior to the group discussion. The group discussion either took place via IRC (Internet Relay Chat), without any information about the communication partners, or f2f.

Before the discussion, the test subjects on average tended to consent to healing chances of 41%. This represented an alternative more aimed at the partner's needs than abiding by valid law. Impartial to the experimental manipulation towards the partner's needs, and thus away from the legal alternative (29% healing chance) [$t(68)$ = 4.45, $p < .001$], the test subjects' attitude changed in the comparison between the measurements before and after the discussion.

To examine the cognitive aspect of the SIDE model, a covariance analysis was calculated with the independent variables *communication medium* and *salient identity category*, the covariate *attitude before the discussion*, and the dependent variable *change of attitude* (difference in healing chance after and before the group discussion).

An interaction between the two independent variables was noted [$F(1, 64)$ = 11.73, $p < .01$]. As was expected, if personal identity is salient, the change in attitude leans more strongly, with high anonymity (i.e., in the case of CMC), towards the individual need to save the partner ($\Delta = 19\%$) than in the nonanonymous communication condition (f2f; $\Delta = 5\%$; see Figure 12.3).

As a norm associated with social identity in groups informally put together for survey purposes, the group members' prevailing opinion can be considered as the group's norm (Turner & Oakes, 1989). In the "f2f/salient social identity" conditions, the change of attitude unsurprisingly leant more toward the group norm (here: orientation to partner's needs, $\Delta = 18\%$) than under the same communication conditions with salient personal identity ($\Delta = 4\%$). The interpretation of the salient social identity group results is more difficult in the case of comparison between both communication media. According to the cognitive aspect of the SIDE model, a tendency towards the group norm should be strengthened more in the case of anonymous CMC, than f2f. Contrary to this hypothesis, there was no change in attitude toward the group norm in the "dominating social identity/CMC" condition ($\Delta = 5\%$). A possible cause for this tendency could be that in the ad hoc groups no dominance of social identity developed with CMC (see also Taylor & McDonald, 1996). Alternately, it is also conceivable that a confounding of identifiability and anonymity effects may be the cause for the findings. This interpretation will be addressed here. Via the manipulation of the medium, identifiability and anonymity were manipulated simultaneously (see also Sassenberg, 2000). This was also the case in other studies on the cognitive aspect of the SIDE model in which anonymity was allegedly manipulated by (a) a variation between anonymous CMC and CMC where the text subjects were all present in the same room during the examination (Spears et al., 1990), or (b) providing or not providing photos of the other group members in the otherwise anonymous CMC (Postmes, 1997).

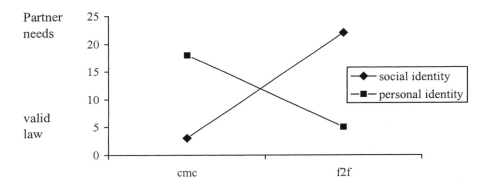

Figure 12.3: Interaction between the two independent variables

In the case of salient personal identity, the predicted attitude change does not change as an effect of the simultaneous manipulation of the identifiability and anonymity. Due to an orientation to valid law, as a norm exhibited by others present, the predicted effect should be reinforced in the f2f condition. In the case of salient social identity, however, an increase in orientation towards the norms of the interacting group is to be expected with increasing identifiability (i.e., with f2f being stronger than CMC). However, in the case of exclusive manipulation of anonymity, a stronger orientation towards the group norm was to be expected in the CMC condition than in the direct communication condition. In total, the presented findings could lead back to a manipulation of identifiability and not to a manipulation of anonymity. Due to the examination paradigm used until now, this cannot be clarified ultimately. We, therefore, conducted a further survey using separate manipulation of anonymity and identifiability (Sassenberg, 1999; Expt. 1).

12.2.4 Examination of the Significance of Identifiability and Anonymity

To successfully implement separate manipulation of identifiability and anonymity, a completely different survey procedure was selected. First, the entire survey was only applied to the salient social identity condition, since the respective group norm can be more precisely predicted than the individual needs which dictate behavior in the case of salient personal identity. The separate examination of the effects of anonymity and identifiability was conducted in the form of a camouflaged public opinion poll on a new car with a prize draw on an advertising agency's WWW page. The different test conditions were presented on appropriately designed pages upon access of the survey's URL address.

In an experiment with a 2 x 2 x 2 x 2 design respondents' alleged identifiability, the anonymity of group members to the respondent and the group's norms were varied. Beyond that, the *test subjects' affiliation to the group* of students or nonstudents was obtained as a fourth, quasi-experimental independent variable in the social category. Dominance of the social identity as a member of one of these two groups was realized via the indication that this was a survey on a comparison of attitudes to the car between students and nonstudents.

Included on the WWW page were statements by eight people who had allegedly test-driven the new car. Four of the people were indicated as students, four weren't. In this manner each test subject, regardless of *group affiliation* (student or nonstudent), was supplied both with statements by members of their own, as well as members of the other, group.

The *own group's norm* was varied with the group members' statements. In each case, the members of a group made positive statements about the design, those in the other group evaluated the car's performance positively in their statements. The characteristics "design" and "performance" were randomized in the student and nonstudent groups. In this way we managed that in each case about half of the students and nonstudents obtained statements on one characteristic from members of the own group, and statements on another characteristic from members of the other group. A confounding of norms and group affiliation can therefore be ruled out.

The *characteristics "design" and "performance"* not only differ from a content perspective, but are examined in a different way from the point of view of "objectivity". Statements on design are evaluations with a strong affective component. However, in the case of statements on performance, facts on actual features are used as arguments, so that an evaluation of the performance can instead be inspected on the basis of physical characteristics.

The two-step manipulation of *identifiability* was carried out in the "nonidentifiable" condition via a separate mailing of the questionnaire for evaluation of personal information. In the "identifiable" condition, however, the test subjects were obliged to indicate their names and address in order to participate in the survey.

In the condition with low *anonymity*, the communicators shown on the WWW page were introduced with their Christian name, group affiliation, occupation or their academic subject, age, and a photograph. In the high anonymity condition, however, apart from communicators' statements, only data on Christian names and group affiliation was presented on the WWW page.

As a *dependent measure*, the global change in attitude before and after reading the statements of the eight persons was collated. In addition, the test subjects had to indicate their degree of agreement with the eight statements. The agreement value was summarized in each case for the four statements on design and the four statements on performance, so that for each test subject an agreement value for the own group's norm, and an agreement value for other group's norm could be determined. Both measures of social influence were implemented to record the effect of anonymity and identifiability. Both the norm of own group, relevant from the cognitive aspect perspective (manipulated by the alleged own group member's statements), and the other group's norm, relevant from a strategic aspect perspective (the automobile manufacturer), contained a positive evaluation of the car. The following hypotheses result from the SIDE model:

- With increasing identifiability, the car was generally evaluated more positively.
- With increasing anonymity the car was evaluated more positively with regard to those dimensions (design or performance) in which statements were made in the own group.
- The influence of the own group is larger than that of the other group.

For five weeks, the WWW site was accessible on the net, and advertised in mailing lists and search engines. In this period, it was accessed by 352 people and completed by 258 who are included in the following presentation of the results. The ratio of broken off questionnaires was influenced significantly by the manipulation of identifiability. In the identifiable condition only 66% of the test subjects filled out the questionnaire completely, 78% in the nonidentifiable condition. 37% of the test subjects were students, 63% indicated being nonstudents. The age of the participants varied between 16 and 78 years, with a mean value of 30 years.

The analysis of the data for change of attitude was computed by means of a five-factorial analysis of variance with measurement repetitions (first or second attitude measurement as a measurement repetition, as well as group affiliation, anonymity, identifiability, group norm), which were calculated respectively for the characteristics *design* and *performance*. The effects of the condition variations on agreement with the text drivers' statements were likewise determined by a five factorial multivariate analysis of variance with the independent variables *anonymity, identifiability, group*

Sassenberg, K. & Boos, M. (1997). Gruppenpolarisation bei computervermittelter Kommunikation: Eine Studie zum SIDE-Modell. *Vortrag auf der 6. Tagung der Fachgruppe Sozialpsychologie der Deutschen Gesellschaft für Psychologie, Konstanz.*

Short, J. A. (1974). Effects of medium of communication on experimental negotiation. *Human Relations, 27*, 225-234.

Short, J. A., Williams, E., & Christie, B. (1976). *The social psychology of telecommunications.* London: John Wiley & Sons.

Siegel, J., Dubrosky, V., Kiesler, S., & McGuire, T. W. (1986). Group processes in computer-mediated communication. *Organizational Behavior and Human Decision Processes, 37*, 157-187.

Simon, B. & Pettigrew, T. F. (1990). Social identity and perceived group homogeneity: Evidence for the ingroup homogeneity effect. *European Journal of Social Psychology, 20*, 269-286.

Spears, R. & Lea, M. (1992). Social influence and the influence of the "social" in computer-mediated communication. In M. Lea (Ed.), *Contexts of computer-mediated communication* (pp. 30-65). New York: Harvester Wheatsheaf.

Spears, R. & Lea, M. (1994). Panacea or panopticon? The hidden power in computer-mediated communication. *Communication Research, 21*, 427-459.

Spears, R., Lea, M., & Lee, S. (1990). De-individuation and group polarization in computer-mediated communication. *British Journal of Social Psychology, 29*, 121-134.

Taylor, J. & MacDonald, J. (1996). *The impact of computer-mediated group interaction on group decision-making, communication, and inter-personal perception.* Paper presented on the 25th International Congress of Psychology.

Turner, J. C., Hogg, M. A., Oakes, P. J., Reicher, S. D., & Wetherell, M. S. (Eds.). (1987). *Rediscovering the social group. A self-categorization theory.* New York: B. Blackwell.

Turner, J. C. & Oakes, P. J. (1989). Self-categorization theory and social influence. In P. B. Paulus (Ed.), *The psychology of group influence* (2nd ed.) (pp. 233-279). Hillsdale, NJ: Erlbaum.

W&V (2000). Agenturen verdoppeln ihren Umsatz. *W&V new media report, 4*, 1-9.

Walther, J. B. (1992). Interpersonal effects in computer-mediated interaction. *Communication Research, 19*, 52-90.

Walther, J. B. (1995). Relational aspects of computer-mediated communication: Experimental observations over time. *Organizational Science, 6*, 186-203.

Walther, J. B. (1997). Group and interpersonal effects in computer-mediated collaboration. *Human Communication Research, 23*, 342-369.

Wilder, D. A. (1990). Some determinants of the persuasive power of in-group and out-group: Organization of information and attribution of interdependence. *Journal of Personality and Social Psychology, 59*, 1202-1213.

13 Theory and Techniques of Conducting Web Experiments

Ulf-Dietrich Reips

In the Internet, there are three main possibilities for collecting data that allow us to draw conclusions on human behavior. These are:

- Nonreactive data collection,
- Online surveys, and
- Web experiments.

Web experiments, the core theme of this chapter, have an advantage over the other two methods because of their ability in proving causal relationships between variables. This advantage implicitly facilitates deductive, hypothesis testing research, in which the much disputed question of representativeness is not posed – in comparison to other study procedures. In the following sections, I will introduce a demonstration of the potential of Web experiments in comparison to the two aforementioned non-experimental online research methods. The first part of the chapter explains the historical and theoretical background for different types of research methods. The second part of the chapter is devoted to several useful techniques for Web experimenting, such as *warm-up*, *password*, *subsampling*, *participant pool*, and *multiple site entry*.

13.1 Nonexperimental Methods

13.1.1 Nonreactive Data Collection

Nonreactive data collection refers to the use and analysis of existing databases, for example server logfiles or newsgroup contributions. This method is referred to as *nonreactive* because, at the time of the investigation, the producer of the data hardly assumes that the information will be used for a study and, therefore, does not behave differently than normal in *reaction* to this fact. Indeed, at the time when the behavior traces are left even the researchers are rarely aware of this fact. Typical characteristics of nonreactive data collection include:

- Investigation of correlations, but not of causalities is possible.
- Data are not gathered by scientists.
- Modest data collection expenditures required.
- Examination of rare behavioral patterns is facilitated.
- Nonmanipulable events can be studied.
- Greater ecological validity provided, i.e., the data are polled without any outside influences ("naturally" so to speak).

An example for the use of nonreactive data is in the study of communicative behavior among members of a mailing list, with the help of interaction frequencies pertaining to e-mail headers in contributions (see Stegbauer & Rausch, this volume).

13.1.2 Online Surveys

The second, and most commonly used method of online research is the survey (see Batinic & Bosnjak, 1997). The frequent use of surveys on the Internet can be explained by the ease with which it seems surveys can be constructed, conducted, and evaluated. In most cases, the motivational factor behind surveys is determined by the potential of reaching conclusions on a greater number of persons (in this case the sampled population) than were actually interviewed (the sample). Representativeness, which is absolutely necessary for the fulfillment of this aim – can only be attained at great cost outside of the Internet. Already the time spent between the survey and its evaluation decreases the data's significance with regard to the "world's" current situation. Representativeness is most likely if each individual member of the sample is randomly selected from that set of persons for whom the results are expected to make general statements upon.

In 1993, Ross Perot, former American presidential candidate, made the painful discovery of the actual extent to which a nonrepresentative survey can bypass reality. He asked TV viewers – in a sort of fit of "nonrandomized" sampling – to fill in a postcard inserted in a magazine called "TV Guide". Ninety seven percent of the entrants answered the question on whether the government should cut spending positively. In a random sample shortly afterwards, the same question only met with 67% approval (Tanur, 1994). Inferring that almost everybody supported spending cuts would be an instructive example for a conclusion reached many years beforehand: "Direct, intuitive observation, accompanied by questioning, imagination, or creative intervention, is a limited and misleading prescientific technique." (Monte, 1975, p.63).

The supposed ease with which surveys can be conducted is, at second glance, a deceiving mirage and does not lead to the source of eternal knowledge, rather into a grinding quagmire teeming with quality control measures. For example, what must be considered when conducting surveys easily filled the 800 pages book by Lyberg, Biemer, Collins, De Leeuw, Dippo, Schwarz, & Trewin (1997). For online surveys, Gräf, Brenner, and Bandilla all describe in their contributions to the present volume how methodological quality can be guaranteed.

The third principal method of collecting data in the Internet is referred to as the *Web experiment* (Musch & Reips, 2000; Reips, 1995b, 1996b, 1998, 2000a), or Internet-based experiment. The characteristics of the experimental method will be discussed in the following section.

13.2 The Experimental Method

13.2.1 Definition and History

A social scientific experiment is a systematic method for exploring and checking causal influences on behavioral patterns of interest. Its effectiveness lies in the fact that only this method is suitable for examining *causal* explanations of behavior (Bredenkamp, 1996; Kirk, 1995; Martin, 2000; Wormser, 1974), and making statements that transcend the claim of a *correlative* connection.

When they hear the word "experiment", many people first think of physical experiments. In the tradition of natural science, experiments are characterized by the fact that the object of research seems to be governed by little natural variance. A piece of metal will always slide down a slope with the same velocity. Consistent with these findings, the natural sciences (except for biology) concentrated on the central aspects of the development of research methods (i.e., the invention of apparatuses and the limitation of measurement errors). On the other hand, it was clear to both the biological and social sciences that differences between various studied objects actually are defined by the characteristics of the object and therefore remain, even if measurement errors can be excluded. In the natural setting of a playground, one can easily observe that, in contrast to a piece of metal, children can slide down a chute differently. Very early on, the task of recording variations of physiology and behavior in a statistical distribution became a necessary component of social and biological scientific research. But how should one proceed to record the data?

Towards the end of the eighteenth century, agricultural scientists accomplished productive and pioneering achievements in the area of conducting experiments, and at the same time advanced the related field of statistics. For instance, faced with the problem that spreading manure in a field under well controlled conditions (in a physical science sense) would yield excellent results on one plot, yet cause an agricultural disaster in another plot, they came to the conclusion that certain factors which probably influenced the field's harvest should be controlled. Also, the various types of manure (i.e., the variations of the target factor) needed to be compared with each other, and the manure conditions needed to be compared with a no treatment condition to see if manure has an effect at all.

The question of if and at which values the differences found in such a comparison could be considered significant were to be answered by statistics, by then a rapidly evolving discipline.

Only recently have the nonbiological natural sciences seen it fit to employ statistic methods for the analysis of occurring variances. (In view of experimental demonstrations in lessons, generations of pupils have had a hunch that there is this necessity...).

13.2.2 Generalizability of Results According to a Hypothetical-Deductive Understanding of Science

The population of Internet users is growing at an extremely fast pace. Various user analyses show that all population parameters are converging with those of the normal population (IntelliQuest Information Group, Inc. http://www.intelliquest.com/about /release41.htm; Graphics, Visualization, & Usability Center, 1997-2001). In the foreseeable future, in "First World" countries the group of Internet users will be nearly as representative as the TV audience is for the general population. This means that, with the expanded spread of Internet access, Web experiments will make experimental research as accessible to just as many participants from the general population as to the "usual subjects" contacted in university cafeterias. Because so few studies exist with confirmatory evidence on other population groups but college students, the limited range in the test participants' characteristics can, from a general point of view, be regarded as a detriment for the significance of experimental research in the social sciences. Nevertheless, representativeness is of relatively little importance in experimental research, because the (inductive) generalization of results plays a minor role in the (deductive) investigation of hypotheses[1]. Results from

---

[1]   Here, a discussion of "representativeness" in the gir-l mailing list (Archive Mailing-List German Internet Research Mailing List gir-l, 1997), and in particular Jochen Musch's contribution dated 17.10.97, is to be mentioned.

survey research conducted online, on the other hand, depend on where and how in the Internet the participants are contacted[2] (Brenner, this volume).

Deduction is the method whereby a conclusion drawn from a general case is applied to a specific case. In hypothetical-deductive research, a verifiable causal hypothesis (symbolized by a small circle in Figure 13.1) is derived from a theory (large circle in Figure 13.1). The hypothesis is then tested in an experiment. In other words, it is compared to data obtained in an empirical test. If the results of the experiment do not repudiate the hypothesis, the theory is (once again) considered confirmed and useful. *Induction* is the process whereby a conclusion drawn from a specific case is applied to the general. An observation leads to a hypothesis around which, following an inductive train of thought, a theory is built. This need not have anything to do with reality apart from the initial observation. The theory does not undergo a *test* (see Figure 13.1). Typical inductive practice is the application of data obtained from a sample to the population of which the sample was extracted from. The actual research procedure as a whole is constantly on the move back and forth between deduction and induction.

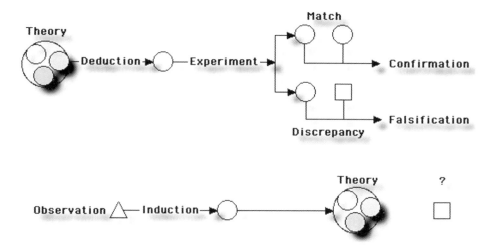

Figure 13.1: Hypothetical-deductive research (top) allows an experimental test of hypotheses, whereas a purely inductive procedure (bottom) does not. Explanation of symbols in text.

---

[2] We recently conducted a Web experiment involving an IQ test with speed components. Resulting distributions were clearly different for two samples gained by placing links on two distinctive Websites.

13.2.3 Characteristics of Experiments

A defining characteristic of an experiment is the *active creation* of specific situations. In an experiment, a situation is actively and methodically produced in which the event to be investigated – and if possible only this event – can unfold in its entirety. Active creation deems the bothersome wait for a spontaneous occurrence of the event of interest unnecessary. Also, it facilitates the preparation of optimal, controlled circumstances that can in no way interfere with the proper interpretation of the situation. The aim of the created situation could be a decision, for instance, if two theories predict different results for one experiment (*experimentum cruxis*). In the simplest case, it could also be the finding of one answer to the question of how manipulation of a variable affects another variable (*explorative experiment*). In most cases, experiments are conducted on the basis of a hypothesis (i.e., in order to investigate theoretically founded hypotheses).

A second important characteristic of the experiment is its *repeatability*, an issue logically related to its active creation characteristic. Because experiments are repeatable, their results can be studied from an inter-subjective perspective.

The third characteristic of experiments is their *variability*. Because the experimenter controls the circumstances, and because experiments are repeatable, she can introduce completely new variables or alter existing variables in further experiments. By varying the variables, through isolation and combination, the effects of independent variables on the dependent variable(s) can be confirmed and quantified.

The fourth characteristic of experiments is the allocation of participants to different experimental conditions[3]. In a typical experiment the participants are allocated one or more variations (*levels*) of the independent variable(s) to be tested against each other. The participants' behavior is then measured on one or more dependent variables.

13.2.4 Experimental Logic

All scientists – and all of us in daily life – try to find out something about relationships between events. In the social sciences, human behavior is permanently in the focus of interest.

In almost every form of examination, even we behavioral scientists encounter problems in generalizing the results of our research when we wish to measure the influence of clearly defined, physically measurable circumstances and their effects on equally clearly defined behavior. Imagine a reaction time experiment in which the

---

[3] Whether this characteristic is of importance is debatable. Tests without this characteristic can be referred to as "incomplete experiments".

participants have to depress a button as quickly as possible after hearing a high, medium, or low frequency sound. An example: The head of a company which develops security systems for atomic power plants is interested in your work and asks you, "Excuse me, I hear you conducted a reaction time experiment. Can you tell me what frequency warning sirens should have so that the security personnel will react within a second?" Because you precisely controlled many different variables in the experiment, you answer, "If you can guarantee that your security personnel is male, 30 years old, mildly extravert, and does not suffer from hearing defects, has a slightly below average IQ of 95, and is sitting in a 4 x 4 x 3 meter, soundproof room at a temperature of 21° Celsius, has nothing else to do and can hear the alarm bells (that are always introduced by a prior warning tone) on a Taka 450xm stereo headphone… – maybe then I could answer your question."

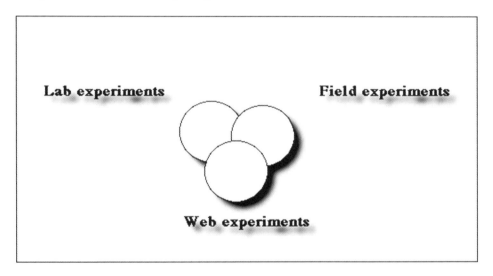

Figure 13.2: "Discovery spotlights" on the *phenomenological space*, as produced by different forms of experiments

In order to avoid research results from being constrained in their significance to an individual combination of situational characteristics, one should avoid *controlling* or *keeping constant* all variables in any given experiment. For, "the more highly controlled the experiment, the less generally applicable the results" (Martin, 2000, p.28). Random variations of the greatest possible amount of variables facilitate generalizability. When participants with whatever traits are randomly allocated to the different conditions of an experiment it cannot be ruled out, but is statistically improbable, that a characteristic manipulated by the experimental conditions systematically influences the differences in the participants' behavior with respect to the dependent variable. A variable that *systematically* varies with the variation of the dependent variable is known as a *confounded* variable.

In contrast to other methods, the characteristics of an experiment (e.g., control groups, randomized allocation of conditions to participants, counterbalancing) allow an examination of causal explanations (for example, assumed reasons for product preferences in shopping behavior).

13.2.5 Types of Experiments

There are three kinds of experiment: laboratory experiments, field experiments, and – more recently – Web experiments (Figure 13.2 symbolizes the three types of experiment as overlapping spotlights on the *phenomenological space*). *Laboratory experiments* are experiments conducted in the traditional sense of the word, for example in a university laboratory. Here, the researchers have the advantage of being able to control many factors precisely. However, the artificial setting can cause the participants to behave in a different manner than usual. For this reason, many researchers tend to go "where life takes place" and conduct experiments in everyday environments. Experiments such as these are known as *field experiments* because of the "naturalness" of such environments. Understandably, anything can cross the researcher's path when the potential for control over the situation is reduced. In consideration, the already classic pioneering study by Muzafer and Carolyn Sherif, who in 1953 conducted an impressive field experiment on group dynamics in a holiday camp, seems all the more remarkable (Sherif & Sherif, 1954). Unfortunately, field experiments are more cost intensive, a reason why they are rarely conducted. Another disadvantage of conducting field experiments is the ethical problem of not informing participants about their involvement in an experiment, because they do not know that they are participating in an experiment. Participants may leave the "action radius", unknowingly creating a methodological problem.

Web experiments (Reips, 1996a, 1996b, 1998, 2001a; see Figure 13.3) are the logical extension of the computer-based laboratory experiment. With the help of a Web browser, the participant can access the laboratory computer – which now is called a *Web server* – from her own computer that may be at a far distant location. In many respects, the experiment is conducted as if the participant were seated in front of a computer in a lab – with the only exception that the experimental information, normally visible on the laboratory computer's monitor, is now transferable to the participant's screen anywhere in the world. Any type of input by the participant, for instance mouse clicks or movements, sound and video signals, text entries or hypertext document requests can be registered by the Web server and answered accordingly. Response times, the name and location of the participant's computer, and the type of browser used are recorded with other data in a logfile. This logfile can be formatted and filtered according to the requirements of the statistical analysis.

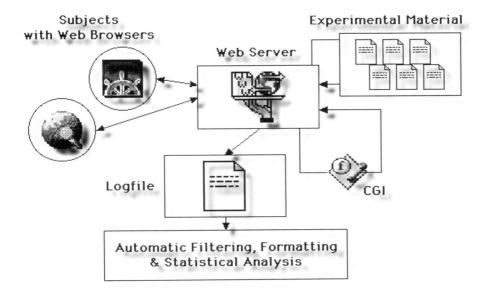

Figure 13.3: Components of a web experimental setup: Web server, web browser, experimental materials to be sent out via Internet, Common Gateway Interface (CGI) scripts, logfile

In contrast to the disadvantages of the lab experimental method, Web experiments offer many advantages:

- Easy access to a large and geographically diverse pool of potential participants, including possible participants from very specific and previously inaccessible target groups.
- The experiment comes to the participant instead of vice versa.
- Ease of acquisition of just the optimal number of participants allows for achieving high statistical power while being able to draw meaningful conclusions from the experiment[4].

---

[4]   Contrary to a widespread belief a study is not generally better the more participants take part in it. At large sample sizes even the tiniest effects become *statistically* "significant", even though they might not be significant in terms of effect size.

- Reduced cost, because neither a laboratory, nor an experimenter assistant are required (More extensive lists of arguments in favor of Web experiments can be found in Reips (1995b, 2000a, 2000b).

First analyses and studies reveal that Web experiments:

- Usually are valid (Krantz, Ballard, & Scher, 1997; Krantz & Dalal, 2000) and sometimes even generate higher quality data than laboratory studies (Birnbaum, 2001; Reips, 2000a),
- facilitate research in previously inaccessible areas (e.g., Bordia, 1996; Coomber, 1997), and
- on the whole, more than even out the scientific and practical disadvantages (Reips, 1997, 2000a).

Figure 13.4: The web experimental psychology lab's logo

The great freedom for participants of being able to begin and discontinue participation in an openly accessible online study at any time has consequences for researchers. On account of this, *self selection* is a problem of great importance. Mostly, questionnaires and experiments on controversial topics are affected. For instance, if one were to post a Web page on the Internet with the title "To take part in an opinion poll on abortion click here" one can rest assured that one will only receive opinions from people generally or specifically interested in the topic of abortions. Before conducting a Web experiment one should consider carefully the likelihood of self-selection and take necessary precautions. These should include factorial design of experiments with variations of the factors, suitable test topics and replications using other samples, which might exist due to other Web connections to an experiment. Also, the multiple site entry technique described later in this chapter can be used to control for biases due to self-selection.

In the summer of 1995, the *Web Experimental Psychology Lab* (Reips, 1995a, 2001a, 2001b) was set up at the University of Tübingen for the purpose of conducting Web experiments (Figure 13.4 shows the Web lab's logo). In 1998, the laboratory moved its physical base to the University of Zürich. At last count (November 2000), the laboratory registered an average of around 4,000 visits per month (for historical numbers see Figure 13.5). Since 1996, a host of further experimental laboratories have been established on the World Wide Web (WWW) (listing in chronological order):

- Interactive CyberLab for Decision-Making Research (http://www.etl.go.jp/~e6930) [April, 1996].
- Laboratory of Social Psychology Jena (http://www.uni-jena.de/~ssw/labor.htm) [June, 1996].
- Experimental Server Trier (http://cogpsy.uni-trier.de:8000/TEServ-e.html) [June, 1997].
- Max-Planck Institute for Biological Cybernetics Tübingen (http://exp.kyb.tuebingen.mpg.de/Web-experiment/index.html) [November, 1997].
- Online Psychology Lab Padua (http://www.psy.unipd.it/personal/laboratorio/surprise/htmltesi/index.html) [May, 1997].
- Decision Research Center (http://psych.fullerton.edu/mbirnbaum/dec.htm) [started online experiments in March, 1998].
- ZUMA Online Research (http://www.or.zuma-mannheim.de/inhalt/onlinelabor/) [May, 1998].
- Psycholinguist Laboratory Scotland (http://surf.to/experiments) [September, 1998].
- PsychExps (http://www.olemiss.edu/PsychExps/) [Fall 1998; invites participation of Web experiments from other researchers].

Further Web experiments can be accessed on the Web experiment list (http://www.genpsy.unizh.ch/Ulf/Lab/webexplist.html), on the classic Web site by the American Psychological Society (http://psych.hanover.edu/APS/exponnet.html), and on William E. Snell Jr.'s Web site to accompany his introductory psychology class on "Psychological Perspectives on Human Behavior" (http://psychology2.semo. edu/websites/web41.htm). Guidelines for conducting experiments in the Web Experimental Psychology Lab can be found on the Web site and in Reips (2000a)[5]. In principle, the Web laboratory is open to cooperative Web experiments.

To complete the picture, the possibility of conducting *undercover* experiments on the WWW (Hänze & Meyer, 1997) should be mentioned. In a series of Web experiments, Hänze and Meyer manipulated images and background colors on the Web pages of a popular icon archive. Hence, for color they were able to replicate the *mere exposure effect* (increasing preferences for often perceived and encountered stimuli) postulated by Kunst-Wilson and Zajonc (1980).

---

[5]   Conditions for the use of the Web lab are listed at http://www.genpsy.unizh.ch/Ulf/Lab/WebLabCond.html

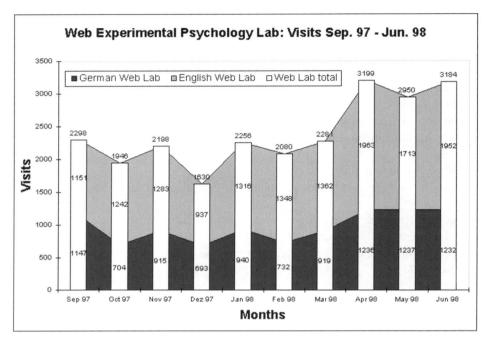

Figure 13.5: Visits to the Tübingen version of the web experimental psychology lab, September 1997 to June 1998

13.3 Motivational Techniques When Conducting Web Experiments

13.3.1 Recruitment and Motivation

Finding and motivating clients and, as in this case, experimental participants to stay on a Web site is a general point of discussion in online business. As will be demonstrated, a few particular characteristics must be regarded when recruiting and encouraging participants to take part in online research projects. To begin with, the Web site should be reasonably attractive to look at. This can be achieved by:

- Incorporating appealing design (e.g., graphics),
- external links to the Web site (registration in search engines),
- comments stating that this part of the Web might be interesting to explore (prize draws, links to press reports, display of awards),

- multilingualism, and
- offering various viewing possibilities (frame/no-frame/text/print versions).

The integrity of the request should be underlined by the corresponding explanation:

- The name(s) of the main institution(s),
- clarification of the scientific value of the project,
- indication of an e-mail contact address, and
- guarantee of data confidentiality (and compliance with this guarantee!).

Participants should be informed of how much time will be required for taking part in the Web experiment. Offering small rewards for taking part and drawing (cash) prizes amongst respondents can be of help. Certainly, an explanation of one's own status in the study as well as receiving information about aim and background of the study both count as further incentives for participating (see Bosnjak & Batinic, in this volume).

13.3.2 Ensuring Incentives for Staying (Dropout Reduction)

Engaging participants for an experiment is one matter, keeping them engaged is another. From a methodological point of view, a low dropout quota is important for a Web experiment. This applies even more to nonexperimental surveys, because a comparison rarely takes place between the different variations of an independent variable. However, whilst the significance of a questionnaire might depend upon the fact that, for example, those who show little interest in the survey will to a greater extent stop answering the questionnaire, selective dropout by participants under one of many different circumstances could be used as a detection device for confounded variables in the Web experiment. This way, potential artifacts could be managed better in the future.

Many Web surfers leave Web sites early because loading times for documents, in particular images, are too long. A proven method of confronting this problem is the *systematic reduction in loading times* the further a respondent advances in the experiment, also called the *High Hurdle Technique*. For instance, most experiments in the Web Experimental Psychology Lab are structured in such a way that the *Web Laboratory page* (http://www.genpsy.unizh.ch/Ulf/Lab/WebExpPsyLab.html) requires the most loading time. The *General Instructions* pages for the various experiments is the second slowest page to load. The *Specific Instructions* pages appear even quicker and the *Experiment Materials* nearly all use text and images that had been used previously, and therefore will be loaded "in no time" from the hard drive's cache. Whoever decides to drop out because of long loading times will be more likely to do this sooner rather than later.

A similar method is advisable when confronting "psychological loading time", (i.e., the "internal barriers" which precede participation). Immediately on the General Instructions page, the participant could be informed of her obligations when deciding to participate, and should be asked to disclose her telephone number or e-mail address. The respondent should also (perhaps with a little test) be notified of the requirement of a certain type of Web browser and should be asked to download the correct software. Furthermore, one should – also for ethical reasons – notify the participant about time needed and other potentially unpleasant aspects of participating in the experiment. The largest hurdle should be straight at the start.

Experienced Web surfers are aware of the fact that they are a "snooping breed". The suggestive power of the term "Web browser" rather implies a sort of drifting or "leafing through" than a planned analysis of contents. What to do with the "snoops"? In order to separate those who are simply peeking from those who are earnestly intent on participating in a Web experiment, the *Warm Up Technique* is a tried method. If, in a Web experiment, the actual experimental manipulation only occurs after a warming up phase, one can deduct that those who ended early did not break off the experiment because of the manipulation.

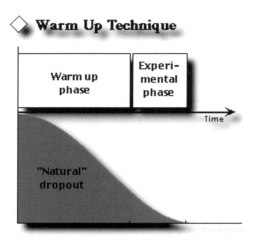

Figure 13.6: The warm up technique separates "snooper" dropout
from dropout in reaction to a Web experiment

Revealing to the participant what awaits him will reduce the likelihood of his leaving the experiment early because of an unpleasant surprise. It is therefore advisable to briefly outline the experiment's contents, e.g., "Instructions – Phase 1: A questionnaire with three questions – Phase 2 – two questionnaires with five questions each. Total time: approximately 25 minutes." One could also notify the participant of his progress during the course of the experiment. If a participant knows how long it will take approximately she is more likely to complete the experiment.

Whether announcements, instructions or questionnaires are used – any text should be written in a positive, personal style. The writing most likely will succeed if the participant is imagined as a partner in a cooperative project (who he/she is anyway.)

13.4 Techniques in Practice

Nearly all of the techniques presented in this chapter were put into practice in the first between subjects experiment conducted on the WWW, which was started in 1995 (Musch & Reips, 2000; Reips, 1996a, 1996b). At http://www.genpsylab.unizh. ch/archiv/first/WWWExpE.html, where this Web experiment is documented, one can put oneself in the position of a participant and experience *the influence of causal mechanism information during acquisition of causal knowledge*. Of a total of 880 participants who took part in this Web experiment with a duration of up to 60 minutes between 18 January and 16 September 1996, 255 dropped out of the experiment during the warming-up phase. During this phase, an additional 29 persons fell victim to technical problems caused on the server side. In total, therefore, 596 participants started the actual experiment. During this phase the dropout ratio added up to less than ten percent (58), with the exception of ten technical faults. "Dropout" during the experimental phase referred of course to the fact that the participants did not complete any of the questionnaires. A subset of the 58 persons could have been "insiders" (other scientists interested in finding out about the method) or "questionnaire shy" people.

Of the remaining 528 participants, these included 25 who refused to reveal their telephone number and/or e-mail address and whose data were excluded as a result. Also excluded were four more sets of data produced within two days after prior participation from the same or only marginally different computer addresses despite different e-mail addresses. The probability that these might have been different people is nevertheless large, since it is likely that people tell their colleagues about the Web experiment, who then also participate from the same office building. Yet, to be on the safe side, all eventualities (e.g., deceptive attempts) must be considered and prevention of data contamination should be a goal with highest priority. No event was registered whereby one person signed up under the same e-mail address or telephone number more than once. To conclude, data from 499 experiment participants on the WWW were included in the statistical analysis.

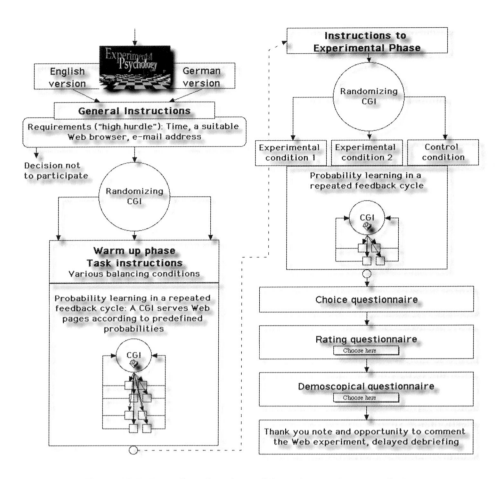

Figure 13.7: Procedure flowchart of the web experiment on the influence of causal mechanism information in the acquisition of
causal knowledge (Reips, 1996a, 1996b, 2000b)

13.5 Control Techniques for Conducting Web Experiments

13.5.1 Avoiding Data Garbage

At the end of the previous section, several techniques were presented which help
avoid collecting unusable data. One need not only check for double e-mail addresses
or IP-addresses, one could also notify participants in advance. One can rest assured

that the majority of the WWW population is not as versed in the medium's technology as to recognize the barriers of inspection of multiple participants. In general, one should be able to count on the goodwill of the participants – previous experience has shown that only very rarely will somebody disregard the request to take part only once (Reips, 1996b, 2000a). To a greater extent, this rule applies to experiments in which participation involves a certain amount of expenditure, because of its length and because of the "high hurdles" for the participant described above. It is equally supportive if the Web site is able to indicate that a genuine contractor or an institution of benefit to the public is involved in the research.

But what should be done with the enthusiastic participants, those that desperately want to see the whole thing again? Offer them a channeling possibility, the option of participating again. This could be implemented via a hyperlink or with a question at the beginning. One should generally try to compile verifiable information with the questions. Other questions can serve as indicators of accuracy and coherence: anyone claiming to be 18 years old and a grandmother at the same time should be handled with caution.

```
<SCRIPT language="JavaScript">
function browsertest (){
document.write("Congratulations, your browser has passed the JavaScript test!!!") }
</SCRIPT>
<FONT size=7>JavaScript Test</FONT>
<SCRIPT LANGUAGE="JavaScript">
{ browsertest(); }
</SCRIPT>
```

Figure 13.8: A JavaScript that tests a web browser's JavaScript
compatibility

Merely from a technical point of view, data garbage can be avoided by testing if the participant's Web browser supports all necessary features such as scroll-down menus and JavaScript (see Figure 13.8). If not, the participant should be referred to a source where the adequate Web browser can be downloaded. With the help of JavaScript one can also detect the participant's set monitor resolution.

13.5.2 Special Techniques

With the aid of certain tricks one can attain more control. For instance, with the installation of *password* technology, truly interested participants can be traced (see Figure 13.9, top). With this procedure, people interested in participating have to register their e-mail and snail-mail addresses and, if necessary, their fax and telephone numbers. Right away, or as soon as a sufficient amount of registrations has been compiled, the users interested in taking part are sent their login and password, although the distribution medium can be altered. (This variation also facilitates a later comparison of those groups that received their password via e-mail, those that received it in the mail and those that had their passwords faxed). Participants can be contacted reliably in the case of further questions. As a result, any participation in the experiment can be attributed to different people.

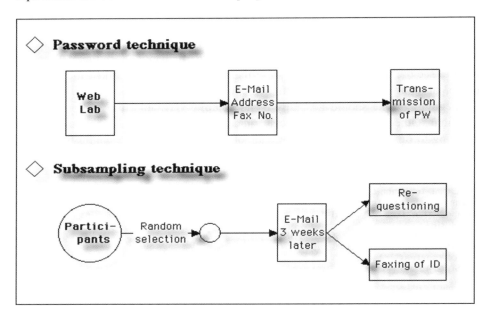

Figure 13.9: Password technique (top) and subsampling technique (bottom)

Another method is a random extraction of a *sub sample* from the total set of all test participants (see Figure 13.9, bottom). The members of this sub sample receive an e-mail that they only need to reply to with an empty e-mail. Firstly, one obtains an estimated value of the proportion of wrong address entries. Secondly, for the participant the expenditure of sending an empty reply is relatively minor, so that one can count on a large response rate. In a further posting the participants are asked to answer certain control questions with reference to the study. One can also request that the people in the sub sample fax back their ID card, and might then contact them repeatedly and rigorously until it is entirely clear who participated only once, and who participated in the experiment on numerous occasions.

Instead of extracting the sub sample after the Web experiment, one can also ensure from the onset that information on the test participants is available. This can be obtained via the *Participant Pool Technique* (see Figure 13.10). Members of a participant pool (also sometimes referred to as an "online panel", e.g., Maruccia, 1999, and similar to a "closed pool" approach, Voracek, Stieger, & Gindl, 2001) must sign an agreement stating their availability to take part in Web experiments or surveys. They enter their demographic data, which of course is processed together with possible test results and experimental data under a strict guarantee of confidentiality. Accordingly, one can reward participants for their participation in the studies. Participant pools also have the advantage of disclosing other studies a participant has taken part in. Additionally, a scientist can also use the data compiled on participants for "ordering" specifically selected persons with particular characteristics (e.g., a ratio of 50% men and 50% women). The participant pool technique (with formation of the pool on the Internet) is an ideal opportunity for researchers in smaller research facilities who have little access to participants and who, despite their use of the Internet, wish to exercise a modicum of control over whom takes part in their studies.

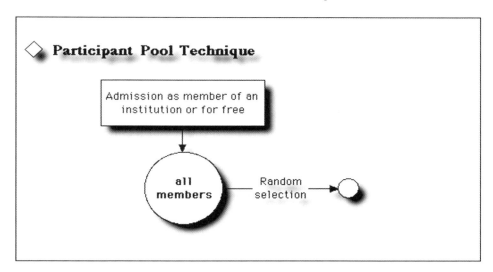

Figure 13.10: The participant pool technique

In the evaluation of data, techniques can also be used to ensure the quality of the data. One example was already mentioned above: only allow and evaluate first participation from one computer address (IP). Also, relative document download times, which are recorded by most Web server programs, can be used as a data filter. In a learning experiment, for example, one would not want to include the data of those participants who took a break during the test. This break can be defined precisely as a certain percentage increase in the average interval time between two learning stages.

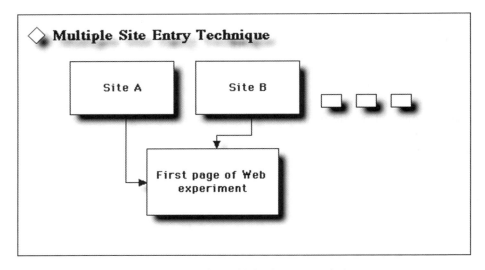

Figure 13.11: The multiple site entry technique

13.6 Epilogue

Web experiments are the method whereby the experimental method is transferred into the virtual world of the WWW. Thanks to the logic of experiments, causal relationships between variables can be examined without being hampered by the quest for representativeness in Internet samples that might be creating a stigma of researchers wandering naïvely into unfamiliar terrain. The WWW is suitable as a space for conducting experiments. The method also holds the promise of working in previously inaccessible areas (for instance with particular groups of people). Should the reader be interested in conducting a Web experiment, then come and visit one of the online laboratories, for example the Web Experimental Psychology Lab, Zürich: http://www .genpsy.unizh.ch/Ulf/Lab/WebExpPsyLab.html.

References

Batinic, B. & Bosnjak, M. (2000). Fragebogenuntersuchungen im Internet [Internet surveys]. In B. Batinic (Ed.), *Internet für Psychologen* (2nd ed.) (pp. 287-317) [Internet for psychologists]. Göttingen: Hogrefe.

Birnbaum, M. H. (2001). Online research and decision making. In U.-D. Reips & M. Bosnjak (Eds.), *Dimensions of Internet science* (pp. 23-55). Lengerich: Pabst Science Publishers.

Bordia, P. (1996). Studying verbal interaction on the Internet: The case of rumor transmission research. *Behavior Research Methods, Instruments, & Computers, 28*, 149-151.

Bredenkamp, J. (1996). Grundlagen experimenteller Methoden [Foundations of experimental methods]. In E. Erdfelder, R. Mausfeld, T. Meiser, & G. Rudinger (Eds.), *Handbuch Quantitative Methoden* (pp. 37-46). Weinheim: Psychologie Verlags Union.

Coomber, R. (1997). Using the Internet for survey research. *Sociological Research Online, 2.* [Online]. Available: http://www.socresonline.org.uk/socresonline/2/2/2.html.

Graphics, Visualization, & Usability Center (1997-2000). *GVU's www user surveys.* [Online]. Availble: http://www.cc.gatech.edu/gvu/user_surveys.

Hänze, M. & Meyer, H. A. (1997). Feldexperimente und nicht-reaktive Datenerhebung im World Wide Web [Field experiments and nonreactive data collection on the world wide web]. In D. Janetzko, B. Batinic, D. Schoder, M. Mattingley-Scott, & G. Strube (Eds.), *CAW-97: cognition & web* (pp.79-92). Freiburg: IIG-Berichte.

Kirk, R. E. (1995). *Experimental design: Procedures for the behavioral sciences* (3rd ed.). Pacific Grove: Brooks/Cole.

Krantz, J. H., Ballard, J., & Scher, J. (1997). Comparing the results of laboratory and world wide web samples on the determinants of female attractiveness. *Behavior Research Methods, Instruments, & Computers, 29,* 264-269.

Krantz, J. H. & Dalal, R. (2000). Validity of web-based psychological research. In M. H. Birnbaum (Ed.), *Psychological Experiments on the Internet* (pp. 35-60). San Diego, CA: Academic Press.

Kunst-Wilson, W. R. & Zajonc, R. B. (1980). Affective discrimination of stimuli that cannot be recognized. *Science, 207,* 557-558.

Lyberg, L., Biemer, P., Collins, M., De Leeuw, E., Dippo, C., Schwarz, N., & Trewin, D. (Eds.). (1997). *Survey measurement and process quality.* New York: Wiley.

Martin, D. W. (2000). *Doing psychology experiments* (5th. ed.). Belmont: Wadsworth.

Maruccia, F. (1999). Online Panels – ein Methodentest [Online panels – a test of method]. In U.-D. Reips, B. Batinic, W. Bandilla, M. Bosnjak, L. Gräf, K. Moser, & A. Werner (Eds.), *Current Internet Science – Trends, Techniques, Results. Aktuelle Online Forschung – Trends, Techniken, Ergebnisse.* [Online]. Available: http://dgof.de/tband99/.

Monte, C. F. (1975). *Psychology's scientific endeavor.* New York: Praeger.

Musch, J. & Reips, U.-D. (2000). A brief history of web experimenting. In M. H. Birnbaum (Ed.), *Psychological experiments on the Internet* (pp. 61-85). San Diego, CA: Academic Press.

Reips, U.-D. (1995a). *The web's experimental psychology lab.* [Online]. Available: http://www.genpsy.unizh.ch/Ulf/Lab/WebExpPsyLab.html.

Reips, U.-D. (1995b). *The web experiment method.* [Online]. Available: http://www.genpsy.unizh.ch/Ulf/Lab/WWWExpMethod.html.

Reips, U.-D. (1996a, April). Experimentieren im World Wide Web [Experimenting in the world wide web] [Abstract]. *Experimentelle Psychologie: Tagung experimentell arbeitender Psychologen* [Proceedings of the experimental psychologist's conference], Germany, 256-257.

Reips, U.-D. (1996b, October). *Experimenting in the world wide web*. Paper presented at the 1996 Society for Computers in Psychology conference, Chicago. [Online]. Available: http://www.genpsy.unizh.ch/reips/slides/scipschicago96.html.

Reips, U.-D. (1997). Forschen im Jahr 2007: Integration von Web-Experimentieren, Online-Publizieren und Multimedia-Kommunikation [Science in the year 2007: Integration of web experimenting, online publishing, and multimedia communication]. In D. Janetzko, B. Batinic, D. Schoder, M. Mattingley-Scott, & G. Strube (Eds.), *CAW-97: Cognition & web* (pp.141-148). Freiburg: IIG-Berichte.

Reips, U.-D. (1998). Web-Experiment [Web experiment]. In F. Dorsch, H. Häcker, & K.-H. Stapf (Eds.), *Psychologisches Wörterbuch* (13, pp. 943-944). Bern, Switzerland: Huber.

Reips, U.-D. (2000a). The web experiment method: Advantages, disadvantages, and solutions. In M. H. Birnbaum (Ed.), *Psychological experiments on the Internet* (pp. 89-114). San Diego, CA: Academic Press.

Reips, U.-D. (2000b). Das psychologische Experimentieren im Internet [Psychological experimenting on the Internet]. In B. Batinic (Ed.), *Internet für Psychologen* (2nd ed.) (pp. 319-343) [Internet for psychologists]. Göttingen, Germany: Hogrefe.

Reips, U.-D. (2001a). Merging field and institution: Running a web laboratory. In U.-D. Reips & M. Bosnjak (Eds.), *Dimensions of Internet science* (pp. 1-22). Lengerich: Pabst Science Publishers.

Reips, U.-D. (2001b). The web experimental psychology lab: Five years of data collection on the Internet. *Behavior Research Methods, Instruments, and Computers, 33*, 201-211.

Repräsentativität. Thread in mailing list (1997). *Archiv Mailingliste German Internet Research List gir-l.* [Online]. Available: http://infosoc.uni-koeln.de/archives/gir-l/msg00 253.html ff.

Schmidt, W. C. (1997). World wide web survey research: Benefits, potential problems, and solutions. *Behavior Research Methods, Instruments, & Computers, 29*, 274-279.

Sherif, M. & Sherif, C. W. (1954). *Groups in harmony and tension*. New York: Harper and Row.

Tanur, J. M. (1994). The trustworthiness of survey research. *Chronicle of Higher Education, 40*, B1-B3.

Voracek, M., Stieger, S., & Gindl, A. (2001). Online replication of results from evolutionary psychology research: Sex differences in sexual jealousy in imagined scenarios of sexual vs. emotional mate infidelity. In U.-D. Reips & M. Bosnjak (Eds.), *Dimensions of Internet science* (pp. 91-112). Lengerich: Pabst Science Publishers.

Wormser, R. (1974). *Experimentelle Psychologie*. München: Reinhardt.

14 Contact Measurement in the WWW

Andreas Werner

As with print and broadcast media, a contact and distribution measurement is also required for the World Wide Web (WWW). In the field of print media, circulation is calculated. In principle, the instrument is fairly simple. The publishing houses that wish to claim audited circulation's register their circulation's, as evident in their bookkeeping, with an ABC (Audit Bureau of Circulation). In Germany, the only institution of this kind is called IVW (Information Organization for the Registration of the Distribution of Advertising Vehicles). For their part, the ABCs publish the numbers and inspect the data. In some countries the data is available on a cost basis, in others the data is free of charge. This is a total census. The results are often referred to as a value for calculating advertising rates, yet, in the case of audience research, only provide marginal indications (see McQuail, 1998).

Representative surveys on online users have, as has already been mentioned repeatedly in this volume, been conducted by the GfK and Germany's public broadcasting institution, the ARD. In most of the relevant Internet markets there are many surveys. The Irish NUA initiative keeps an archive with abstracts of such studies. In the USA, the market research institute Nielsen conducted such surveys at a very early phase. In Germany, it took a little longer until the GfK (see Bronold, 1999) could acquire comparable values. In addition, there are also numerous studies in the most important advertising markets, where interviews are conducted on the basis of relatively large representative samples. In this manner, clarification is gained on the demography and consumer habits of the recipients. Broadcast media are also taken into account in the surveys. There is also another technical measurement tool for broadcast media: telemetry. In a panel of households that receive broadcast media, a measuring instrument is connected to the broadcast apparatus to log media use. In order to find out how many persons use the medium in each case, the panel participants (see Ang, 1991) have to log themselves on and off by pressing appropriate keys on a remote control apparatus. The methods specified in this section describe procedures which calculate values of use, and which are prone to certain error rates in the acquisition of data (see Noelle, Neumann, & Petersen, 1996).

In the Internet, the advertising market consists of two components. First, companies may advertise by maintaining a presence (site). In order for this site to be found, they promote the site (see Werner & Stephan, 1998). One tool for this type of site promotion is banner advertising (clickable graphics) on frequently visited presence's (see Werner, 2000). Understandably, the advertisers want to know how often people are exposed to their banners. For this purpose, a contact measurement is required. Due to the specific characteristics of the Internet this measurement should be a non-reactive total census. However, because of the specific characteristics inherent in the Internet, new measuring problems crop up. As will be demonstrated, this procedure is also suitable for deployment in scientific research, and in particular as an acquisition module for online experiments.

In this contribution, the measurement model conceived and developed by various German media organizations (amongst others: VDZ, BDZV, and dmmv), and first employed by the IVW in October 1997, will be described. In some features, this model differs from procedures used outside of Germany. The ABC interactive procedure, frequently distributed in the USA, will be used as comparison. Most of the differences are particularly obvious in the areas of data privacy and error rates.

14.1 The Measurement Principle

Online media can be classified as screen media. As a result, one may think that measurement should also be conducted according to the same method as broadcast media. Unfortunately, this does not apply (at least not entirely so, as will be discussed later). Regarding sites on the WWW, and the access offered to the information, one is instantly aware of the fact that content categories, at least in the beginning (1993 to 1997), correspond more to print media than to broadcast media. Transmission of information is a further characteristic crucial to measurement. In contrast to classic media, data is requested – and accessed individually. Why should these requests for data not simply be recorded in order to conduct the measuring procedure?

Obviously, this procedure may almost seem simple to execute. Why? WWW servers register all access activity and each request for a file in logfiles. By evaluating these files, the results should be straightforward to determine – and in the form of a sum census without distortions. Unfortunately, one has another thing coming. The Internet is a heterogeneous network based on the protocols TCP/IP (Transmission Control Protocol / Internet Protocol). One of the principles of the Net is (or should be) the minimization of data transfer volume. For this purpose, proxy servers are used which store frequently requested files in certain areas of the net, so that this data does not have to cover the full distance over the Internet.

One may ask oneself how current information can be accessed repeatedly? As a rule, the proxy server "asks" the source whether the information it has buffered is still up to date. This procedure is also logged. Unfortunately, this process only occurs "as a rule" – not all proxy servers are programmed as mindfully that they always inquire. This is also one of the most serious measuring problems on the WWW, but also an indication of the necessity of analysis of the technical structure of the Net (see also Werner, 1997).

14.2 Critical Factors

The data transferred via HTTP (Hypertext Transfer Protocol) is recorded in the logfiles. Normally, – one might assume – such a protocol, which represents a central network entity, should always be used and interpreted instantly. Unfortunately, that is not the case. There are a whole series of critical factors that influence the use of the log.

We can locate these problems at different points. Different computer platforms are connected to the Internet. These refer to different hardware configurations with different operating systems, which in turn also run different servers (programs!). In order to ensure consistent acquisition and evaluation, each possible configuration must use and document the same HTTP variables. Unfortunately, it is neither necessary to use all variables, nor are the same variables recorded automatically. However, modern servers can normally be programmed in such a manner that all servers included in a measurement system can produce equivalent logfiles, according to an agreement of the variables (in the correct sequence). This is necessary in order to evaluate logfiles with the same instrument, regardless of the operating system. There are no further problems, since the logfiles are all text files based on ASCII-format. The log should therefore not pose a problem.

More difficulties arise with proxy servers. Whilst the servers of the institutions participating in the measurement procedure can be manipulated – as stated, one can reach agreements on certain situations, which need to be standardized – this does not apply to proxy servers. What should prompt an organization, which does not want to produce data according to a netwide uniform standard, to configure their proxy server in such a manner that will facilitate documentation of the necessary variables? In the hybrid medium of the Internet, conventions are difficult to enforce, and convincing reasons hard to find without the support of central organizational instances. Therefore, the solution must consist in technically circumventing the inhomogeneous behavior of proxy servers, or searching for suitable auxiliary constructions to minimize deficits.

The situation is complicated further by the browsers. Netscape and Microsoft account for more than 90% market share with their products. Unfortunately, in this case, measuring software is also expected to attain comparable results on different platforms (Windows 3.x, 95, 98, NT; Apple; Unix). Since these products also vary from version to version in their "behavior" and "interpretation" of HTTP, a certain degree of uniformity must also be ensured.

Further, the user also has a whole range of possibilities to accommodate for auxiliary functions when configuring the browser. Accordingly, cookies[1] may be suitable for identifying individual computers, yet only on condition that the user accepts cookies or has not disabled the function. Additionally, there is still legal uncertainty in Germany over whether the use of the cookies for such a purpose, or without prior consent of the users, is permitted. The use of cookies also leads to yet further problems: the user can delete them, different users might use the same browser, the same user might use a different browser[2], etc.

Not only can the user disable cookies. Java, JavaScript, and Active X are additional programming languages, whose implementation permits more "interactivity" on the WWW. In order to eliminate another problem addressed further below JavaScript was used. A majority of users also has this option activated in their computers. JavaScript also frequently causes "errors" and system failures, in particular in Apple computers. It therefore seems as if Netscape JavaScript script interpreters do not function equally on all platforms. Besides, the problems referred to provoke some users to disable JavaScript. In this case as well, supplementary solutions are also required. Altogether, one should – if somehow possible – limit the acquisition of data to sources that are reliable despite different configurations. The focus is on finding the smallest common denominator. The values to be determined should, as far as possible, correspond to real values.

14.2.1 The Page Impression

Our next concern is to determine contact values. In the case of newspapers, one can control the distributed circulation, and thus an exemplary value. In the case of television, audience numbers can be gathered using meter technology. In the Internet, Page Impressions are the easiest size to measure. Page Impressions refer to all page contacts. In Germany, the official definition of the IVW is as follows:

Page Impressions (previously known as PageViews) designate the number of visual contacts by any user with a potential, advertisement carrying HyperText Markup Language (HTML) -page. They provide a measure of use for individual pages in a certain presence. If a presence contains screen pages consisting of one or more frames (frameset), then only the contents of one frame are counted as a unit of content. The primary request for a frameset therefore only counts as one Page Impression, just as each further change induced by the user in the appropriate content

---

[1] Cookies are identification strings written in a text file.
[2] It still depends on whether the browsers use the same or different cookie files.

frames. Only one Page Impression is counted per user action. In order to ensure a census consistent with this definition, the content provider can, in each case, only load the described content into one frame per frameset (http://www.ivw.de/).

Let us begin with a serious problem in the acquisition and definition. Numerous advertising vehicles on the WWW use frame technology. The browser window is then composed of different HTML files. The advantage for the provider is that less elements necessary for navigation of the site have to loaded, as opposed to a design that demands that these elements have to be transferred with every new click. In the case of carefully planned frame design this can facilitate navigation for the user.

However, when using frame designs, several page requests can be induced by a single user action ("click") – each frame window has its own HTML file. Yet only user actions should be measured. This is quite obviously an action-oriented variable, the interpretation of which is made more difficult by a distortion of user actions. Unfortunately, this is not made clear by IVW's definition. It reads: "In order to ensure a census consistent with this definition, the content provider can, in each case, only load the described content into one frame per frameset". This quite plainly interferes in the advertising vehicle's design autonomy, which is by no means necessary, from the point of view of measurement technology. The measurement is registered – as already suggested above – by the request of a transparent image via a Common Gateway Interface (CGI) script. This request is included in the HTML file to be counted. The IVW clause should therefore read: "In order to ensure a census consistent with this definition, the content provider can, in each case, only load one distinctly characterized file per user action". In this manner, the provider's freedom of design remains in tact, and precise measurement still feasible.

14.2.1.1   Push Elements

Push elements do not refer to Push technologies such as PointCast, Marimba or NetCaster. Instead, these are elements that are loaded into the browser window without any further actions executed by the user. The measurement problem crops up when HTML pages are reloaded automatically, in order to obtain determined effects, and if a new request were to be counted each time. The internal regulations of the IVW exclude this procedure. This is unfortunately not spelled out in the Page Impression definition. A change of definition – as was suggested in the course of the measurement of framed offers – would also amend this problem. Only one Page Impression should be counted per user action. Unfortunately, different international audit organizations hold different concepts. If one is to examine whether data is comparable in this instance, one would need to first examine whether the technology is in accordance with the site.

14.2.1.2   Convincing Proxy Servers

As mentioned above, some proxy servers do not independently inform the server of an advertising medium whether determined documents have been requested. In the IVW measurement concept these are convinced by a "CGI" script. In the business, this procedure is known as cachebusting. Once again of interest in this context: the comparison of the systems in the USA and Germany. In the USA, sites can use various cachebusting procedures, but are not required to conform to the underlying measurement system. In Germany, the procedure is completely standardized. Only one survey method may be used. In the USA, different survey methods may be used and inevitably lead to different results.

A further critical instance in the measurement procedure is the browser. These must recognize and acknowledge the CGI instructions in exactly the same manner as the proxy servers. This is required in order to measure the use of the "back" buttons – defined as a user action. It quickly became obvious that the Microsoft Internet Explorer does not support CGI commands in all versions[3].

The IVW tried to master the problem with the use of JavaScript. Despite the fact that the Script needs to be integrated into every file, and would therefore lead to an increase in data traffic, a whole series of further problems crop up. As already mentioned above, the Script can cause system failures on Macintosh computers. Additionally, JavaScript interpretation can be disabled. Valid measurement would therefore seem impossible.

Alternately, another method seems passable. Should the hypothesis apply that Netscape Navigator (or Communicator) and Microsoft Internet Explorers users are equal in their use behavior patterns. Then the effect of the use of "back" buttons can also be computed. This would spare a detour via the implementation of JavaScripts.

14.2.1.3   Agents

In the meantime, a relatively large number of accesses to WWW sites are carried out via search engine spiders, or other types of agents. Since only requests induced by users are to be counted, all that is needed is the user-agent HTTP variable in order to attain a positive sample. Only those entries made by a browser's user agent are counted. Altavista's spider "Scooter", for example, cannot be included. In this instance, procedure is similar in both the USA and Germany. Only human requests are to be counted. However, the system common in Germany seems somewhat more secure since it is based on CGI, not on file, requests. CGIs are hardly ever requested by agents.

---

[3]   As in so many other cases, Microsoft does not abide by general specifications. The aim is to lull users into believing that their product is quicker than Netscape's. This problem was particularly severe in some of the 3.xx versions.

14.2.2 The Visit: "Visits" Do Not Mean "Visitors"

The number of page contacts is not sufficient to adequately illustrate patterns of use on a WWW Site. The number of the visitors would also be of interest. Unfortunately, this type of measurement is not possible, because users who access the Internet via a dial-up line are, in most cases, dynamically assigned a certain IP address that in each case only applies to one Internet session. If an Internet address is registered in the logfile one can only assume a single user. Yet there are often several. Consequently, this form of addressing is not suitable for measuring visitors.

In America this measurement was tried via obligatory user identification with the use of a password. As a result this led to a decrease in visitors on particular sites – as with Hotwired. As a rule, a method that has such grave repercussions for the test result cannot be considered useful.

A further component used to identify visitors (without actually knowing who it was) is the cookie developed by Netscape. Cookies are files that are installed in the users' computers, which contain certain content providers' identification strings (combinations of characters). These combinations of characters should save the users from having to enter a password repeatedly when visiting sites where individual settings are possible. Naturally, this string could also be used to identify visitors. Unfortunately, this procedure has several catches. If the user were to enter his e-mail address or his name on such a site, then the data could provide personal information. From the point of view of privacy, the evaluation would be considered suspicious. This is not the only instance that hinders valid measurement with the use of cookies. Users can disable the function or write-protect the file. For that reason, a valid measurement cannot be ensured.

Because cookies were considered precarious in light of data privacy demands in the USA, different companies developed an Open Profiling Standard (OPS). In the meantime OPS was integrated into P3P, W3C's Privacy Preference Project. With this standard the user is to be put in the position of being able to determine when and where they hand over which data. I would like to take the liberty of making the prognosis that P3P would not be feasible in Germany for measuring visitors. The sensibility in Germany regarding privacy laws it is so extreme that useful information will only reach servers in the rarest of cases. The opportunities are substantially higher in America, even if one can count on systematic losses to distort the results.

What now?

If no visitors can be measured, then at least visits should be measured. As can be expected, there are once again hurdles in HTTP characteristic. A time of access and request can be measured, yet no time for site departure. For this reason, one would have to make an informed guess on when a user left a site: after 5, 10, 15, or perhaps

30 minutes. Since Internet addresses are multiply assigned, it can unfortunately also occur that another user can make a request with the same address. The phenomenon is further increased if access is via a proxy server. Visits that were longer than eight hours were occasionally measured yet were not recognized as stemming from the same user due to other criteria. Since the time factor in this case would lead to strong distortions in the measurement, thereby rendering it invalid, another criterion is required. HTTP in its current version 1.0 also recognizes the referrer variable. This indicates the last file requested. It is easy to determine whether a user has accessed the presence from the outside. The definition reads: A visit designates a coherent use procedure (Visit) of a WWW presence. It defines the contact with the advertising medium. Technically speaking, a use procedure counts as a successful page request by an Internet browser for the current presence, if it takes place from the outside (http://www.ivw.de/).

One might be able to argue about whether the definition was solely "developed" technically, and therefore bears no resemblance to actual user behavior. What is meant is the fact that a visitor on a search engine very often generates very short visits. The reason for this is as follows: every time a user receives a search engine's list of results, clicks on all links on the results page, and then onto the "back" button, he would, according to the IVW software, be generating a new visit with each click on this button. If asked, probably not one user would claim to have made several visits. The value therefore contradicts "user actions" in its very conception.

A definition, which is so dependent on its technology, can unfortunately not be formulated in any other way for the purpose of measuring contacts for a generally accepted system. In any other case, the content structure of the site to be measured by the IVW would have to be determined and examined by the IVW. In this manner, one could somewhat approximate the census technique and the value's definition with users' actual behavior. As long as advertising revenues remain as low as they are, what may seem logical in an individual case, will be impossible to implement in a system with over one hundred participating sites.

However, acquisition technology that implements referrals is not 100% reliable either. The variable is not passed on by some proxy servers. With an algorithm consisting of the HTTP-headers Forward, Via, and User-Agent, as well as the time factor, one will gain another variable apart from Internet addresses. In the USA, one hardly bothers with standardizing Visit measurements. There are numerous definitions and measuring procedures. Cookies or time intervals are normally implemented. The rule of thumb is, for example: "if there hasn't been an access via the same Internet address, a new Visit is counted." Problems crop up particularly often with ISPs. Europe's largest ISP – T-Online – (still) processes individual requests via different proxy servers. In this case, a measurement using the space procedure could never be executed.

14.2.3 ViewTime – "Viewing Time" or "Activity Time"?

Time measurements are already common in print media research: reading times are measured – backed up by a highly advanced questionnaire methodology. In the context of broadcast media, times are calculated using different methods – differences crop up. Why shouldn't view times for pages and/or sites also be culled online? The question is justified, yet does not quite adopt the right approach. First, one should ask for the reason why "view times" are counted for print objects and the broadcast media. These studies are conducted because connections in effect between "view times" and advertising success can be traced back to advertising recall! When analyzing the medium a little more, one will soon discover that banner advertising on online advertising media serves primarily to reroute the advertising vehicle's user to the advertiser's Web site. Thus, actions are demanded and not only cognitive effects. A click on a banner can be measured exactly. What is the point in examining view time and cognitive effects, except – perhaps – for reasons of pure scientific interest?

If there were only banners, as we have come to know so far, one would not need a value for banner planning – it is insignificant and only complicates planning procedure. If, however, one is concerned with improving individual sites, then knowing how long users are occupied with which contents is extremely important. "Activity times" are equally important in advertising contents, which are not only a banner, but permit interactivity within a file (e.g., JavaApplets, Shockwaves, Flash movies etc.). The advertising success also arises due to interest in a file via cognitive processes. Actions "within" can only be measured with a standardized process with enormous difficulties since the files often differ in their programming language, and the executable commands no longer keep to relatively simple mechanisms of hypertext and form.

Therefore, – regardless of whether one wants to or not – interpretation models similar to those used in classical media, have to be implemented for the time being. Survey methods for measuring "activity time" are required.

Measuring ViewTime

The procedure for measuring ViewTime is anything but simple. Only version 1.0 of HTTP allows for documentation of the time of transmission of a file, but not for the time of departure from a site (e.g., by clicking on an external link). In the logfile (n) times are listed for file requests. With these (n) requests, (n-1) time spans can be calculated. The "view time" period for the last pages of a Visit is omitted.

Various suggestions were made during the course of the development of the IVW software. It was first suggested that each last page of a Visit be granted 30 seconds' "view time". The result would be equally invalid if one were to grant the last page of a Visit the average "view time" of all measurable pages. This mathematical formula does not pose a viable solution. The next step was the implementation of a JavaScript. If one only wanted to measure the content's "view time" in which the factor, as described above, plays a role, then the use of Java Scripts is quite feasible. When using the content, the feature is normally required to enable it in the Browser anyway. To that extent, a measurement of the addressed content could be executed. The acquisition of data cannot, however, be completed validly. JavaScript can only register user actions within the browser environment.

What the user does besides looking at the browser on his computer is not included in the measurement: he might change to another program, he can cut the modem connection, the system can crash, he might switch off his computer without ending the programs appropriately etc. From a wholly technical point of view two options remain for employing Java Scripts: it can announce when a certain hyperlink is activated, or it can send impulses in regular intervals. The first possibility was discussed in the context of the IVW implementation. The latter can be used, for example, in the context of test procedures for measuring how long a user remains on a test site before breaking off.

Consequently, gaining valid and comparable for the entire online business is hardly possible. In the case of a scientific survey of sites, a pulse generator can be installed in the pages, and the transmission of impulses suppressed by JavaScript.

14.2.4 Measurement Differences in AdServers

The Internet is a heterogeneous network. From the user's view, it does not matter which files come from which servers in order to be formed into a viewable and usable page in the browser window. The Net makes interactivity possible and, due to the ability to record user actions easily, permits improving advertising campaigns. In addition, AdServers are necessary. These special servers facilitate handling advertising banners. For example, in this way it is possible to reserve advertising inventory only at certain times of day or prevent banner burnout. The AdClickRate, i.e., the number of banner clicks in relation to the visual contacts on a page, sinks along with an increase in visual contacts. This situation is known as banner burnout.

In most cases, AdServers come installed with their own technology for measuring Impressions. Since the products normally come from North America, however, the collection and analysis software function differently from those used in the IVW system. Differences crop up when determining Page Impressions. With most standard products the command line cannot be adapted to the requirements of the IVW. For the time being, the differences will have to be tolerated. If advertising vehicles use AdServers the results are hardly decisive. The client rarely notices anything of the difference. However, if the standard products are used by planning and allocation agencies difficulties can arise, since the difference can add up to ten percent or more.

14.2.5 Susceptibility to Manipulation

A collection system, which like the GfK Meter and the remaining IVW figures, contributes to shaping the market must naturally also be immune against manipulation.
After all, advertising revenues are set in relation to contact numbers. The Nielsen and
GfK meters include controls that examine via telephone whether what is noted by
meters is also correct. The IVW inspects the publishers' bookkeeping records in order to validate circulation numbers. Similar control mechanisms must also be integrated into the Internet – only what sort?

Logfiles are simple text files. Nothing would be simpler than increasing the file
via copy and paste. Obviously, it is not quite as simple as that. The time of request is
also recorded in the logfiles. Using a simple algorithm, manipulations would be de-
tectable. Although the situation could be further complicated if a service provider
were to feign "human" requests with an accordingly programmed agent. Depending
upon the expenditure invested by the advertising medium, detecting manipulation is
virtually impossible. However, in this case, expenditure and possible results would
be out of proportion. Those intent on manipulating results would have to inaugurate a
lot of people, so that the manipulation could be discovered entirely "nonvirtually".

14.2.6 Overall Assessment

Despite the numerous problems mentioned, the IVW's collection technology is relatively precise. One should not forget that this is a total census without statistic falsification. The procedure provides minimum values. And Page Impressions can be
measured more precisely than Visits. The two core values probably suffice for a media planner – scientists normally want to know a little more. The IVW software also
accommodates for this. The acquisition module also documents an SQL-compatible
database sorted according to Click Streams, which can be evaluated according to
preference using the appropriate statistics or data base programs. In Germany it will
nevertheless take time until more information is available on users and their request
for certain contents. Since 1997, W3C has been occupied with developing P3P (Platform for Privacy Preferences). Its main interest is to allow users to decide which data
they surrender to the site's administrators. If the user can decide for himself, the data
record of information that can be evaluated will be very heterogeneous. There will be
an enormous amount of missing values.

Yet the method's largest deficit lies in the fact that contact figures and usage mi-
grations can "only" be determined for individual sites. Usage migration on the Net
cannot be documented with the aid of this nonreactive procedure. Instead, this can be
measured by analyzing the very proxy servers that were described above as being so
annoying (see Berker's contribution in this volume). What must be considered is that

the evaluation of proxy logfiles is unfortunately only applicable to behavior patterns demonstrated by a sub population of Web users.

In general, the search for the audience – if one is allowed to call it that – may still take some time. In line with Ien Ang's (1991) own words for describing television research, – "Desperately Seeking the Audience" – and in the hope that in such an early stage of research activity, no despair should arise just yet.

References

Ang, I. (1991). *Desperately seeking the audience*. London. New York: Routledge.

Eimeren, B. v., Oehmichen, E., & Schröter, C. (1997). ARD-Online-Studie 1997: Online-nutzung in Deutschland. Nutzung und Bewertung der Onlineangebote von Radio- und Fernsehsendern. *Media-Perspektiven, 10*, 548-557.

McQuail, D. (1998). *Audience analysis*. Thousand Oaks, London, New Dehli: SAGE.

Noelle-Neumann, E. & Petersen, T. (1996). *Alle, nicht jeder. Einführung in die Methoden der Demoskopie*. München: dtv.

Werner, A. (2000). *Site promotion*. Heidelberg: dpunkt.verlag.

Werner, A. (1997). Werbeträgerkontakt- und -verbreitungsmessung im WWW. In K.- P. Boden & M. Barabas (Eds.), *Internet – von der Technologie zum Wirtschaftsfaktor* (pp. 119-128). Heidelberg: dpunkt.

Werner, A. & Stephan, R. (1998). *Marketing-Instrument Internet* (2nd ed.). Heidelberg: dpunkt.verlag.

15 Lurkers in Mailing Lists

Christian Stegbauer & Alexander Rausch

Numerous publications on the Internet and on Internet-based communication groups are based upon speculation, and do not refer to empirical data. When studies are based on data, then these are normally derived from surveys, or observations of particularly active users. Both methods, the use of reactive instruments[1], but in particular selective awareness of individual users, can lead to biased results. Often, a small part of the entire usership's behavior spectrum is extracted and applied to all participants – sometimes even to an entire generation of actors. Such data is also frequently used when characterizing Internet-based social spaces as a whole (e.g., Turkle, 1995; Tapscott, 1998). In contrast, the study presented here uses neither a reactive instrument, nor does it generalize the analysis of a minority of active participants. Instead, passive users are the focus of attention. Hopefully, a more balanced overall view of Internet-based communication forums may be possible.

This contribution is based on data culled from a *series of participant registers* and text archives in mailing lists, in other words, from longitudinal data. The examination is aimed at finding out the role of passive users in mailing lists (i.e., passive participants). The survey thereby picks up on a phenomenon whose interpretation has already provoked a broad of spectrum of opinions and conjecture. On the one hand, lurkers are reviled as freeriders since they collect information communicated by active users without making a contribution in return (e.g., Kollock & Smith, 1994). Other considerations state that lurkers are unnecessary for communication, if not an obstruction; they only exhaust bandwidth (Schoenberger, 1998).

Lurking is often thought of as spying, or even more seriously as voyeurism. Obviously, some participants find it unpleasant that their messages are distributed to a larger number of users without these being recognizable as an audience. Another view describes lurking as a fleeting phenomenon: in netiquettes one is requested to follow the discussion first for a while in order to become active later on, having gained more knowledge of the topic, the status of discussion, and the regulations within the communication space. In this manner, the communication space is pro-

---

[1] If opinions are requested, the risk is great that known judgments on effects are reproduced. Schmutzer (1997) expresses an opinion on this topic.

tected against redundant and unqualified contributions, and fewer references need to be made to generally accepted rules of conduct. A third view is held by Stegbauer and Rausch (1999) who state that lurking is considered structurally necessary in order to avoid "information overload". Lurkers also contribute to guaranteeing the "conditions of the possibility of communication", and are thus indispensably necessary for enabling communication, in particular in larger user groups.

15.1 Problems in Defining Lurking

When authors write about lurking it is remarkable how vague the respective authors' conception of this phenomenon is. As a result, completely passive users are sometimes referred to as lurkers. Yet it can also be that those participants have not written a contribution within the last month but are still identified as lurkers (Sproull & Faraj, 1997). The only consensus is on the fact that there are numerous lurkers. Accordingly, Fassler (1997), for example, quotes a survey stating that 90% of participants remained passive.

Such numbers are based on estimations or speculation since so far no method has been found to determine the number or proportion of lurkers. Consequently, empirical analysis is necessary. First, though, a clear definition is required.

It is not even clear what lurking means. Is passivity a feature that is static, and remains that way? In other words, is it an individual characteristic of or an intention of a section of the participants? It would seem reasonable to assume that this is correct if one takes into account the insults or the above mentioned studies. Another facet is also possible: passive users only wait for topics of interest before becoming active[2]. Another hypothesis would be that a constant ebb and flow in users is to be found in discussion forums, and that many users behave similarly to zappers in front of a television set, or to aimless surfers in the World Wide Web (WWW) who visit the forum briefly and leave immediately.

In order to characterize the phenomenon, two levels must be isolated: the individual behavior level and the level of the respective communication space's structure. Irregardless of whether lurking is a static phenomenon on the individual level or only a transition phase from a passive to an active user, one can ask whether social space

---

[2] Such a situation is described by Baym (1997, p.111) who examined an American newsgroup on soap operas: "A lurker alluded to this responsibility when she responded to a post that thanked her for unlurking to post a New Yorker magazine article about AMC (AMC is the abbreviation for the television series concerned. It means: All My Children): I'm also glad for the chance to add something to this ongoing stimulating dialogue!! I've been lurking for several weeks now, but rarely post, since you all seem to already have so many fun things to say!"

requires such a position and what sort of function such a position, which can be occupied by completely different people, would have.

A definition and operationalization would also have to be aimed at the researcher's particular focus of interest.

Lurkers can hardly be tracked down by means of classical Internet research methods. Cross section surveys are not suitable for obtaining data on a phenomenon potentially dependent on progression. Passive, or practically invisible users cannot be observed either. Whilst lurkers seem completely inaccessible in newsgroups, the member register and text archives at least offer some sort of a reference point for a quantification of the proportion of lurkers. However, when counting the membership register, relatively high (to date indefinite) fluctuation must be taken into account with the result that a survey using this method seems just as doubtful.

The approach taken here combines archive data analysis with the analysis of a sufficiently long series of member registers. In mailing lists, normally all messages intended for the social space are archived. These files are normally accessible to all members, and sometimes to outsiders. As far as accessibility is concerned, the same also applies to member registers. These are not archived, but updated at each modification. The modifications are usually not logged. The basis of observations conducted in this survey were the member registers of a number of topically related mailing lists, which were accessed monthly over a period of two years. In this manner, by combining this information with the archives, each individual user's behavior patterns can be drawn up.

15.2 Database

The observation period ran from September 1996 until September 1998. The behavior of those people who subscribed to one of the lists (see Table 15.1) between September 1996 and September 1997 was tracked. However, that was not feasible for all of the included mailing lists: the "Popper" list has not published its register since December 1997.

Table 15.1: Different mailing lists were included in the survey

List name	E-mail address of the list server	List exists since
Critical-Café	Majordomo@mjmail.eeng.dcu.ie	November 1995
Descartes L	listserv@bucknell.edu	July 1995
Hegel L	listserv@bucknell.edu	April 1995
Kant L	listserv@bucknell.edu	January 1994
Logic L	listserv@bucknell.edu	March 1994
Phil-Logic	listserv@bucknell.edu	June 1995
Popper	listserv@maelstrom.stjohns.edu	October 1995

Lurking is defined in an operational sense of the term here: lurkers are those participants who did not make a contribution in the first 12 months after subscribing to
the list. In this way, an individual time scale can be plotted for each participant. This
scale determines the entrance time as month "0", the month of subscription. By combining these with archive data, one can determine which subscribers went active at
which point in time during the observation period, and who remained passive. Apart
from examining lurking, a chronological profile of activity can be created on the
newly subscribed posters.

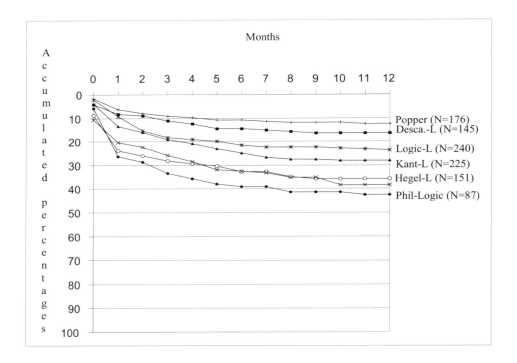

Figure 15.1: Time until the first contribution in months (participants who subscribed
to the mailing list for less than twelve months were also included)

In an examination of all of the included mailing lists, on average only 30% of all selected subscribers went active within 12 month. In other words, about 70% of the
users can be defined as lurkers. All of the newly subscribed members of the various
mailing lists are entered in the above diagram. First, one can observe that the proportion of lurkers varies according to the lists. In all lists, lurkers make up the majority
of new members. In the list with the lowest lurker proportion, Phil-logic, their pro-

portion amounts to about 55%. The most lurkers amongst those newly subscribed during the test period could be found in the Popper list, about 85%.

Figure 15.1 indicates one disadvantage: those participants who left the communication forum again shortly after subscribing are also subtracted. Therefore, Figure 15.2 only shows those users who were members in their respective communication space for at least one year.

It can be noted that they made their first contribution relatively shortly after subscribing. After approximately four months the probability that a user who was inactive until then will contribute is very small.

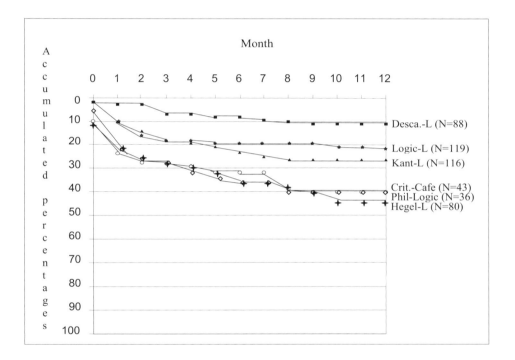

Figure 15.2: Time until the first contribution in months (participants who subscribed to the mailing list for less than twelve months were also included)

As a result, it can be stated: among the majority of users, lurking is not a transitional phenomenon but a fixed behavior pattern.

The very different proportion of lurkers is however not obviously related to the content or respective topics of the mailing list. Instead it depends heavily on the volume of messages in each individual social space. The next diagram (see Figure 15.3) shows this relationship: the smaller the volume of postings, the higher the proportion of lurkers.

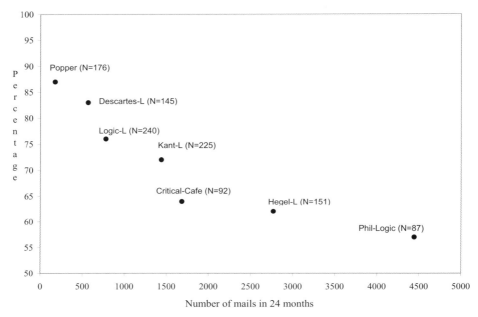

Figure 15.3: Proportion of lurkers versus mail volume (on the basis
of all newly subscribed participants)

This relation can be explained as a result of the differences between the individual effort, the time spent reading all of the detailed messages and dealing with them, and the user's individual interest. To sum up, this means that the costs of participation in various mailing lists increases with the number of the dispatched mails. In this fashion, selection amongst users sets in fairly rapidly – only those really interested stay, the rest shy away from the excessive number of messages in their mailboxes and withdraw again fairly quickly. In a list with a small volume of messages, however, occasional postings are accepted, and are considered less of a nuisance. Furthermore, the possible deletion of a posting causes less effort than looking up the mail server address and unsubscribing. In addition: the less messages on a certain mailing list are received, the longer it takes for a user to be in the picture on the respective list. What is possible in larger lists within a few days can take months in a rarely frequented list. For example, the Popper-List has a volume of 7 mails per month whilst Phil-logic has 185. A participant on the Popper list would need to spend more than two years to read exactly the same amount of messages a Phil-logic subscriber receives in one month.

In this respect, the procedure presented here is somewhat vague. Since the member registers were only retrieved once a month, a documentation gap arises for those participants who were "passagers" (i.e., those who simply took a brief look into the list and disappeared again quickly).

15.2.1 Characterization of Passive Users

With the help of information supplied by the e-mail address, lurkers can be described more exactly in comparison to the active users. The users come from all over the world, whereby North America, with approximately 65% of all users, and Europe, with about 22%, are clearly dominant. Due to the language problems and behavior patterns specific to different nationalities in mailing lists, as found in another context (Stegbauer & Rausch, 1999), one must assume that the proportion of lurkers is larger in peripheral areas than in the hubs in North America and Europe. This assumption could not be confirmed, at least not with the help of the relatively inaccurate top level domain analysis[3]. Only a weak, and insignificant indication of our hypothesis was found when top level domains were arranged according to the language sets "English" and "not English"[4].

15.2.2 Affiliation to the Community

Homans (1961) was of the opinion that one could measure relationships between humans or between humans and groups with the help of communication frequency. If one follows this, not at all undisputed, view[5], less community affiliation is to be expected amongst passive users than amongst the active users. Less affiliation would be measured by a higher proportion of users who had unsubscribed. In the operation-

---

[3] Top level domains are the letter combinations at the end of e-mail addresses. This analysis is inaccurate because the origin cannot always be indicated precisely, as is the case with "de". The "com" ending, for example, is used internationally by some providers.

[4] It is possible that the effect assumed by us is covered by an interaction. Whilst specialists are occupied with the lists in the peripheral areas, further classes, with access to the center, then operate as lurkers more so than the highly interested participants in the peripheral areas. Otherwise, maybe those communication forums that are apparently boundless play a stronger role in the peripheral areas since the informal channels are absent in the scientific audience due to a lack of mass.

[5] For a critical review see Neidthardt (1983).

alization, users who only contributed one message were differentiated to those who wrote more than one message.

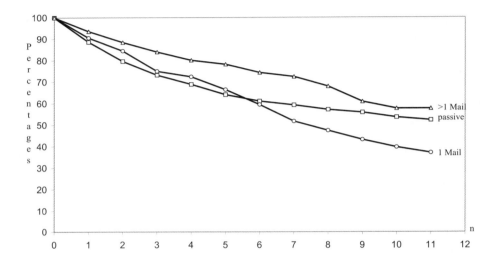

Figure 15.4: Proportion participants still subscribed after n months
(Critical-Cafe, Descartes-L, Hegel-L, Kant-L, Logic-L, Phil-Logic;
passive: 668 participants, active: 272 participants; of these: 1 mail
116 participants; and: >1 mail 156 participants)

This hypothesis is partly confirmed by the data: of those who contributed more than one message, scarcely 60% were still subscribed to the list after 12 months; of those who only wrote one message, fewer than 40% were still enlisted after one year (see Figure 15.4). Those that participate more frequently are less inclined to give up their membership than lurkers. A far larger proportion of those who only write one message is liable to give up their membership. It seems as if the users classified in this category are more likely to engage in an instrumental relationship with the mailing list. In other words, the one message written is instrumental in discovering information (for instance, on literature for a thesis (diploma) or the likes). After receiving the answer, their interest in the contents of the mailing list also fades.

15.2.3 Intersections in Social Spaces

The question was asked above whether lurkers represent a fixed social position that might be necessary to ensure communication at all in view of the threat of "information overload". This question cannot be answered with the help of this data. One can however explore whether it is always the same people who behave passively in different lists. If lurkers really were necessary as a social position this does not mean that this position is always occupied by the same people. Therefore, one must distinguish between the social position as such which always exists even if divergent participants fall into this category, and the position an individual user earns in a certain social space[6]. It seems evident that such a social position exists (Stegbauer & Rausch, 1999), but that this position is always occupied by the same persons is not evident. If individual people are subscribed to several mailing lists, they could be active in one, yet listening passively in another.

Since the lists included are all forums concerned with a similar topic, this suggests a synoptic outlook. Are lurkers on one list also passive in others? Of the 823 participants who subscribed to one of the observed mailing lists between September 1996 and September 1997, 25 participants can be found who count to the lurkers in one or more mailing lists, yet are simultaneously active in one or two other lists. This is not a high proportion, however. Altogether, there are only 89 intersections.

When the synoptic view is expanded to active participation in the Usenet the picture changes[7]. Nevertheless, 28% of those who behaved passively in the examined mailing lists sent postings to newsgroups during the test period. The proportion of posters amongst the active mailing list members is only barely higher at 34%.

Not all lurkers are also passive in other discussion forums. This suggests that the social status of passive membership is not always occupied by the same participants. With this important realization, the attitude towards lurkers, as quoted above, can be brought into relation (Kollock & Smith, 1994; Schoenberger, 1998). Even if they remain passive in some mailing lists, a not so small proportion of lurkers can be active in other social spaces. Lurkers, just like active members, could thereby fulfill a function by connecting otherwise isolated social spaces. They possibly contribute to the passing on of contents between mailing lists and from mailing lists into the Usenet. Precisely this sort of slight group affiliation, or so-called "weak ties" (Granovetter, 1973; 1982; Feldman, 1987) as Burt (1992) demonstrated in his contemplation on structural holes, is essential for the transfer of knowledge between social spaces otherwise separated from each other. Such a function thereby helps to hinder repeatedly feared fragmentation (e.g., Wehner, 1997) or to reduce it, and make content available beyond the subscriber base of a mailing list.

---

[6] Nadel (1957) offers the initiating theory on roles and status for the later development of empirical surveys with the aid of the block model analysis (White et al., 1976).

[7] On one of the news search engines, in this case Dejanews, everybody's activities in the Usenet can be traced (with a few exceptions).

15.3 Discussion

We introduced a method for analysis of a class of participants, which had hitherto been classed as unable to investigate. One can draw on the data traces left behind in the data networks by individuals invisible elsewhere. On the one hand, it was proven that those participants who do not become active soon after subscription would hardly change this behavior. On the other hand, there are those participants among lurkers who can be quite active in other contexts.

When talking about passive users are we dealing with freeloaders, or can the role of the lurker be otherwise reassessed? On the basis of the studies conducted for this contribution, several arguments can be derived which are of importance for the role of the lurker in mailing lists.

If one were to argue that lurkers really are just freeloaders, then one would have to assume that their proportions are largest in those lists with large messaging volumes because these are the most rewarding. However, these lists exhibited the smallest proportion of passive members, at least amongst those who were newly subscribed during the survey period. Obviously, a type of "law of inertia" can be applied instead, which turns curious passers-by into lurkers. If only a few messages emanate from a communication space the decision of what function to attribute to membership is hardly forced upon the participant, since it only costs little attention.

One can see in broad sections that lurkers basically do not remain equally passive in all social spaces. For example, many contribute to the exchange of ideas in news-groups. Via weak ties they might even occupy a function in stuffing so-called structural holes (Burt, 1992). In light of strict segregation between individual communication spaces, this function is particularly important in order to avoid too great a degree of fragmentation.

Those who contribute actively to a mailing list obtain the possibility of forming an identity and attaining prestige on account of this. Even passive users form an audience and, in so doing, partake in the formation and distribution of prestige.

In those lists where participants can reap the most benefits by listening in (i.e., in lists with high message volumes), lurkers contribute to the preservation of the requirements for potential communication. These lists would probably be threatened by a further increase in communication sequences.

Lurkers do not actually disturb communication; as an active participant one does not acknowledge them. The actual community is only created by those participants who are perceptible to others via an identity. Amongst active participants these only form a small minority.

Numerous messages, in mailing lists too, which actually serve as scientific communication, only wish to inform members about certain things. It should nevertheless be legitimate not to want to miss such information without having to contribute actively.

The question remains why lurkers are nonetheless frequently harangued as freeloaders. Despite the fact that the results of this analysis are not accessible to everyone, one could interpret such conduct as a sign of social bonding – even though this is paradox since participation is welcomed. For lack of any other easily recognizable features in the type of segregation, a simple substitute explanation could be found in the general condemnation of a user caste.

References

Baym, N. K. (1997). Interpreting soap operas and creating community: Inside an electronic fan culture. In S. Kiesler (Ed.), *Culture of the Internet* (pp. 103-120). Mahwah, NJ: Erlbaum.

Burt, R. S. (1992). *Structural holes: The social structure of competition.* Cambridge, Mass.: Harvard University Press.

Faßler, M. (1997). Sphinx "Netz". Die Wirklichkeit computerbasierter Netzwerke. *Medienpädagogik online, 2,* 4-9.

Feldman, M. S. (1987). Electronic mail and weak ties in organisations. *Office, Technology, and People, 3,* 83-101.

Granovetter, M. S. (1973). The strength of weak ties. *American Journal of Sociology, 78,* 1360-1380.

Granovetter, M. S. (1982). The strength of weak ties: A network theory revisited. In P. Marden & N. Lin (Eds.), *Social structure and network analysis* (pp. 105-30). Beverly Hills, CA: Sage.

Homans, G. C. (1961). *Social beahvior. Its elementary forms.* Hartcourt, Brace, & World.

Kollock, P. & Smith, M. (1994). *Managing the virtual commons: Co-operation and conflict in computer communities.* [Online]. Available: http://www.sscnet.ucla.edu/soc/csoc/papers/virtcomm/.

Nadel, S. F. (1957). *The theory of social structure.* New York: Free Press.

Neidhardt, F. (1983). Themen und Thesen zur Gruppensoziologie. In F. Neidhardt (Ed.), *Gruppensoziologie. Perspektiven und Materialien. Sonderheft der Kölner Zeitschrift für Soziologie und Sozialpsychologie, 25,* 12-34.

Schmutzer, R. (1997). Vorstellungen über die Merkmale und die Folgen von neuen Medien. In L. Gräf & M. Krajewski (Eds.), *Soziologie des Internet. Handeln im elektronischen Web-Werk* (pp. 216-234). Frankfurt: Campus.

Schönberger, K. (1998). *An Alle: Von „Lurkers", „Flames" und Datenmüll. Begegnungen im Internet.* [Online]. Available: http://max.lui.uni-tuebingen.de/fp/glossen.htm.

Smith, M. A. (1997). *Netscan: Measuring and mapping the social structure of usenet.* Paper presented at the 17th annual international sunbelt social network conference. San Diego, California. [Online]. Available: http://netscan.sscnet.ucla.edu/csoc/papers/sunbelt97/Sunbelt_Talk.html.

Sproull, L. & Faraj, S. (1997). Atheism, sex, and databases: The Net as a social technology. In S. Kiesler (Ed.), *Culture of the Internet* (pp. 35-51). Mahwah, NJ: Erlbaum.

Stegbauer, C. & Rausch, A. (1999). Ungleichheit in virtuellen Gemeinschaften. *Soziale Welt, 50*, 93-110.

Tapscott, D. (1997). *Growing up digital. The rise of the Net generation.* New York: McGraw-Hill.

Turkle, S. (1995). *Life on the screen. Identity in the age of the Internet.* New York: Simon & Schuster.

Wehner, J. (1997). Interaktive Medien – Ende der Massenkommunikation? *Zeitschrift für Soziologie, 26*, 96-114.

White, H. C., Boorman, S. A., & Breiger, R. L. (1976). Social structure from multiple networks I. Blockmodels of roles and positions. *American Journal of Sociology, 81*, 730-780.

16 Forms of Research in MUDs

Sonja Utz

MUDs (multi user dungeons / domains) are a type of role playing adventure game on the Internet. In comparison to the World Wide Web (WWW), Newsgroups, or IRC, they are a less well-known type of computer-mediated communication. The inhabitants of these virtual worlds form a specific subculture in the Internet. Nevertheless, a whole set of sociological and psychological questions can be researched in MUDs. In the following contribution, the empirical methods at the researcher's disposal will be presented. Prior to that, however, the author will clarify what MUDs are and how they differentiate themselves from other forms of CMC (computer-mediated communication). Next, the possibilities and limits of MUD research and the various research levels will be discussed. Besides basic problems in defining samples, the pros and cons of the most common and, in this context, frequently used methods of qualitative and quantitative social research will be presented: (participatory) observation, interview, and questionnaire based surveys.

16.1 MUDs – Definition and Characteristics

Multi user dungeons, or in short MUDs, are text-based multi user virtual worlds. In principle, MUDs are simply adventure role-playing games, which can be played over the Internet. They are oriented towards conventional role-playing games like "Advanced Dungeons and Dragons". In other words, most MUDs are set in a fantasy world with elves, dwarves, demons etc. The purpose of the game is to solve various tasks with a game figure, the so-called "character", and thus score points to reach further levels in the game. When a certain score is achieved one can actively take part as a so-called "wizard" in the further expansion of the MUD by programming new objects, areas, or quests.

Besides classical, adventure-oriented MUDs there are numerous other forms: socially oriented MUDs, graphic MUDs or MUDs that can be used in training or learning contexts.

The distinctiveness of all MUDs is determined by their computer-mediated communication, and less by man-machine interaction. Becoming acquainted and chatting with the fellow players makes up a majority of MUD time.

MUDs are interactive, and communication in them takes place in real time. Therefore, they are characterized as a prototype for synchronous, computer-mediated communication. On the other hand, they differ from other forms of CMC via a set of characteristics. These characteristics are to be shed light upon in the following section, before dealing with how to conduct scientific research in MUDs. Three points appear to be particularly important.

16.1.1 Identity/Role Playing

As mentioned above, MUDs are *role-playing* games. They therefore pose explicit opportunities for toying with identity. In general, CMC is, at least at the onset, characterized by the anonymity of the individual participants. Usually, one does not see one's CMC-interaction partner. Whilst at least an e-mail address may be recognizable in some forms of CMC, it is commonplace in chats to select a self-chosen name, or so-called nickname. On the Internet, one is therefore given the opportunity of selective self-presentation (Walther, 1996). It is possible to indicate a real name, but also to slip into the role of for instance the other sex. Particularly in asynchronous CMC forms (e.g., newsgroups), messages can be contemplated in peace, and leave time to consider one's own depiction exactly. In MUDs however, this sort of slipping into another role is not only a possibility, but the focus of attention. When logging in for the first time, a name, gender, and race (e.g., dwarf, elf) have to be selected for the character. Additionally, most MUDs offer the possibility to describe the game figure more closely in a short text, the so-called "description". Information can be given on appearance, personality characteristics, and, in addition, on the fictitious character's momentary disposition. In other forms of CMC, it is often considered a break of confidence if somebody dons a false identity. In contrast, MUD rules explicitly state that one is to behave consistently with one's selected role. In some MUDs the role-playing component is so strongly stressed that private conversations have to be transferred into special out-of-character channels (see for example http://www.xyllomer .de:80/l_guide.html#part3). In others, the borders between imaginary and real life characters are blurred. It is also fairly common for one person to play several characters, each endowed with different traits.

16.1.2 Virtual Worlds

A further point in which MUDs differ from other forms of CMC is that they portray *virtual worlds* in the truest sense of the term. In many other CMC-forms such as newsgroups or mailing-lists, "only" text can be found on certain topics in the form of questions and answers, and discussions that are typed instead of spoken. Even the synchronous chat channels are topic related in the broadest sense, although they often only deal with small talk. MUDs, in comparison, offer a gaming environment "related" to the real world: there are landscapes, forests, lakes, roads, mountains, cities with shops, taverns, and temples etc. All this is described in a few lines of text, a description of the area where one is located. Each of these elements can be inspected more closely and the objects can be integrated into the game play. All possible exits of a virtual room are indicated so that one can wander through the virtual world like in the real world. An analogy to real life is formed, one is given the impression of being in a three-dimensional area. The descriptions of space and time further supply references about the social context the respective situation is embedded in. They can signal danger in a dark, uncanny forest, liveliness in a pub or reverent behavior in a temple. But, not only are the locations described in MUDs; the players can also define their character with a description. MUDs therefore take on a strange intermediate position: on the one hand, by using analogies they show a close proximity to well-known structures in the real world. On the other hand, these worlds are expressly fantasy worlds. The frequently specified CMC characteristic "absence of social context cues" does not apply to MUDs. Reid (1994) expressly states that MUDs are context, not text.

16.1.3 Feelings and Emotes

Computer-mediated communication has often been deemed impersonal and unsuitable for the exchange of socio-emotional contents. These findings have been disproved in field studies anyway. It turned out that CMC users develope their own expression tools, for example the well-known Smileys, in order to textualize nonverbal communication acts (Walther, 1992). However, MUDs go far beyond that. They possess a number of features to express different feelings. There are so-called "Feelings", predesignated verbs. Over a hundred Feelings exist which can be activated with abbreviations. On the communication partner's screen, a longer description can then be seen. In Tapp-Mud it looks like this:

> tears

> Big tear drops are falling down from your eyes when you start to cry silently.

> fall

> You fall down laughing.

In this fashion one can smile, laugh, dance, embrace somebody else, kiss them, stick out one's tongue, etc. Additionally, the verbs can be combined with adjectives. For example, one can smile in many ways: merrily, sadly, understandingly, ironically, amusedly, admiringly or knowingly. Feelings facilitate expressing emotional circumstances decidedly and without having to type out lengthy sentences. If a player prefers an individual mode of expression, then this is possible with so-called "Emotes". In this case, any sort of text can be attached to the individual's name by using the appropriate command. To prevent abuse, the individual's name must remain in front, for example, to avoid another player acting on behalf of someone else. Player Gundar can only write, "Gundar kicks you" on the screen, but not "Anna kicks you."

MUDs thereby exhibit some characteristics different from other CMC forms. They explicitly incite users to play with their identity, they can depict social contexts with text descriptions, and they allow emotions to be expressed with special features. The "classical" characteristics of CMC, absence of regulatory feedback, dramaturgical limitations, few reference impulses on status and position, as well as social anonymity (Kiesler, Seal, & McGuire, 1984) do not apply, or only to a smaller extent (see Reid, 1994). These characteristics refer to short term effects of CMC, as they occur in laboratory groups. MUDs need to be observed under a different aspect of time. Many players spend years of several hours per week in these virtual worlds (19.7 months, 12.3 hours/week (Utz, 2000b); similar values with Bruckman, 1992; Curtis, 1992; Zielke, Schildmann, & Wirausky, 1995). During the course of this time, a relatively constant identity is gradually developed.

16.2 Possibilities and Limits of MUD Research

It becomes clear from these remarks that MUDs represent a specific subculture on the Internet. Findings obtained in MUDs cannot be generalized for all Internet users. Above all, MUDders form a very homogeneous group, if one takes regard of the socio-demographic structure. Various studies (Bruckman, 1992; Curtis, 1992; Utz, 1996, 1999; Zielke, Schildmann, & Wirausky, 1995) have found that "the average MUDder" is male, between 20 and 25 years old, and a student of natural science or technology. Nevertheless, quite a number of phenomena can be studied in MUDs at different levels of analysis.

16.2.1 Personal Level

On a personal level, the effects on the personality can be examined. Playing with identity and testing different roles enables completely new experiences. Bruckman (1992) calls MUDs identity workshops, which offer a free space for character development. Skeptics fear playing MUDs will cause isolation and loneliness. Whether, and to what extent, role-playing games in virtual worlds affect personality can definitely be researched.

16.2.2 Group Level

In MUDs friendships and relations also develop (Parks & Roberts, 1998), or groups are formed. Conflicts and disputes happen which are sometimes more violent than in real life (Leyde, 1994). On the group level, communications structures (e.g., Serpentelli, 1992) or social psychological processes in group formation can be observed. Also, the results of CMC specific conditions such as anonymity, physical isolation, identifiability, and copresence for the salience of a certain identity – and thus orientation towards personal or group norms, as specified in the SIDE model (Spears & Lea, 1994) – correspond to possible research objectives.

16.2.3 MUDs as Virtual Communities

From an even more superordinate perspective, MUDs can be regarded as virtual communities and examined as a whole. Does a sense of affiliation develop, and which rules and standards are created? Because MUDs, as depicted above, are virtual worlds, problems also result in them that also arise in "real" society. The ideal of an equal, hierarchy free community must usually be abandoned quickly as soon as the MUD grows larger and the number of players increases (Reid, 1994). Somebody has to be responsible for it for the outside world. Who programs what and what can and cannot be introduced into the MUD has to be coordinated. How are these problems solved? Which forms of regulation are to be found? Can everyone participate in the organization of MUDs, or do hierarchic structures crystallize quickly? How are these legitimized: by appointment of the MUD God, or in democratic elections? Questions like these have been studied for example by Duval Smith (1999) and Reid (1999). Leyde (1994, pp. 30/31) correctly describes MUDs as a *society en miniature*, in which not only identities, but political concepts can also be tested.

Certainly, this portrayal is not comprehensive. It only serves to point out that MUDs offer multi-layered possibilities for research. General (socio)psychological and sociological phenomena and principles can be observed and examined here, even if the results cannot be generalized to all forms of CMC.

16.3 Investigation Forms in MUDs

16.3.1 General Problems

The question about suitable research methods is now approached. In principle, one can differentiate between qualitative and quantitative methods of data acquisition in the field of social research. The former interpretatively evaluates verbal data, the latter deals with the statistic analysis of measured values. Methods can also be classified according to reactive and nonreactive procedures. In reactive procedure, the subjects are aware of the investigation and can (more or less) intentionally falsify the results. Theoretically, all methods can be used in MUDs; however, (past) MUD research largely consisted of field investigations and was mainly concerned with questions concerning applied social science. The following chapter will present the most frequently used procedures: (participatory) observation, interview, and questionnaire.

Before dealing with the pro and cons of the individual research methods, the problem of sample representativeness needs to be discussed. Theoretically, one should bear in mind that MUDders are not representative of other Internet-users, or even for the remainder of the population. As mentioned above, they are mostly young men who study a natural science subject. Nevertheless, one must assume that gender ratio, and possibly also age distribution will change in the years to come. What must also be considered is that within conventional fantasy role-playing games, the male ratio is predominant as well, and the average age is probably even lower than that of MUDders.

The question remains whether one can at least acquire a representative cross section of the MUDder population. Here, a factor that weighs heavily is willingness to participate. The larger the sample, the smaller the sampling error in all probability. Internet research is hampered by the problem that no exact numbers are available on the total population. In MUDs, however, these can be defined to some extent since at least the number of player files is known or available via the "wizards". This would however only represent an upper limit since many MUDders play with several characters. Findings by Utz (2000b), for example, indicated that 51% of participants only have one figure. 35% played with two, 9% with three, and 5% with four or more of characters. With this data a projection can be made, brought into relation with the number of player files, and the rate participation measured.

The size of the population in MUDs can therefore be estimated relatively accurately, compared to other services such as newsgroups, where the number of "lurkers" is unknown (Stegbauer & Rausch, this volume).

The willingness to participate is also dependent on how the participants are won. The survey can be announced in the appropriate general newsgroups (e.g., de.alt

.mud). In this manner a large number of MUDders can be reached, yet irritation has been expressed over the number of studies being conducted without ever hearing anything of the results. According to experience, participation is greater when approaching potential participants openly (e.g., by announcing the study in the internal news sections in selected MUDs). MUDders are generally relatively open when it comes to participating in studies and also show great interest in the results (cf. McKenna & Lee, 1996 (n = 200); Utz, 1999 (n = 217).

Another problem is the effects of sample selection that generally arise in empirical social research. Either voluntary and thereby more motivated subjects only take part in the studies (self-selection) or subtle persuasion has to be exerted. Studies with psychology students, who are bound by exam regulations to clock a certain number of participant hours, may serve as an example of the latter. This not entirely voluntary type of participation can however lead to falsified answers. Because of the anonymity in MUDs there is little risk that social pressure is exerted on the MUDders. Instead, one fear is that only the more motivated MUDders will participate in the survey. This cannot be excluded, but controlled. Accordingly, data on MUD behavior should also be included in the survey. On the basis of values on MUD time distribution, in general and per week, conclusions can be made on whether a broad cross section was reached. If only subjects with at least two years of "mudding" experience and a schedule of at least 20 hours per week can be observed in the sample, then this is indicative of a highly selected and involved sample. In order to study the effects of "mudding", however, high variances in MUD time are advantageous. High and low frequency "mudding" subjects, beginners and experienced MUDders can then be compared. Normally, the standard deviations of reported hours and/or months of MUD time is quite high. For example, the following values were recorded in Utz (1999): total MUD time: $M = 28$, $SD = 21$; hours per week: $M = 14.3$, $SD = 13.9$. Zielke et al. (1995) compared participant data with player files and found corresponding values. However, this comparison is only possible if the survey is limited to one MUD.

16.3.2 Selected Methods

As already mentioned above, the methods of data acquisition can be differentiated according the aspects quantitative vs. qualitative, and reactive vs. nonreactive. These characteristics do not apply to one method per se, but in each case to a different extent. A mode of observation can, for example, be reactive and quantitative (in the laboratory, use of rating questionnaires), even if the procedure in the field is qualitative and nonreactive in most cases. According to whether the study is intended to generate or verify a hypothesis, whether one wants to record behavior patterns or attitudes, different methods can be employed. In the following section, the three most common procedures in MUD will be introduced. The general description of the method will be kept to a minimum. Instead, I will describe in detail which method is particularly suitable for which objective and what must be considered at the time of carrying it out. The theoretical remarks are accompanied by examples from empirical studies.

16.3.2.1   (Participatory) Observation

One nonreactive method is (participatory) observation. It is applied above all by ethnologists, cultural anthropologists, and sociologists, and is usually evaluated qualitatively. One of its key characteristics is the deployment of this method in the test subjects' natural environment (i.e., the researcher takes part in the group's everyday life).

Observation methods are appropriate when researching behavior. In order to research attitudes, opinions, feelings etc. questionnaire techniques are more suitable. Observation can take place in a participatory or nonparticipatory, in a structured or unstructured, in an active or passive manner (see Lamnek, 1993). To date, participatory observation has been used most frequently when investigating MUDs (e.g., Curtis, 1992; Leyde, 1994; Reid, 1994). This can either be conducted openly or incognito (i.e., the observes either know that they are the subject of observation or they do not). Both methods have their pros and cons. If the observation is acknowledged, reactivity phenomena can adjust themselves in that the behavior of interest is not revealed or differently revealed. In the case of incognito observation, the researcher can obtain more information, yet is confronted with ethical problems of research.

Whilst observations in real life entail substantial documentation expenditure for the researcher, MUDs at least theoretically offer technical potential for simplifying this process. As a result, MUD sessions can be logged without any further problems. Here one only obtains those procedures that can be traced on one's own monitor (i.e., discussions lead by oneself, or shouts audible for the whole MUD). However, "wizards" have a "Snoop" command at their disposal so they can follow actions of certain players. Technically, it is possible to log absolutely everything. As a consequence, the local and temporal limits are eliminated, by which observing researchers are constricted in real life. Likewise, errors of observation – caused by researchers' selective perception and limited documentation capacity – can be avoided.

However, logging all activity raises considerable ethical questions. There have already been severe discussions on "snooping" in several MUDs, so that the command predominantly requires the agreement of those concerned (see Leyde, 1994). Since the majority of MUDders not only lead discussions on the game, but also private discussions (Utz, 1996, more than 70%), one cannot assume that the analysis of this data would be tolerated. Logging of activity and evaluating this data without prior consent of those involved is illegal from an ethical point of view. In addition, the anonymity of the subjects should always be ensured for reasons of privacy.

Even in the case of open observation, a further problem is posed by how to announce the survey. MUDs are characterized by a permanent coming and going of players so that the announcement would have to be repeated frequently. Besides, one should not count on all players reading the news. A message when logging in will possibly be overseen since text is often scrolled from the screen quite quickly in the greetings.

Despite these restrictions and problems, this method can be employed in numerous cases. This procedure is particularly suitable for hypothesis generating and explorative studies. McKenna and Lee (1996) used this approach, but employed it in addition to in-depth interviews and a questionnaire survey. For three months, they spent 50 hours per week in various MUDs. Above all, they learned about the different types of MUDs and their specific rules and atmosphere. They report that they thereby gained larger understanding for the MUDders and established a type of comradeship. The majority of the players welcomed the study and commented positively on the venture for more understanding.

Observation methods are therefore appropriate when generating hypotheses or supplementing background information. As long as ethical aspects are considered, (i.e., not keeping a record without permission), and the focus is on (observable) behavior and not on attitudes or personal attributes, this is the method of choice. Behavior observation is recommendable particularly in those aspects that are strongly influenced by socially desirable norms. This is where indicated attitudes and actual behavior often lie worlds apart (e.g., hostility, xenophobia).

16.3.2.2   Qualitative (In-Depth) Interview

For recording attitudes, opinions, and feelings qualitatively, the interview method is suitable. It is often referred to as the ideal method for qualitative social research and thus takes on the role of counterpart to the experiment in laboratory research. Methodically and methodologically it is attributed with a high status since it is recorded in its entirety. Therefore, factors such as selective perception play no role in observation. The transcription makes the interpretation comprehensible for all readers. Many different forms can be differentiated, depending upon intention, standardization, the structure of the respondents, the kinds of questions etc. No closer attention will be paid to these, instead the relevant literature for qualitative social research will be indicated (Lamnek, 1993).

Interviews are frequently used in MUD research (Bruckman, 1992; Stodart, 1997; McKenna & Lee, 1996). MUDs facilitate problem-free, undetected documentation without having to use additional technical equipment such as tape or video camera. The advantage of interviews as opposed to questionnaires is its flexibility and openness. With the exception of fully standardized interviews the answers are not forced into prefabricated categories (although the content analytical evaluation does imply a reduction into certain categories). The interviewer can fully devote himself to the respondent and pose specific questions at certain points. As a result, substantially more detailed and in-depth information is attainable. With questionnaires one only has a response pattern, yet does not know why a person has chosen a certain category, if this fully and completely corresponds to his opinion, or if it only represents the most fitting category. The respondents' thoughts are not necessarily intelligible.

A further advantage of interviews in MUDs is the fact that the problem of anonymity is fairly well solved. Since the players have nicknames anyway, privacy can thereby already be ensured. If the researcher plays MUD him/herself, it can naturally occur that one might already know the respondent. From experience one can assume that the MUDder will not object. Stodart offers an elegant solution in her study (1997). The participants were recruited via postings in newsgroups and had to enlist themselves via e-mail. Subsequently an interview appointment was arranged in a MUD foreign to them. The potential respondent was to log himself in as a "guest", the interviewer announced her name there and the password was agreed upon. This procedure makes an anonymous recording of the interview possible since the e-mail addresses are deleted immediately. Stodart registered good encounters with willingness to participate; more people were interested than could even be interviewed.

With interviews, no further ethical problems are posed due to the announcement of the survey and the possibility of remaining anonymous. The respondents can, after all, refuse to answer specific questions.

The largest disadvantage of interviews lies in the comparatively large time expenditure. Both acquisition and evaluation are relatively lengthy. The commonplace transcription of tape may be void in MUDs, yet content-analytical procedures are still necessary for evaluation (see Roessler, this volume, for more information on content analysis). The answers need to be partitioned into individual statements and coded accordingly, so results often tend to be rather quantitative at the end. The cost in effort automatically leads to a smaller sample size. This may reduce the general validity of the results considerably since the sample's representativeness for the total population of MUDders is not given. However, the considerable advantage of this procedure lies in the opportunity for producing differentiated typologies or obtaining hypotheses on relevant characteristics in order to acquire such typologies.

The interview therefore presents a good method for surveying and analyzing MUDders' attitudes, feelings, etc. in detail. Specific, extensive descriptions of different game modes can be obtained. The only warning to be heeded is of rash generalization. The interview can also be employed as supplement to quantitative procedures, in order to illustrate data with real examples.

16.3.2.3 Questionnaires

If there are already specific hypotheses which shall be tested within a large sample, then questionnaires are a suitable method of data acquisition. They have numerous advantages. First, they are relatively economical since they do not take up a lot of time and are cost-effective. Additionally, standardized procedures can be used, making a comparison with a control group possible. Questionnaires can collect "hard data" which are evaluated by quantitative, statistic procedures. Accordingly, statements on the size of correlations or on percentage of explained variance can be made. In longitudinal studies, causal connection hypotheses can be examined.

In principle, the researcher can select from one of several possibilities. Questionnaires can be distributed in a conventional paper-pencil-procedure, via e-mail, or posted on the WWW.

The paper-pencil-procedure has the advantage of being more comfortable for Internet beginners. This increases the chances of a representative sample.

More elegant for the examiner, yet technically more complex, are surveys on the net. E-mail surveys are relatively frequently used (e.g., McKenna & Lee, 1996; Zielke et al., 1995). These are technically speaking easy to conduct, and the researcher seldom needs an external programming aid. The questionnaire can either be a circular posted to all participants of a MUD. This normally fails however, because of the fact that the e-mail addresses are not publicly accessible. Unwanted dispatching of questionnaires can also be considered a nuisance. If one uses the internal MUD mail program one might likewise encounter problems. MUDders with several characters will receive several questionnaires. Furthermore, these programs usually have fewer functions than the usual e-mail clients. It is therefore better to announce the survey in the (MUD internal) news and only to post questionnaires to those MUDders who showed interest.

The advantages of e-mail questionnaires lie in the small expenditure: dispatch is quick, they can also be answered in another window opened next to the MUD, and they eliminate the walk to a mailbox. All of these factors should increase the motivation to participate (for other motivating factors see Bosnjak & Batinic, this volume). One problem is posed by anonymity since the e-mail address of the sender is recognizable. One could mask these by use of an anon server, yet this procedure is relatively complicated. It would be simpler to guarantee the participant that the e-mail address will be separated from the remaining data to be evaluated.

Questionnaires are also conducted on the WWW. This is technically complex since additional, complicated programming scripts (Common Gateway Interface (CGI) script or JavaScript) are required. The abbreviation CGI stands for common gateway interface, these scripts are mostly written in Perl and ensure, for example, that text entered into the page on the WWW is submitted to the researcher, or recorded in a data file. With the help of these scripts a whole set of further options can be realized. Response sensitive questionnaires can be constructed which allocate other items, depending upon the selected alternative. The participant can be designated randomly or depending on certain characteristics to a particular condition, in case one wanted to include experimental elements (for experiments in the WWW see Reips, this volume). Even parts of the evaluation can be managed by scripts. The personal totals or average values can be sent in reply to the participants.

One of the advantages of presentation on the WWW lies in the fact that one can reach a very large number of persons (world wide) at a stable cost; postage or online fees do not have to be paid each time a questionnaire is filled in. Meanwhile, many sophisticated tools have been developed to create online surveys. CGI- or javascripts are available for free in the Internet. Therefore, in the future WWW questionnaires will probably outnumber paper-pencil and e-mail-questionnaires by far.

Regardless of which method of presentation one chooses questionnaires prove themselves to be particularly suitable for the testing of specific hypotheses on a large sample. The quantitative data facilitate comprehensive statistical evaluations and tests of significance.

16.4 Research Outlook

To sum up one can conclude that researchers have at their disposal a set of methods for studying MUDs that have proven satisfactory in the field of qualitative and quantitative social research. In fact, the computer medium assists in the implementation of studies since data is documented automatically. What applies to empirical research in general also applies to studies in MUDs. Methods can only be evaluated in connection with content objectives, since they are all in each case more or less suitable for a specific line of questioning.

For what sorts of questions do MUDs offer a suitable framework? As was demonstrated MUDders form a highly selective sample; they embody a subculture on the Internet (Reid, 1994). Nevertheless, results acquired in MUDs are relevant beyond that. A short outlook on research will clarify this.

Roughly speaking, three objectives can be differentiated. On the one hand, there is the *scientific testing of theory*, primarily concerned with the examination of hypotheses and scientific increase in understanding. Besides this, MUDs must be examined as to what extent they function not only as game environments, but are also suitable as *learning and working environments*. Thirdly, MUDs can be regarded as representative for other *virtual communities*. The results found in MUDs could be applied in less playful contexts.

MUDs offer a favorable investigative environment for a number of scientific disciplines, spanning from computer science (Leyde, 1994) to psychology and sociology. Alone social psychology comprises a set of theories that can be examined in these virtual worlds: group formation, coherence, co-operation, leadership, social influence, interpersonal attraction, to name not all but a few.

Virtual communities are created in MUDs. This makes them particularly interesting for sociologists. Without great expenditure one can observe how in time a community is created by individual persons who more or less coincidentally logged into a MUD. What holds this community together, what norms develop, and how are these created? Most larger MUDs have a differentiated system of guilds and hierarchies. Guild leaders are selected and "wizard" conferences are held. How does this complex social structure function? MUDs form a microcosm, given that social processes often occur more quickly than in real life. They represent an experimentation area where insights can be made which can be transferred onto society.

Besides social structure, the topic of "identity" can also be studied in MUDs. MUDs as role-playing games incite slipping into another role, even that of another gender. What effects does this have on the personality? Turkle (1995) is concerned with this question. She regards the Internet as an opportunity to discover one's own identity, and to put into practice facets that would otherwise remain hidden. Her colleague Bruckman (1992) examined MUDs explicitly and dubbed them identity workshops. She has also taken a closer look at the phenomenon of *gender swapping* (1993). Why do men pose as women and vice versa? Do experiences made in such a way have repercussions in their real lives? A whole series of research questions is aimed at this phenomenon. The studies mentioned here are only the beginning. The potential of MUDs as a research space is a long way off from being fully taken advantage of.

In MUDs not only can scientific theories be tested, they can be employed directly as a learning or working environment. In this context, pedagogical science can examine ideal training/learning conditions. New didactic concepts can be tested. As a result, some MUDs will be used as virtual work teams. Probably the most renowned of these is the Media MOO initiated by Bruckman at the Massachusetts Institute of Technology. It offers scientists dedicated to new media opportunities for making new contacts and for presenting and discussing their research results. *Educational MUDs* were installed for different faculties. Here no frontal tutoring, as in class rooms, takes place, instead the pupils are actively involved in the exercises, they can program scenarios, play roles, exchange their thoughts and documents. One speaks of *active* or *searching learning*. In the meantime, graphic MUDs have also been developed in order to illustrate situations graphically. An open research question is for instance to what extent additional key skills can be acquired in MUDs, and how these can be applied later in career life (transfer). MUDs are also suitable for forms of telelearning. People separated by space can meet in the virtual learning environment. Experiments with new teaching methods should be examined complementarily in order to obtain insights into lesson design in the information age.

The knowledge gained in MUDs can also be used practically in other contexts. One such applied discipline is industrial and organizational psychology. Virtual work groups and virtual corporations are a current topic and many firms have introduced this kind of teamwork. For years, MUDs have been based on this work principle. "Wizards" consider them large programming projects and mention also gaining experiences in teamwork apart from programming knowledge (Utz, 1996). The individual tasks have to be distributed, coordinated, and have to be in tune with one another if a coherent, functional virtual world is to be developed. How project management and co-operation function in the MUD, or how efficiently they function could also be examined. Does less conflict occur if the programming "wizards" additionally have Feelings and Emotes at their disposal? These features could increase the medial depth and thus the suitability of the medium for complex tasks (Daft & Lengel, 1986). Questions such as these and others can be examined in MUDs and are of practical importance for the implementation of virtual working groups in companies (Utz, 2000a).

This research outlook may not be complete, yet it shows clearly that there are a number of questions that can be studied in MUDs. MUDs form an inexhaustible research area – take the right method and explore them!

References

Bortz, J. & Döring, N. (1995). *Forschungsmethoden und Evaluation für Sozialwissenschaftler*. Berlin: Springer.

Bruckman, A. (1992). *Emergent social and psychological phenomena in text-based virtual reality. Xerox parc.* [Online]. Available: ftp://ftp.lambda.moo.mud.org/pub/Moo/papers /identity-workshop.rtf.

Bruckman, A. (1993). *Gender-swapping on the Internet.* [Online]. Available: ftp://ftp.lamda .moo.mud.org/pub/Moo/papers/gender-swapping.txt.

Curtis, P. (1992). *Mudding. Social phenomena in text-based virtual realities. Xerox parc.* [Online]. Available: ftp://ftp.lambda.moo.mud.org/pub/Moo/papers/DIAC92.ps.

Daft, R. L. & Lengel, R. H. (1986). Organizational information requirements, media richness, and structural design. *Management Science, 32,* 554-571.

Duval Smith, A. (1999). Problems of conflict management in virtual communities. In M. A. Smith & P. Kollock (Eds.), *Communities in cyberspace* (pp.134-163). London: Routledge.

Kiesler, S., Siegel, J., & McGuire, T. (1984). Social psychological aspects of computer-mediated communication. *American Psychologist, 39,* 1123-1134.

Lamnek, S. (1993). *Qualitative Sozialforschung. Bd. 2 Methoden und Techniken*. Weinheim: Psychologie Verlags Union.

Leyde, I. (1994). *Technische und soziale Strukturen virtueller Welten am Beispiel von Tub-Mud. (Bericht 94-38)*. Berlin: TU, Fachbereich 13, Informatik.

McKenna, K. Y. A. & Lee, S. (1996). *A love affair with MUDs: Flow and social interaction in multi user dungeons.* Paper presented at the annual meetings of the international communication association, Chicago. [Online]. Available: http://oak.cats.ohiou.edu/~sl302186/mud.htm.

Parks, M. R. & Roberts, L. D. (1998). "Making MOOsic": The development of personal relationships online and a comparison to their offline counterparts. *Journal of Social and Personal Relationships, 15*, 517-537.

Reid, E. (1994). *Cultural Formations in text-based virtual realities*. [Online]. Available: ftp://ftp.lambda.moo.mud.org/pub/Moo/papers/CulturalFormations.txt.

Reid, E. (1999). Hierarchy and power: Social control in cyberspace. In M. A. Smith & P. Kollock (Eds.), *Communities in cyberspace* (pp. 107-133). London: Routledge.

Serpentelli, J. (1992). *Conversational structure and personality correlates of electronic communication*. [Online]. Available: ftp://ftp.lambda.moo.mud.org/pub/Moo/papers/conv_structure.txt.

Spears, R. & Lea, M. (1994). Panacea or panopticon? The hidden power in computer-mediated communication. *Communication Research, 21*, 427-459.

Turkle, S. (1995). *Life on the screen: Identity in the age of the Internet*. New York, NY: Simon and Schuster.

Utz, S. (1996). *Kommunikationsstrukturen und Persönlichkeitsaspekte bei MUD-Nutzern. Unpublished Thesis, Kath. Universität Eichstätt*. [Online]. Available: http://www.tu-chemnitz.de/phil/psych/professuren/sozpsy/Mitarbeiter/Utz/Diplom1.htm.

Utz, S. (1999). *Soziale Identifikation mit virtuellen Gemeinschaften – Bedingungen und Konsequenzen*. Lengerich: Pabst.

Utz, S. (2000a). Identifikation mit virtuellen Arbeitsgruppen und Organisationen. In M. Boos, K. J. Jonas, & K. Sassenberg (Eds.), *Computervermittelte Kommunikation in Organisationen* (pp. 41-55). Göttingen: Hogrefe.

Utz, S. (2000b). Social information processing in MUDs: The development of friendships in virtual worlds. *Journal of Online Behavior, 1*. [Online]. Available: http://www.behavior.net/JOB/v1n1/utz.html.

Walther, J. B. (1992). Interpersonal effects in computer-mediated interaction: A relational perspective. *Communication Research, 1*, 52-90.

Walther, J. B. (1996). Computer-mediated communication: Impersonal, interpersonal, and hyperpersonal interaction. *Communication Research, 23*, 1-43.

Zielke, A., Schildmann, S., & Wirausky, H. (1995). *Spiel- und Sozialverhalten im Morgengrauen*. [Online]. Available: http://www.mud.de/Forschung/verhalten.html.

17 Content Analysis in Online Communication: A Challenge for Traditional Methodology

Patrick Rössler

The contents of communication represent an essential element of the communication process as a whole. In recent years, the description and analysis of these communication contents have grown to be a central preoccupation of communication scholars. Since the early 1970's, an increasing number of studies based on a standardized media content analysis have been published in scientific journals. This indicates that it has reached the status of an important and well-approved instrument of empirical research (Merten & Grossmann, 1996, p.70f). Obviously, to assess the social relevance of a new communication environment such as the Internet, careful and systematic observation of its contents seems inevitable. In the long run, all assumptions about the possible impact of online communication must take into account the very nature of the communicated content in order to be more than pure speculation and storytelling. But before developing a completely new approach for this purpose, it seems reasonable to argue against the background of experiences made in the past with content analysis of traditional mass media, since they may provide a guideline for the analysis of the "new channel" of Internet content (Krippendorff, 1980, p.10).

Since its early development in the first decades of this century, content analysis has undergone a process of modification, improvement, and criticism. This evolution is not discussed here, but is easily accessible in the standard literature of the field (see Früh, 1998; Krippendorf, 1980; Merten, 1995; Rosengren, 1981; Weber, 1990). The same holds true for the basic rationale of content analysis, its epistemology and methodological practice. Instead, this chapter will elaborate on particular problems that emerge when the traditional approach of content analysis is transferred to online communication content. Space restrictions require that we assume the reader is familiar with the method in general. Due to the immaturity of online content research, the chapter will raise more questions than answers are given or solutions presented. The problems addressed range in scope from very fundamental issues down to some simple practical obstacles that concern content analysis research.

Although some empirical studies based on Web content analysis have been published by German scholars (see Dahm & Rössler, 1997; Rössler, 1998; Bruns, Marcinkowski, & Schierl, 1997; Rössler & Eichhorn, 1999; Heddergott & Loosen,

1999), their results are not of particular interest here, because they do not provide more than a snapshot of what was encountered within the fast-moving world of cyberspace at a particular time. Instead, the experiences drawn from these efforts to describe online content are organized along three main issues in content analysis – sampling, standardizing, and recording (Krippendorff, p.52f, Figure 15.7). Before these issues are addressed, some theoretical considerations will discuss the definitions of content analysis and the applicability of these definitions, focusing on the similarities and differences between traditional media and online communication. Next, the decision what material should be coded (sampling) is discussed, as well as the specification of the units of analysis (standardizing). A short section will elaborate on the organization of the coding process itself, particularly on the archival management of the material to code. The final remarks shed some light on the interpretation of data, referring to the results of German pilot studies based on content analyses of the World Wide Web (WWW) as mentioned above.

17.1 Theoretical Considerations: Definitions and Modifications

Every textbook on content analysis practice includes at least one definition of the method. An American and a German example are quoted here:

> "Content analysis is a research technique for making replicable and valid inferences from data to their context." (Krippendorff, 1980, p.21)

> "Content analysis is an empirical method for the systematically and inter-subjectively reproducible description of formal and content characteristics of messages." (Früh, 1998, p.25)

According to these definitions, the content of online communication can be a subject for this research technique. But two elements of the cited definition are particularly challenged by net-based communication: The inferences that should be allowed to describe the context of data, and the replicability or inter-subjective reproducibility. With regard to the first problem, three dimensions of inference can be achieved by content analysis: inference from media content (1) on the communicator; (2) on the reader or viewer; and (3) on the situation in terms of historical, political or social developments etc. (Merten, 1995, p.16; Weber, 1990, p.9). In the case of online communication, (1) and (2) are difficult to separate from each other, because the roles labeled "communicator" and "user" are not as determined as they are in the case of traditional mass media. Consequently, every kind of inference must take into account that:

- The term "communicator" does not imply that journalists are responsible for the messages, rather a heterogeneous mass of people with different motivations, intentions, and skills for communication (see Rössler, 1999).
- An inference made concerning a prototypical "user" is problematic as users themselves have a strong influence on the messages perceived, the content is in part produced by the users themselves (see Rössler & Eichhorn, 1999).
- Thus "communicator" and "user" very often switch their roles within the same communication process.
- The interaction of "communicators" and "users" is not yet based on long-term development of learned rules for either the presentation or perception of contents (see Rössler, 1998).
- And finally some caution is called for if online contents should be used for inference on the situation, as it is difficult to ascertain the reliability and trustworthiness of the information received (see Rössler & Wirth, 1999).

Due to limitations of space, these aspects cannot be gone into in detail, but they point to the fact that the interpretation of Internet content analysis data should always consider the specific nature of the respective online communication process it is based upon in its reflection. The third type of inference, aimed at the situational context, is important for online content analysis, given the fact that the institutional processes related to the worldwide distribution of the Internet are in rapid change. Four dimensions of content analyses in institutional contexts (as mentioned by Krippendorff, 1980, pp.9-46) become relevant fields of research:

legal matters, including the regulation of Internet, discussions on hardcore pornography, censorship, etc.;

economic matters, concerning home shopping, digital payment, and e-cash, etc.;

sociopolitical matters, with regard to the representation and articulation of minorities, the formation of virtual communities, the establishment of a counter-audience, etc.; and,

technical-structural matters, taking the diffusion of new technologies, software and Internet access into account.

The problem of *inter-subjective reproducibility* has theoretical and practical implications. Within this context, replicability means that the instrument developed by the researcher leads to the same results when applied repeatedly to the same data: "The rules that govern it must be explicit and equally applicable to all units of analysis" (Krippendorff, 1980, p.21). The data to be studied does not change because of the measurement, and the analysis can be repeated as often as desired with the same results (Früh, 1998, p.37f) – an assumption which holds perfectly true for the traditional mass media. Reactivity has to be taken into account only on the side of coders as soon as they are forced to make decisions, not on a simply syntactical level but on a level where his or her individual competence is required. Apart from that, there is usually no reactivity during data collection, because the nature of every single unit in the media content sample controlled by the communicator is not changed between two coding procedures.

Certain types of online communication content may violate this assumption – namely those, which rely on random requests from a larger database (e.g., ad banners, home shopping catalogs etc.). Following the discussion stimulated by Berelson's (1952) disputed definition of content analysis, researchers did not focus exclusively on the manifest content of media messages. Instead, it was postulated that the material has to be manifest in a basic and broader sense, since it is required to exist in terms of a manifestation of reality physically identifiable in an unambiguous manner (Kepplinger, 1997, p.6). In the case of online communication, the transaction with and by the medium exerts an important influence on the production of communication content itself, emphasizing the important role of the single user for the creation of the manifest content. The consequences for empirical content analysis are obvious. Although all contents are manifest in terms of their physical presence (and some only for a short period of time, such as chat messages) and in the form of a sequence of digitized information units which can be saved in data files, the description of these data files does not reflect the user-dependent communication content of the Net (apart from more technical problems concerning the archiving of these files, see below).

To illustrate this problem, again a comparison with traditional media may be useful. Here, user behavior was a minor problem for content analysis because it could be assumed that (1) due to the rules of media economics, the content of a medium was required to have a certain degree of acceptance within its target group; and (2) single messages did not vary between the screens of the spectators or the readers' pages. Now, there are at least three reasons why the messages may lack their manifest character from one user to another within the online communication process:

- Going online with a Web homepage or a posting in a newsgroup does not mean that the respective content contributes automatically to the online communication process. It is part of this process in so far as the content is published somewhere; but it is not a relevant part of this process unless it is found and consumed by at least one other user.
- On many occasions, generating the contents requires user decisions (e.g., within the coding process). As these decisions depend on the content to be studied, general rules for the procedure, that could be included in a codebook, are difficult to establish. Therefore, the user (in this particular case: the coder) exerts an influence on the analyzed material.

- From a more practical point of view, the idea of integrating large databases from which content is generated into a coding seems rather unrealistic as the number of single items is usually too large. Instead, the researcher has to decide whether the variation of database content is relevant for his research.

Generally speaking, the traditional notion that content analysis is a nonreactive and unobtrusive research technique, without the measurement process influencing the subject (Krippendorff, 1980, p.29; Weber, 1990, p.10), must be revised for online communication, starting at the level of message generation and collection. As a consequence, inter-subjective reproducibility is not ascertained by content analysis in general, but needs to be considered independently for each analysis. Hence the character of online communication questions basic assumptions of the method's application, particularly as far as further decisions about research units, sampling or the definition of coding units are concerned. The following chapters discuss these implications, referring to problems of research practice.

17.2 Deciding What to Code

17.2.1 Traditional Media and Online Communication

Most of the research on media content has analyzed material codified in written language, particularly articles in newspapers or magazines. There are many reasons for this procedure. Printed media are easily accessible, even a long time after the date of publishing. They are usually archived completely in public libraries, handling of the material requires no technical support – and in the realm of political communication (an area of high interest to scholars), the coverage of quality newspapers is frequently taken as a surrogate for the variety of political journalism in general. Coding then focuses on the content of the written text; in general, the codebook marginalizes the role of pictures.

When it comes to content analysis in audiovisual media, researchers conducting a systematic and quantitative content analysis very often neglect the *higher complexity* of the material under examination. (1) Radio messages are transcribed and interpreted similar to press texts, while nonverbal elements such as the pronunciation and accentuation of the respective speaker are not coded. (2) In television content analysis, the material that has to be coded is usually transferred into text, either (2a) by limiting the analysis to the textual elements of the programs (e.g., spoken words, subtitles) or (2b) by analyzing only related printed meta-media (e.g., program guides), which serve as a surrogate for the inspection of videotapes (Merten & Grossmann, 1996, p.71f). Again, relevant characteristics of visual communication – nonverbal codes displayed by TV persons, the dramaturgy of the material, or the whole range of formal aspects such as cutting and montage – remain unconsidered. The reason for this severe reduction lies in the predominance of certain topics in empirical communication research: scholars interested in the political impact of media messages only occasionally include the aesthetics of audiovisual media, traditionally studied with more qualitative methods of film or discourse analysis.

Given the particular nature of online communication, authors stress the fact that, within this net-based media environment, different *configurations of communication* are merged with different modalities (Rössler, 1998, p.28f). Following the distinction for traditional media, three types of modalities can be excluded on analytical grounds:

- *Text-based elements:* as with print media coverage, a great part of online communication is text-based as well. As long as these texts grow from and are presented in a corresponding manner, the application of classical content analysis strategies seems appropriate.
- *Audiovisual elements:* content known from radio or television (sound files, video files, and animations) can be digitalized and subsequently integrated into online communication. Coding of these elements would require a detailed codebook and an enormous effort if a complete recording is to be carried out.
- *Online elements:* virtual reality allows the implementation of contents usually not encountered in other media, both on the level of text (e.g., hypertext elements), visuals (e.g., three-dimensional simulations) or other animations (e.g., Java-Scripts). For the coding of these elements, there are little or no guidelines that can be derived from classical content analysis.

Depending on the research questions to be addressed by standardized content analysis, scholars need to decide which elements should be included with what kind of mediality in their coding process. If it can be assumed that audiovisual and online elements play a crucial role for the topic under examination, their coding seems to be inevitable in order to take online communication and its particular characteristics seriously. As a consequence, the coding process gets more complex and time-consuming.

17.2.2 Configurations of Communication

As Morris and Ogan (1996, p.42) put it, within the new communication environment of the Internet, different configurations of communication can be distinguished. All these configurations share a common technical platform – the Internet – but applications can be described by different technical features or have different functions for the user and therefore play different roles in the communication environment (for a detailed description, see Rössler, 1998, p.30f). The four most common applications are listed in order below to check their suitability for standardized content analysis.

- *WWW:* The most popular and most successful configuration is the WWW where a still growing number of organizations, companies, parties, interest groups, and private persons form a never-ending stream of online content serving both information and entertainment needs of the users. Interactivity is restricted more or less to a type of "interselectivity", where the user has the opportunity to choose from an extraordinary large variety of prepared content; variations occur only within a planned randomization, or as a reaction to a user's data entry. As a consequence for content analysis, Web sites are obviously the case where the most ambitious research efforts in online content analysis are to be found.
- *Usenet:* The Usenet is organized as a great number of thematically ordered bulletin boards where each user can post his own messages. Communication is largely text-based, as most of the newsgroups see themselves as a platform for discussions where facts and opinions are exchanged. The quality of the textual messages lies somewhere between scientific or newspaper level on the one hand, and simple statements of love and hate on the other hand. An ordinary coding scheme as applied in most content analysis of press texts will be appropriate after some modification. Furthermore, several boards also include pictures, video, and sound files posted by users. Again, the decision whether these elements are relevant for the research issue at hand must precede the decision whether and what kind of coding scheme has to be developed for these elements.
- *e-mail:* The personal variant of the Usenet consists of individual messages not intended to be read by the public, but distributed to a limited number of persons. Apart from the fact that, out of ethical reasons, it is unlikely that researchers will gain legal access to a larger amount of these messages, content analysis would have to focus on the basic level of written text, considering the possibility of attached data files as mentioned above. A special case of e-mail communication, the mailing lists which distribute messages to a larger number of subscribers, seem to be a more fruitful realm for content analysis, as they may provide insight into the dynamics of issue building and opinion formation in virtual communities.
- *Internet Relay Chat:* Although being largely text-based, too, the communication in chat-rooms appears to be less important for quantitative content analysis. Instead, the traditional methods of analyzing interpersonal communication can be modified for this purpose as the nature of chat communication already indicates (Wetzstein, Dahm, Steinmetz, Lentes, Schampaul, & Eckert, 1995, p.48f.).

Generally spoken, researchers have to bear in mind that the *standardized and quantitative type of content analysis* was conceptualized for detecting structures within mass media messages which themselves are produced in a highly standardized manner, and occur in great number. Research questions referring to facts that are not suitable to this kind of conception should therefore be analyzed using a different method. As a consequence, the WWW, being most closely oriented towards the traditional mass media metaphor, should be the most important field for online content analysis. On the other hand, many Web sites offer interfaces to other applications (e.g., a political party may offer a bulletin board for users to discuss current issues, a live-chat with a prominent party member or the opportunity to send e-mails to a contact person). In this case, the Web site serves as a melting pot for different forms of online communication, and it has to be clearly defined which elements are to be included, and which should be excluded from analysis.

Sampling of relevant material

Depending on the research question, the material relevant for coding has to be determined. No matter whether a random or systematic sampling seems appropriate with regard to the research question (Krippendorff, 1980, p.66f), a selection from the enormous amount of communication content has to be made. In traditional content analysis of mass media, there are five criteria for the selection of content:

- The time span to be considered.
- The type of media to be analyzed.
- The particular media (channels, newspapers, etc.).
- The relevant section of the media (news shows, economy pages etc.).
- The single program or article included.

Not all five sampling steps are always applicable (see Weber, 1990, p.42), but usually the coding team ends up with a definition like "four weeks of television news on ABC, CBS, and NBC, only the main news show in the evening". The particular selection is based on a quite valid information on the population of media messages. Although they are numerous, precise data about the number of television channels, the programs aired, the radio stations, the number and distribution of newspapers and magazines is available.

When adjusting these criteria to the sampling procedure for online content, some caution is required. Quite similar to the problems in online survey research, the population of messages for the described filtering process is only occasionally and vaguely known, as online content is under rapid change. Nevertheless, the validity and the generality of the results is dramatically reduced when the relationship between the material analyzed and the content to which the research question refers remains unclear. With regard to sampling, four types of content have to be distinguished:

- *Content addressed at a broad audience:* In this case communicators are strongly interested in reaching a large number of users and will, therefore, take measures to "get noticed" in cyberspace. To accumulate a population of messages for the sampling process, search engines, link lists, relevant Web directories or other metastructures within the Internet can be used. Nevertheless, scholars have to keep in mind that, due to the rapidly changing content, all sampling procedures fall short in precision.

- *Content which is aimed at a limited audience:* Particularly in the case of mailing lists or newsgroups, which focus on certain topics, participants tend to document their communication if the messages posted or sent are kept in an archive. Again, on the level of metastructures, comprehensive lists of accessible newsgroups or mailing lists exist or can be generated for sampling.

- *Content which is not intended to be perceived by the general public, but only by insiders, often a conspirative group:* Although this type occurs in an infinitely small number of cases, the respective content is often an important topic for research in social sciences. Sampling these contents calls for another selection process, following the guidelines of criminal or journalistic investigations rather than those of random selection. From a statistical point of view this is unproblematic as a generalization of the results is not intended anyway.

- *Content that must be paid for:* Some services require registration and payment by the user. Access to these outlets is restricted and therefore cannot be compared to other online content without detailed explanation. As the costs for this kind of Internet service quickly amount to large sums of money, coding will either omit these contents completely or focus particularly on this segment, then with appropriate funding for the research project.

One general problem of any sampling procedure is the fact that a reference in a metastructure does not imply that the specified outlet still exists, that it exists under the same URL, and that it is technically accessible at the moment.

Taking periodicity into account, in most cases, traditional mass media publish their messages on a regular schedule. Apart from breaking news stories such as the assassination of John F. Kennedy, their update is predictable – either for physical reasons, as newspapers are published in daily issues, or due to the formatting of broadcast media, where certain programs are scheduled to repeat at certain times. In general, there is a *definable sequentiality* and a *limited parallelism* of messages: the number of outlets is large but reasonably limited. Both characteristics are not true in cyberspace. Due to its virtual nature and easy and free access, we find an endless number of simultaneous outlets that update their messages constantly (or at least not according to a shared and predictable procedure) – possibly a serious obstacle for performing certain types of longitudinal analyses. This may not be true for distinct types of online communication, such as Net editions of traditional media, but in general, researchers have to face the fact that the periodicity of surveying data has to be oriented towards the periodicity of the type of online communication under examination.

One simple solution for this problem would be to collect the material for coding in retrospect. While traditional media content that was printed or broadcast is documented in libraries or video archives, and thus manifest in another sense, online communication content so far only exists in cyberspace itself. Sampling at a latter point in time assumes (1) that all relevant content is still online (usually not true); (2) that the content has not changed since its creation (older versions will often be deleted); and particularly (3) that any changes made do not interfere with the topic under examination, as would be in the case of explicit content manipulation. Generally spoken, online content analysis has to pay special attention to the authenticity of the material under examination compared to traditional content analysis.

Units of analysis

One of the most important decisions a content analysis researcher has to make is the *selection of sampling as recording units* (Weber, 1990, p.21; see also Krippendorff, 1980, p.57ff). This decision determines on which level results will be attained, and at the same time it determines the scope of empirical work. In traditional content analysis, a set of significant units of analysis can be retrieved from past studies for each of the different media. Taking newspapers as an example, the single article is a frequently analyzed recording unit. Particular statements or words are mentioned on a micro-level below the complete article, and the respective section of the newspaper (e.g., the front page) or the newspaper issue, as a whole, represents a more general level of analysis. Similar levels exist for the content analysis of other types of media. All these units may seem appropriate depending on the specific research question.

From this point of view, online content encountered in different configurations of communication can be also coded according to different levels of analysis. The recording units most appropriate for research are similar to the units used in traditional media content analysis. For example, Usenet messages can be studied on the level of each single posting (with regard to topic, date, length, etc.). They can be studied on the level of statements within a posting (arguments, valence, writing style, etc.), or they can be studied on the level of whole newsgroups (number of postings, participants, issues, and so on). A more complex type of communication, such as the WWW, allows for a set of different units of analysis. As it embraces a variety of textual, visual, auditive, and animated elements, coding can refer to all these elements, and therefore require a differentiated set of coding instructions for many coding units independent of one another.

Because some of these elements – and above all the hypertext structure – do not have any counterpart among traditional mass media, defining the sampling units for a

WWW content analysis is often a difficult and unsatisfying task. The Web site (representing the most evident unit for many research questions) has no physical borders in the usual sense, which could help determine its onset and ending. Using the URL as a criteria may lead to mistakes, either if parts of a site are located on a different server, or the other way around, if different sites with different content are located on the same server. For example, it is very common for the Web sites of international companies to offer local information in national departments with different domains within the same Web site.

The distinction is even more blurred if one takes into account that hypertextuality turns far-away Web sites into neighbors: the same operation – clicking on a link – may lead to another page on the same site, or to another site which has little to do with its predecessor. As a consequence, the site as a sampling unit has to be defined according to its coherence in layout, content or aesthetics: "natural" borders of a Web site do not exist.

Another main problem in defining the units of analysis deals with the increasing popularity of splitting the screen into frames. Additional frames may aid navigation within the site, but they may also open a second area of information content or advertisement. Problems emerge for example when a navigation frame is always present while the user moves within a Web site – if pages are the units to be recorded, does the navigation area have to be coded again and again with every subsequent page? Do navigation frames have to be coded at all? Do applications like Java applets constitute own units of analysis? How are additional windows, which open up during a session, treated? How are pages addressed by different links on different pages treated? These are only some of the questions that arise from hypertextuality and framing techniques, when defining the units of a WWW content analysis. To avoid numerous problems during the coding process, researchers need to work intensively on detailed regulations that cover most of these very common Web site characteristics.

Which parts of a Web site have to be analyzed, and in particular how deep the coding needs to go into the structure of a Web site, also depends on the research question. As Web design continues to develop elaborate options for content presentation, coding a whole Web site on the level of single pages takes more and more effort. By using superficial, general indicators for the entire Web site, important information about the overall network structure of the site is lost. Yet this data is needed to calculate well-known indicators in social science network analysis, such as network density and degree of centralization (see Roessler, 1997, p.263 for an application). A practical solution would be to include into the sampling unit Web pages down to a certain depth away from the homepage. This means that all pages of a site not further away from the homepage than a certain number of clicks (usually two or three clicks) are coded. This procedure, however, favors "flat" Web sites with strong interlinking of pages, while other more hierarchically organized sites may be under-represented.

17.3 Organization of Coding

Archiving content

Even if a certain amount of reactivity in data collection has to be accepted, as mentioned above, online content analysis should ascertain at least some degree of replicability by saving the content under examination in data files and archives. Although this point may sound trivial and archiving is inevitable if the coding takes place post facto, very often the coding has to be performed "live" and online. This means that the coder fills in the codesheets while moving in real-time in cyberspace. Unfortunately, some parts of Web content are unique at a certain point in time (e.g., live webcam transmissions), or outstanding because they depend on randomized selection as mentioned above. One outcome for research practice is that (lacking reproducibility) reliability tests are no longer conductible, leaving an external observer without the most important indicators for the quality of data collection (Krippendorff, 1980, p.129ff). Thus, the intersubjective testability, regarded as a more adequate formulation of what is generally meant by "objectivity" in science (Andrén, 1981, p.48), is already challenged at an earlier stage than in the case of traditional media content analysis, where the material printed or aired remains unchanged over a long period of time and can be reproduced arbitrarily (Weber, 1990, p.10).

When comparing online coding with a post-hoc analysis, it is extremely time-consuming to download and save Web content, even if only a limited number of outlets is considered. Installing an archive is easier for other more text-based and non hypertext-related configurations of communication, such as the Usenet and mailing lists. Additionally, the periodicity of the pages (see above) sometimes calls for constant downloading because content is permanently updated (e.g., in the case of online news channels). All of a Web site's details and subpages can hardly ever be archived; selecting content to be saved (sometimes equivalent to what is to be coded) has to be considered carefully. In particular, leaving out "difficult" elements very often means restricting the analysis to simple and well-known features – a procedure that does not take seriously the innovative features of online communication content. In particular with regard to these elements, documenting the Web site with screen-shots or print-outs falls short. Preserving material in part coded "live" allows at least some control over what was coded.

Technical and formal requirements

Textual, visual, and audio presentation of online content depends on the computer system's local configuration. For example, the standard typeface, monitor resolution, image, and color settings or the bandwidth of Net access usually vary among different terminal configurations. As a consequence, the selection of preferences applied in content analysis has to consider two different aspects of validity:

- For ascertaining *external validity* the researcher's system needs to equal with regard to the kind of inference intended; e.g., if the research question addresses inferences about users' perceptions of content, system parameters should resemble the users' systems' configuration.
- For ascertaining *internal validity*, system parameters need to be standardized across all computers used in analysis, particularly the browser characteristics specified. Hence, the coding manual has to give exact instructions on which hardware is to be used, and how the relevant software options should be set.

As far as the coder's technical capabilities are concerned, a basic understanding of cyberspace, hypertextuality, and the different types of communication is required. Particularly if the material needs to be coded online many unsubstantiated situations may emerge that require a coder's online skill. Content analysis relies heavily on the observer's dual qualification – being familiar with the nature of the material, but also being capable of reliably handling the categories and data language terms (Krippendorff, 1980, p.72).

17.4 Some Conclusions

The more widespread the Internet becomes, the more the content of online communication needs to be described and analyzed. The present essay intended to address some of the problems that emerge when the usual instruments of content analysis are applied without serious reflection. In particular, online communication has to be conceptualized from a dynamic-transactional perspective where different types of communication can be included simultaneously – and which does not adhere to traditional research paradigms where the recipient uses prepared, unique media messages (see Roessler & Eichhorn, 1999, p.163). During the online communication process, reactivity is inevitable because many contents are generated interactively. As a consequence, reactivity becomes more than a factor influencing research quality – the degree of reactivity itself represents a possible variable to describe online content. Measuring interactive features requires strong coder participation. Coders must interact with the content in order to generate it. Thus, coder training needs to be intensified and must be taken seriously. The same applies to the degree of precision of the coding instructions. Sometimes they will include rules for the evaluation of Web sites by the coders, rather than a simple list of the features encountered.

Some confusion may be caused by the fact that traditional mass media sites represent some of the most important and most frequently used contents on the WWW. It comes as no surprise that, in particular mass communication scholars focus their research efforts on the uses and effects of these sites (and related topics such as online journalism). On the other hand, taking media sites as their topic of analysis, researchers are tempted to apply methods and instruments they are familiar with from their experience with traditional media. Online newspapers are in the first place "online", and only secondarily can be considered as newspapers, Web TV is not exactly the same as ordinary television, and radio station Web sites in general offer a lot more than radio programs on air. Transferring this observation from the media realm to a more general level of reflection, online content has to deal with a basic problem that can be traced back to the general relationship between the online world and real world. If an inference of the results about social reality is intended, it has to be clarified whether *virtual* social reality as it is encountered in cyberspace, or *real-life* social reality with online communication being part of a larger social environment is indicated. The mutual interactions between the two represent a crucial point for any kind of Internet related research (Roessler, 1998).

Starting with traditional applications of content analysis with regard to mass media communication, German researchers have to date conducted a small number of online studies. There is a certain emphasis on Web site content analysis, and recently the first *continuous Web monitoring effort* was launched by the "Medien Tenor", a commercial research institute which has gained accolades for performing the only permanent and systematic content analysis of leading German media outlets. Since early 1999, a set of German Web pages is coded on a daily basis with respect to political and economic news. The sites of various *home shopping companies* were the topic of the first German Web content analysis carried out in June 1996 (see Roessler, 1997; Dahm & Roessler, 1997). Following the idea of network analysis, the link structure of the sites could be described by the respective parameters (e.g., the network density varied between .17 and .80). The instrument included a coder's rating of Web sites that considered a set of evaluative dimensions (e.g., professionalism, originality, and complexity). Bruns, Marcinkowski, and Schierl (1997) studied Web sites of 150 companies with respect to their usability, topics addressed, topicality, interactivity, and multimedia features. Their analysis focused on *complete Web sites* as recording units, mainly allowing for rather superficial comparisons of different branches. The world soccer championship in 1998 served as a background for Heddergott and Loosen's (2000) case study of two selected *sports Web sites*, where they encountered a large amount of stereotyped coverage. In their methodological considerations, the authors emphasize the problem of arriving at meaningful inferences from the data, and predict that Web content analysis will serve mainly descriptive purposes in the future.

In their analysis of *car manufacturer Web sites*, Roessler and Eichhorn (1999) divided their coding scheme into four sections related to different fields of interest:

- *Structural features:* clarity, user guidance and navigation, degree of interlinking, Web site size in general, etc.
- *Design features:* text or visual ratio, use of audio and video elements or animation, banner ads, language, overall visual impression, etc.
- *Interactive features:* user contact, features such as prize competitions, surveys, chat rooms, mail contact, download options, user passwords, etc.
- *Content-related features:* topics and issues addressed, opinions given, content sources named, all aspects related to content, and purpose of the site.

Results revealed strong differences between the examined Web sites for all types of features. As an indicator of its structure, they calculated the relationship between internal and external links within one site. Additionally, multivariate statistics are recommended for a comprehensive analysis of Web content.

It seems rather obvious that Internet content which already exists in digitalized form should become a central field for the application of computer-assisted content analysis (CCA). In fact, text data included in Web sites can easily be processed by different software tools previously developed for CCA of traditional mass media (e.g., Weber, 1990, p.24ff; Klein, 1998). As a consequence, the well-known limitations of this research strategy have not yet been overcome, for example the numerous problems associated with the identification of meaning (especially in German). Furthermore, more complex link structures, multimedia features, as well as database information, ftp and gopher services, e-mail forms, or other interactive elements still have to be excluded from the analysis (Klein, 1998). Any kind of analysis based on these restrictions ignores the characteristics of online communication, and will ultimately lead to superficial results; more appropriate tools to analyze Web content are being developed at this time.

A final point must refer to the problem of content analyzing Internet communication other than Web sites – the issue of privacy of personal data and research ethics. Although chat room sessions, Usenet postings and mailing list messages can be documented, whether these contents may be used as a subject of research without informing the participating users needs to be discussed. In particular in the case of logfile content analyses, users must remain unidentified. While different academic research communities are committed to developing codes of conduct to tackle the ethical dimension of online research, there seem to be few measures that prevent improper use by market researchers. After all, in the case of a user's rights being violated, legal procedure for prosecution differs greatly between countries, even in the western hemisphere.

Due to lack of experience, standardized instruments, and general consensus on online content analysis, devising a satisfactory research design in terms of scientific merit is still a difficult and costly task. Unfortunately, the efforts to be taken are reflected by the restricted plausibility of the results in the fast-changing communication environment. Online content analysis is a lot of work with little gains but yet an important and responsible task because today's content on the Net cannot be reproduced or studied by communication scholars in the future. The Net has no past, virtually at least.

References

Andrén, G. (1981). Reliability and content analysis. In K. E. Rosengren (Ed.), *Advances in content analysis* (pp. 43-67). Beverly Hills, CA: Sage.

Berelson, B. (1952). *Content analysis in communication research*. Glencoe, Ill.: Free Press.

Bruns, T., Marcinkowski, F., & Schierl, T. (1997). Marktkommunikation deutscher Unternehmen im Internet. Eine quantitative Inhaltsanalyse ausgewählter Web sites. *pro online, 1*. Duisburg: Universität Duisburg.

Dahm, H. & Rössler, P. (1997). Marktplatz der Sensationen? Deutsche Anbieter von Online-Shopping im Test. *Media Spectrum, 3*, 32-36.

Früh, W. (1998). *Inhaltsanalyse. Theorie und Praxis* (4th ed.). München: Ölschläger.

Heddergott, K. & Loosen, W. (1999). *Ins Netz gegangen? Eine Inhaltsanalyse im Umfeld der Fußball-WM 1998 im World Wide Web*. Paper presented to the Annual Convention of the German Association of Communication Research (DGPuK), Utrecht.

Kepplinger, H. M. (1997). Zum Charakter des manifesten Inhalts von Kommunikation. *Medien Journal, 21*, 4-10.

Klein, H. (1998). *Text analysis of data in the world wide web*. Paper presented to the 14th world congress of sociology, Montréal.

Krippendorff, K. (1980). *Content analysis. An introduction to its methodology*. Beverly Hills, London: Sage.

Merten, K. (1995). *Inhaltsanalyse. Einführung in Theorie, Methode und Praxis* (2nd ed.). Opladen: Westdeutscher Verlag.

Merten, K. (1996). Reactivity in content analysis. *Communications, 21*, 65-76.

Merten, K. & Großmann, B. (1996). Möglichkeiten und Grenzen der Inhaltsanalyse. *Rundfunk und Fernsehen, 44*, 70-85.

Rössler, P. (1997). Standardisierte Inhaltsanalysen im World Wide Web. Überlegungen zur Anwendung der Methode am Beispiel einer Studie zu Online-Shopping-Angeboten. In K. Beck & G. Vowe (Eds.), *Computernetze – ein Medium öffentlicher Kommunikation?* (pp. 245-267). Berlin: Wissenschaftsverlag Volker Spiess.

Rössler, P. (1998). Wirkungsmodelle: die digitale Herausforderung. Überlegungen zu einer Inventur bestehender Erklärungsansätze der Medienwirkungsforschung. In P. Rössler (Ed.), *Online-Kommunikation. Beiträge zu Nutzung und Wirkung* (pp. 113-139). Opladen: Westdeutscher Verlag.

Rössler, P. (1999). „Wir sehen betroffen: die Netze voll und alle Schleusen offen..." NET-SELEKT – eine Befragung zur Auswahl von Web-Inhalten durch Online-Gatekeeper. In W. Wirth & W. Schweiger (Eds.), *Selektion im Internet* (pp. 113-139). Opladen: Westdeutscher Verlag.

Rössler, P. & Eichhorn, W. (1999). WebCanal – ein Instrument zur Beschreibung von Inhalten im World Wide Web. In B. Batinic, A. Werner, L. Gräf, & W. Bandilla (Eds.), *Online Research. Methoden, Anwendungen und Ergebnisse* (pp. 263-276). Göttingen: Hogrefe.

Rössler, P. & Wirth, W. (1999). *Glaubwürdigkeit im Internet. Fragestellungen, Modelle, empirische Befunde.* München: R. Fischer.

Rosengren, K. E. (Ed.). (1981). *Advances in content analysis.* Beverly Hills, CA: Sage.

Weber, R. (1990). *Basic content analysis* (2nd ed.). Newbury Park: Sage.

Wester, F. (1996). Comments on Klaus Merten: Reactivity in content analysis? *Communications, 21*, 199-202.

Wetzstein, T., Dahm, H., Steinmetz, L., Lentes, A., Schampaul, S., & Eckert, R. (1995). *Datenreisende. Die Kultur der Computernetze.* Opladen: Westdeutscher Verlag.

18 "Let a Thousand Proposals Bloom" – Mailing Lists as Research Sources

Jeanette Hofmann

Mailing lists belong to the electronic communications services that are much older than the Internet. They are based on a simple program that duplicates a received posting and sends it to all of the list's subscribers. Shirky (1995, p.61) describes mailing lists as one of the first and most simple examples of a public "multi user space on the Net."

Distributed communication forms support particular segments of the general public. These are located somewhere between public spaces generated by physical presence, and those formed by the mass media (Hasse & Wehner, 1997, p.64; Vogelsang, Steinmetz, & Wetzstein, 1995). Mailing lists constitute "translocal" spaces where peers with similar interests and qualifications correspond with each other as if they were face-to-face. The communication services on the Internet evoke not only new social experiences, but also facilitate previously unknown forms of observation. Reading mailing lists opens new "windows" onto the research terrain. It differs from common forms of surveying by the type of presence one adopts. "Lurking", i.e., silent observation, corresponds to a type of participation that remains more or less unnoticed. Now, how does this virtual presence affect research findings? Which insights can be won on mailing lists that cannot, for example, be gained in interviews?

The purpose of this contribution is to get to the bottom of a personal bewilderment with this topic. Against my expectations, reading mailing lists ousted my usual favorites – qualitative interviews and document analyses – from their pole positions. Meanwhile, controversial debates held on the Internet have become my most important data resource. A obvious explanation can be found in the subject matter of the research. The "Internet as a Cultural Space" project group devoted its attention to the Internet from an interior point of view[1]. We examined the Net as a social space characterized by its own set of rules determining use and development. Our research focused on the digital space's socio-technical manner of organizing itself. In particu-

---

[1] In the context of a project promoted by the Volkswagen Foundation: "Interactive spaces: the Internet. Network culture and network organization in open computer networks" (see Helmers, Hoffmann, & Hofmann, 1996; 1998).

lar, this pertained to the interrelations between technical and social conventions that govern the Net's change. Bearing this in mind, it seems plausible that the Net's communication services occupy a particular position amongst the available information sources. E-mail, mailing lists, file transfer, and the World Wide Web (WWW) allow close co-operation among the internationally distributed Internet community – and thereby, if one so wishes, the self-regulation of the Internet. The question of the particular methodological characteristics of mailing lists, however, remains untouched by this focus. How can this part of reality, as generated and transmitted by this communication service, be characterized?

To answer this question, this contribution will undertake an excursion into the inner life of a mailing list. Using an episode that took place some time ago, the exchange among network engineers will be explored with a view to finding out how mailing lists reflect technology development via the Internet. The events will be presented in chronological order, even if they occasionally occurred simultaneously or circularly, and organized in seven acts. Excerpts from approximately six months of discussion threads aim at giving exemplary insight into the network technicians' routines and trains of thought. What and how all the individual occurrences happened can, in contrast to most stories written in "real life", be reviewed word for word in the archives of the mailing list[2]. The second part of the contribution revolves around an interview with the story's protagonist in which he explains the events from his point of view. Where differences can be found, and what these tell us about mailing lists and interviews as forms of research is then discussed.

The chosen mailing list bears the prosaic name "Internet Protocol next generation", in short: IPng. It serves as a forum for discussion for the eponymous working group – one of the 124 existing working groups assembled in the Internet engineering Task Force (IETF). The IETF sees itself as an open network consisting of technicians, scientists, and technology service providers responsible for the constant operation and further progress of the Internet[3]. A constantly growing number of network engineers of different backgrounds uses the mailing lists and the quarter yearly IETF meetings to participate in the joint development of new technical norms for the Internet (or "protocols" as technical norms are known in the community language). In its role as a comprehensive international and corporate co-operation body, the association is bequeathed with official standardization organizations. In contrast to the latter, the IETF sees itself as an informal collective without binding rules of membership.

---

[2] The IPng mailing list file can be found in the Internet at: ftp://playground.sun.com/pub /ipng/mail files.

[3] The IETF homepage, with information on their working groups, mailing lists and technical specifications, has the following address: http://www.ietf.org. The IPng working group "Charta" is at: http://www.ietf.org/html.charters/ipngwg-charter.html.

Mailing lists, meetings, and the standards derived from these, are open to anyone interested.[4]

The IPng mailing list was brought to life simultaneously to the working group's conception in 1994. The list is the successor to an IETF list called "BIG-I" where the entire Internet community initially led a general type of discussion on the Internet's future. This list spawned the IPng list and working group, which, in contrast to their predecessors, has a specific task[5]. Its aim is to develop the next generation Internet Protocol (IP) until ripe for application. By the end of 1996, the project's progress was being followed by 1,400 mainly "lurking" subscribers.

The story that will be told began at a time when fundamental decisions on IP had long been made, and an increasing amount of users were waiting for the new protocol's readiness for use.

18.1 The Rise and Fall of a Technical Idea – A Play in Seven Acts

The year is 1996. Three years of development, and all in all five years of heated discussion lie behind us. The topic, after all, is the technical nerve center of the Internet. IP, the "lingua franca of Cyberspace" (December 1996) that made global data transmission possible in the first place, is to be updated to accommodate for the growth of the Net. The current version "IPv4" hailed from the early eighties. Not only was it conceived for a significantly smaller network, but also for less demanding forms of data transmission.

Following lengthy arguments on the next generation, IPng, one eventually agreed upon a catalogue of features and named it IPv6. At last, the preparation and test phases for the technical specifications have reached their end. The introduction of IPv6 seems almost close enough to touch. But then, right in the middle of a peaceful work routine, the unexpected occurs. A new technical idea appears.

18.1.1 Act 1: 8+8 – A Technical Occurrence Is Announced

Shortly before midnight on a Saturday evening in October, we receive an e-mail. Under the number 2200, the following posting appears on our mailing list:

---

[4]   Cf. "The Tao of IETF" (RFC 1718; a summary is at: http://www.ietf.cnri.reston.va.us/tao .html).

[5]   On the development of IPng, Bradner & Mankin, 1996; Helmers, Hoffmann, & Hofmann, 1997.

```
Date sent:    Sat, 5 Oct 1996 23:57:23 -0400 (EDT)
From:         mo@UU.NET (Mike O'Dell)
To:           ipng@sunroof.Eng.Sun.COM
Subject:      (IPng 2200) 8+8...

imagine that. i have a draft that i'm finishing up
which details an 8+8 proposal....

-mo
```

Under the heading "8+8..." a person named "mo" heralds a document of which he obviously supposes that we take its occurrence for at least unlikely: "imagine that", and that we are also aware of what is meant by 8+8.

Active mailing lists with a stable subscriber base of many years become a type of social biotope where collective experiences are deposited in specific patterns of behavior, argots, and spelling[6]. The IETF mailing lists consist of a substantial repertoire of acronyms and puns whose recognition separates the native from the newcomer. The concise cipher 8+8 apparently refers to a familiar issue in the history of IP.

Three weeks pass by, and since nobody has reacted to this elusive announcement, we have long forgotten this unknown object called 8+8. And then, suddenly...

18.1.2 Act 2: 8+8 – The Official Statement

The "IETF announcement list", responsible for general notifications such as the publication of new documents, informs us about a new Internet draft:

```
I-D ACTION: draft-odell-8+8-00.txt

Internet-Drafts@ietf.org
Fri, 25 Oct 1996 09:27:18 -0400

A New Internet-Draft is available from the online
Internet-Drafts directories.

Title: 8+8 - An Alternate Addressing Architecture for
IPv6
Author(s):  M. O'Dell
```

---

[6] In this context Knoblauch speaks of "a type of *secondary traditionalization*" (ibid. 1995, p.237; emphasis added by author). The coordination of intentions requires a higher degree of classification and conventionalisation in medial communication than in direct communication, which has a larger reservoir of physical communication media at its disposal. This stock of conventions does not only settle "on an interactive level; it has to be learned like reading, software and culture." (ibid; see also Reid, 1996; Fassler, 1996, p.404)

```
Filename  :   draft-odell-8+8-00.txt
Pages  :  20
Date:    10/24/1996

This  document  presents  an  alternative  addressing  ar-
chitecture  for  IPv6  which  controls  global  routing
growth  with  very  aggressive  topological  aggregation.
It  also  includes  support  for  scalable  multihoming  as
a  distinguished  service  while  freeing  sites  and  ser-
vice  resellers  from  the  tyranny  of  CIDR-based  aggre-
gation  by  providing  transparent  rehoming  of  both.
```

Stages of technical evolution on the Internet are chronicled in documents. Their publication underlies a formalized procedure that in itself is the topic of many documents. That has not always been the case[7]. Various categories of document give information on the status or the degree of readiness of a technical solution. 8+8 is still in the drawing board stages and therefore begins its career as an Internet draft[8].

8+8, as the summary informs us, represents an alternative addressing architecture for the new Internet protocol. It promises to contain the growth of routing information and, beyond that, to free us from a tyranny called "CIDR". "Routing growth", "multihoming" and "rehoming" are keywords that show the initiated the draft's conceptual direction. All three terms point out current problem areas in the operation of the global Net. The larger the Net becomes and the more complex its property and usage relationships, the higher will be the costs of determining suitable routes between sender and recipient addresses for the routers. The summary informs us indirectly that IPv6's presently envisaged addressing architecture does not convincingly accommodate for this bottleneck.

And how do the IPv6 developers respond to such a loud-mouthed announcement? The reactions are manifold.

---

[7] The heightened degree of formalism stems from the fact that the status of technical documentation has changed in light of the commercialization of the Internet. Internet standards have become an economic factor. The location of individual bytes in a transmission protocol can determine the fate of companies, as an IETF member recently put it (see also RFC 1958).

[8] Basically, one can differentiate between two publication series: Internet-Drafts and Requests for Comment (RFC). Drafts contain initial blueprints for technical ideas or specifications. They have a life span of six months. Afterwards, they are deleted from the official IETF files. Only the technical idea survives for which the community shows so much interest that it is raised again and – in the form of new documents – developed. RFCs are divided into different genres. The most important describe Internet standards (standards track). Further categories are informational, experimental and BCP (Best Current Practice); (cf. for instance RFC 1796 and RFC 2026).

18.1.3 Act 3: 8+8 – Applause and Whistles

The first contribution under the header "Mike's 8+8" is confined to a further reading
hint. In view of the flood of new Internet drafts advertised daily on the announcement
list, there obviously seems to be some interest that 8+8 reaches the attention of the
list's members:

```
Date sent:   Fri, 25 Oct 1996 10:19:37 -0400
From:        Scott Bradner <sob@deas.harvard.edu>
To:          ipng@sunroof.Eng.Sun.COM
Subject:     (IPng 2375) Mike's 8+8

I'd suggest that people take a look at this ID - it
seems to me to be quite a win.

Scott
```

The lax diction with which 8+8 is recommended is not
arbitrary. Scott belongs to the Internet community's
first generation. His technical and social qualifications are so highly recognized that even the most
sparsely dosed comments receive attention. The next
contribution endorses Scott's comment and also undertakes a first review of the document: (IPng 2378)

```
Re: Mike's 8+8
bound@zk3.dec.com
Mon, 28 Oct 96 02:05:33 -0500

I really hope all check this out a.s.a.p. I think
it's really important and fixes a day-1 architecture
problem for IPv6 that needs fixing if this protocol
is to be widely deployed. I also think it should be
part of the IPng WG agenda.

/jim
```

IPv6, which we had assumed to be in the test phase, reveals itself as unexpectedly
hampered with problems. 8+8 seems to focus upon a previously known weak point
that needs to be fixed, should IPv6 assert itself on the Net. Accordingly, "/jim" en-
courages assessment of 8+8 "as soon as possible", and to put it on the agenda of the
next working group meeting.

In the next reply, however, we encounter a different tone of voice:

```
From:        Masataka Ohta
Subject:     (IPng 2380) Re: Mike's 8+8
To:          bound@zk3.dec.com
```

```
Date sent:  Mon, 28 Oct 96 16:31:55 JST
Copies to:  ipng@sunroof.Eng.Sun.COM

jim > I really hope all check this out a.s.a.p. I
think it's
jim > really important and fixes a day-1 architecture
problem
jim > for IPv6 that needs fixing if this protocol is
to be
jim > widely deployed.

It's almost identical to my FIRST proposal of 8+8
proposed even before the day-1 and is no good.

Why? Dig the ML archive.

Masataka Ohta
```

Obviously written to oppose /jim's partially cited comment, Masataka Ohta not only claims copyright to 8+8, but also cast doubt upon the draft's quality. Simultaneously, we receive a further piece of advice to plow through the mailing list's archive!

8+8, we read from this, already has a longer past. "Day −1" symbolizes the approximate time span in which the Internet community agreed upon the ground rules of the new protocol and installed the IPng mailing list with the aim of formulating it.

Not unwelcomed by us outsiders, Ohta's objection prompts a short recapitulation of 8+8's past. Following /jim, 8+8's author also utters a statement:

18.1.4 Act 4: 8+8 – Reconstructing the History of an Idea

```
From:         bound@zk3.dec.com
To:   Masataka Ohta <mohta@necom830.hpcl.titech.ac.jp>
Copies to: ipng@sunroof.Eng.Sun.COM
Subject:   (IPng 2400) Re: Mike's 8+8
Date sent: Tue, 29 Oct 96 00:29:26 -0500

For example the first 8+8 like idea I recall was Paul
Francis's PIP in 1992 I think. It was not for address-
ing but routing but implied the same idea. Very
tricky to prove the idea. This was also a major point
of contention at the IPng Big Ten meeting (see RFC
1752) at an IPng Directorate meeting in Chicago June
1994 I think (off the top of my head). I think Mike
has finally crystalized an 8+8 proposal that will
work but more importantly can be implemented. But I
```

am just one person and open to hear issues I may have
missed in the draft.

/jim

To: Masataka Ohta <mohta@necom830.hpcl.titech.ac.jp>
Copies to: bound@ZK3.DEC.COM,
              ipng@sunroof.Eng.Sun.COM
Subject: (IPng 2403) Re: Mike's 8+8
Date sent: Tue, 29 Oct 1996 05:08:43 -0500
From: "Mike O'Dell" <mo@UU.NET>

Ohtasan,

Sorry you feel slighted.

To my knowledge, this idea was first suggested by
Dave Clark quite a while ago in the early 8/16 discussions and that's where *I* first heard it. I even
have the e-mail stored here somewhere... [....]
cheers,
-mo (O'Dell, IPng 2403)

8+8 proves to be the brainchild of many parents. Its origin remains unclear. Additionally, we find out that its curriculum vitae has crossed paths with IPv6 before. A
reference is made to "PIP" and an "IPng Big Ten meeting" – both milestones in
IPng's or IPv6's difficult history. Under different guises, 8+8 has been discussed by
different people at different stages of development, however without the necessary
support. Now, at the last minute, we come across another and possibly the last attempt to enforce the idea.

Whilst Masataka Ohta ("Ohtasan") vies for the recognition of his personal contribution to 8+8 without success, a topical debate on 8+8 commences. The spark comes
from an occurrence outside of the mailing list. In December all teams will meet in
San Jose, California, for the last of their third annually held conferences. For five
days all of those questions not answered on the mailing list are dealt with in one to
two sittings per working group. For the first time, 8+8 is to be presented and debated
"in real life". Consequently the draft has been read by many in the meantime. Already
before the IPng team has conferred for the first time, the settlement on its aims and

possible implications begins in the "Terminal Room" of the conference hotel: "Of course (sez Mike who is sitting next to me)..." (Carpenter, IPng, 2570)[9].

Shortly after the meeting in San Jose, the minutes are distributed on the mailing list. On the 8+8 discussion it says: "Long discussion. Many questions. Chairs will make decision on how to proceed." (Hinden, IPng 2638).

It dawns upon the working group that 8+8 is, despite or due to its history, is not as clear and comprehensible as it may have seemed at first glance. Debate on the mailing list notes that the document is difficult to understand, not precise enough, and, consequently, there is considerable demand for interpretation.

18.1.5 Act 5: Text Exegesis – What Exactly Does 8+8 Mean?

The explanation of 8+8 begins with a general brooding over its description. Many of the contributions refer to the Internet draft and end with questions directed at the author. The text exegetic phase exemplifies the atmosphere in which collective reasoning occurs in the IETF mailing lists:

```
Mike,

I havn't formed an opinion on 8+8 as I don't really
understand all ramifications of the proposal. At this
point, I am only asking questions in hope to get to
understand it better. (Haskin, IPng 2751)

Is there something that I missed on this subject that
will solve this issue? (Durand, IPng 2763)

However, i don't yet feel like i exactly and com-
pletely understand how all of this would work at a
"systems" level. (Stewart III, IPng, 2738)

This reasoning is faulty. I'd urge a rereading of
Mike's draft. (Atkinson, IPng 2772)

So the conclusion I reach, and which I didn't expect
is this: (Crawford, IPng 2732)
```

---

[9] The debates on the mailing lists also continue during the IETF meetings. The reason for this being that not all of those involved can participate in the gatherings; another being that distributed communication on the Internet bears no substitute for real-life meetings, but has attained its own merit. Each IETF meeting location is therefore equipped with a Terminal Room that enables the approximately 2,000 attendees to communicate publicly with absentees, as well as attendees.

```
It may be just me but I still fail to understand how
your hybrid approach is different from the current
provider based approach. (Haskin, IPng 2809)

Are you proposing two kinds of routers? (Narten, IPng
2820)

Also I assume you do not want to alter the destina-
tion address in the packet? Is that correct? (Bound,
IPng 2822)
```

Without restraint, the limits of one's own competence are revealed, questions of understanding are posed and unexpected insights put forward. A willingness to think
over and revise is visible. By reading, one listens to the others. Given the repeated
and looping queries, "mo," the 8+8's author, is running out of patience.

```
sigh - here we go again
IPv4 addresses are not globally unique (O'Dell, IPng
2805)

... he is immediately called to order.

mo> sigh - here we go again

We have to go over a lot, you have proposed something
radical, Mike. We need to understand it. You have
been thinking about this problem, I am sure, for a
long time before you sent out the draft. (Bound, IPng
2808)
```

The predominant form of understanding in the specialized public domain of an IETF
mailing list differs decidedly from the sort of ritualized discussion seen in parlia-
ments, the mass media or conferences. The frankness with which the possible advantages of a still nebulous technical solution are sized up against its opponent almost seems enticing.

One will only be able to appreciate this conceptual frankness when one recalls that
the founding fathers of the Internet also contribute to these mailing lists. Some of
those who so modestly turn up as inquirers now enjoy a reputation as heroes.

An explanation for their cooperative modus operandi may lie in the special public
space created by the IETF's mailing lists. Its audience consists of the international
aristocracy of network engineering: self-perceived pioneers exploring new technical
terrain. The questions they ask are aimed at domesticating this terrain. In other
words, the questions posed are not from beginners but highly qualified specialists and
pioneer. An acknowledgment of ignorance is therefore not interpreted as a personal
shortcoming, but rather as a ritualized expression of a general need for clarification.

In fact, 8+8 is regarded as technically unexplored territory. Unlike the IPv6 drafted addressing architecture, which follows on where IPv4's contemporary architecture left off, there is little or no experience with 8+8:

```
I do feel comfortable with an architecture in which
the main limitations are already well understood
[...] A new architecture represents a jump in the
dark. (Roque, IPng 2766)

The unknown tends to be somewhat scary. (I think this
con also applies to the current 8+8 proposal, which I
consider a hybrid.) (Tracey, IPng 2776)

I don't think that it is a question of desirable or
undesirable. There are a set of tradeoffs with either
approach. The fact is that today, we have a pretty
good understanding of the pros and cons of combining
both functions into the address (and there are defi-
nitely drawbacks). I think we have a much sketchier
understanding of the other approach. What existing
systems have used this approach? How well do they
scale? (Narten, IPng 2778)
```

8+8, there seems to be a consensus, is a shot in the dark. The solution deviates from addressing procedures currently in practice, yet the architectural consequences of implementing these differences are unforeseeable. Despite this limited perspective, a decision has to be made: "We need to decide whether 8+8 is the right thing to do engineering-wise" (Carpenter, IPng 2908).

How then can the strengths and weaknesses of two such differently researched models be weighed up against each other? How can one find out whether 8+8 is the technically proper solution if, given the size of the Internet, field studies with new addressing models have to be ruled out?

18.1.6 Act 6: In Search of Order – Playing 8+8 Scene by Scene

The ensuing debate allows us to follow the process whereby the technicians gradually bring light to the end of the tunnel. It is a mental ordering process, which breaks the unknown down into definable questions. And, already at an early stage, 8+8 does tend to show first signs of dissolution. In the path of its exploration the conceptual construct is separated into individual elements. This procedure continues until each

piece reaches a size manageable enough to determine its features[10]. These features
are then questioned as to their compatibility with the current network environment.
Among other things, this concerns the addressing mode:

Can 8+8 guarantee its global uniqueness, and, if not, does it differ significantly
from IPv4? Under which circumstances does 8+8 allow a modification of addresses,
and which of its segments are affected? Which role does 8+8 attribute to the routers
in this relationship? Are they permitted to overwrite the data packages' addresses,
should the (topological) location of the sender change over the course of data transmission? And what consequences would this have for open connections? On the
other hand, fears about security are linked to these questions: Does 8+8 facilitate
hijacking data packages or header spoofing? How can data authenticity be verified if
the sender's representation has been altered underway? Does 8+8 demand that all
data traffic be encrypted in future?

The actual evaluation of 8+8's characteristics is conducted with the aid of varying
case hypotheses: "That depends on what scenarios you think are likely" (Carpenter,
IPng 2770). Little scenic scripts are then created which attribute different roles to the
involved network objects. It is interesting to observe which dramaturgical and verbal
forms these mind games adopt:

> Individual hosts would know exactly what their global
> addresses were and could select an appropriate source
> on their own. (Harrington, IPng 2703)

> I don't like the idea of the host having to know so
> much about network addresses or topology, which it
> would have to do to intelligently make that decision.
> (...) The translation of addresses, tunneling, rout-
> ing decisions, etc. are the jobs of routers, which
> are more incline to be aware of the factors involved
> and the current network topology. (Black, IPng 2713)

> By moving the decision of source prefix to routers
> and hiding it from hosts, hosts have no way to detect
> whenever they need to generate special control traf-
> fic... (Roque, IPng 2766)

> Allow border routers to rewrite the addresses...
> (Malcom IPng 2712)

---

[10] The reverse is described in a "First of April" RFC: "It is always possible to agglutinate
multiple separate problems into a single complex interdependent solution. In most cases
this is a bad idea" (RFC 1925). Obviously, this is RFC is categorized as "informational".

```
The sending host cannot reasonably be asked to do RG.
Only the routing system can possess that knowledge.
(Carpenter, IPng 2908)
```

An intellectual world unravels itself in front of our eyes, in which variations of relations between technical objects are discussed. 8+8 represents such a set of rules that define the relationship between hosts and routers. Largely, this set of rules is concerned with the distribution of information over the network environment, and the responsibility for decisions that are based on this information. The instructions or algorithms, according to which this knowledge is generated, selected, and distributed, need to be established. Whilst all imaginable models are looked over, the nodes seem to come to life:

```
If a host inside the firewall can ask the firewall to
create a hole for some external host... (Ohta, IPng
2742)
```

```
A node roaming into a provider's domain can negotiate
a provider routing goop across all providers accross
from London to San Francisco... (Bound, IPng 2745)
```

Assuming all the routers understand all the formats and can figure out when to look at how much of the address to use for forwarding... (O'Dell, IPng 2771)

```
How are endpoints assured that a claimed source iden-
tifier is true? (Tracey, IPng 2753)
```

Hosts and routers appear as questioners, negotiators, and understanders who mutually supply each other with information on the identity and availability of their neighbors – information they may choose to trust or not. The differences between machine operations and human action, between technical and social rules or protocols seem to blur in these scenarios. The interaction among program-controlled artifacts is described in the same terms as those among living beings. Where does this come from? Is an "anthropomorphisation" taking place?

Unlike a textbook or manual, where we go through the functions and rules of technical systems, the mailing list allows us to observe the development of such rules. And while the textbook presupposes the logic of such rules as a given, the mailing list presents the ongoing struggle and negotiation of a technology's rationality. Hosts and routers appear as agents because they act representatively for the engineers who consider how a general set of rules should be best assembled. From the perspective of such a set of rules, however, no principle difference exists between data traffic managed by humans or machines. The instructions that define behavior remain the same.[11]

Technology development implies processes of negotiation, because thinking about meaningful ordering criteria reveals different possibilities, which also bring more or less unwanted side effects with them. Each mode of distributing competencies between routers and hosts seems to correspond to an impending information deficit, as the comments on the mailing list suggest. And the technical procedures or conventions the community will finally agree upon are the result of weighing and selecting various options, whose conclusiveness or logic is possibly brought to light only ex post – by manuals, for example.

Meanwhile the dismantling of 8+8 shows unexpectedly wide repercussions. The debate is no longer confined to understanding and evaluating 8+8, its features, potential advantages, and problems; the addressing principles of the Internet per se are now at stake. This, however, leaves neither 8+8 nor IPv6 unaffected. "Flat 16" or "IP classic", as IPv6 is occasionally referred to in contrast to 8+8, has meanwhile become a recognized problem child: "As for frozen, IPv6 ain't even cool" (O'Dell, IPng 3158), as the author of 8+8 states cleverly. At the same time, 8+8 begins to take on another form.

18.1.7 Act 7: Metamorphosis

Still in its investigation phase, concerned with understanding "all ramifications of the proposal" (Hasking, IPng 2751), a differentiation commences. From originally two components 8+8, three are developed, and 8+8 becomes a generic name for the various combination proposals:

> Assuming that the WG decides to explore the 8+8 alternative (or 6+2+8 which seamed to have better support)...(Roque, IPng 2569)

> I follow with interest the O'Dell/Ohta-san or Ohta-san/O'Dell addressing architecture development (maybe we should call it the O+O architecture instead). (Perkins, IPng 2667)

---

[11] This notion follows from Bettina Heintz's work on the Turing machine (Heintz, 1993) where algorithms are introduced as a "mechanical" obeying of evident instructions. It also follows Bruno Latour's approach to technology, the conceptual pivot of which lies in the delegation and distribution of authority between human and nonhuman "actors" (Latour, 1992).

```
But, it's not 8+2+6. It's 6+2+8 now. (Ohta, IPng 2723)


The 2 bytes in the 8+8 models (6+2+8 or 8+2+6), as
they are not unique, do not carry enough information
to make routing decisions _inside_ a site. (Durrant,
IPng 2763)


Mike's original proposal could have been characterised
as 8+2+6 (exterior routing/interior routing/interface
ID). My slight revision of Mike's proposal is 6+2+8
(exterior/interior/interface   ID)  (Atkinson,   IPng
2787)
```

8+8 reveals itself to be an inconsistent occurrence. While it first seemed clear in its objectives, and was only submitted for evaluation, it evoked a general debate on addressing principles. The individual parts of 8+8 are synthesized in changing forms. For a brief period 8+8 oscillates between 8+2+6 and 6+2+8. After 6+2+8 has established itself as a probable consensual version, the author writes up a new Internet-Draft[12] which documents the changes in relation to the first draft, and at the same time undertakes a further name change because:

```
GSE means Global-Site-ESD - tying the name to byte
boundaries became less amusing when it stopped being
"8+8". (O'Dell, IPng 3071)


Let me start by saying that I support the general
thrust of the gseaddr draft (and 8+8 before that).
(Elz, IPng 3108)


I am not convinced that GSE as it stands today is
ready for rubber stamping. Equally, GSE+ attempts to
be a long term solution. (Hunter, IPng 3112)


New draft will be called "Aggregation-Based Unicast
Address Formats". This will replace RFC-2073 "An IPv6
Provider Based Unicast Address Format" (Hinden, IPng
3558)
```

---

[12] The title of the meantime invalid Draft reads: "GSE – An Alternate Addressing Architecture for IPv6" (draft-ietf-IPngwg-gseaddr-00.txt).

> GSE is also endowed with proposals for correction,
> one of which is properly named: GSE+. Then the meta-
> morphoses of 8+8 come to a halt. GSE and GSE+ are not
> considered "ready for rubber stamping". (Hunter, IPng
> 3112)

By the way, the decision against 8+8 did not take place on the mailing list. The problem proved too complex to be mastered exclusively via electronic communication; more "bandwidth" was needed. To discuss GSE, formerly known as 6+2+8, a public "interim meeting" was arranged between two regular IETF meetings. The result of this meeting is a further text that at least provisionally brings 8+8's career to a conclusion. It comprises a comprehensive analysis of GSE which – embedded in a discussion of the Internet's present addressing and routing principles – systematically discusses its characteristics.[13]

For a short time, the analysis of GSE is still the subject of text exegetic considerations. The next IETF conference is imminent, however, and the mailing list set its sights on a revision of the classical addressing format. The competitive addressing model is also rejected. The new draft, called "Aggregation-Based Unicast Address Format14"[14], differs significantly from the original version, and takes at least one of 8+8's objectives into account. Its central intention, segmenting the localization and identification function of numeric network addresses, cannot become generally accepted, however – not because it would have been considered wrong or not feasible in principle, but because it breaks with "one of the strong design hypotheses of IPv6" (Huitema, IPng 2747). The associated risks and side effects seem too excessive.

18.2 8+8: The author's Narration

A few months after 8+8's decay in August 1997, the IETF met in Munich, resulting in an opportunity for an interview with its author. Towards the end of a conversation lasting several hours, I came to realize the expectations which had directed my questions. The curtain would open and reveal the real events taking place beyond the debate on the mailing list. Mailing lists constitute public areas which disclose only those facets of events that their subscribers express coram publico. Meanwhile, addi-

---

[13] IPng analysis of the GSE Proposal (draft-ietf-ipngwg-esd-analysis-00.txt). The Internet Draft, in the meantime invalid, can be found in the mailing list file at IPng 3440. In the meantime, a fifth version of the analysis of GSE is available (www.ietf.org/internet-drafts/draft-ietf-ipngwg-esd-analysis-05.txt).

[14] The draft has become a standard in the meantime: An IPv6 Aggregatable Global Unicast Address Format (RFC 2374).

tional considerations and strategies are exchanged in private messages surrounding the public realm; these remain invisible.[15]

Of course, an interview cannot reveal what is to remain secret. It nevertheless gives the opportunity to inquire about what was said and arranged outside of the mailing list. As a matter of fact, the author's narration did actually circle around an event which was only indirectly visible as a report on the mailing list: the interim meeting between the two IETF conferences, crucial for 8+8's fate, arranged to decide its final approval or rejection:

> There'd been a lot of discussion saying "Gee, if we'd just done xyz, this would be a lot better." What the GSE document did was try to take a lot of those things and scrape them up into one pile and produce the alternate reality (...) and try to understand what the implications of that are. In fact, it was a huge experiment. The way it was done was there was a meeting in Palo Alto. The amount of intellectual horsepower in that room was terrifying, a whole bunch of seriously smart people. We looked at this alternate universe and we said "What if the rules worked this way, what are the implications of changing all these rules?" We really did work all the way through to the edges. We didn't just say "Oh yeah, it sort of looks like it's going to be okay," we really followed all the strings and pulled them all the way out of the carpet. I believe the Net result was that a lot of these things got thought about a lot harder than they'd ever been thought about before.

In the interview, the story is told with hindsight and structured around its outcome. The fact that 8+8 is a very old idea, which had already been discussed in the early days of network design, is only mentioned as an aside as was the statement that "people had been after me for 18 months" to present 8+8 as an addressing model for the Internet in the form of a draft for discussion. The thrust of his narrative, however, is aimed at how, by whom, and with what result 8+8 was rejected.

---

[15]   Haase & Wehner state that specialized audiences withdraw from the "familiar dichotomy public vs. private" because they are based on topics that cannot be generalized (ibid. 1997, p.54). This can be countered by the point that specialized communities on mailing lists also border on closed spheres or explicitly generate these – more or less via bilateral communication among list members. As Kerckhove puts it, the Net is the first medium which simultaneously articulates itself privately and publicly (ibid. 1996, p.146; see also Samarajiva & Shields, 1997).

The people who met in Palo Alto were the particularly bright heads of the community[16]. And they succeeded in illuminating the 8+8's effects right into the last detail so that "a lot of these things" were more comprehensively thought through than before. – Then follows the narration's dramatic climax:

> ... and I basically got up at noon on the second day
> and said "First of all, just to make sure nobody is
> in the hot seat here, as author I'm willing to take
> this thing off the table and say "This is a fine ex-
> ercise, but basically, it isn't going anywhere." and
> all of us can get a plane home a day early. (...) As
> the author of an obviously broken thing, I will no
> longer impose on anybody else's time." The answer was
> "No, we want to think this through, this has led to
> some enlightenments and we want to squeeze out all
> the juice we can get out of the exercise."

> The exercise was to break the whole thing up into its pieces and figure out if
> some of these are valuable (...). People went off and spent a tremendous amount
> of time that night and came back with workarounds and think throughs. We got
> through it and that's how the addressing design stuff got respun.

Instead of closing the meeting prematurely, following the unanimous decision against 8+8, the remaining time was used to draw as many insights as possible from the discussion of the "alternate universe", and at least save parts of the idea for IPv6's revision. So, 8+8 was once again divided into its components. And because the intellectual quality of this "exercise" was so exceptional, 8+8's defeat still seemed profitable:

> "I'm personally very gratified with what happened.
> (...) The result of going through it was that we un-
> derstand a lot more about how IPv4 works. There are
> some incredibly subtle things in the way IPv4 is put
> together. Some of the people that did it (i.e., de-
> signed IPv4, J.H.) were there and they said: „We were
> not smart enough to do this from first principle, we
> weren't smart enough to get this right." This is a
> case where being lucky accounts for a lot, they had
> the right intuition..."

---

[16] This point is also referred to in the GSE analysis: "The well-attended meeting generated high caliber, focused technical discussions on the issues involved, with participation by almost all of the attendees" (IPng 3440).

Bringing 8+8 to paper and discussing it, the author's original intention, was not a waste of time. The effects on the current draft of IPv6 may be marginal, yet a lasting success can still be noted. Possibly the most important facet, however, materialized unexpectedly: the investigation of 8+8 deepened the understanding of the Internet's functional environment. Procedures, which had once been developed intuitively only revealed their underlying logic when they were seriously put to the test for the first time. 8+8 contravenes this logic and could therefore probably only be realized as an axiom of its own network architecture: "The lesson I came away with from very strongly is (...) that [it] has to be the first axiom. Everything else is done cognizant of that" (O'Dell). 8+8 thereby evoked two progressive insights: an old idea in limbo was endowed with distinct characteristics and implementation requirements. At the same time, the well-known characteristics of the IP Internet protocol received a degree of foundation unknown beforehand.

18.3 8+8 on the Mailing List and in the Interview: Ways of Ordering and Representing the Event

Did the author's narration provide the anticipated view behind the mailing list's curtain? Did it add dimensions to 8+8's story that had remained hidden on the Net? The answer is both yes and no and it leads back to the question raised initially about the special window mailing lists open on occurrences on the Net. A review of the impressions of 8+8 as portrayed by the debates on the mailing list and by the author's account exposes a set of differences between the two research sources. Interestingly enough, these are found less in specific facts, than in the way those facts are brought into relationship with one another: presentation and ordering.

18.3.1 The Direction of Time – The Remains of 8+8

The remains of 8+8 form the pivotal point in the author's narration: a remarkable advance in insight. This is put in contrast to the "school of thought" in whose place it stepped: "I belonged to the school of thought that believed "If you could just split this apart' was the road to making things good." Looking back, 8+8 seems to have undergone a metamorphosis. That cloudy and complex idea, which went through several transformations before finally being rejected, turned back into what it was at the beginning: an axiom, a clear and coherent set of rules.

Compared to the debate on the Net, the author's account seems very selective. Nothing is mentioned about how long the community strove to illuminate the technical obscurity, and to what degree the object changed during the course of this illumination. The events are reduced to a few episodes and aspects. Yet, the author's narrative nevertheless enables what debates on mailing lists seem almost to refuse: an overview. Seen from the author's perspective, 8+8 is embedded in a before and after, in a framework as it were, and endowed with a fixed and plausible definition.

On the mailing list, however, the present prevails. The impression of "live participation" does not even fade, when reconstructing the debate on 8+8 from the electronical archives. As readers we always gather the substance of a story in the sum of the contributions, which are spun further in succession from one mail to the next. The controversial and occasionally meandering nature of the debates on the Net tends to obstruct the view of those aspects that are usually put to the forefront by retrospective accounts: causal connections between events and what is regarded as typical for these events. The review in the interview lends the events an explanatory order. It offers interpretations on the basis of which we will read the same debates on the Net differently.

However, different levels of time and reflection levels in mailing lists and interviews are only one of the factors that determined the appearance of 8+8.

18.3.2 The Role of the Addressee: 8+8 for Outsiders

A comparison of the author's account to his contributions on the mailing list reveals, in addition to narrative deviations, also remarkable language differences. Unlike the discussion on the Net, which devoted itself to every detail of 8+8 separately, the talk in the interview is rather vague when referring to "incredible subtle things", "addressing design stuff" and an "alternate universe". 8+8's technical dimension remained almost hidden. Several queries were necessary before the author rather reluctantly shared his view of the decisive reasons for 8+8's refusal. The focus of his story was not on the actual technical problem, but on what the story illustrates in his eyes: the very special working rituals of the IETF, and the (mostly unacknowledged) mixture of intuition, experience, and luck, which has always determined the development of network technology.

One reason for this topical focus lies in the character of our conversation. The context in which the story is told exerts influence on the type of presentation. How detailed answers are, which terms are used and which causal references are made depends on the addressees. Accordingly, an observer (and above all: a sociological observer) will probably receive other explanations than the technical savvy community. For the interviewer is by definition an outsider, and the discussion she has initiated takes place outside of the topic's usual context.

The arranged character of the interview poses a well-known quandary to this source of research. Inevitably it affects the very subject it wishes to gain information upon – not only by way of questioning which points the discussion in a certain direction, but also by means of the person who places the questions and thereby becomes the point of reference for the answers[17].

On the IETF's mailing lists, engineers do talk among themselves. The language used within the community is largely incomprehensible to laymen. No translation takes place, no term or acronym is explained, and no correlation described (unless someone expressly asks for it). Whether or not outsiders attend the arguments seems to be of no influence. Lurkers do not have any recognizable relevance for occurrences on the mailing list. This aspect refers to one of the properties of mailing lists as a source of research. In contrast to the interview, the observer is not an addressee here. She is not only invisible – like in a public space constituted by the mass media – she does not even form an audience. Neither does she initiate a discussion, nor does she intervene involuntarily. It is probably the collective interior orientation of the participants that lends the act of reading mailing lists the impression of "peeking over the fence": Everyday life situations, rituals, and traditions, which are hardly made explicit in an interview, can be pursued from a close, virtual proximity. And depending upon the speaker, our point of view of the occurrence may change.

18.3.3 The Role of the Informant: The Hows and Whys of 8+8

The interview authorizes one person as a speaker, while many voices struggle to be heard on the mailing list[18]. While the monological interview tends to portray individual certainties, the coexistence of conflicting views on the Net serves to qualify these convictions. Convictions, which in the context of surveys may only prove contentious after several interviews, would provoke ongoing controversies as soon as they were expressed on an IETF mailing list. Thus, the hypothetical question becomes what reactions would be expressed by the community due to the author's retrospective on 8+8 in the interview? Would they share his conclusions? Applause and whistles are the likely result.

---

[17] The approach of Symbolic Interactionism is based on the idea that the meaning of situations is produced interactively and, therefore, dependent on the contexts in which it became subject of discussion or action (e.g., Blumer, 1969).

[18] During the GOR Workshop the objection was raised that mailing lists could not be compared with individual, but only with group interviews. Admittedly, group interviews are also capable of bringing controversies to light. However, discussions on mailing lists cannot be repeated in the same form as group interviews. Apart from the fact that such a large number of people could hardly be gathered around one table, an interview would create a special situation that differs from the Net's common working environment. What is more, unlike real-life conversations, the asynchronous mailing list service enables a simultaneous overlapping speech (see Black et al., 1983). Even the discussions during the IETF meetings indicate stronger hierarchical patterns than those on the mailing lists.

The mailing list is a collective and polyphonic informant. Their "dangling conversations" (Black, Levin, & Quinn, 1983, p.62) bring to light the community's entire spectrum of opinions, and thereby illuminate the discord, or ambivalence, inherent in the process of developing technical norms. The IETF mailing lists illustrate the difficulty in reaching agreements on what is technically right and wrong. At least implicitly, mailing lists deny a quality of the Internet's technical development. Individual narrations gladly attribute the qualities of coherent rationality and objective logic superior to their conceivable alternatives to the Internet. From a methodical point of view, the insights into the contingency of technology developments, gained by studying such controversies, may constitute the most valuable characteristic of the mailing list.

Nevertheless, the polyphonic nature of the Net does not permit the conclusion that mailing lists are per se superior to other research sources, or in fact capable of replacing these. By no means do the yields of these two forms of investigation differ from one another in their proximity to reality or authenticity. For monological interviews, like meandering mailing list debates, always offer, as Latour writes "texts or stories bearing on *something else*" (Latour 1988, p.169). It is this distance between reflection and reality, this "something else", that remains the same in both cases.

The difference between these two windows onto the inner world of the Internet cannot be found in the reliability of the depiction but in the manner they represent reality – in other words, in the narrative ordering to which the events, and their complicated subplots, are subjected.

To conclude one may say, interviews emphasize causal connections between events or matters and thereby offer answers to analytically-oriented "why questions". By contrast, the IETF's mailing lists reflect a collective effort to establish a common plane of interpretation. The fully-fledged routines and rituals, observable in the development of new technical ground, offer answers to phenomenological-inspired "how questions". Nevertheless, the two research sources are complementary.

References

Black, S. D., Levin, J. A., & Quinn, C. N. (1983). Real and nonreal time interaction: "Unraveling multiple threads of discourse". *Discourse Processes, 6*, 59–75.

Blumer, H. (1969). *Symbolic interactionism: Perspective and method.* Englewood Cliffs: Prentice-Hall.

Bradner, S. O. & Mankin, A. (Eds.). (1996). *IPng. Internet protocol next generation.* Reading: Addison-Wesley.

December, J. (1996). Units of analysis for Internet communication. *Journal of Communication, 46.* [Online]. Available: http://www.usc.edu/dept/annenberg/vol1/ssue4/december.html.

Faßler, M. (1996). *Mediale Interaktion. Speicher – Individualität – Öffentlichkeit.* München: Wilhelm Fink Verlag.

Heintz, B. (1993). *Die Herrschaft der Regel. Zur Grundlagengeschichte des Computers.* Frankfurt a. M.: Campus.

Helmers, S., Hoffmann, U., & Hofmann, J. (1996). *Netzkultur und Netzwerkorganisation. Das Projekt „Interaktionsraum Internet".* WZB discussion paper FS II 96-103. [Online]. Available: http/duplox.wz-berlin.de/dokumente.html.

Helmers, S., Hoffmann, U., & Hofmann, J. (1997). Standard development as techno-social ordering: The case of the next generation of the Internet protocol. In T. Buland et al. (Eds.), *Management and network technology, Proceedings from the COST A3 workshop* (pp. 35–57). Trondheim, Norway; EC: Brussels.

Helmers, S., Hoffmann, U., & Hofmann, J. (1998). *Internet... The final frontier: An ethnographic account. Exploring the cultural space of the Net from the inside. WZB discussion paper FS II 98-112 (English Version: WZB discussion paper FS II 00-101).* [Online]. Available: http/duplox.wz-berlin.de/dokumente.html.

Knoblauch, H. (1995). *Kommunikationskultur- Die kommunikative Konstruktion kultureller Kontexte.* Berlin: Walter de Gruyter.

Kerckhove De, D. (1996). Jenseits des globalen Dorfs. Infragestellen der Öffentlichkeit. In R. Maresch (Ed.), *Medien und Öffentlichkeit. Positionierungen – Symptome – Simulationsbrüche* (pp. 135–148). Boer.

Latour, B. (1992). Where are the missing masses? The sociology of a few mundane artifacts. In W. E. Bijker & J. Law (Eds.), *Shaping technology/building society. Studies in sociotechnical change* (pp. 225–258). Cambridge: MIT Press.

Latour, B. (1988). The politics of explanation: An alternative. In S. Woolgar (Ed.), *Knowledge and reflexivity. New frontiers in the sociology of knowledge* (pp. 155–176). London: Sage.

Reid, E. M. (1996). Communication and community on Internet relay chat: Constructing communities. In P. Ludlow (Ed.), *HIGH NOON on the electronic frontier. Conceptual issues in cyberspace* (pp. 397–411). Cambridge: MIT Press.

RFC 1718: The IETF secretariat & Gary Malkin (1994). *The tao of IETF – A guide for new attendees of the Internet engineering task force.*

RFC 1796: Christian Huitema, Jon Postel, & Steve Crocker (1995). *Not all RFCs are standards.*

RFC 1925: Ross Callon (1996). *The twelve networking truths.*

RFC 1958: Brian Carpenter (1996). *Architectural principles of the Internet.*

RFC 2026: Scott Bradner (1996). *The Internet standards process – Revision 3.*

Samarajiva, R. & Shields, P. (1997). Telecommunication networks as social space: Implications for research and policy and an exemplar. *Media Culture and Society, 19,* 535–555.

Shirky, C. (1995). *Voices from the net.* Emeryville: Ziff-Davis.

Vogelsang, W., Steinmetz, L., & Wetzstein, T. (1995). Öffentliche und verborgene Kommunikation in Computernetzen. *Rundfunk und Fernsehen, 43,* 538–548.

19 Studying Online Love and Cyber Romance

Nicola Döring

The fact that people fall in love on the net, and truly experience deep feelings during the course of their cyber romance, has been demonstrated too often to still be denied. Nevertheless, it is often doubted that *genuine* love relationships exist on the net. How can it be possible to lead a close, intimate relationship if participants are only there for each other primarily via their computer-mediated messages? The first section of this contribution argues that cyber romance should no longer be treated as an exotic fringe phenomenon, and, instead, should be regarded as a serious sociopsychological research topic. The second section discusses the most important data collection methods used to study cyber romance.

19.1 Why Study Cyber Romance?

Studying cyber romance is significant for three reasons: first, cyber romantic relationships can be reconstructed theoretically in the form of normal social relationships (19.1.1). Besides, they are quite common among people active on the Net (19.1.2). Finally, in the context of social relationships research, cyber romantic relationships provoke a number of interesting new research questions (19.1.3).

19.1.1 Definition of Cyber Romance

In order to clarify whether, or under which circumstances, a cyber romance counts as a genuine romantic relationship or merely represents a pseudo relationship, we must first clarify the term relationship.

A social relationship develops between two people if they repeatedly have contact with one another, be it in form of asynchronous communication (e.g., letters, notes) or synchronous interaction (e.g., telephone calls, personal conversations, joint activities). In contrast to a social contact as an individual event, social relationships continue over a period of several occasions, so that each individual contact is affected both by the preceding contacts and by expectations of future contacts. During the course of the development of the relationship, participants get to know each other and have to negotiate a common relationship definition, for instance by mutually spelling out their expectations and by continually renewing their commitment to the relationship. Since the relationship continues in the periods between individual contacts, apart from open communication and interactive behavior patterns, emotional, motivational, and cognitive processes within each partner (e.g., a feeling of longing, preparing for the next meeting, remembering common experiences) also play an important role in the quality and continuity of the relationship. This sociopsychological interpretation of personal relationships (see Hinde, 1997) places no restrictions on the type of media used for the individual contacts, and thereby allows one, theoretically, to speak of genuine social relationships when the participants predominantly or exclusively contact each other in a computer-mediated environment.

Such relationships based on contacts mediated primarily via computers, where the first contact normally takes place on the net, are today called *online relationships* or *cyber relationships*. This distinguishes them from "conventional" relationships, where the first contact and the important following contacts take place face-to-face. In Net discourse, these conventional relationships are now called *offline relationships*, *real life relationships*, *3D relationships*, or *in person relationships*.

Social relationships can roughly be divided into formal (e.g., salesman-customer) and personal (e.g., father-son) relationships, whereby personal relationships are further divided into strong (e.g., friendship) and weak (e.g., acquaintance) ties. Romantic relationships (to a large extent synonymous with love affairs or partnerships) are strong personal bonds which clearly differ from family and friendship relationships because of their open sexuality. Passion, intimacy, and commitment are three of the core elements of romantic relationships (Steinberg, 1986). Theoretically, nothing can be held against the fact that a love relationship is primarily or exclusively based on Net contacts, since in principle, passion (e.g., shared arousal when articulating sexual fantasies), intimacy (e.g., support in times of personal problems), and commitment (e.g., regular contact) can also be passed on via the asynchronous or synchronous exchange of digital text, tone, or image messages. Whether and how people on the Net make use of these options and thereby actually lead *genuine romantic online relationships* (synonymous with cyber love affairs, cyber romance) must, in contrast, be ascertained with the help of empirical analysis. If one of the participants in a cyber romance also lives in a committed relationship outside of the net, then the cyber romance is called a *cyber affair*.

19.1.2 Pervasiveness of Cyber Romance

How common are romantic online relationships? Although a majority of Net contacts occur between people who already know each other offline (which affects the *density of the social network;* see Hamman, 1998), many people also find new contacts directly after accessing the Net (which affects the *size of the social network,* see Wellman & Gulia, 1999). Most of the new online relationships are *weak ties:* information is exchanged with colleagues overseas or the last episode of a favorite TV series is discussed with other fans worldwide. Those people who develop *strong ties* on the Net in the form of friendships or romantic relationships represent a minority of the online population. A minority which nevertheless might, in absolute numbers, include several million people worldwide. In a representative telephone survey in 1995, 14% of n = 601 US citizens who had access to the Net reported having become acquainted with people on the Net whom they would refer to as "friends". Unfortunately, no differentiation was made between romantic and nonromantic relationships (Katz & Aspden, 1997). In surveys aimed at persons active in newsgroups, the portion of those who maintain close relationships on the Net increases to 61% (53% friendships, 8% romantic relationships; Park & Floyd, 1996). If one considers MUD (multi user dungeons/domains) participants only, the portion of those with close Net relationships shoots up to 91% (Schildmann, Wirausky, & Zielke, 1995), or 93% (67% friendships, 26% romantic relationships; Park & Robert, 1997). Among people who use chat forums, cyber romance seems to be especially prevalent, as most online chat forums promote flirting and fooling around.

In summary: romantic Net relationships neither represent an exotic fringe phenomenon nor an epidemic mass phenomenon. Instead, Net relationships are an experience that belongs to the everyday life of a considerable portion of the Net population, and one which is growing exponentially. Furthermore, an increasing number of people are also indirectly affected by cyber romance and cyber affairs, because friends, relatives, partners or clients fall in love online. According to the results of an ongoing public WWW questionnaire on cyber romance that has been conducted since 1997 by the *Self-Help & Psychology* Online Magazine, as of October 1999 the majority (70% of n = 2,174) of respondents (64% women, 36% men) admitted having experienced at least one case of cyber romance in their immediate social surroundings (Maheu, 1999). Psychologist Storm King, active in the areas of clinical and socio-psychological Internet research, provides the following anecdotal evidence that demonstrates the everyday nature of cyber romantic affairs:

> This author has presented at several psychology conferences, talking about Internet interpersonal relationships. At each of four presentations, the audience, composed of psychologists and mental health workers, was asked to raise their hand if they knew of someone (friend, family or client) that had partaken in a

cyber romance. Each time, of the approximately 50 people in the audience, about half the hands went up. (King, 1999)

The fact that most cyber romantic relationships are also cyber *affairs* is a result of the socio-statistic composition of the Net population, in which singles are the minority. Of the 9,177 people active on the Net (14% women, 86% men), who participated in Cooper, Scherer, Boies, and Gordon's (1999) WWW survey, 80% had a steady partner and approximately 50% were married, which mirrors the situation outside of the net: even today's hi-tech nations are *not* "single societies".

19.1.3 Research Questions

Who is most likely to actually fall in love on the net? Which Net forums are particularly suitable for making romantic acquaintances or for strengthening existing relationships? What personal and behavioral characteristics are indicative of interpersonal (and particularly of erotic) attraction, if we confront each other on the Net only in the form of our text contributions written on machines? After becoming acquainted via a Chat, a MUD or a Web site, how, when, and why do people agree to switch over to private e-mail contact, telephone calls, exchange of pictures, or personal meetings? How, when, and why do they consciously abstain from such a change in media, and thus maintain the "virtual" character of the relationship? How do people involved in a cyber romantic relationship deal with the fact that one can control one's own self-presentation much better via computer-mediated text communication than in face-to-face situations? What effect does tactical self-presentation in online love (e.g., consciously withholding certain personal traits, or information) have on misgivings, or an increase in them, for the other partner? How widely spread is "love at first byte" really, or at what point in time in the media mediated acquaintance do participants claim to have fallen in love, or actually love each other? How do online lovers officially seal their status as a couple? What is their degree of commitment to their cyber romance? If, during the course of the strengthening of a cyber romance, various media changes took place before the face-to-face meeting, the romantic relationship is considered less of an online relationship and more of an offline relationship. Which definition criteria do participants apply to the relationship in order to illustrate the dichotomous online versus offline relationship construction in the continuum of the relative significance of Net communication? How large is the share of multinational and long distance relationships amongst cyber romantic relationships? How do online lovers deal with the (sometimes considerable) geographical distances, and cultural differences? Such research questions are initially aimed at establishing a detailed definition. Systematic studies may thereby help to qualify the occurrence frequency and/or subjective meaning of those characteristics of cyber romance, which so often arouse interest in the public eye (e.g., cyber weddings or online gender swapping).

Foremost, a descriptive examination of cyber romance is necessary but studies which use the Net context as a new test bed for well-known impression formation, self-presentation, attraction, and social relationship theories are also required. Even if other people are initially invisible on the net, one nevertheless gets a general impression of what someone is like on the basis of their communication behavior. In interpersonal exchange outside of as well as within the net, co-operation, sincerity, spontaneity, and empathy for others are valued traits. The fear those who are egocentric, socially incompetent, and incapable of forming relationships can comfortably "consume" social contacts without any risk merely by pushing a button on a keyboard should be analyzed in view of this background. After all, even on the net, compassion for other people is a prerequisite for getting to know somebody more closely. Concepts such as intimacy, self-disclosure, social skills or interpersonal proximity should be examined according to the role they play in a particular medium. "Genuine" interpersonal proximity, as is always maintained intuitively, requires face-to-face contact, even though the psychosocial dimensions of such categorical claims are not confirmed. The common fear that Net relationships, which will play an increasingly important role for younger generations, cause deficits in social skills is also questionable: computer-mediated relationships also require, apart from technical expertise in operating the system, various social skills, such as explicitly articulating one's feelings in absence of nonverbal communication.

If teenagers' first loves are increasingly online love relationships, will certain development psychology and socialization theory concepts have to be reformulated? If cyber romance particularly stresses emotional intimacy, because the partners usually communicate with each other for days, weeks, or months on an exclusively verbal basis, and otherwise do not pursue common activities, should they then be characterized as "female" forms of communication? Or wouldn't they pose a reason, in view of the amount of male participation, to question the hypothesis of two distinctly gender specific communication styles? It is not the repeatedly alleged possibility of falling for a gender switch, or of presenting oneself on the Net as a neuter that make cyber relationships so interesting from a gender theory point of view. Instead, it is the fact that we encounter and desire each other on the Net explicitly as men or as women, while we realize unusual forms of self-presentation and of coming closer which may deviate from traditional gender roles and from conventional rituals of homosexual, heterosexual or bisexual paradigms.

Studies on cyber romance not only contribute to basic scientific research into social relationships, they are also relevant from the perspective of applied science. Under certain circumstances, excessive devotion to cyber romantic relationships can be an indicator, or catalyst, of psychosocial problems and disturbances. As a result, some people limit their radius of behavior drastically during the course of a cyber romance, and then increase their Net activities even if these already have serious negative consequences within their psychological, physical or social environment. If a person is on her computer for nights on end in order to chat with her online love, neglects all other areas of life and nevertheless tends to increase her time online, then this is often referred to as an "online addiction" (see Young, 1998). Such pathological labeling can, however, be problematic. Loss of control, development of tolerance, and withdrawal symptoms may be characteristic for addictions as well as for falling in love. Overly enthusiastic Net activity seldom is caused by an obsession with technology in itself. Rather it is a symptom of a – more or less conflicted – search for interpersonal proximity. With regard to problematic patterns of Net use, the focus of research needs to be centered on pathological relationship behavior, its determinants and moderators, instead of projecting the problem onto the medium itself. Since computer-mediated communication is a part of the everyday lifestyle of growing portion of the population, cyber romance and cyber affairs will increasingly become a topic in the context of psychological consultation and therapy (see Cooper et al., 1999; Greenfield & Cooper, 1999). An expert treatment of these new forms of relationships and their various psychosocial functions, (e.g., escapism, compensation or exploration) is therefore required and should be based on sound social scientific research instead of on storytelling and prejudices (see Döring, 1999).

19.2 How to Study Cyber Romance?

If one wants to get a precise idea of the characteristics of romantic Net relationships, different data collection *methods* are at our disposal. Observational studies (19.2.1), interviews and surveys (19.2.2), personal narratives (19.2.3), and practical suggestions (19.2.4) are four particularly important sources of data.

Due to space restrictions, this chapter focuses on data collection and does not go into data analysis. In the case of offline data about online love, all the conventional analytical methods are applicable. In the case of online data, conventional data analysis methods can also be used for standardized online interviews or surveys whose data output can easily be processed by the common statistical packages. More difficult to analyze are natural online data such as chat conversations, newsgroup postings or Web sites. As Rössler (this volume) points out, a content analysis of natural online data is a challenge for traditional methodology in many ways. "Online content analysis," he summarizes, "is a lot of work with little gains but yet an important and responsible task because content on the Net cannot be reproduced or studied by communication scholars in the future." In fact, natural online data on cyber romances are not only historically but also psychologically unique since the most important discourses on the phenomenon take place online. Even though we know that the analysis of natural online data is not an easy task, it should not stop us from collecting such data. On the contrary, even purely exploratory data collection and inspection are key prerequisites of any further development in online methodology as well as in our understanding of online social phenomena.

19.2.1 Observational Studies

Observation of computer-mediated communication and interaction processes is facilitated by the fact that the medium allows complete documentation of interpersonal events without any additional technology and without the target persons noticing the documentation process. For example, we can completely log public behavior in mailing lists, newsgroups, chat forums or MUDs (multi user dungeons) for hours, days, and weeks, and on the basis of this observation data examine flirtation behavior, acquaintance processes, but also communication within couples. *Automatically compiled observation logs* can be analyzed qualitatively, and/or quantitatively. Since romantic online encounters are so prevalent and online (participatory) observation in Chats and MUDs is quite a well-known data collection method (see Utz, this volume) it's surprising that there have been as yet no online observational studies examining romantic Net relationships systematically on the basis of automatic observation logs. As illustrated on the basis of two chat interaction logfiles, such observational studies could contribute to our understanding of cyber romance.

The first logfile documents a meeting between *Bekin* and *ABC* on the mainly German language chat channel #germany (February 18th, 1999; only the messages of the two focus persons will be listed). Bekin and ABC both address their respective names, home towns, and leisure interests during the first ten minutes of the online dialogue. The interspersed smileys underscore the friendly atmosphere, while the rapid reactions show mutual interest. Just as in face-to-face situations, small talk normally takes place at the beginning of a potential Net relationship:

[18:16] <Bekin> are u here ABC

[18:16] <abc> yes

[18:16] <Bekin> ok

[18:17] <Bekin> whats ur name

[18:17] <abc> Sandra

[18:17] <Bekin> my name is bekin

[18:17] <abc> Nice to meet you bekin:)

[18:17] <Bekin> and i am Turkish

[18:17] <abc>:)

[18:18] <Bekin> do u speak german

[18:18] <abc> so, when did you came into germany?

[18:18] <abc> No, I can understand, but can't speak

[18:18] <Bekin> i born here

[18:19] <abc> I have learned german language in primary school

[18:19] <Bekin>: -)

[18:19] <abc> but as I am working in english language, I have forgot lots of words

[18:19] <Bekin> and i learned English in Primary scool

[18:19] <abc>:)

[18:20] <abc> I am trying to learn German language again

[18:20] <Bekin> Wow thats great

[18:20] <abc> thanks

[18:21] <Bekin> do u speak Tuerkish? -)

[18:21] <abc> No, just Bosnian... but we have some similar words

[18:21] <Bekin> what a words?

[18:22] <abc> I don't know precisely but lots of Bosnian words are Turkish origin

[18:23] <Bekin> yes

[18:23] <Bekin> are u visit Germany?

[18:23] <abc> Long time ago

[18:23] <Bekin> when?

[18:23] <abc> I was in Koeln

[18:24] <Bekin> Koeln is a Wunderfull City

[18:24] <abc> 1987

[18:24] <abc> yes, it is

[18:24] <Bekin> but the city where i leave is better

[18:24] <abc> where do you live?

[18:25] <Bekin> Mannheim

[18:25] <Bekin> u know

[18:25] <abc> yes I know, but I never been there

[18:26] <abc> what are you doing except working

The second logfile documents romantic communication on the #38plus-de (February 19th, 1999) chat channel. Morrison and Janina, who are officially a couple, refer to each other with their nicknames (Morri, Jani, sweetie). To a third person (BlueMan), Janina stresses the monogamous nature of her relationship with Morrison. She kisses

Morrison virtually and publicly. Morrison plays a love song for Janina on the channel. What becomes clear is the way the partners use verbal and nonverbal means of expression via computer-mediated communication, in order to create a friendly, attentive first contact (Bekin and ABC) or an euphoric, amorous rendezvous (Janina and Morrison):

[15:31] * * * Joins: Morrison (user5@146.usk.de)

[15:31] <Morrison> morning fans:))

[15:31] <janina> morri!!!!

[15:32] <Morrison> jani,:)))))))))))))))))))))))

[15:34] <Morrison> how are we feeling today?

[15:35] * janina is sad, because she has to go soon

[15:37] <BlueMan> janina: you have to leave so soon???

[15:38] <janina> morri, my sweetie, were you also here yesterday?????

[15:38] <Morrison> jani, not me

[15:38] <janina> blueman, well I'll stay for a bit

[15:39] <BlueMan> janina: *smile*

[15:39] <janina> blueman, also *smile* (however don't cuddle me again, otherwise morri will get mad)

[15:40] <BlueMan> janina: I don't care *grin*

* Morrison plays ☐ i can't stop loving you.mp³☐ 3304kb ☐

[15:47] <janina> morri, No. 10 is simply the most beautiful song *kiss*

[15:47] <Morrison> jani, I can't play it often enough

[15:48] <janina> morri, here's a rose @-;-;---;-- for you

Field observations, which include longer participation in selected Net forums, as well as field interviews with their participants, permit the reconstruction of romantic Net relationships from the first encounter to the happy ending, the split-up or the change of the relationship. Active participation in the respective Net forum and private contacts to members of the forum during field research provide insight into the participants' biographies. From his one year of field observation in various Compuserve chat forums (SIGs: Special Interest Groups), Sannicolas (1997) offers the following information on the "success ratio" of romantic chat relationships:

> In the year that this researcher has spent visiting SIG's I have seen approximately 50 relationships form online. In many of those instances, one party has moved a great distance to be with the other person, without giving much time to spend time together face-to-face getting to know one another. All of the knowl-

edge about the other person has come from their interaction over the "puter". Thus, it is not surprising that out of these approximately 50 relationships, only a very small number (3) have worked out to last more than 6 months. (Sanni-colas, 1997)

As a participating observer, Debatin (1997) frequented an anonymous CompuServe chat room between December 1995 and July 1997, and thereby gained insight into the resident virtual group's structure as well as into the relationships between the individual group members. The author presents observation logs of individual chan-nel discussions and interprets these against the background of his own experiences on the channel. As a result, he managed to solve an alleged forum participant's leukemia death as a dramatized retreat from a complicated online love affair:

> E. was suffering, as she had told many regulars in confidence, from leukemia. After her disappearance from the forum it was said that she had died. Her death was received mournfully in the forum, and Showan, her cyber lover, disap-peared from the forum for several months. Later, we found out that E. had only feigned her illness and death in order to free herself from an emotionally com-plicated affair with Showan. Approx. 15 years younger and a single Showan wanted to begin a "new life" with E., who was tied up in an unhappy marriage. This was out of the question for her. Some months later, E. got back in contact with Showan, and even occasionally returned to the forum. (Debatin, 1997)

Automatic observation logs document participants' behavior in public forums. Be-yond that, by means of participatory field observation we can gain information on the happening behind the scenes and on the partakers' subjective experiences. Outsiders cannot register how private Net communication comes about in detail, but even more so by the participants themselves. Many mail clients not only store sent messages, but also receive e-mails, meaning that a glance in his or her private mailbox is all a Net user needs to be able give precise information on the communication with his or her cyber love:

> It has been 2 months now that we've been together and so far I have received a total of 140 e-mail messages and he has approx. 160 from me. (Story 20 in the Archive of Cyber Love Stories: http://www.lovelife.com/LS/)

People who are active on the Net usually archive large parts of their e-mail corre-spondence, and in particular their electronic love letters. Occasionally, they will also record their private online discussions, which is unproblematic for many chat and MUD programs to execute (without the opposite side's knowledge). In this manner, we can cull objective behavior data on intimate social events, which normally remain undocumented and can at most be recalled from memory if the participants do not associate with one another via media. Logs of private (and more or less openly sexual) Net contacts in the context of cyber romance are occasionally incorporated into personal narratives (see section 19.2.3). They can also be used as data for empirical social research, provided the participants agree to supply the appropriate documents.

Automatic registration of computer-mediated communication processes generally presents a particularly economically and ecologically viable form of data acquisition. It is, however, afflicted by ethical problems. One of the core problems is the fact that nowadays privacy is the subject of extremely controversial debate in most Net contexts. The argument postulated by participants and outsiders states that any open group communication on the Net is public domain, in principle, and thereby qua implicit agreement open for documentation by anybody interested, just as the case may be with, for instance, television talk shows or panel discussions on political meetings. The opposite viewpoint states that Net forums are not addressed at a dispersed, broad audience, and instead fulfill an internal exchange aimed at only those people who are currently enlisted. Incognito logging of group interactions in the Net would thus be equivalent to the secret recording of a table conversation in a restaurant or a multi-person chat at a party, and would represent an unethical infringement of privacy laws. Ethical problems in the context of online observational studies cannot be resolved by simply applying overall guidelines. Rather, we should make conscious decisions for each study based on our respective research aim as well as on the specific social norms of the observed forum. In light of these considerations, the names and computer addresses of all persons involved in the two logfiles presented in this section have, for purposes of data privacy, been changed. Anonymity is still ensured, even though the names of the forums and the times at which the interactions took place have been listed for purposes of documentation.

19.2.2 Interviews and Surveys

Interviews and surveys are particularly suitable for researching romantic online relationships, since they can equally address past events and future expectations, and can also include those contacts that remain hidden to observation.

In *interviews*, direct dialogue is established between the researcher and the respondent. Research interviews can be conducted face-to-face, over the telephone, or in a chat or MUD. Standardized interviews stick to a fixed catalog of questions and give the respondent a choice of answers from a set of preselected alternatives. In this way, a lot of people can be interviewed efficiently, and the responses can be easily compared (for a standardized telephone survey on personal Net relationships see Katz & Aspden, 1997). In contrast, semi-open or open interviews adapt the questions to the course of the interview. Additionally, the respondents have the opportunity of expressing themselves in their own words. The variety and quantity of the data gained in this way with a relatively small numbers of informants permit detailed descriptions of individual cases, however, it hardly permits generalizations on how common or typical the described phenomena and constellations are. Face-to-face interviews, which focus on Net relationships among other things, were either conducted as semi-open interviews, such as those carried out by Wetzstein, Dahm, Steinmetz, Lentes, Schampaul, and Eckert (1995) or as open or clinical interviews, such as those by Turkle (1995). In both studies, the interviews are, unfortunately, only documented in the form of individual quotations. In his open interview study, Shaw (1997) gave his $n = 12$ student informants the option of sharing information on their experiences with gay chat contacts either via e-mail, chat, or over the telephone. Albright and Conran (1995) interviewed $n = 33$ chatters on their cyber romantic relationships by asking the following questions:

> *Initial meeting and Attraction*
> Where and how did you meet the person or persons with whom you became intimately involved? What first attracted you? What got you interested? What fascinated you most? How did you know this person (or persons) was "right" for you?

> *Development of Relationship*
> What was the frequency, intensity, and content of your online communications? How did you augment and shape your messages for each other? Did you speak on the telephone, send photos, and plan a time to flesh meet? If you did some or all of these, how was it decided and what happened? How did your relationship transform, grow, or end over time? Did you develop an offline relationship? If so, how did that evolve, and what, if any online communication was still used?

> *Truth and Deception*
> How did you learn to trust the other or others? How quickly did you experience a meeting of the minds, a sense of intimacy? What, if any, nice surprises or disappointments did you experience? What, if any, fantasies or simulations did you do online?

In *surveys* there is no direct contact between researcher and respondent. The questions in the questionnaire are fixed and the answers are entered there. The questionnaire can be handed out personally on paper, or sent via the postal service, as a private e-mail, as a posting to a mailing list or newsgroup, or be made available as an online document on the WWW. The choice of distribution medium affects the composition of the sample.

Communications scientist, Traci Anderson, (1999a) is currently examining cyber love on the basis of a WWW questionnaire. The questionnaire includes closed questions (e.g., multiple choice question on the communication media used) and open questions (e.g., "How do you feel about online romantic relationships compared to in-person romantic relationships?" or "How do you feel about your current or most recent online romantic partner?"). Additionally, general attitudes towards romantic love are measured on a scale (example item: "I believe that to be truly in love is to be in love forever."). A second WWW questionnaire (Anderson, 1999b) is concerned with cyber affairs. Apart from questions on quantity and quality of Internet use and on personal dispositions, it also asks about direct participation in or indirect suffering caused by cyber affairs. For three years, the current WWW Self-Help and Psychology Magazine questionnaire (Maheu, 1999) has in particular been concerned with the sexual dimensions of cyber romance (example item: "Can cyber sex be as satisfying as physical sex?"), and also allows the respondents to enter a personal statement "pro" or "contra" cyber romance. In her online romance survey, psychologist Pamela McManus (1999) addresses, among other things, the announcement of cyber relationships in the social network (e.g., to parents or friends), as well as the ensuing reactions from the direct social environment.

WWW surveys employing self-selected samples (for instance, Anderson, 1999a, 1999b, Maheu, 1999, McManus, 1999), are more likely to be answered by people who are both particularly active on the Internet (and therefore more likely to find the questionnaire in the first place) and particularly interested in questions concerning romance and love on the Net (and thus more motivated to answer the questionnaire). Surveys based on self-selected online samples therefore have a tendency to *overrate* the frequency, intensity, and significance of online romance. In contrast to this, the studies of Parks and Floyd (1995), and Parks and Robert's (1997) using random online samples are protected against such distortions (for generalizability issues in Internet-based survey research see Brenner, this volume).

In the field of Net relationships, research interviews and surveys are more common than observational studies. Since interviews and surveys are reactive methods, the volunteers must give explicit consent to the investigation, which eliminates a lot of ethical problems related to observational studies. As Sassenberg and Kreutz (this volume) point out, anonymity is a crucial issue in online surveys influencing both participation rate and honesty of answers. Whenever we guarantee the anonymity of an online survey to make our respondents feel safe, we should make an extra effort to ensure actual nonidentifiability. In some cases (depending on the survey design) we should direct potential respondents to anonymous e-mailing or surfing services to prevent them from inadvertently handing over delicate information such as their personal e-mail or IP addresses in the course of responding to the survey. Since the results of a Web survey are online themselves one has to make sure that the respective data file cannot be downloaded or inspected by any third party, which inadvertently was the case in one of the above-mentioned cyber romance surveys.

19.2.3 Personal Narratives

Firsthand personal narratives can be found in some of the standard *sociopsychological literature* on cyber romance. In the rarest cases they originate from the social scientists themselves, who would – according to prevailing social norms in academia – possibly endanger their professional integrity if they were to reveal self-aspects related to love and sexuality. Instead, guest contributions are used. In the anthology *Wired Women* the programmer Liv Ullman (1996) talks about e-mail love; in the online magazine *Cybersociology* an anonymous author Sue (1997), who is likewise foreign to the social sciences, reports of her cyber liaisons. The anthropologist Cleo Odzer (1997) combines the descriptive and detailed reports of her own romantic and sexual Net experiences with general reflections based on feminism and cultural criticism; as an independent writer, she is unconstrained by academic norms.

Without a doubt, the largest collection of personal narratives on online love affairs can be found on the Net itself. Contrary to frequent claims in the context of Net communication, an inspection of the narratives does not indicate fictitious self-portrayals being produced on a large scale, a process sometimes referred to as "masquerade". Besides, from a psychological point of view, it seems implausible that people should invest so much time and trouble in publishing fictitious accounts under a fictitious alias if they have the opportunity of expressing that which really moves them without having to fear a loss of face or discrimination in their direct social environment (e.g., family, colleagues).

What a psychology student from Switzerland experienced under her nickname *Priscilla* in the net, in particular her romantic Net relationship with *MrNorth*, is illustrated in her online diary on a separate Web site (Priscilla, 1999) purposely not linked to her personal homepage. Again and again, Priscilla invites her readers to send reactions to her often meta-reflexive diary entries, and also publishes some of the detailed comments, so that dialogues develop (e.g., on unfaithfulness). Between April 1998 and May 1999, Priscilla wrote entries in her online diary on a nearly daily basis. Then she said farewell to the Internet world that over the months had started to seem more and more shallow and futile to her. With her diploma thesis, the separation from her boyfriend and her retreat from MrNorth behind her, she was about to begin her first career.

> *14th December 1998*
> How words can grab hold of you. MrNorth was so far away from me, I did not know him in person – and nevertheless I thought of him so often. The little flag on my e-mail program, which possibly indicated a new message from him, was the center of my attention. And the evenings we arranged to chat were the highlights of my day. I do not know anymore what we always talked about. I only know that I sat there for hours, with an empty stomach a lot of the time, because I had skipped dinner to be online, and I laughed. It was unbelievable.

As absurd as it seemed to me to sit in the office at night and laugh with not a soul in the house. We played with words, invented dream worlds, strange irrealities, we split ourselves up into several people and let four people speak with each other, we were horses, elephants, bears, sailed across the sea in a Viking galleon – it was an unbelievably fantastic playground which we filled together with life, a world, as it had never existed before, neither for him, nor for me. And in this fairytale world feelings also arose [...]

15th December 1998
When does infidelity begin? The longer this continued, the more I was surprised at myself by the way MrNorth accompanied me in my everyday life. I bought a jumper and asked myself whether it would please him. I walked down the streets and watched for men with short, blond hair – in the meantime he had revealed that much about his looks. I lay in the arms of my boyfriend – and thought of the man who I had never seen nor heard.

What is infidelity? I had a bad conscience. One evening I told my boyfriend about my unbelievable experiences, wanted to let him in on the secret, warn him, what do I know – but he did not get what it really meant. Language is not his thing, and he probably had no idea of how very much this world was displaced to his. So I remained alone and tried to get along in this new ground [...]

Shorter autobiographic accounts, which are typically incorporated into the personal homepage, are more common than complete online diaries. Cyber couples like to link their homepages with each other's, or even offer a joint homepage. Online diaries or private homepages, which contain empirical reports on cyber romantic relationships, are individually accessible over search engines, or bundled in the appropriate *webrings*. The most common webrings (http://www.webring.org/) are *Love Online* (62 homepages), *Love at first Byte* (82 homepages), *Internet Romance* (184 homepages), or *I Met My Mate on the Net* (241 homepages), whereby most usually involve heterosexual couples. Reports on gay or lesbian cyber romantic relationships can be found individually, for example in the *Queer Wedding Webring* (e.g., Kim & Kellie, 1999) or in the *Women Loving Women Webring* (e.g., Pedds & Birdie, 1999).

Finally, various free online archives are also accessible, which publish personal narratives on online romances. Some archives allow users to submit their own narratives into the archives via an online form. In this way, 170 contributions have so far been submitted to the *Archive of Cyber Love Stories*, which is administered by a chat forum, Hawaii Chat Universe (HCU: http://www.lovelife.com/LS/). The lack of editorial control of these archives is most apparent in the fact that 54 of the 170 contributions are either double postings, or off topic (e.g., description of offline romances). The actual database therefore consists of $n = 116$ empirical reports of cyber romantic relationships (valid: October 1999): 78% ($n = 89$) of these contributions came from women, 22% ($n = 26$) were contributed by men; in one case no gender could be allocated. All of the described relationships are heterosexual relationships. This indicates that the relatively small rate of male participation in the cyber romance and cyber sex discourse has nothing to do with lack of experience in the phenomenon and can instead be attributed to less willingness to bring the subject up for discussion. The contributors age spectrum ranges from 15 to 55 years, and the cyber romances described are accordingly of different biographic values in each case. In 59% of the cases ($n = 68$), a reference was found to the participants' hometowns. Geographical distance was small in only 9 cases (e.g., neighboring town, same city), whilst in all other cases distances of several hundred miles were registered, as well as different countries and even continents of origin. Nearly every fourth cyber romance was a cyber affair with at least one person married ($n = 15$), or living in a committed relationship ($n = 12$).

In other archives, new entries are made by the archives' administrators to whom the material has been submitted via e-mail. The central archives administration facilitates selecting and classifying the contributions. The administrator of the *Safer Dating* Web site (http://www.saferdating.com/) offers archives with $n = 37$ *True Stories* (valid: October 1999).

One must assume that in the entire spectrum of experiences with cyber romantic relationships, spectacular cases will be somewhat over-represented in the personal narratives, since unusually positive or negative experiences are the first thing that motivate people to produce and publish a contribution. From an ethical perspective, personal narratives published on the WWW can be interpreted as freely available for social scientific purposes (providing correct citation is used), since the potential audience on the WWW is far larger and more uncontrollable than the target group of a scientific publication. Therefore, the use of WWW contributions does not pose an infringement of privacy laws. The reference to the Web source frequently does not contain any reference to the author's identity, since these archived contributions usually only indicate the author's nickname. If one were, to a larger extent, to use individuals' narratives, and if the authors concerned can be identified or at least contacted, then information on the research project would be appropriate. A critical issue for the authors of online contributions is not only an unwanted distribution of their accounts in front of a larger audience, but also an undesirable recontextualization, including quoting out of context which would suggest an interpretation of their personal narratives that they might not agree with (Sharf, 1999, p.248).

19.2.4 Practical Suggestions

If we wanted to know how to flirt successfully on the net, how to unmask unfaithful cyber lovers, or get to grips with the unhappy ending of a cyber romance, it would be

futile to turn to the sociopsychological literature in search of assistance. In the meantime, the market for *counseling literature* has adopted this topic. Typically, the so-
called experts are all people who have either had the required personal Net experiences (e.g., Phlegar, 1996; Skrilloff & Gould, 1997; Theman, 1997) or have a psychological or psychotherapeutic background (e.g., Adamse & Motta, 1996; Booth &
Jung, 1996; Gwinnell, 1998). Such counseling books are strongly shaded by their
authors' personal opinions, and may give questionable advice ("Cyber sex: most
women – if they're honest about it – have faked one orgasm or two. Just fake one on
the screen", "Check his fidelity: change your screen name and try seducing him in
your new persona", Skrilloff & Gould, 1997, p.70, p.97). Some of the counseling
literature can nevertheless provide researchers with interesting suggestions and case
descriptions.

Besides the conventional book publications, counseling literature written by experts is also available on the net, in the form of *online magazines*, which may not
primarily, but at least marginally address cyber romance. These include the *Self-Help
and Psychology Magazine* (http://www.shpm.com/), the *Friends and Lovers – Relationship Magazine* (http://www.friends-lovers.com/), *Cybergrrl* (http://www.cyber
grrl.com/) or the *Love, Romance & Relationships* Web site (http://www.lovingyou
.com/).

However, even more frequently, lay persons meet to assist and support each other
on the Net in *discussion forums* and *online self-help groups*. This typically takes
place on newsboards in the WWW, newsgroups in the Usenet, in mailing lists as well
as in chat forums. Of relevance in cases of problems with cyber romance and cyber
affairs are the newsboard *Cyber Romance* (http://members.lovingyou.com/boards/),
the "Cyberdating" mailing list (http://www.onlinelist.com/), and the alt.irc.romance
newsgroup. The following excerpts from a thread in the Web newsboard *Cyber Romance* address typical problems and uncertainties from different perspectives:

1st contribution (5.10.1999)
Subject: Am I insane or is it possible?

Hi, Ok this is the story about a month ago I was chatting on ICQ and I was in
the Romance room, I usually go to these rooms just for the fun of it. I was already seeing someone in real life so I wasn't really looking for anything new.
Well I was scrolling the names and I came across a name that I really thought
was interesting. So I began a chat with this guy, we chatted for over five hours
and neither of us had even realized it. We were so absorbed in our conversation
that time no longer seemed to matter. During that first talk, we discovered so
much about each other. It was like we could feel each other. I don't really know
how to explain it. All I knew was that from the moment I talked with him I had
this deep longing and caring for him. He felt the same for me. We've talked
every day since this first meeting, as I said about a month, and we feel more and

more for each other. I love him, I know I do, but what I'm asking is how can this be? I mean is it wrong to care so deeply for someone I have never even met in person and have only known a short time? We have exchanged pictures and I have to admit that having his picture and knowing what he looks like just cements my feelings more. He lives in Italy and I live in the States so that makes our relationship even more frustrating. The logical side of me is saying that I'm crazy and that it isn't right, but my heart is saying how can someone who makes me feel so good about myself and makes me happy be wrong. So can anyone give me some advice? Are things going too fast or what??

2nd contribution (5.10.1999)
Sometimes you just meet "the one". You don't know when or where. And it's not wrong to feel this way at all. HOWEVER, you are dating someone now. How do you really feel about him? How serious is your relationship with your bf? It's good to be friends but if you are thinking about more than friends then you have to decide who you want. Don't let distance stop you or your heart. My fiancé is 1300 miles from me and we just celebrated our 9th month together. Just don't start a new love relationship unless you are finished with the old.

4th contribution (5.10.1999)
Hey, I just wanted to tell you that I think it's really cool that you met someone you have so much in common with, and that i know how you feel. I have fallen in love with someone online, and I know how frustrating it is, because he lives in Germany and I live in the states. So, hang in there. It doesn't sound like you're going too fast, to me. But, it's always best to listen to your heart. That's the easiest way to tell if you are going too fast or not, and no matter what...never listen to anyone else's advice, comments, etc.

5th contribution (10.10.1999)
Believe me I know what you are feeling. The same thing happened to me too. I had been happily married for 21 yrs when I played around in a chat room and met a man that would forever change my life. We connected right away and are now engaged. I am leaving my husband and children in Dec. for a new life with him in Hawaii. He is also leaving his marriage and family also. It sounds worst than it really is. Anyway, like I did, You just gotta follow your heart and listen to No one.

7th contribution (13.10.1999)
First, I thought the reason that people posted in this forum was to get advice...now everyone is saying don't follow anyone's advice (sorry I don't get it). [...] I think we all know that there is no such thing as a "perfect" relationship and they all have their ups and downs. I've always said that if we worked

half as hard at making our current relationships work as we do complaining about them and eyeing others life would be so much better. I think it's right that you have to do what is in your heart...but in this case I think she knows in her heart this is not a good situation and will only cause problems in the long run (the distance thing alone). Why cause problems for yourself if you don't have to? I've never understood that.

If quotations from a public Net forum (i.e., Web newsboards) are used here for illustration purposes, then only with indication of the date, but without mention of the authors' names. In this manner, the authors of the newsboard postings are only identifiable (if at all) to those who have the necessary competence and motivation to read the appropriate Net forums themselves. In contrast to Web newsboard contributions that seldom reveal the authors' e-mail addresses, in mailing lists and newsgroups every posting comes with an e-mail address. This means that explicit agreement for the use of quotations can be obtained, and the mode of citation can be coordinated (e.g., anonymous or with mention of the name). Beyond the ethical purpose of informed consent, contacting the respective authors of the online contributions analyzed may provide valuable additional background information (Sharf, 1999, p.251). But getting in touch with posters is not always possible. If postings whose publication date is several years old are used for analyses, then one must assume that many of the indicated e-mail addresses are already outdated. If a larger amount of postings is analyzed, contacting all posters might be too costly. In addition, some posters of worthwhile online contributions will be slow or unreliable when it comes to responding to a researcher's request for citation permission. Furthermore, many researchers feel that data collection without explicit permission is ethical if a content analysis of the postings is conducted and the published results summarize individual statements. The lack of general ethical rules in online research should encourage us to discuss our respective ethical decisions and their implications in more detail.

19.3 Conclusion

For the investigation of cyber romance, data can be collected via observational studies, interviews, and surveys as well as via naturally occurring personal narratives and practical suggestions. The possibility of logging and documenting online communication automatically, unnoticed by the participants, and without the use of any additional technical equipment is a major advantage of online research. In addition, the fact that many lay persons publish their experiences with and attitudes towards cyber romantic relationships makes Net forums valuable data sources, whereby there is no cause to generally doubt the accounts' authenticity. In view of diverging concepts of privacy and copyright, harvesting Net documents raises ethical problems, which have to be solved individually in each specific context.

Although research activities in the field of cyber romance are on the rise and several characteristics of cyber romances have meanwhile been well-replicated (e.g., accelerated self-disclosure), there is still call for systematic empirical data. The economy of online data collection may, on the one hand, be conducive for relatively unprepared ad-hoc studies, but can, on the other hand, save resources better invested in designing the study. Representative results can be obtained from observational studies, interviews, and surveys for example by selecting Net forums, observation times or respondent samples from defined populations according to random sample principles. In contrast, analyses based on personal narratives or discussion contributions cannot be regarded as representative since we still know too little about the motives that prompt certain Net users to publicly tell the story of their online love or to publicly give advice on cyber romance. It would be worthwhile to examine in which respect descriptions of cyber romance published on the Internet deviate from descriptions recollected in the framework of representative studies. So it must be assumed that personal narratives published on the Net turn out to be more spectacular and eccentric.

That cyber romance is not a homogeneous phenomenon determined by media technology is easily proven through an explorative analysis of personal narratives, in which totally different experiences are represented (Archive of Cyber Love Stories: http://www.lovelife.com/LS/):

"Love is hard. CyberLove is impossible. I have learned this." (Story 130)

"A sad cyberlove story, but a true one. On one hand the skeptics were right, it didn't work out, but it did for 3 months, and those three months, were among the best of my life." (Story 119)

"I have found my one true love and for anyone that thinks that it can't happen online, you are wrong! Love can be found online!" (Story 161)

If one takes into account that people clearly differ both in the way they build social relationships, and in how they deal with computer-mediated communication, then it is not surprising to which extent the experiences are heterogeneous. If further research activities manage to process this heterogeneity, then mono-causal explanation models, which either attribute the existence of cyber romance to personal deficits ("Only the social inept, lonely computer freak searches for love on the net."), and/or are directly derived from media characteristics ("In the computer-based virtual reality illusionary love flourishes and people get addicted to those mock feelings."), should lose some of their persuasive power.

Contrasting virtuality with reality, the mind against the flesh, or the online relationship against the offline relationship is doubtful and at the same time necessary. Doubtful because dichotomous schematizing as a willful neglect of ambiguity and interdependence generally has the disadvantage of oversimplification. Contrasting is necessary, however, because the participants themselves frequently interpret their experiences in terms of dichotomous concepts, and then tend to contrast for example the "virtual life" with the "real life". The hypothesis of two distinct experiential realms prove then to be illusory when instructive irritations crop up:

> Of course I then asked myself what MrNorth looks like. That means: first I simply had an imaginary picture of him. Approx. 1.85 meters [6 ' 1"] tall, brown hair, brown eyes. How on earth did I deduce that? Lautrec says it isn't cool to ask a new chat acquaintance about their looks. And nevertheless most do it. MrNorth and I were cool. We did not ask each other for a long time. But nevertheless it did once strike me that that he might have a moustache and wire-framed spectacles. After that I had to ask nevertheless. He asked whether I knew Cyrano de Bergerac – that was him. He neither wears a moustache, nor spectacles, but is 1.65 meters [5' 5"] tall. How that frightened me. It disappointed me – I had wished him to be taller. The idea of chatting with such a small man dampened my joy in our talks. And then frightened me again. His looks meant that much to me? Me, who always stressed the importance of values? Now that was definitely uncool. And it was all different again. It turned out to be a joke – my virtual interlocutor had wanted to put me to the test. In reality he is some centimeters taller than I am. Although the "joke" had annoyed me a little – it had had its effect. I began to have second thoughts about my expectations. And discovered in me some completely narrow-minded ideal conceptions which I thought I had long overcome. That on the one hand – and on the other hand I became conscious of what is really important to me in a man's looks. Some other ideas, hitherto unquestioned, also changed. (Priscilla, 1999, December 9th, 1998)

An online love affair does not necessarily lend itself to better self-realization, though. Instead, dispositions independent of media technology might be decisive here (e.g., cognitive and motivational requirements for self-reflection).

About fifteen years ago, computer-mediated contacts were accused of being impersonal, unemotional, and solely determined by facts and logic due to their "technological nature." Today the exact opposite is claimed. Communication technology is blamed for inventing a dreamland, encouraging people to quickly and openly express romantic feelings and sexual attraction instead of sticking to a matter-of-fact information exchange. Caution and reserve when dealing with Net acquaintances are frequently advised these days in order to resist the temptations of online love and cyber romance. For further research into online relationships, it seems particularly sensible not to interpret anonymity and intimacy, physical distance, and sensual presence, the ability to control and unpredictability as pairs of opposites, but instead to explore them as interrelated complements that affect the quality of both our online and offline romances.

References

Adamse, M. & Motta, S. (1996). *Online friendship, chat-room romance, and cybersex. Your guide to affairs of the net.* Deerfield Beach, FL: Health Communications Inc.

Albright, J. & Conran, T. (1995). *Online love: Sex, gender, and relationships in cyberspace.* [Online]. Available: http://www-scf.usc.edu/~albright/onlineluv.txt.

Anderson, T. (1999a). *The experience of online romance.* [Online]. Available: http://members.aol.com/andersontl/surveys/romancesurvey.htm.

Anderson, T. (1999b). *Perceptions of online relationships and affairs.* [Online]. Available: http://members.aol.com/andersontl/surveys/CMRTsurvey.htm.

Booth, R. & Jung, M. (1996). *Romancing the net. A "Tell-All" guide to love online.* Rocklin, CA: Prima Publishing.

Cooper, A., Scherer, C., Boies, S., & Gordon, B. (1999). Sexuality on the Internet: From sexual exploration to pathological expression. *Professional psychology: Research and practice, 30,* 154–164.

Debatin, B. (1997). *Analyse einer öffentlichen Gruppenkonversation im Chat-Room. Referenzformen, kommunikationspraktische Regularitäten und soziale Strukturen in einem kontextarmen Medium (Vortrag gehalten auf der Jahrestagung der Fachgruppe Computervermittelte Kommunikation der DGPuK in München 1997).* [Online]. Available: http://www.uni-leipzig.de/~debatin/German/Chat.htm.

Döring, N. (2000). Romantische Beziehungen im Netz [Romantic Online Relationships]. In C. Thimm (Ed.), *Soziales im Netz. Sprache, Beziehungen und Kommunikationskulturen im Netz* [The Social on the Net. Language, Social Relationships, and Communication Cultures on the Net] (pp. 39-70). Opladen: Westdeutscher Verlag.

Döring, N. (1999). Sozialpsychologie des Internet [Social psychology of the Internet]. Göttingen: Hogrefe.

Greenfield, D. & Cooper, A. (o.J.). *Crossing the line – On line. Self-help and psychology magazine, rubrik "cyber affairs".* [Online]. Available: http://www.shpm.com/articles/sex/sexcross.html.

Gwinnell, E. (1998). *Online seductions. Falling in love with strangers on the Internet.* New York, NY: Kodansha International.

Hamman, R. (1998). *The online/offline dichotomy: Debunking some myths about AOL users and the affects of their being online upon offline friendships and offline community (MPhil dissertation, university of Liverpool, department of communication studies).* [Online]. Available: http://www.cybersoc.com/mphil.html.

Hinde, R. A. (1997). *Relationships: A dialectical perspective.* Hove, East Sussex: Psychology Press.

Katz, J. & Aspden, P. (1997). A nation of strangers? Friendship patterns and community involvement of Internet users. *Communications of the ACM, 40,* 81–86.

Kim & Kellie (1999). *Kim and Kellie's commitment ceremony.* [Online]. Available: http://www.geocities.com/WestHollywood/Village/6400/cc.html.

King, S. A. (1999). Internet gambling and pornography: Illustrative examples of the psychological consequences of communication anarchy. *CyberPsychology and Behavior, 2,* 175-184.

Maheu, M. M. (1999). *Cyber affairs survey results. Self-help & psychology magazine, rubrik "cyber affairs".* [Online]. Available: http://www.shpm.com/articles/cyber_rom ance/.

McManus, P. (1999). *Online romantic relationship survey.* [Online]. Available: http://www. shsu.edu/~ccp_pwm/.

Odzer, C. (1997). Virtual spaces. Sex and the cyber citizen. New York, NY: Berkley Books.

Parks, M. & Floyd, K. (1996). Making friends in cyberspace. *Journal of Computer-Mediated Communication, 1,* March. [Online]. Available: http://www.ascusc.org/jcmc/vol1 /issue4/parks.html.

Parks, M. & Roberts, L. (1997). *"Making MOOsic": The development of personal relationships online and a comparison to their offline counterparts.* Paper presented at the annual conference of the western speech communication association. Monterey, California. [Online]. Available: http://psych.curtin.edu.au/people/robertsl/moosic.htm.

Pedds & Birdie (1999). *Peddler & nitebird's beachouse.* [Online]. Available: http:// members.xoom.com/Beachouse/.

Phlegar, P. (1996). *Love online: A practical guide to digital dating.* Cambridge, MA: Addison Wesley Longman.

Priscilla (1999). *Priscillas Tagebuch.* [Online]. Available: http://www.priscilla.ch/ or Mirror-Site Available: http://paeps.psi.uni-heidelberg.de/doering/priscilla/.

Sannicolas, N. (1997). Erving Goffman, dramaturgy, and online relationships. *Cybersociology Magazine, 1.* [Online]. Available: http://members.aol.com/Cybersoc/is1nikki.html.

Schildmann, I., Wirausky, H., & Zielke, A. (1995). *Spiel- und Sozialverhalten im Morgen-Grauen.* [Online]. Available: http://www.mud.de/Forschung/verhalten.html.

Sharf, B. F. (1999). Beyond netiquette: The ethics of doing naturalistic discourse research on the Internet. In S. Jones (Ed.), *Doing Internet research. Critical issues and methods for examining the Net* (pp. 243-256). Thousand Oaks, CA: Sage.

Shaw, D. (1997). Gay men and computer communication: A discourse of sex and identity in cyberspace. In S. G. Jones (Ed.), *Virtual culture. Identity and communication in cybersociety* (pp. 133-145). London: Sage.

Skrilloff, L. & Gould, J. (1997). *Men are from cyberspace. The single woman's guide to flirting, dating, and finding love online.* New York, NY: St. Martin's Press.

Sternberg, R. (1986). A triangular theory of love. *Psychological Review, 93,* 119-135.

Sue (1997). *New to cyber liaisons. Cybersociology Magazine 1.* [Online]. Available: http://members.aol.com/Cybersoc/is1sue.html.

Theman, D. (1997). *Beyond cybersex: Charming her online, meeting her offline.* San Francisco, CA: Liberty Publishing.

Turkle, S. (1995). *Life on the screen: Identity in the age of the Internet.* New York, NY: Simon and Schuster.

Ullman, E. (1996). Come in, cq: The body and the wire. In L. Cherny & E. Weise (Eds.), *Wired Women. Gender, and new realities in cyberspace* (pp. 3-23). Seattle: Seal Press.

Wellman, B. & Gulia, M. (1999). Virtual communities as communities. Net surfers don't ride alone. In M. A. Smith & P. Kollock (Eds.), *Communities in cyberspace* (pp. 167-194). London & New York: Routledge.

Wetzstein, T., Dahm, H., Steinmetz, L., Lentes, A., Schampaul, S., & Eckert, R. (1995). *Datenreisende. Die Kultur der Computernetze.* Opladen: Westdeutscher Verlag.

Young, K. (1998). *Caught in the net: How to recognize the signs of Internet addiction and a winning strategy for recovery.* New York: Wiley.

20 Artificial Dialogues – Dialogue and Interview Bots for the World Wide Web

Dietmar Janetzko

The immense spread of the World Wide Web (WWW) is being followed closely by empirical social researchers. A lot of attention is currently dedicated to questions of the possibilities and restrictions of implementing "classical" sociological methods such as questionnaires and experiments on the WWW. In comparison, only a very little amount of attention has been paid to a, in no way lesser classical sociological method, the interview. The following is intended to cast light on the potential of this method for use on the WWW. Furthermore, we shall demonstrate that interviews can be conducted via the WWW even if one of the interview participants is not a human, but a computer program conceived for this purpose. Systems of this kind are reminiscent of the computer program ELIZA, which more or less convincingly simulated a speech therapist (Weizenbaum, 1966). Strangely enough, the discussion following ELIZA was reduced to a few aspects (computer credibility, ritualized communication, etc.). Serious consideration has still not been given to using such systems as a dialogue or interview partner with the user being informed beforehand that he is dealing with a computer program.

The systems introduced here are defined by different aims to those of ELIZA. Instead of acting as instruments for the exploration of natural languages, they are instead employed for user oriented dialogue systems with many possibilities for implementation. The goal of this contribution is to present their usage in carrying out standardized interviews. When polling data on the WWW, dialogue systems can add to the arsenal of methods of empirical social research. Instead of using the term "interview," we will be using the more general term "dialogue". The reason for this is that methods of dialogue steerage are suitable for modeling other forms of dyadic communication (e.g., consulting dialogues).

In order to avoid any misunderstandings, we would like to stress right from the beginning that in this contribution we are primarily concerned with simple dialogue systems (dialogue and interview bots, see below) not conceived for interpreting natural language (see Smith & Hipp, 1995). In Germany, natural language (translation) systems are being developed at great cost for the BMBF Organization's VERBMO-BIL project (Wahlster, 1993). The majority of the immense problems posed by the development of natural language dialogue systems – most of which have not been satisfactorily solved yet – do not apply to the systems sketched here (e.g., grapheme-morpheme conversion, word segmentation, syntactic and semantic analysis, text pro-duction, etc.). Certainly, simply avoiding classic problems when analyzing and syn-thesizing natural language has its price. The user of the systems introduced here will be presented with canned text (i.e., with preformulated questions or answers). What should become clear with this contribution is that, even when implementing rela-tively simple dialogue and interview bots, interesting questions of research and de-velopment crop up, and open application perspectives hitherto rarely used.

We assume that linguistic and psycholinguistic knowledge can give valuable in-formation when designing dialogue compatible systems and can help improve their acceptance. Therefore, a strictly defined selection of fundamental results of surveys of dialogues will be introduced. In particular, attention will be paid to aspects of dialogue management, since research conducted in this field is of crucial importance for developing dialogue systems. In the following section, dialogue "bots" will be presented, which count to a new efficient generation of tools for the Internet (Schroder & Janetzko, 1998). Finally, three basic types of systems will be outlined that can be differentiated by their potential for dialogue management.

20.1 Dialogue Structures

A general empirically based theory of dialogue formation that describes, explains, and projects the sequential arrangement of speaker's contributions and the coherence in dialogues does not exist. However, some results on partial aspects of dialogue structures are available, which can certainly be used for development of dialogue formation systems.

In the investigation of dialogs, great use has been derived from distinguishing between individual conversational contributions (*turns*) on the one hand and their sequential connection on the other hand. It seems obvious that a classification of both aspects is also important for the development of dialogue formation systems.

20.1.1 Dialogue Elements

An orientation towards Austin (1962) and Searle's (1969) speech act theory is al-ready discernible in the concept of *dialogue acts* itself. According to the speech act theory (inspired by Wittgenstein's later philosophy), three simultaneous aspects or dimensions can be distinguished. In the *locutionary* dimension, the fact that some-thing is being said is expressed. The *illocutionary* dimension signalizes that the speaker is doing something. The *perlocutionary* dimension is designated as the dimension where something happens to the hearer because of the speech act. The speech act theory – in its form first conceived by J. L. Austin – has been modified on numerous occasions, and one of the branches of modification led to the dialogue act concept and its application in the development of dialogue directing systems. A good example is the application of dialogue acts in the VERBMOBIL project (e.g., Schmitz & Quantz, 1996), which in itself is associated with Bunt's findings (1981, 1994). Different classes of dialogue acts are defined according to the combination of aspects of achievement (*illocutionary*) and the amount of (*propositional*) meaning (Schmitz & Quantz, 1996). Following this train of thought, speech acts such as

> A: What about Thursday?
>
> B: I would suggest Thursday.

can be listed under the dialogue act of a proposal for a rendezvous. Additionally, one should note that when automatically defining such dialogue acts, details from different sources are evaluated. Besides syntactic and semantic details, keywords, and above all the use of linguistic conventions such as neighboring pairs of the genus "Request for a rendezvous" and "Proposal for a rendezvous" (*adjacency pairs*) are included as well.

20.1.2 Dialogue Formation

While the examination of dialogue acts is in certain respects aimed at the individual building blocks, dialogue formation deals more the relationship between them. The initiative for dialogue formation can be one-sided or equally distributed for both dialogue partners. In "real life" the socio-cultural context normally decides on which side the initiative for dialogue formation lies. Examples for a particularly one-sided version of dialogue formation can be found in job interviews or consulting talks.

In the given context, certain aspects of dialogue formation can be of particular importance, since the bots to be introduced below distinguish themselves from the directors of dialogues especially in consideration of initiation. Dialogue formation is normally steered via *local* and *global strategies* (Stein, 1995). Competence in local dialogue formation manifests itself by replying to a reaction with adequate ensuing feedback. Competence in global dialogue formation consists of maneuvering a dialogue in such a way that it can be considered "meaningful". What is considered "meaningful" depends on the context (e.g., from the general to the exceptional, discussing all relevant points, etc.).

When designing dialogue systems a body of rules that could regulate the dialogue sequencing would be advantageous. Until now, however, all efforts to establish a set of rules have remained unsuccessful since what is to be considered a "meaningful" association of conversational contributions depends strongly on the context. An example of this is discussed by Levinson (1983):

> A: I have a fourteen year old son.
> B: Well that's alright.
> A: I also have a dog.
> B: Oh I'm sorry.

Isolated from its original context, this dialogue may seem strange. If one knows that A is introducing himself to B, because A wants to rent B's apartment, the dialogue definitely seems significant. However, the absence of dialogue shaping rules cannot be considered a hindrance for developing dialogue systems. During computer-sided or bot-sided control over the system, the system must be equipped with mechanisms that can allocate local as well as global dialogue formation. In the most simple case, this can be facilitated via dialogue scripts (Stein, 1995). With this technique, a whole range of possible combinations of conversational contributions can be plotted out beforehand and can be implemented in the actual dialogue formation. Dialogue scripts are particularly suitable for the dialogue systems we are dealing with here where all conversational contributions are defined beforehand in the form of menus.

Table 20.1: Interview strategies according to Cleary and Bareiss (1994)

Jump-starting	Introduction of new, untreated aspects
Chaining	Beginning and continuation of a topic
Mining	Thorough discussion of a topic
Proposing possibilities	Proposals for various possibilities
Recognizing hotspots	Realizing important topics
Backtracking	Return to previously discussed topics
Gambit-walking	Choice of sequence for asking questions

While dialogue scripts may be a simple formal method for implementing dialogue strategies they do not in themselves represent proper dialogue strategies. A summary of such strategies for interview situations can be found in Cleary and Bareiss (1994), who examined empirical interview data in respect of the implemented strategies (see Table 20.1 and 20.2).

Table 20.2: Types of interview strategy: "mining" according to
Cleary and Bareiss (1994)

Context	Question of the context the topic belongs to
Specifics	Question of an example or details
Causes/Earlier Events	Question on development
Results/Later Events	Question on results
Analogies	Question on similar situations or analogue situations
Alternatives	Question on alternative possibilities of dealing with a situation
Opportunities	Question on aspects which can be of use in a situation
Warnings	Question on aspects which need to be regarded in a situation

20.2 Bots

The words "Bots", "Softbots" or even "Knowbots" are derived from the terms "Software Robots" or "Knowledge Robots" (Etzioni, 1994; Schroder & Janetzko, 1998). Bots are systems that are supplied via the Internet and that simulate, amend or even substitute the human user for the purpose of obtaining (i.e., reception of data), reflecting (i.e., execution of inferences) and acting (e.g., drawing up of data). The demarcation from terms such as "Internet agent", which in themselves are not clearly defined, can be problematic. Table 20.3 lists a summary of the most important types of Bots.

Table 20.3: Types of bots

Watcher bots	Observation of sites and information when changes occur
Search bots	Information retrieval, above all as search engine providers
Shopping / bargain bots	Categorization of product and price information
IRC bots	Disturbances (war bots) and disturbance defense (channel-protection bots) in Internet Relay Chats (IRC)
Chatter bots	Implementation of dyadic communication
Dialog / interview bots	Systems designed for the implementation of dialogues or interviews

20.3 Designing Dialogue or Interview Bots

In the following section, three types of interview and dialogue bots are introduced and discussed in reference to their respective development requirements and to their deployment possibilities:

- Type I User asks – Bot answers.
- Type II Bot asks – User answers.
- Type III User/Bot asks – Bot/User answers.

I – User asks – Bot answers. This is the simplest form of interview or dialogue bot. When developing this and other bots with similar functions a large amount of questions (e.g., a FAQ list) is advantageous. Certainly, parallels to the use of FAQs are recognizable. However, this can only be true when the design options outlined below (e.g., context sensitive directional instruments) cannot be implemented. Even in a simple bot that operates only on top of a list of frequently asked questions, a motivational effect is to be expected as a result of the dynamic interactions that can be conducted with such a bot. Design options exist in the choice of implementation of how the user can ask questions. In the simplest case, this can be solved with a pull-down menu. When dealing with extensive lists, this sort of application can become complicated. In this case, a partitioned question catalog or a context sensitive compilation of such lists would be more effective. Bots of this sort can be used as consultative or informational systems. At the University of Freiburg in Germany, the Faculty of Cognitive Science uses a simple bot of this kind for student advice: http://cogweb. iig.uni-freiburg.de/STUDIENTIPS/.

II – Bot asks – User answers. This type seems to be a simple reversal of the first type of bot. However, a new, important aspect has to be considered in addition: this bot has to be equipped with mechanisms for dialogue formation, since it lacks a mechanism for leading, steering or controlling dialogues. This requires a rationale of local and global directional strategies. In other words, this bot needs a more powerful device for steering dialogues. The options for the answers given by the user can be implemented with the aid of one or more menu catalogs, which can, if necessary, be varied to match the context. In addition, where applicable, a context sensitive context field should be included for short entries (e.g., numerical entries). Bots of this kind can be used as diagnosis systems (all kinds of interviews, job interviews over the WWW, assessment tests for language courses at evening colleges, etc.).

III – User/Bot asks – Bot/User answers. Of all of the systems introduced here, this type of Bot is the most complicated to develop. All that has been said for Type 2 as far as answer options and dialogue formation mechanisms is concerned, applies to this type as well. However, a steering mechanism for the change in speakers (*turn-taking*) must also be included. Various mechanisms are at our disposal. The change in speaker can either occur via an offered change (e.g., "Do you have any further questions?"), an acquired change (e.g., "Maybe I could ask a question to you?") or a chronologically dependent change (after longer conversational gaps). The concept of dialogue acts is particularly suitable for situations with extensive amounts of questions and answers. For example, when structuring material, dialogue acts can be useful by defining classes of equivalent questions and answers. Bots of this sort can be implemented as complex diagnosis and advisory systems where expert systems technologies are implemented. Furthermore, Bots such as these can be used as intelligent interfaces (e.g., as dialogue formational components in search engines or as interfaces to other bots, for example *bargain bots*).

20.4 Conclusion

Language processing systems are expected to play a key role in the realization of man-machine communication. In future, one can also count on an increased deployment of language processing systems on the WWW. The Bots introduced in this contribution represent simple language processing systems that further enhance the distribution and processing of information via the Internet. Such systems are especially of interest for social empirical research that makes use of interviews on the WWW. In particular, the second system outlined here ("Bot asks – User answers") is suitable as an interview and dialogue Bot. One of the advantages of such systems is their availability "around the clock". Furthermore, in comparison to usual forms of interviews, the extensive content analytical evaluation and calculation of the interrater reliability (Breakwell, 1995) is annulled since question and answer options are fixed beforehand and can be recorded easily by the use of Common Gateway Interface (CGI) scripts. In contrast to (simple) Internet questionnaires, a dialog and interview Bot can omit individual questions or highlight others. A further motivational stimulus can be found in the interactive nature of dialog and interview Bots. However, one must calculate for disadvantages in comparison to common interviews. Flexible, even emphatic attention towards the interview partner can, of course, not be expected from interview Bots.

For this reason, this type cannot be implemented in interviews on topics that demand a relationship of trust. These systems are suitable for situations and themes with expressly factual topic matter and when the user is highly motivated (e.g., questions on financial savings).

In addition to interviews, another emphasis of implementation lies in the field of consulting dialogues (Janetzko, 1998) starting with student advisors and going beyond advice on how to fill in tax deduction slips. This could even include error diagnoses for software systems or technical installations. Such systems could replace existing telephone services (e.g., hotlines services).

In any case, the user should be informed expressly that a computer program is being used. Otherwise one might easily provoke an unwitting game of hide-and-seek in which the user, with the aid of cunning questioning, wishes to find out if the system is human or machine. With an increasing expertise in the methods of processing natural language, the limits of the simple Bots introduced here (*canned text*, fixed amounts of questions and answers) will lessen. But even the more simpler variants of dialogue and interview bots will allow for an improved evaluation of information on the WWW or of the information the users of the WWW provide us.

References

Austin, J. L. (1962). *How to do things with words.* Oxford: University Press.

Breakwell, G. M. (1995). Interviewing. In G. M. Breakwell, S. Hammond, & C. Fife-Schaw (Eds.), *Research methods in psychology* (pp. 230-242). London: Sage.

Bunt, H. C. (1981). Rules for interpretation, evaluation, and generation of dialogue acts. *IPO Annual Progress Report, 16*, 99-107.

Bunt, H. C. (1994). Context and dialogue control. *Think, 3*, 19-31.

Cleary, C. & Barreis, R. (1994). A descriptive model of question asking during story acquisition interview. *Proceedings of the sixteenth conference of the cognitive science society.* Hillsdale, NJ: Lawrence Erlbaum.

Etzioni, O. & Weld, D. (1994). A softbot-based interface to the Internet. *Communications of the ACM, 37*, 72-76.

Janetzko, D. (1998). *Der automatische WWW-Studienberater für das Fach Kognitionswissenschaft.* [Online]. Available: http://cogweb.iig.uni-freiburg.de/STUDIENTIPS/.

Levinson, St. C. (1983). *Pragmatics.* Cambridge: University Press.

Schmitz, B. & Quantz, J. J. (1996). Dialogue acts in automating dialogue interpretation. *VERBMOBIL-Report, 173*, TU Berlin.

Schoder, D. & Janetzko, D. (1998). Bots. *Wirtschaftsinformtik, 40*, 341-343.

Searle, J. R. (1969). *Speech acts. An essay in the philosophy of language.* Cambridge.

Smith, R. W. & Hipp, D. R. (1995). *Spoken natural language dialog-systems: A practical approach.* Oxford: University Press.

Stein, A. (1995). Dialogstrategien für kooperative Informationssysteme: Ein komplexes Modell multimodaler Interaktion. *Sprache und Datenverarbeitung, 19*, 19-31.

Stenström. A.-B. (1994). *An introduction to spoken interaction.* London: Longman.

Wahlster, W. (1993). Übersetzung von Verhandlungsdialogen. *VERBMOBIL-Report, 1.* DFKI Saarbrücken.

Weizenbaum, J. (1966). ELIZA – A computer program for the study of natural language communications between man and machine. *Communications of the ACM, 9*, 36-45.

21 World Wide Web Use at a German University – Computers, Sex, and Imported Names. Results of a Logfile Analysis

Thomas Berker

"Amongst them there was one who investigated them from the beneath the ground: Ginster. Sometimes, he would be surprised about how they could jump around so cheerfully in the schoolyard while he was calculating the checksum of their behavior. His judgment over them was determined by small incidents they themselves had no knowledge of." (Siegfried Kracauer, Ginster, 1928)

21.1 Talking About the Internet...

Although comparatively small, Internet use has become normal for a segment of the population in industrialized states. A substantial element of this normality is attributed to use of the World Wide Web (WWW); substantial above all because of the pivotal role the introduction of this technology (in 1993 for the first time with a graphic interface) has played since then in the unsurpassed career of the Internet. The goal of the empirical research project presented here is to contribute to the depiction of the present normality of WWW use.

When referring to the Internet, it is evident, both in an academic and nonacademic context, how strong a role technically including and excluding factors play. One either has "access" to the Internet or one doesn't. The logfile analysis procedure presented here can make a contribution by describing patterns of use beyond the reach of participatory observation, yet on this side of the census of opinions of those who "already" have access. Nevertheless or therefore, the execution of a logfile analysis remains a balancing act between the engineering and social sciences, between technology and the sociological search for knowledge. The question always arises at which point the simplifying reduction of technical aspects crosses the border of falsehood, and at which point sociological interpretation is stalled by technical details. Finding an arrangement between both poles is a suggestion. All who on the one hand do not wish to leave the future of the Internet in the hands of the technicians, yet hold no high regard for the baseless guesswork practiced in the "waffle subjects" will agree upon this.

21.2 Logfiles as Sociological Empirical Material

21.2.1 The Technical Aspect[1]

Logfiles are a widespread in everyday computer procedures. They contain as complete a transcript of information as possible on processes executed by users or programs. Normally, such files are used if a performance or error analysis is necessary. They are usually deleted after a certain period as automatically as they are created. Their appearance can vary to a certain degree, and the logs used here document one action per line:

- Time of action.
- Type of action (including technical details).
- Success or failure of the action.

We speak of large amounts of data, the basic materials for this analysis document approximately three entries for each second of computer operation, which in itself is not insignificant for the analysis which has to proceed extremely selectively and accumulatively. A further fundamental problem lies in differentiating between actions executed by machines and those caused by the user. Despite expert knowledge of the logged procedures this is only scarcely possible in a sufficient manner, as the following section will demonstrate.

Server-Side vs. Client-Side Logfiles

In the case of WWW use, approximately a half dozen logfiles are of interest. Technically, they are distinguishable in server-side and client-side files, although the client side rarely registers logs whilst executing Net applications. It is nevertheless possible to accommodate for this demand.

While a user at his computer A (the client) sends a request for contents (a document, image, etc.) on computer B (the server) the execution of this action can be registered both in computer A as well as in B. Under ideal circumstances, we would be able to find out on the server side when and from where (using which program) a user has requested an accessible file. This is interesting, for example, for advertisers

---

[1] In the following section, the phrase "in the simplest terms" could be included in each sentence.

who can turn a site's appeal (i.e., the number of accesses) into money (see Werner, in this volume). However, in order to get the proper picture of happenings on the WWW a sufficiently large number of such logfiles would need to be compiled. Indeed, rankings that are compiled with this method do not differ fundamentally from those presented below, they are however limited to the co-operating servers.

On the client side the situation it is similar. Only when several client logs, which are not automatically generated under normal conditions, are compiled can an impression of the actual use of a population be made. This is the method postulated by Catledge and Pitkow (o.J.) and Graham-Cumming (o.J.). The advantage over server-side analysis is that the observed events are selected according to a particular user sample and not, as in the first case, according to certain presence's.

The problem in both cases is the decentralized structure of the WWW. In order to log a large of amount of users' usage patterns a needle eye between client and server is required. This can either be constructed via compilation of data that is available or needs to be generated, or by installing a network monitor (see Abrams & Williams, 1996), at a not entirely insignificant technical and organizational cost.

However, increasingly successful proxy technology can supply all required data.

Proxy Server

Proxy servers (also known as proxies or plural proxies) are located between client and server, yet closer to the Client so to speak. The user's request at computer A is first handed to the proxy. The proxy operates first as a server. Then it passes on the request to server B, which was actually addressed, and is now the client. In many cases the reason for such a stopover is to establish a so-called firewall, a kind of safety wall between a local intranet and the Internet. Usually, however, the main technical argument for inserting a proxy is to establish a connection to a local cache, (i.e., contents that had been requested briefly before by another proxy user are buffered locally and do not have to be requested from a server further away), provided the contents have not changed.

A side effect of this reduction in resources is that WWW use is logged centrally for all of those users who have their proxy "switched on". The advantage of a logfile analysis conducted here is obvious. The data is already available.

The specific disadvantage results from the fact that proxy use is voluntary. In many cases, this "sample extraction" leads to refusal of the procedure[2]. In fact, to a large extent proxy use is voluntary amongst the sample population culled for this logfile analysis. In an e-mail survey on use of the Frankfurt University computer center, conducted simultaneously to the logfiles census, proxy application was also surveyed. Of 871 respondents, 55% indicated not usually using proxies or not know-

---

[2] cf. similar to Abrams & Williams (1996)

ing what a proxy is, which is probably equivalent to nonuse. Upon comparing proxy users' behavior patterns with those of the nonusers, as is reflected in the questionnaire, amazingly few systematic differences are evident. The most substantial bias is apparent in gender, in favor of men. However, as with other deviations, this is statistically insignificant.

Technical Problems and Their Handling

Finally, to conclude the technical section, one must refer to five technically induced problems, which do not only apply to proxy logfile analyses, but to the method of logfile analyses on the whole.

Caches. The further away the logfile's location from the request location, the more caches (buffer) can lie in between. The described caches in connection with a proxy can be a problem, above all for server-side logs, if the request is served from the cache. A whole set of suggestions has been made on how to switch off this bias (see Pitkow). These can only specify approximate values, owing to the net's heterogeneous structure. Even proxy logs can be deceived by caches installed by browser applications on the user's computer. The only way to avoid this is by making the browser log each action itself. However, the bias caused by this method, which inevitably demands the user's co-operation, may have far more serious repercussions. One must also note that above all contents requested particularly frequently by a user do not further appear in proxy logs, a bias towards larger heterogeneity of use.

Man or machine? Inferring user actions on the basis of network activities registered in the logfile is, as has already been ascertained, not entirely unproblematic. The bottom line is selecting the logfile entries relevant for analysis. For example, when a user clicks on a link to Frankfurt University's address it looks like this in the logfile:

On 11th February 2002, at 2 o'clock, 11 minutes, and 3 seconds a user requested the address http://www.uni-frankfurt.de/ via modem (NAF stands for Network Access Facility). The request is rerouted:

```
887159464.562    71 NAF88rz.uni-frankfurt.de  TCP_HIT/200
3057 GET http://www.rz.uni-frankfurt.de/unihome/ - NONE/-
text/html
```

This page contains three images:

```
887159466.741    52 NAF88rz.uni-frankfurt.de  TCP_HIT/200
324 GET http://www.rz.uni-frankfurt.de/unigifs/goethe.gif
- NONE/- image/gif
```

```
887159466.958      68  NAF88rz.uni-frankfurt.de  TCP_HIT/200
4094 GET http://www.rz.uni-frankfurt.de/unigifs/bgd.gif -
NONE/- image/gif
```

```
887159467.299     169 NAF88rz.uni-frankfurt.de  TCP_HIT/200
10422 GET http://www.rz.uni-frankfurt.de/unigifs/jwgu.gif
- NONE/- image/gif
```

Approximately ten seconds later, the user selects the option Yahoo! in the Netscape browser's menu which (probably unnoticed by him or her) is linked to a connection to home.netscape.com server.

```
887159474.762     433 NAF88rz.uni-frankfurt.de  TCP_REFRESH
_HIT/200   213   GET   http://home.netscape.com/bookmark/4/
yahoo.html - PARENT_HIT/ frankfurt.www-cache.dfn.de text/
html
```

Finally, he/she reaches Yahoo:

```
887159476.757     1183 NAF88rz.uni-frankfurt.de  TCP_CLIENT
_REFRESH/200 9384 GET http://www.yahoo.com/ - PARENT_HIT/
spock.rz.uni-frankfurt.de - text/html
```

This example makes two things clear: the selective criteria must exclude images and the like, since pages with a lot of pictures would be over-represented in the census. This can either be handled by controlling the extensions (the last letters of the file name) or the MIME type[3] indicated in the last field of the logfile entry. Unfortunately, this entry is frequently not correct, causing systematic distortions. One is left with a distinction according to file names or their extensions. In the logfile analysis conducted here, images were not excluded, instead only requests were included for files which included the "htm" extension as well full server addresses, possibly with indication of a path but without file names. The HyperText Markup Language (HTML) side is still *the* basic integration element for supply of data on the WWW. To that extent, strict limitation can be justified.

Nonetheless, we should bear in mind: pages that are not de facto classified as being standard HTML or are related (SHTML, etc..), or that do not explicitly define their files as such are underrepresented. Currently this affects search engines on the one hand whose search queries, and results, are dispatched in the HTML format, yet are hardly recognizable as such, and on the other hand presences where on can chat over the WWW.

---

[3]   MIME (Multipurpose Internet Mail Extensions) is a standard according to which file types can be clearly designated (and classified).

A further source of error can be found in a skillful move implemented by the manufacturers of the software needed to access the WWW. They install the program with a preset connection to their own URL addresses. This connection is established as soon as the program is launched, or, as could be seen in the example, when a menu option is activated. This can be changed by the user, but not all users are ware of this.

At the same time, these URL addresses (e.g., home.netscape.com) are also of some value, e.g., by offering the possibility of searching the Internet. Graham-Cumming (o.J.) reports registering a high user-side abort rate especially on these pages, which indicates that the encountered dominance of Netscape et al. is rather to be attributed to the technically induced connection as opposed to user behavior. Since this problem only concerns some addresses it is not as serious as those specified before.

Finally, the problem of "frames" must be mentioned. Pages that are split up into several simultaneously visible files are over-represented in the census. In order to reduce this effect all actions that were initiated by the user less than one second after each other were excluded from the logfile. This is based on the assumption that a user can only be this quick in the rarest of cases.

Anonymization. Since the originator of an action is also recorded in the proxy log, it is possible to trace these actions back to the individual user. In terms of privacy, the precariousness of collecting data without the knowledge of the users is obvious. In the pretest it was underlined that all logfiles were to be separated from this data. Unfortunately, one no longer has the opportunity of differentiating between sessions; one can only aggregate the data globally. In the main census the originator field of the logfile was therefore coded in such a way as to be able to differentiate between sessions. On the user level, however, no profiles could be reconstructed beyond this analytical component. The specific form of this anonymization made it necessary to return to a purely definitive version of the analysis unit. A session is therefore to be defined as a sequence of actions by the same user unit not interrupted by a pause of a minimum of 20 minutes. In comparison to literature on this topic a rather restrictive measure[4] was decided upon, since it should not be suggested that the analysis units are individual users. The risk of dividing one person's WWW use into two or more sessions because this person was doing something else in between was taken into account. What is gained hereby is to be on the safe side of recording one session before making false assumptions on the behavior of two persons.

---

[4]   see Catledge & Pitkow, who consider approx. 30 minutes of inactivity as a session limit

Interpretation. A last problem leads us to the next point: the fundamental question about the status of data collected in such a manner. It would surely be naive to assume – particularly for an unnoticed observer – that a logfile analysis would deliver positive knowledge on user behavior. If hitherto terms such as use, user behavior, action, page or even action have been used more or less equivalently then this is indicative of the fact that more methodological reflection is required.

21.2.2 Logfiles as Nonreactively Collected Data

According to the canon of sociological empirical methodology, logfile analyses are filed under the nonreactive procedure category.

These suffer a comparatively miserable existence beside their dominating competitor, reactive procedures, which above all take shape in the form of more or less standardized interviews.

Nonreactive Methods

When Webb (1975) argued against the supremacy of interviews as sociological methodology in the middle of the 60's, he had good arguments. The first chapter was dedicated to a monograph on nonreactive measuring procedures, the reactive measuring effects that can crop up in the different levels of a census. Researchers, interviewers, respondents, etc. are all involved and exert influence, intentionally or inadvertently. That, for example, gender or perhaps even hair color can affect the results of an interview has long been proven in experiments.

Even after thirty years of methodical debate, the author is to be respected, both in the criticism, as in the classification of nonreactive measuring procedures, yet above all in his restraint when he argued "no research method is without error. Interviews and questionnaires must be supplemented by methods that examine the same sociological variables, yet possess different methodical weaknesses" (Webb, 1975, p.15).

Logfile Analysis as Observation

According to Webb's classification, logfile analyses would be referred to as "planned observation". This is how they paraphrase every form of observation in whose contexts the researchers decide "to actively change the course of observation, or substitute human bookkeeping with "hardware" methods." (Webb, 1975, p.181) Amongst the particular advantages are the objectivity of the recording devices, and the elimination of error the observer passes onto the observation because "humans are observation instruments of little reliability." (Webb, 1975)

However, since we cannot choose the conditions of recording in the case of the proxy logfiles yet another category comes into play. Webb refers to the measurement of physical traces as a form of nonreactive methodology. Similar to the way the floor in front of a particularly attractive museum exhibit will tend to be more worn out, patterns of WWW use also accumulate in the logfiles. Some of the substantial problems connected with this method of survey can also be found in the logfile analysis. When Webb asks about deposit measurements, "... whether the data selectively outlasted or was deposited selectively..." (Webb, 1975, p.73) one is reminded of the technical problems described in the previous chapter. The reference to population distortions (Webb, 1975, p.73) is also virulent in our case. Recording logfiles is nevertheless an incomparably more precise and more significant measuring instrument than for example surveying the contents of household garbage. That is above all due to the fact that "physical traces" are bound more strongly to their instigators, so that that their actions can be located more clearly in space and time.

Behaviorism?

Guenter Albrecht reconciled the discussion on nonreactive measuring methods with the controversy over behaviorism in the human sciences (see Albrecht, 1975, p.9). Indeed, for the social scientist oriented towards the behaviorist paradigm, what happens in the individual's black box is to a large extent unknown and irrelevant. The observable action (user X clicks on address Y) is what he is interested in. He is furthermore preoccupied with measuring regularities and/or calculating simple correlations. This already offers a description of what nonreactive measuring methods can achieve. Or according to the words of Bungard and Lücks: "an uncompromising nonreactive measurement inevitably only provides a restrictive survey of individual behavior components, with the decreased possibility of significant interpretation of the meaning for participants..." (Bungard & Lueck, 1991, p.203).

Whether the sociologist's soul is entirely sold to behaviorism with the application of nonreactive methods is doubtful. It is more important that we are conscious of the limits to which this form of empirical analysis is subjected. This not only refers to the throwback "to individual behavior components", as Bungard and Lück write. The potential for theoretical interpretation is also very constrained. Schnell, Hill, and Esser (1993, p.423) point this out when they talk of restricting the method in order to verify only "very simple instrument theories."

Perhaps the following outlined results can demonstrate how large the range actually is.

21.3 Results of a Logfile Analysis[5]

In the context of a logfile analysis, three analytical units seem plausible: the contacted servers (server names would be more exact), the requested pages, sessions, or the individual using the WWW.

The latter is omitted for reasons of data privacy. It is substituted by the anonymized session to which we will turn our attention following the overview of servers and pages.

21.3.1 Server, Pages

The abundance of data makes reductions essential. The objective is therefore to categorize the contents requested by users. The "page" unit would surely be one of the more significant analysis objects. Since, however, a large number of pages on one server can easily be assigned to a single category, the server address will form the basis of our categorization.

Categorization was conducted manually in the ME&E manner ("mutually exclusive and exhausting", see Bakeman & Gottman, 1987, p.33). In individual cases, intersections were certainly not to be avoided. Also, at the time of evaluation (approximately two months later) a whole row of servers was no longer available (category 9, see below), or unable to be categorized due to linguistic or other obstacles. To that extent, categorization is to be referred to as explorative.

During the two week survey period (20th January until 4th February 1998) nearly 30,000 different servers were contacted by the proxy users of Frankfurt University's computer centers, via modem and in the largest accessible terminal area ("Grapool"). In a ranking according to contact frequency the 878 servers, which constituted the "upper" 50%, were included in the categorization.

Homogeneity of Use

Scarcely three percent of the servers make up 50% of all requests. Every tenth request is directed at one of the twelve first servers. An examination of these "Top 12" provides us with a first result we will come across again on different levels, and which we will have to differentiate in the following sections. Only four kinds of servers are apparent here: On the one hand, as mentioned above, the preset sites or server addresses of the different browsers (http://home.netscape.com/, http://www.rz. uni-frankfurt.de/, etc.); on the other hand, addresses where nudity can be found

---

[5] The processing and analysis of the data was executed with the programming language PERL, and the statistics analysis package SPSS. My gratitude goes out to CL for cooperation in anonymization and supplying the logs.

(http://www.voyeurweb.com/, http://www.aec.co.at/, etc.), thirdly search services (http://www.yahoo.de/, http://www.dino-online.de/, etc.), and finally servers which offer a whole host of different services under one name, so-called provider addresses (http://www.geocities.com/, http://home.t-online.de/, etc.). The most remarkable facet of the "Top 12" is how many German-language variants can be found in these four relatively dominant categories.

The individual categories (for preset sites, see above):

- *Search:* if we total Yahoo!'s German-language service with the international service then Yahoo! is the most frequent request at 56%. One must assume that the absence of so-called "search engines" is linked with the type of data processing.
- *Provider addresses:* with the increasing significance of commercial providers their importance for use also rises. An examination of the single pages that were requested at these addresses did not indicate any dominance, e.g., of commercial providers. To a greater extent the calculated attention was focused upon private pages and their various services.
- *Sex:* the two main URL addresses from this category that made it into the "Top 12" are rather exceptional for their "category". Both the Austrian Erotic Centre (http://www.aec.co.at/) and Voyeurweb (http://www.voyeurweb.com/) offer rather discreet nudity, and on the other hand are characterized by a strong impression of amateurism, voyeurism, and the commonplace.

Stability of the Results

Before we go further into the detail another situation has to be clarified. The restriction of logfiles, as conducted here for reasons of capacity, to a period of two weeks could be inadmissible with strong fluctuation of use. A comparison of the results with those of the two weeks afterwards (5th until 18th February 1998) only indicated marginal deviations, above all as far as the illustrated focus on use was concerned. In the second two weeks we nevertheless found 365 new server addresses in the top 50%, yet situated in the lower ranks of rankings according to access. The highest scoring "newcomer" in the second week (http://www.tourism-db.co.at/) is on position 24. The fifth highest scoring "newcomer", the Frankfurt Eintracht Soccer Team homepage (http://www.eintracht.frankfurt-online.de/), which was relaunched during this period, only ranked position 55.

To sum up, in terms of homogeneity and stability, a relatively large, stable core is apparent. Though, this core loses some of its outline at the edges.

21.3.2 Categories

If we extend the focus of attention to the aforementioned "most successful" 878 server addresses, consulting the more strongly aggregated analysis unit of category becomes essential. The 172,995 requests were coded by hand (Table 21.1).

Table 21.1: 33 criteria according to content

Rang	Category	Number	%	cum. %
1	Sex	41,643	24.07	24.07
2	Multipurpose1 (homepages)	21,852	12.63	36.70
3	Multipurpose2 (NS, MS, Uni-Fr.)	15,990	9.24	45.95
4	Software, drivers, support	14,866	8.59	54.54
5	Navigation	14,726	8.51	63.05
6	Old' media	13,707	7.92	70.98
7	Unidentified	6,756	3.91	74.88
8	Stock exchange, capital market	5,156	2.98	77.86
9	Computer magazines	4,233	2.45	80.31
10	Computer related consume	3,659	2.12	82.42
11	Universities	3,383	1.96	84.38
12	(Study related) professional infor.	3,233	1.87	86.25
13	(Computer-)Games	2,712	1.57	87.82
14	Telecommunication	2,661	1.54	89.35
15	Information from official sources	2,360	1.36	90.72
16	Shopping, travelling	2,281	1.32	92.04
17	Serials, warez, filez, cracks	2,178	1.26	93.30
18	Cinema and music	1,723	1.00	94.29
19	Online banking	1,457	0.84	95.13
20	Local information (e.g., events)	1,267	0.73	95.87
21	Mail	1,124	0.65	96.52
22	Schedules (plains, rail, & buses)	1,100	0.64	97.15
23	Chat	826	0.48	97.63
24	Bibliographic informations	719	0.42	98.04
25	Cars	706	0.41	98.45
26	Sports	587	0.34	98.79
27	Web design	545	0.32	99.11
28	Special offers for fans	316	0.18	99.29
29	Virtual communities	297	0.17	99.46
30	Jobs and job-seeking	269	0.16	99.62
31	Regional information	228	0.13	99.75
32	Weather	224	0.13	99.88
33	Esoteric, religion	211	0.12	100.00

Because of limitations in space the individual categories cannot be described in detail, yet clear tendencies can be pointed out.

To the four categories we already know, i.e., "general purpose 1", meaning the "preset" sites, "general purpose 2", usually private homepages on commercial provider servers, "sex", and "search", the search engines and indexes, we can add two more frequently requested content types. These categories are referred to as "software, drivers, support", and "old media". The first category includes all addresses devoted to software and hardware, but which do not explicitly sell any items. Usually, information on products, free software, installation hints, FAQs (Frequently Asked Questions), or also links to other sources of information can be accessed here. If we add further computer and Internet-oriented categories (e.g., important online magazines, computer sales, computer games etc.), we are dealing with the most important form of use (16.3% of all requests) following the "sex" category (24.1% of requests). This self-reference to the Internet is not surprising. After all, computers, their application, and problems are a topic that unites many users, and hence creates a community with perhaps otherwise divergent patterns of use.

"Old" media comprises all addresses with a counterpart in another media market. Usually, additional information is supplied bearing the respective print or TV medium's name, or the already existing contents of the parent medium are simply transferred into the new medium. The appeal of such sites may be partly explainable due to synergy effects. Since the introduction of double marketing tactics, using different channels in the book and cinema markets is a tried and tested means of increasing sales. Alternately, the professional editorial teams working for the online presence of a popular print medium can often publish more up-to-date news, and can feature contents better. Lastly, it is apparent that hardly any of these information services goes without content types that proved attractive in the above categorization: search engine, information on computers and on the Internet, stock exchange news, and, in the case of the digital version of the Bild newspaper, even "nudity" is featured.

The convergence of different media channels has already begun, at least in this area, yet not on the frequently reported hardware side of things (see Web TV). Instead, the connection caused by multiple marketing of a name or of specific contents is decisive.

To conclude the above section, this contribution's provocative title needs to be brought into relation. The heading "specialized information" refers to all Web sites, which can clearly be allocated to different academic subjects. Also, categories such as "Online Banking", "information from official carriers", or the latest stock exchange news need to be allocated differently to the more broadly discussed patterns of use. In conclusion, however, one must acknowledge that services featuring nudity, computer-related subjects, and contents from other previously well-known media constitute the lion's share.

When differentiating more precisely according to contents, much speaks for the theory that the categories general purpose 2 and search replicate contents of the remaining categories, and can therefore be excluded for now. Moreover, as a purely technically induced category, general purpose 1 is to be excluded from the census, and the selection of 878 server addresses, not based on a random sampling, can nevertheless be evaluated representatively. If we follow all of these assumptions, then more than a third of all WWW use is to be filed under the heading "sex", nearly a quarter is computer and Internet related, and a good tenth can be allocated to the various other ("old") media brands. Together, these categories make up a share of scarcely 70% of all server requests.

21.3.3 Sessions

With the change of focus to the analytical unit of a "session" we will go further into detail in the description of patterns of use. The center of attention is not so much the "What" of WWW use, but instead the "How".

Sessions were defined above as a user unit's surfing activity enveloped by periods of inactivity of at least 1,200 seconds (20 minutes). As mentioned before, the same person who returns to using the WWW after a break of 20 minutes, without having broken the connection in the meantime, can be responsible for two or more sessions. This definition, enforced to a greater part due to requirements concerning data privacy, also reveals previous conceptions of WWW use. Strictly speaking, this thereby only encompasses active participation illustrated by a string of documents usually linked to each other via hypertext. Other forms of use, such as reading longer documents on screen or playing with Java gimmicks are thereby excluded.

Preparation

This restriction is conducted above all with the aid of plausibility tests. For example, sessions whose average internal inactivity times lay under three seconds were categorized as probably "not induced by humans", and were deleted accordingly. Today, a great deal of programs for all sorts of purposes use automatic connections to the WWW (via a proxy too). In this context, increasingly popular programs need to be mentioned with whose assistance contents on the WWW can automatically be accessed, and then read offline at home.

In this manner, 6,033 sessions could be distinguished for the survey period. Originally, the data record contained over 10,000 sessions, yet since a tight rein was kept on the plausibility criteria, one can estimate the actual number of sessions between these two values.

For each session formal details were polled, such as overall length, as well as the length of average time of inactivity per session, the number of contacted server addresses, which categories, and requests. Furthermore, the above category system was brought into the play if sessions were classified according to the most frequently requested category. Lastly, we can differentiate between sessions according to the time of day and the first page requested.

At certain times of day[6] certain categories appear more frequently. If, in the following section, differences are described on the basis of categorization and time of day, this by no means suggests a causal model. Whether effects based on the time of day (e.g., the distinction between leisure time and working hours), are decisive for the observed formal differences in use, or for the decision to access certain contents, will be difficult to discern. On the basis of the described restriction of nonreactive measurements via logfile, we can initially only conclude that certain times of the day are accompanied by usage contents with certain formal characteristics. The emphasis is to be placed upon those three categories identified above as particularly important: "sex", "computers", and "old media".

Temporal Differentiation

Whilst use of services allocated to the "old media" peaks during the late afternoon (3-6 o'clock pm), the other two content categories are distributed more evenly during the day (see Figure 21.1). Nevertheless, they do reveal differences. While the number of sessions whose use is strictly speaking computer-related (software, drivers, and support) reaches its peak at midnight approximately and hardly plays a role from then on, "sex sessions" carry on until deep into the night. Applied to the rules described above (exclusion of general purpose categories etc.), 40%[7] of the sessions that can be categorized between midnight and 6 o'clock in the morning are devoted to "nudity".

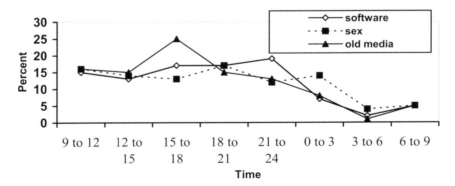

Figure 21.1: Temporal differentiation

---

[6]   Operationalized as the categorized median value of the starting and finishing time.
[7]   Whilst the percentage figures in the diagram refer to the sum of sessions dominated by a category, this number refers to the sum of all sessions at a particular time of day.

Starting Pages

This impression is confirmed if we look at the kind of offers that are requested first in a session (see Figure 21.2). What is evident here, however, is the high percentage, at approximately 16% to 25% of sessions that begin with a server where we assume that access involves preset settings in the browser. This portion varies strongly according to the time of day; it is smallest in the afternoon (12 to 3 o'clock in the afternoon), and highest in the morning (6 to 9 o'clock). It stands to assume that these fluctuations are related to population fluctuations. Therefore, in the afternoon, we would predominantly come across users who are not willing or able to change these preset settings. Only two other categories crop up with a similar frequency as the start category: search and server names in the nudity category, yet only between midnight and 6 o'clock am.

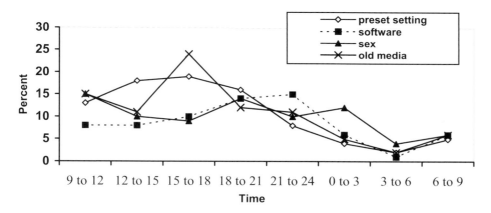

Figure 21.2: Starting pages

Surfing at Night

The average length of a session lies at 23 minutes, a value that is influenced significantly by our initial analytical definition. Nevertheless, the average session times are affected comparatively according to our categories. At an average time of 16.5 minutes, the duration of computer related sessions lies clearly below average. Clearly above average are the "sex" category sessions with 35 minutes' duration.

This result is also reflected when observing the number of server contacts or different server addresses within a session. Indeed, these values bear strong correlations. For this purpose, an artificial variable was formed in order to measure the number of different server addresses per minute. As a result, a measure indicating the "speed" of server changes can be developed (see Figure 21.3).

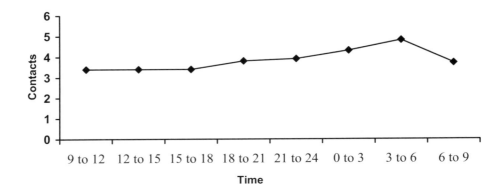

Figure 21.3: Server contacts per minute

Differentiated according to the time of day, it is clear that the average value of this variable remains fairly stable during the day and in the evening with an approximate value of 3.4 different servers per minute. At night it increases to 4.8 during the early hours of the morning (4 to 6 o'clock).

Since the average session duration climbs in accordance with this value, and also with night coming to a close it is difficult not to immediately think of the frequently reported phenomenon of surfing. According to these findings, this would be a phenomenon attributed to the late hours, whilst daytime is reserved for functional sessions.

21.4 Summary

If one follows the procedure suggested here, a contoured picture of the virtual WWW user at a German university is depicted. He sits in front of his monitor, most of all late at night, scouring one server after another, and stares at nude models. In order to quickly obtain information on computers and on the Internet he has likewise learned to appreciate what the WWW has to offer. Finally, and most likely in the afternoon, he gladly accesses the online services of a print medium or a television station. Within all three areas he will read, so it seems, the German-language counterpart. Extensive surf sessions are reserved for late at night. During the day, he favors a more functional access to information.

According to the results presented here, whoever recognizes him or herself in this picture may consider themselves as typical. Yet many questions are left open, among them some quite substantial. Are only a few, very active users responsible for this picture? Furthermore, due to the relatively large significance attached to the "sex" category, the issue of gender specific use is of great importance. In order to understand use of the "old media" category, we would need to find out how WWW use is related to further media use.

The logfile analysis method will not be able to contribute much more to this. A qualitative evaluation of a smaller number of sessions would be feasible and certainly also worthwhile. But in order to get more detailed results, a combination of these results with other methods would be essential.

References

Abrams, M. & Williams, St. (1996). *Complementing surveying and demographics with automated network monitoring.* [Online]. Available: http://www.cs.vt.edu/~chitra/docs/96w3j/96w3j.html.

Albrecht, G. (1975). Nicht-reaktive Messung und Anwendung historischer Methoden. In J. Koolwijk (Ed.), *Techniken der empirischen Sozialforschung: ein Lehrbuch in 8 Bänden. Bd. 2. Untersuchungsformen* (pp. 9-81). München: Oldenbourg.

Bakeman, R. & Gottman, J. M. (1987). *Observing interaction: an introduction to sequential analysis.* Cambridge: University Press.

Bungard, W. & Lück, H. (1991). Nichtreaktive Verfahren. In U. Flick (Ed.), *Handbuch Qualitative Sozialforschung: Grundlagen, Konzepte, Methoden und Anwendungen* (pp. 198-202). München: Psychologie-Verlags-Union.

Catledge, L. & Pitkow, J. (o.J.). *Characterizing browsing strategies in the world wide web.* [Online]. Available: http://www.igd.fhg.de/www/www95/papers/80/userpatterns/Userpatterns.Paper4.formatted.html.

Graham-Cumming, J. (o.J.). *Hits and misses: A year watching the web.* [Online]. Available: http://proceedings.www6conf.org/HyperNews/get/PAPER131.html.

Kracauer, S. (1928, 1990). *Ginster.* Frankfurt/Main: Suhrkamp.

Pitkow, J. (o.J.). *In search of: Reliable usage data on the www.* [Online]. Available: http://www6.nttlabs.com/HyperNews/get/PAPER126.html.

Schnell, R., Hill, P. B., & Esser, E. (1993). *Methoden der empirischen Sozialforschung* (4. ed.). München: Oldenbourg.

Webb, E. (1975). *Nichtreaktive Meßverfahren.* Weinheim, Basel: Beltz.

22 Academic Communication and Internet Discussion Groups: What Kinds of Benefits for Whom?

Uwe Matzat

This paper analyzes the implications of Internet discussion groups for informal academic communication. The first part reviews different hypotheses of the benefits of academic mailing lists and newsgroups for individual researchers. Moreover, special attention is given to the various forms of impact on the macro system of informal communication networks. Hypotheses are presented suggesting equalizing effects on the distribution of communication opportunities for researchers. Other studies suggest that mailing lists could contribute to a "Balkanization" of the academic communication system. The sparse empirical evidence for and against these hypotheses is summarized. The last part concentrates on differences in the use of these communication tools in various academic disciplines. It discusses a number of hypotheses that try to predict which groups of researchers will use mailing lists or newsgroups more often.

22.1 Introduction

There is much speculation about the potential of new information technologies. Predictions are made that the "information superhighway" will transform the world into a global village, and that the communication revolution will lead to "[t] he death of distance" (Cairncross, 1997). In the academic education system, there is the virtual university and in the research system, the Internet is seen by some as a communications-technology quantum transition (Pascha, 1995). What is *certain* is that the growth of the Internet has been accompanied by an explosion of predictions of the coming technological utopia, within academic circles as well as in the general public (Kling & Iacono, 1995).

A lively discussion among researchers about the potential of the new communication tools the Internet offers is understandable: formal and informal communication is crucial for the research community (Garvey, 1979; Meadows, 1974). New possibilities for their promotion are thus very important. The potential of the World Wide

Web (WWW) for online publishing is influencing the formal publication system (Peek & Newby, 1996). Academic mailing lists and newsgroups have been adopted as tools for informal communication between researchers.

These Internet discussion groups (IDGs), as I will call mailing lists and newsgroups here, can be traced back to electronic conference systems used as early as the 1970s (see e.g., Hiltz, 1984). Despite 20 years of use there are still various hopes for improvement of the communication system as well as concern for the detrimental consequences IDGs may have for informal communication in the research community. The next section shows that questions remain about the effects of IDG usage. A clarification of possible benefits or disadvantages of IDGs for the academic communication system is needed for at least two reasons:

Firstly, the number of academic IDGs increased to cover almost every discipline by the middle of the 1990s (Kovacs & the Directory Team, 1996; Mailbase, 1999a). In some countries, computing services were founded to promote and support the initiation and use of academic mailing lists. These services receive official funds from science foundations (e.g., Mailbase, 1999b; H-Net Webstaff, 1999). Much time, money, and effort is invested in IDGs with distinct target groups – not to mention the time individual researchers spend on the maintenance of IDGs as moderators or as readers/contributors.[1] The use of IDGs is no longer restricted to a minority of technically interested academics. Many researchers use them, and many lists noted a growing number of users in the 1990s (Mailbase, 1999c). A careful analysis can show what benefits IDGs really have for the research community, and which expectations are unwarranted. Such an analysis serves as a basis for judging whether increased expenditure in mental and financial resources for the maintenance of IDGs is justified. It prevents the expenditure of resources for certain ends that may not be attainable via these means.

Secondly, the success and failure of communication technologies depend crucially on the social context in which they are used. Unfortunately, little is known about which conditions are favorable for successful adoption of a communication technology. Rather, different tools and pathways of communication exist in the different disciplines within the research community, and tools successful within one field are adopted in other research fields under different conditions (Kling & McKim, 2000). The costs of such diffusion by trial-and-error could be avoided if we knew more about the interplay between a communication tool and the communication conditions of a discipline. Thus, what is necessary is a better understanding of the actual usage

---

[1]   Conner (1992) mentions that he spends on the average about 10 hours per week for active moderation of an IDG within the humanities. Other listowners or moderators also complain about the required time (Berge & Collins, 1993). Moreover, active mailing lists aggravate the problem of information overload for every user (McCarty, 1992; Whittaker & Sidner, 1997).

and impact of different communication technologies *under different conditions* (Walsh & Bayma, 1996a). The analysis of the *use of IDGs by researchers in a variety of different disciplines* offers some insights into general effects of IDG usage by researchers in different disciplines *with distinct communication habits and needs.* This makes it possible to compare the same computer-mediated communication tool under different conditions. The analysis of IDGs offers accordingly general insights into the question of which communication needs are fulfilled under what condition. These insights could help to predict some effects of other computer-mediated communication tools.

This paper tries to clarify possible outcomes of the use of IDGs for the informal communication system. The next section reviews some hypotheses of the potential benefits and negative effects of the use of IDGs for researchers and for the informal communication system. The empirical evidence is summarized, and the drawbacks and limitations of existing empirical studies are described. I show what the likely answers are to some questions relating to possible consequences of IDGs, and which questions are still to be answered. The important question of what determines the use of IDGs by researchers is explored in the third section. It focuses on differences in the adoption of IDGs by researchers in different disciplines. Several hypotheses identifying specific aspects of the spread of IDG use in different disciplines are discussed. The final section draws some conclusions about what kind of research is needed to answer at least a few of the many questions still unanswered. The main aim of this paper is to show that there exists a set of related hypotheses about academic IDGs that can help to steer future empirical research.

22.2 Potential Effects of Academic Internet Discussion Groups

As early as the 1970s, first predictions appeared of the opportunities so-called electronic conference systems will offer academic communication (Hiltz & Turoff, 1978). Although similar optimism regarding the potential of IDGs can be found in the 1990s among some academics (Gresham, 1994; Turoff & Hiltz, 1998), some skeptical voices have also been raised expressing doubts about the general relevance of some IDGs (Bainbridge, 1995) or even suggesting that the use of IDGs might have detrimental consequences for the informal communication system (Alstyne & Brynjolfsson, 1996a).

At first glance it is surprising to find optimistic as well as skeptical evaluations of IDG use more than 20 years after its inception (e.g., compare Alstyne & Brynjolfsson, 1996; Bainbridge, 1995; Gresham 1994; Turoff & Hiltz, 1998). The question whether and how IDGs can serve the objectives of academic research is discussed not only among observers, but also among IDG users, who have different views of how IDGs should work (Conner, 1992; McCarty, 1992). The range of different views makes it more difficult to judge the relevance of IDGs.

However, although there might be different specific consequences for different researchers, not all of them are of importance for the general population of academic users. I would like to concentrate on the claims of many IDG proponents for universal IDG effects on academic communication. To simplify the discussion, I will make a distinction between two different general groups of potential effects relevant for the large majority of researchers. I categorize them as either being information effects or contact effects.

22.2.1 Information Production, Information Transmission or Information Overload?

Hiltz and Turoff (1978) brought up many different potential benefits IDGs can have for either individual researchers or for a whole research field.[2] According to them, IDGs could generate new research *ideas* or *proposals for research* among academics, from which every active and passive user of an IDG could profit.

Moreover, computer conferences could allow *informal exchange of research results or of other helpful information between researchers*. The authors compare such an exchange with informal discussions on the fringe of academic conferences. Many benefits of conferences are not gained through listening to the official presentations of other researchers. Rather, they are gained through discussions within a small group or through bilateral discussions between individual researchers (Menzel, 1962). A problem of such discussions is that researchers have to be willing to provide help and information to colleagues. The help provider does not get something in return for such a provision, reducing his motivation to do so. The information transfer and provision of help within an IDG, however, take place in front of an audience and are usually recorded. Accordingly, Hiltz and Turoff (1978) expect an increase in the motivation to provide help.

The authors are of the opinion that the most important intellectual benefits of IDGs are those that affect the whole research community. It might profit from the enhanced opportunities for discussions: electronic conferences could help *to resolve or develop* theoretical, methodological, and ethical *controversies of a research field*. This, in turn, might *speed up the development of whole research fields* (Hiltz & Turoff, 1978, pp.210-239).

---

[2] The authors themselves analyze "computerized conferencing" and not mailing lists or newsgroups. However, their ideas can be found in many analyses of IDGs (e.g., Gresham, 1994; Lewenstein, 1995; McCarty, 1992). Turoff & Hiltz (1998) explicitly include newsgroups in their later statements.

Many empirical studies of IDGs and electronic conferences have been inspired by the ideas of Hiltz, Turoff, and their colleagues. Most of them consist of case studies of single or a few intentionally selected IDGs or electronic conferences. Usually the users were asked to enumerate advantages or disadvantages of IDG use, or to describe benefits they obtained or problems they experienced with IDG use (see e.g., Tombaugh, 1984; Harasim & Winkelmans, 1990; Rojo & Ragdale, 1997a, 1997b). Other empirical evidence is rather anecdotal and consists of descriptions by moderators of what happened in "their" IDGs (Conner, 1992; McCarty, 1992; Berge & Collins, 1993).

These studies show that *users evaluate positively* the opportunities IDGs offer for the *creation of new ideas, for the provision of research information, and other helpful advice*. Such users tell of referral to new literature mentioned by other IDG users. Others were able to get help from people they otherwise had no chance of contacting (Conner, 1992; McCarty, 1992).

On the other hand, many users complained about the *low quality* or the *low amount of discussion* within discussion groups. These complaints can be found among users or moderators of a variety of different IDGs (Conner, 1992; McCarty, 1992; Rooy 1996). Some studies mention explicitly that IDGs are not well suited for the discussion or the solution of intellectual controversies between researchers (Hiltz, 1984; Harasim & Winkelmans, 1990; Lewenstein, 1995; Tombaugh, 1984).

This does not mean discussions do not take place. Rather, if they take place, they are often abandoned before the resolution of a problem. Discussion participants inform each other and the passive readers of the discussion about their positions and about "the state of the art". Yet it is not the rule that this leads to a resolution of controversies (e.g., Hiltz, 1984).

Only single studies try to assess how large the amount of discussion in an IDG is in comparison to messages that contain questions, answers, announcements etc. Lewenstein (1995) analyzed how the newsgroup sci.physics.fusion was used between March 1989 and June 1992. On March 23, 1989 two electrochemists from the University of Utah announced that they had discovered a method for creating nuclear fusion at room temperature with simple equipment. Despite the *important role* the newsgroup sci.physics.fusion played in the *distribution of information* about cold fusion, Lewenstein (1995) concludes that it was hardly used by the researchers who were most active in the field. It was most of all used by nonprofessional observers who wanted to stay informed. The newsgroup was *not used* by researchers *to discuss* or judge colleagues' new findings; this happened at conferences. The author of another study comes to a similar conclusion relating to the amount of discussion within an IDG. Rooy (1996) grouped the e-mail messages of a scientific mailing list according to whether they contained a) discussion contributions, b) requests for information, reactions to these requests or summaries of already conducted research projects, c) administrative messages or d) announcements. He found that only three per-cent of the messages were discussion contributions.

I conclude from these findings that the *transmission of already existing knowledge* is much *more common* in IDGs than the *production of new knowledge*. If IDGs have a *general information potential* for academic communication, this potential is grounded most of all in the possibilities for a *transfer of information*. However, even the claim that IDGs are a valuable tool for researchers to get access to information and the knowledge of their colleagues rests on shaky ground.[3]

The empirical evidence for these claims consists of studies with many drawbacks and limitations.[4] The evidence often consists of *subjective descriptions of user experiences* within single *deliberately selected IDGs* which can be very untypical for the general population of IDGs used by researchers (e.g., Tombaugh, 1984; Harasim & Winkelmans, 1990). Only Rojo and Ragsdale (1997a, 1997b) studied a larger number of IDGs. Furthermore, few of these studies conduct a *systematic comparison of users with nonusers of IDGs*. It is therefore unclear whether the use of IDGs really leads to benefits that could not be obtained in a different way. Cohen (1996) analyses the use of computer-mediated communication tools in a random sample of full-time faculty in chemistry, philosophy, sociology, and political science in US institutions that are members of the Association of Jesuit Colleges and Universities. He found in a bivariate analysis that the more intensively the faculty used IDGs the more posi-tively they assessed "...how electronic mail and network access have benefited .. scholarly activities..." with regard to "more timely access to information" and "access to new kinds of information for .. research" (ibid., p.56). Scholl, Pelz, & Rade, (1996) use data of a random sample of German university researchers in the social sciences. They compare researchers who are intensive users of e-mail and IDGs with those who do not use IDGs, and who use e-mail less often. Both groups had to assess how far their use of computer-mediated communication (CMC) improved their in-formation gathering and stimulated new ideas for research. The intensive users as-sessed their improvements significantly higher than the less intensive users (Scholl et al., 1996; Scholl & Pelz, 1997). However, the data did not allow for a distinction between the effects of IDG use and the effects of general e-mail use.

---

[3]   I leave out a serious negative effect of IDGs, namely, that they aggravate the problem of information overload. This is an obvious effect of IDGs with a high number of messages (McCarty, 1992).

[4]   In the following, I concentrate on the evidence for benefits relating to the transfer of information. I do not consider the evidence for the creation of new ideas through the help of IDGs. The same limitations of the empirical studies are valid for both kinds of evidence. I think it is possible to overcome the drawbacks in studying whether or not IDGs provide information advantages, however, this is hardly possible with regard to the analysis of the creation of new ideas.

In addition, there were no effective controls for spuriousness of the found effects and their claimed relevance. Intensive users of e-mail and IDGs will differ from non-users in many aspects. Maybe the information benefits are due to other, noncontrolled factors and not to the use of IDGs and e-mail. *No study systematically controls whether information effects are IDG-induced.* This is crucial for evaluating the potential of IDGs.

Another disadvantage of most studies is that the experienced *information benefits are expressed in very abstract ways.* Scholl and Pelz (1997) asked their respondents whether they received "more information", whether they received information "quicker" or "easier" (ibid., 355 – own translation, U. M.). Rojo and Ragsdale (1997, p.334) mention as benefits "keep[ing] updated", "get[ting] materials" and "get[ting] answers". But it was *never asked what kind of information IDG users received.* This makes it hard to make any judgments on the specific relevance of the information that is gained from IDGs. Does the information enhance the theoretical knowledge of researchers about their research field or is it advice related to practical problems the researchers have?

Finally, the authors always associate the information benefits with the use of the IDG (e.g., Rojo & Ragsdale, 1997a; 1997b; Scholl et al., 1996). It was asked whether the use of an IDG led to some benefits (e.g., more information). It is never clear whether these benefits were really obtained through the use of IDGs or whether intensive users justified their time consuming use of IDGs for themselves by assuming that it led to benefits. There are *no measures of the effects (benefits) that are independent from the assumed causes (IDG use).*

As a consequence it is not surprising that since the mid-1990s there are more and more researchers who doubt the general relevance of IDGs for academic communication. Lewenstein (1995) argues that smaller electronic spaces with more limited access than newsgroups might be better for active researchers. This resembles the observation of Bainbridge (1995), who argues that public newsgroups have too high a noise rate. Many researchers would react by leaving these groups and concentrating on more restricted mailing lists.

However, the available data, lacking any systematic evaluation, doesn't allow a judgment of these assessments.

22.2.2 Transformation of Invisible Colleges, Peripherality Effects, or the "Balkanization" of the Sciences?

Some researchers regard the discussion in IDGs as low quality research more resembling party conversation than serious academic communication and stop using them (Bainbridge, 1995; Conner, 1992). One might counter that this kind of electronic conversation is important for the interactive formulation of new ideas (Conner,

1992). Conversation, however, does more than stimulate the formation of new ideas. Studies of the academic communication system demonstrate that the benefits of informal communication are only to a small extent the intended result of planned action. They are often a by-product of interactions initiated for other reasons (Menzel, 1962, 1966). Such by-products can nevertheless lead to important new *contacts* between researchers.

The discussion within an IDG is sometimes compared to discussions on the fringe of conferences (Gresham, 1994; Hiltz & Turoff, 1978). E-mail communication is a peculiar mixture of textual and conversational elements (McCarty, 1992; Rice, 1997). This suggests that e-mail not only facilitates the transmission of impersonal information on research questions, but also acts as a social medium in which personal information is exchanged. Empirical studies show that e-mail communication makes possible the sending out of social cues about the sender especially during longer-lasting communication processes (e.g., Korenman & Wyatt, 1996; Walther, 1995).

These considerations have become more important since the 1980s because science policy gives clear incentives for collaboration and co-operation between researchers (Ziman, 1994). Empirical indications for an increase in co-operation and networking within the research system exist (Hicks & Katz, 1996). The formation of a collaboration between researchers, however, is dependent on their cognitive backgrounds as well as on social and economic considerations (Traore & Landry, 1997; Luukkonen, Persson, & Sivertsen, 1992). Moreover, the frequency of interaction between researchers plays a role (Hagstrom, 1965; Katz & Martin, 1997). Kraut, Egido, & Galegher (1990) and Kraut, Galegher, & Egido (1987) argue that frequent communication provides opportunities for an easy assessment of the qualities of a potential co-operation partner. These opportunities for a first preliminary assessment can be given in an active IDG as well.

Accordingly, one of the important possibilities of IDGs is the *creation of new contacts between individual researchers or the intensification of already existing contacts* (Hiltz & Turoff, 1978). Furthermore, many analysts have taken a look at the impact on the *macro level* of the whole communication system.

The possibility of creating new links has particularly attracted their attention. This potential to change the informal communication network of the whole academic system, and not just the networks of single researchers, is sometimes regarded as a remedy for existing problems and disadvantages (e.g., Gresham, 1994). Others look upon it with the skepticism that the use of IDGs might also create new problems, at least if IDGs are used by numerous researchers (Alstyne & Brynjolfsson, 1996a). Both points of view expect that the emergence of new contacts will not take place randomly. Hopeful analysts expect the creation of new links to diminish existing disadvantages in the informal communication structure *within research areas*. The skeptical view concentrates on the possible detrimental consequences for the communication structure *between different research areas.*

Optimistic analysts believe that electronic communication will put an end to some of the negative effects of the so-called "invisible colleges" which have traditionally characterized the informal academic communication structure. An invisible college consists of a small number of very active researchers who regularly exchange information or papers about the newest progress on the research front (Price, 1963; Crane, 1972). Such invisible colleges have been found in a variety of different disciplines within the natural sciences, social sciences, and humanities (e.g., Price & Beaver, 1966; Crane, 1969, 1972; Gaston, 1972; Weedman 1993; Zaltman 1974). They mediate large parts of the informal communication within many research fields. As a result of its limited size and restricted access opportunities, the existence of an invisible college leads to a very *unequal distribution of communication possibilities.* There is a status hierarchy that corresponds to the opportunities for access to communication channels. Those few very active researchers in the center of an invisible college have the most possibilities (Price & Beaver, 1966; Price, 1971). The large number of researchers without access to any member of an invisible college has very few communication opportunities (Garvey & Griffith, 1966). This especially affects younger researchers, who are prevented from reaching their full potential, and making the maximum possible contribution to their discipline (Cronin, 1982).

Proponents of IDGs hope that IDGs enhance the information flow between low status and high status researchers and that especially disadvantaged researchers will profit from the opportunities of creating new contacts (Hiltz & Turoff, 1978). IDGs could thereby, it is hoped, counteract the Matthew Effect in science (Merton, 1973), which postulates that those in the research system who are already recognized will cumulatively be more advantaged compared to those who are less recognized. Researchers have different expectations about the extent to which this inequality will be diminished.

Some researchers expect a *peripherality effect* of those computer-mediated communication tools for which there are few access restrictions (Walsh & Bayma, 1996b; Hesse, Sproull, Kiesler, & Walsh, 1993).[5] Peripheral researchers (younger researchers and those in less prestigious institutions) will be more able to participate in the informal communication system of a research field through the use of these CMC tools, and will extend their communication networks (Walsh & Bayma, 1996b). The peripherality hypothesis is often mentioned in connection with the study of Hesse et al. (1993). They found that peripheral researchers in the field of oceanography profited more from the use of CMC tools, including several bulletin boards, than integrated researchers did (see below). The hypothesis does not predict sweeping changes in the significance of a researcher's status for control over access opportunities to communication channels (Walsh & Bayma, 1996b). It also leaves open the question whether there are any substantial effects for well-integrated researchers and whether the differential effects will be large enough to have a *fundamental* impact on the inequality in the distribution of access opportunities in general (ibid.).[6] Nevertheless, it suggests an effect that *reduces these inequalities at least to some degree* (Hesse et al., 1993; Walsh, 1998).

A more explicit variant of this hope states that IDGs will extend the contact networks of researchers in general. Gresham (1994) predicts that invisible colleges will increase in size and that their exclusiveness will be overcome through the use of IDGs. Members of an invisible college, as well as other researchers, will make use of mailing lists, newsgroups, and other forms of online conferences. Peripheral researchers will have new possibilities for participating in the flow of ideas, information, and unpublished research papers, which usually takes place only between members of an invisible college. They will easily make contacts with experts in their research area. Everyone will profit from these opportunities to a considerable degree. The formerly limited networks of invisible colleges will expand into international networks of enormous size. According to Gresham (1994) the character of invisible colleges will be changed fundamentally through the use of IDGs because their elitism will disappear.

Consequently, the two variants differ relating to the expected scope of the change in the networks. According to the peripherality hypothesis, it is possible that the communication networks of well-established researchers using IDGs are minimally affected whereas those of traditionally disadvantaged researchers benefit from access to more established researchers. Gresham (1994) is much more explicit with regard to the expected effects. However, both versions expect consequences of the use of IDGs that will reduce the traditionally existing inequalities in the distribution of access opportunities.

Alstyne and Brynjolfsson (1996a, 1996b) are more skeptical about the consequences of increased use of mailing lists and the Internet in general. They also expect that the Internet and academic mailing lists will offer opportunities for the creation of new contacts. Their starting point, however, is not the unequal distribution of access

---

[5] Free access to CMC tools like e-mail and IDGs is practically given for Western European and US researchers.

[6] Furthermore, Walsh & Bayma (1996b, 357) explicitly mention another scenario. They note that top researchers may profit more because they are the targets of those researchers who initiate e-mail-contact in hopes of collaboration. However, the only differential effects found were larger for peripheral researchers (see below). Moreover, Walsh (1998) refers to the peripherality hypothesis as implying peripheral researchers profit disproportionately.

opportunities within a research area. Rather, they are concerned with the possible effects on interdisciplinary contact between different research areas. They take into account that the increasing possibilities the Internet offers for extending one's network might lead to a "global village", as it is often stated. At the same time, they emphasize that the emergence of a "global village" is just one possible outcome. An alternate, completely different outcome may be increasing fragmentation among insulated research communities supported by very narrowly specialized mailing lists (Alstyne & Brynjolfsson, 1996b). In a nutshell, their argument reads as follows:

The Internet and its different tools offer a variety of opportunities for information access and contact with other researchers. The geographical limitations of the past can be overcome by the Internet. However, researchers have a limited amount of time and attention at their disposal. The increase in opportunities of choice demands an increase in selectivity: it becomes necessary to filter out the most favored information and contacts. Researchers have to focus on those colleagues that interest them most, regardless of their geographical location. Other colleagues have to be excluded (Alstyne & Brynjolfsson, 1996a). Whether fragmentation occurs depends on the nature of the researcher's interest: is it more concentrated in his own field or in the developments of other research fields? *If* the interest is based on *similarity* and *if* the preference for similarity is so *strong* that it leads to more contacts of the same sort than are available locally (e.g., based on the same discipline or on the same research field), the increase in choice opportunities will lead to an increased balkanization of the research system (Alstyne & Brynjolfsson, 1996b). Researchers will then favor depth in their interactions with colleagues at the cost of breadth.

This consequence is not inevitable. If researchers prefer diversity in their contacts, there will be no increase in balkanization. On the other hand, specialization is often beneficial for the individual researcher. Especially in research fields with high pressure for publication there will be less time to cross the borders of one's own specialty (Alstyne & Brynjolfsson, 1996a). The authors view the increasing use of technological filter mechanisms for the selection of information and the retreat of researchers into ever more restricted *mailing lists* as indicators that a balkanization is indeed possible. At the same time, they stress that in the second half of the 1990s these changes are just beginning. The direction of the change, either towards a "global village" or "balkanized electronic communities" can still be influenced by the research system. The emergence of a "global village", however, should not be taken for granted (ibid.).

The *empirical evidence* for contact benefits of IDGs is weaker than the evidence for the information and idea benefits. Lubanski and Matthew (1998) and Ziesemer (1996) give some examples of researchers that created new contacts by using Internet tools (including IDGs). Hiltz (1984) found in her study of four research groups using a computer conference system that intensive system use increased the communication between the researchers. Freeman (1984) studied the use of an electronic conference system by a small number of social network researchers. He found that during the seven months of system use, the mutual awareness and mutual acquaintance between pairs of researchers increased. Rojo and Ragsdale (1997a) found in their study of eleven mailing lists that only a minority of researchers (37 out of 124) had become more aware of other researchers. Lewenstein (1995) reports few possibilities for the creation of new contacts between researchers in one studied physics newsgroup. None of these studies compared users with nonusers of IDGs or distinguished peripheral researchers from other ones. Scholl et al. (1996) asked researchers whether e-mail use led to an intensification of contacts to other researchers. They found that those who were intensive e-mail and IDG users attributed a significantly higher value to its usefulness in intensifying contacts. Cohen (1996) found in his study that the more intensively the faculty used IDGs the more positively they assessed "...how electronic mail and network access have benefited .. scholarly activities..." with regard to "enhanced contact" and the "ability to collaborate with colleagues at other campuses" (ibid., p.56).

Hesse et al. (1993) made a distinction between different groups of researchers. They studied the use of computer networks (including IDGs) by 257 researchers within the field of oceanography. In a multivariate analysis, they found positive associations between CMC use and the number of published articles, professional recognition, and the number of oceanographers known by the respondent. The first two effects were stronger for researchers at peripheral research institutes or for less experienced researchers. Other studies of the general use of CMC found positive associations between the use of CMC tools and the amount of collaboration between researchers. However, stronger effects of general CMC use for peripheral researchers were not always found (Cohen, 1996; Walsh, 1998).

I do not know of any study that analyses the possible impact of IDG use on the diversity of researchers' contact networks.

Some studies investigate the effects of general e-mail use on the creation of new contacts between researchers. Carley and Wendt (1991) studied a small group of researchers at geographically dispersed locations. They found that e-mail was used to enhance existing contacts but not to create new ones. Meadows and Buckle (1992) also argue that the use of e-mail for informal communication by British researchers did not reduce social barriers to the circulation of important pieces of information like preprints of research papers.

This data does not lead to any firm conclusions. The existing evidence for contact benefits often suffers from the same drawbacks as the evidence for information benefits. It is not clear if IDGs lead to an increase in informal contacts among researchers. Furthermore, it is unclear whether there are differential effects that reduce existing inequalities. Contact benefits even for a limited group of researchers could be important for the research system. However, it remains unclear what benefit these hypothetical new contacts may have and for whom. Are they opportunities for posing single questions, or can they become more regular information channels? Qualitative information about the nature of these new links is minimal. This makes it even more difficult to evaluate whether IDGs can reduce inequalities, or if they narrow the focus of interactions between researchers.

22.3 Disciplinary Differences in the Use of Internet Discussion Groups

The hypotheses that were presented in the previous section have a very broad scope in the sense that they do not make a distinction between researchers in different disciplines. However, different disciplines have distinct communication traditions (Becher, 1989). Many researchers argue that these differences have an influence on how researchers use the Internet (Goodman, Press, Ruth, & Rutkowski, 1994; Kling & Covi, 1995). This leads to the question: Are there differences in the prevalence of IDGs use among different disciplines? If so, how can these differences be explained?

The common view is to regard researchers in the natural sciences as the most advanced Internet users (Goodman et al., 1994; Scholl et al., 1996). Some even forecast that researchers in other disciplines, after a time lag, will adopt the Internet tools most successful in the natural sciences, and that finally all disciplines will converge to use the same tools in similar ways (Odlyzko, 1996). Other analysts emphasize disciplinary differences in communication habits. They think disciplinary differences in the use of computer-mediated communication tools will continue to exist (Kling & McKim, 2000).

Little research has been done on general differences in the use of e-mail, IDGs or computer-mediated communication tools among the different academic disciplines (Harrison & Stephen, 1996). Most analysts adopt ideas from organizational studies or from diffusion of innovation studies (Rogers, 1995). The basic idea of these studies is that not only the potential of a technology, but also the working and communication traditions and the personal interests of its potential users influence the way it will be used.

In a study of researchers in mathematics, physics, chemistry, and experimental biology, Walsh and Bayma (1996a) identified a number of conditions which, according to their view, influence how a researcher will make use of a computer-mediated communication tool if he has access to the technology. They argue that a high *degree of interdependency* between the projects of researchers within a research field will facilitate the adoption of computer-mediated communication (CMC). In such fields CMC is a useful tool for informal communication, helping to coordinate, and adjust research activities among researchers. Another factor is the strength of the *link to the (commercial) market* within a research field. If this link is strong, much of the information is too valuable for researchers to spread it informally, inhibiting the use of CMC. An additional determinant might be *the size of a research field.* Walsh and Bayma (1996a) think that in large research fields many researchers are unknown to one another, leading to complications in informal communication. This would discourage researchers from communicating informally with each other via CMC. Finally, the *match between routine working traditions and CMC* might be important. If it is difficult to integrate the CMC tool into the working routine of researchers, its usage would be avoided.[7]

Kling and McKim (2000) argue that *problems of trust* between researchers have a pivotal influence on the use of CMC by researchers. They discuss various conditions related to the usage of CMC tools by researchers in different disciplines, and how they may affect these problems. Two kinds of problems of trust have an impact on the use of CMC in research fields. Firstly, researchers who use CMC tools to receive information in an informal way have to trust the sender that the information is reliable. Reliability is necessary for the information to have some value. Secondly, researchers who use CMC tools to send information informally to others have to be confident that sharing information does not harm their own career advancement. Kling and McKim (2000) regard four conditions of research fields as crucial for these problems of trust that may inhibit the use of CMC tools.

If there is a *high degree of mutual visibility* of research projects, the risk of sharing information may be lower. A higher visibility of the projects in a research field results in the distributed information having a value which is less dependent on its secrecy. Moreover, Kling and McKim (2000) argue that the *degree of concentration of communication channels* is important. If the research results in a field are published in a small number of journals, researchers are much more visible. This visibility, in turn, lowers the risk of sharing information (see above). As a third condition, they consider the *commercial consequences* of research projects as important. Commercial consequences of research results cause researchers to be more conservative about sharing information and data. Finally, according to the authors, *high research project costs* can have several effects. They can give incentives to collaborate more often and may make researchers more visible within their research field. At the same time, high costs give rise to stronger internal controls of the reliability of the distributed results of a project.[8]

---

[7]   As an additional remark, Walsh & Bayma (1996a) regard the publication time lag of research journals as an important factor in the use of CMC tools.

[8]   I regard this last effect as ambiguous. It may reduce the problem of trust for the receiver of the information. On the other hand, it can increase it for the sender.

These hypotheses have not been tested explicitly. In principle, they should apply to the use of IDGs among different disciplines. Presently the only way to assess their validity is to examine existing studies that describe disciplinary differences in the use of IDGs.

Harrison and Stephen (1996) conclude from the growth of the number of academic mailing lists in the first half of the 1990s that it is unlikely that there is a discipline that does not make any use of IDGs. However, representative data on the use of e-mail, IDGs, electronic archives or other forms of computer-mediated communication tools in a variety of different disciplines is not available. The study of Scholl et al. (1996) suggests that German researchers in the natural sciences used e-mail more often than researchers in the social sciences did. Walsh and Bayma (1996a) found in a study among US-researchers that mathematicians and physicists used e-mail more often than experimental biologists or chemists. Mathematicians mentioned the use of mailing lists most often. Cohen (1996) shows that in his study chemists used CMC tools more often than social scientists, who used them more often than philosophers. In another study, Merz (1998) notes that only a few theoretical physicists use mailing lists or newsgroups.

These studies cannot be used to evaluate any of the hypotheses systematically: Many factors are confounded when we look at outcomes compiled from different disciplines. Walsh and Bayma (1996a) comment on their findings that, for instance, mathematicians work in small research fields that have a weak link to commercial markets. One has to compare researchers in different fields to find out whether the small field size or the low amount of commercial consequences is the crucial factor. As another important aspect, these studies suggest that even *within the same discipline different CMC tools can be used completely differently*. Although physicists may use e-mail very often, they may avoid IDGs.

I regard this as a hint to consider very carefully *which communication needs can be fulfilled with which CMC tool*. It might indeed be possible that *problems of trust* inhibit the use of IDGs among researchers within some research fields. Empirical research that looks carefully at the differences between distinct research fields is needed to verify this. However, it might also be that researchers in fields with a large diversity of communication channels (journals) use IDGs because they have special communication needs. They may use IDGs to stay informed e.g., about ongoing conferences, which is more difficult in a field with diverse communication channels. This implies that a diversity of communication channels does not inhibit the use of IDGs. Rather, it gives incentives to use them.

22.4 Summary

This paper reviewed a number of hypotheses with regard to the possible effects of IDGs on the informal academic communication system. It looked at possible benefits for individual researchers and at the possible consequences of the use of IDGs for the structure of the informal communication system.

The individual benefits were categorized as information or contact benefits. Existing studies suggest IDGs may *facilitate the transfer of information*, yet may *not* stimulate *the production of new knowledge*. The creation of *new contacts* or the *intensification of existing contacts* are often mentioned as potential contact benefits. However, existing studies have not yet succeeded in giving clear evidence that the use of IDGs really results in information or contact advantages.

Different hypotheses were presented that focused on distinct consequences of the use of IDGs for the informal communication networks of researchers. Many analysts expect IDGs will *equalize access to communication channels*: those with fewer opportunities to communicate will profit disproportionately from the use of IDGs. Other analysts look at the effects of intensified Internet and mailing list use on the fragmentation of research fields. They emphasize that the emergence of a global village should not be taken for granted. A *balkanization of the academic communication network* is another possible outcome. Empirical evidence for either scenario is limited.

Finally, differences in the use of IDGs in various disciplines were discussed. Some studies focus on problems of trust between researchers that might inhibit CMC use. The sparse empirical evidence relating to disciplinary differences in the use of IDGs suggests that conditions, which may facilitate the use of one CMC tool, do not necessarily facilitate the use of another tool. One has to take into consideration how the communication needs of researchers in a field relate to a CMC tool. Otherwise it is difficult to generalize predictions for one CMC tool to another one.

Most empirical studies have the disadvantage of only concentrating on restricted parts of the research system. They focus either on single IDGs or on a few groups of researchers. They do not take into account the differences in communication behavior, communication needs, and research traditions of different disciplines. In summary, one can say that many empirical studies lack theory. Exactly such a *theory-guided comparative view* is required to evaluate the validity of far-reaching claims. Some of our expectations about the effects of the Internet and its communication tools on research have not been met, but many others still exist. It is time to replace speculation with evidence. Data collection, however, should be steered by theory. I hope to have shown that there is a set of related hypotheses empirical studies should take into account. If this paper is to give some direction for future research, it can be considered a first useful step in understanding the effects of the Internet on research practice.

References

Alstyne, M. van & Brynjolfsson, E. (1996a). Could the Internet balkanize science? *Science, 274*, 1479-1480.

Alstyne, M. van & Brynjolfsson, E. (1996b). *Electronic communities: Global village or cyberbalkans?* Paper presented at the 17th international conference on information cystems, Cleveland, OH.

Bainbridge, W. S. (1995). Sociology on the world wide web. *Social Science Computer Review, 13*, 508-523.

Becher, T. (1989). *Academic tribes and territories. Intellectual enquiry and the cultures of the disciplines.* The society for research into higher education & open university press.

Berge, Z. L. & Collins, M. (1993). *The founding and managing of IPCT-L: A listowners' perspective. Interpersonal Computing and Technology, 1.* [Online]. Available: http://star.ucc.nau.edu/~mauri/papers/founding.html.

Cairncross, F. (1997). *The death of distance: How the communication revolution will change our lives.* Orion Business.

Carley, K. & Wendt, K. (1991). Electronic mail and scientific communication. *Knowledge: Creation, Diffusion, Utilization, 12*, 406-440.

Cohen, J. (1996). Computer-mediated communication and publication productivity among faculty. *Internet Research, 6*, 41-63.

Conner, P. W. (1992). Networking in the humanities: Lessons from ANSAXNET. *Computers and the Humanities, 26*, 195-204.

Crane, D. (1972). *Invisible colleges. Diffusion of knowledge in scientific communities.* Chicago: University Press.

Crane, D. (1969). Social structure in a group of scientists: A test of the "invisible college" hypothesis. *American Sociological Review, 34*, 335-352.

Cronin, B. (1982). Progress in documentation: Invisible colleges and information transfer. *Journal of Documentation, 38*, 212-236.

Freeman, L. C. (1984). The impact of computer based communication on the social structure of an emerging scientific specialty. *Social Networks, 6*, 201-221.

Garvey, W. D. (1979). *Communication: The essence of science.* Oxford: Pergamon Press.

Garvey, W. D. & Griffith, B. C. (1966). Studies of social innovations in scientific communication in psychology. *American Psychologist, 21*, 1019-1036.

Gaston, J. (1972). Communication and the reward system of science: A study of a national "invisible college". In P. Halmos & M. Albrow (Eds.), *The sociology of science* (pp. 25-41). J. H. Bookes Limited.

Goodman, S. E., Press, L. I., Ruth, S. R., & Rutkowski, A. M. (1994). The global diffusion of the Internet: Patterns and problems. *Communications of the Association for Computing Machinery (ACM), 37*, 27-31.

Gresham, J. L. Jr. (1994). From invisible college to cyberspace college: Computer conferencing and the transformation of informal scholarly communication networks. *Interpersonal Computing and Technology: An Electronic Journal for the 21st Century, 2*, 37-52.

Hagstrom, W. (1965). *The scientific community*. New York: Basic Books.

Harasim, L. M. & Winkelmans, T. (1990). Computer-mediated collaboration. A case study of an international online educational workshop. *Knowledge: Creation, Diffusion, Utilization, 11*, 382-409.

Harrison, M. T. & Stephen, T. (1996). Computer networking, communication, and scholarship. In M. T. Harrison & T. Stephen (Eds.), *Computer networking and scholarly communication in the twenty-first-century University* (pp. 3-36). State University of New York.

Hesse, B. W., Sproull, L. S., Kiesler, S. B., & Walsh, J. P. (1993). Returns to science: Computer networks in Oceanography. *Communications of the Association for Computing Machinery (ACM)*, 90-101.

Hicks, D. M. & Katz, J. S. (1996). Where is science going? *Science, Technology, & Human Values, 21*, 379-406.

Hiltz, S. R. (1984). *Online communities. A case study of the office of the future*. Norwood, New Jersey: Ablex Publishing Corporation.

Hiltz, S. R. & Turoff, M. (1978). *The network nation: Human communication via computer*. Cambridge: MIT Press.

H-Net Webstaff (1999). *What is h-net?* [Online]. Available: http://www.h-net.msu.edu/about/.

Katz, J. S. & Martin, B. R. (1997). What is research collaboration? *Research Policy, 26*, 1-18.

Kling, R. & Covi, L. (1995). Electronic journals and legitimate media in the systems of scholarly communication. *The Information Society, 11*, 261-271.

Kling, R. & Iacono, S. (1995). Computerization movements and the mobilization of support for computerization. In S. L. Star (Ed.), *Ecologies of knowledge* (pp. 119-153). Albany: SUNY Press.

Kling, R. & McKim, G. (2000). Not just a matter of time: Field differences and the shaping of electronic media in supporting scientific communication. *Journal of the American Society for Information Science, 51*, 1-13. [Online]. Available: http://xxx.lanl.gov/ftp/cs/papers/9909/9909008.pdf.

Korenman, J. & Wyatt, N. (1996). Group dynamics in an e-mail forum. In S. C. Herring (Ed.), *Computer-mediated communication. Linguistic, social, and cross-cultural perspectives* (pp. 225-242). Amsterdam-Philadelphia: John Benjamin.

Kovacs, D. K. & The Directory Team. (1996). *11th revision directory of scholarly and professional e-conferences*. [Online]. Available: http://www.n2h2.com/kovacs/whatis.html.

Kraut, R. E., Egido, C., & Galegher, J. (1990). Patterns of contact and communication in scientific research collaboration. In J. Galegher, R. E. Kraut, & C. Egido (Eds.), *Intellectual teamwork. Social and technological foundations of cooperative work* (pp. 149-171). Hillsdale: Lawrence Erlbaum.

Kraut, R. E., Galegher, J., & Egido, C. (1987). Relationships and tasks in scientific research collaboration. *Human Computer Interaction, 3*, 31-58.

Lewenstein, B. V. (1995). Do public electronic bulletin boards help create scientific knowledge? The cold fusion case. *Science, Technology, & Human Values, 20*, 123-149.

Lubanski, A. & Matthew, L. (1998). *Socio-economic impact of the Internet in the academic research environment*. Paper presented at the IRISS 98 conference. [Online]. Available: http://www.sosig.ac.uk/iriss/papers/paper18.html.

Luukkonen, T., Persson, O., & Sivertsen, G. (1992). Understanding patterns of international scientific collaboration. *Science, Technology, & Human Values, 17*, 101-126.

Mailbase. (1999a). *The mailbase service: More than just mailing lists*. [Online]. Available: http://www.mailbase.ac.uk/lists.html.

Mailbase. (1999b). *Mailbase: An overview*. [Online]. Available: http://www.mailbase.ac.uk /docs/overview.html.

Mailbase. (1999c). *Growth in the number of members (June '93 – January '99)*. [Online]. Available: http://www.mailbase.ac.uk/stats/members-growth.html.

McCarty, W. (1992). Humanist: Lessons from a global electronic seminar. *Computers and the Humanities, 26*, 205-222.

Meadows, A. J. (1974). *Communication in science*. London: Butterworths.

Meadows, A. J. & Buckle, P. (1992). Changing communication activities in the British scientific community. *Journal of Documentation, 48*, 276-290.

Menzel, H. (1962). Planned and unplanned scientific communication. In B. Barber & W. Hirsch (Eds.), *The sociology of science* (pp. 417-441). NY: Free Press of Glancoe.

Menzel, H. (1966). Scientific communication: Five themes from social science research. *American Psychologist, 21*, 999-1004.

Merton, R. K. (1973). The Matthew effect in science. In R. K. Merton (Ed.), *The sociology of science. Theoretical and empirical investigations* (pp. 439-459). Chicago: University Press.

Merz, M. (1998). "Nobody can force you when you are across the ocean"-Face-to-face and e-mail exchanges between theoretical physicists. In C. Smith & J. Agar (Eds.), *Making space for science. Territorial themes in the shaping of knowledge* (pp. 313-329). Centre for the history of science, technology, and medicine, University of Manchester.

Odlyzko, A. M. (1996). Tragic loss or riddance? The impending demise of traditional scholarly journals. In R. Peek & G. Newby (Eds.), *Scholarly publishing. The electronic frontier* (pp. 91-102). Cambridge: MIT Press.

Pascha, L. (1995). *Japan im Netz. Eine Materialsammlung zur Nutzung des Internet*. Center for East-Asian Studies (Institut fuer Ostasienwissenschaften), Duisburger Arbeitspapiere Ostasienwissenschaften, 2.

Peek, R. P. & Newby, B. (1996). *Scholarly publishing. The electronic frontier*. Cambridge: MIT Press.

Price, D. J. de S. (1963). *Little science, big science*. New York: Columbia University Press.

Price, D. J. de S. (1971). Some remarks on elitism in information and the invisible college phenomenon in science. *Journal of the American Society for Information Science, 22*, 74-75.

Price, D. J. de S. & Beaver, D. (1966). Collaboration in an invisible college. *American Psychologist, 21*, 1011-1018.

Rice, R. P. (1997). An analysis of stylistic variables in electronic mail. *Journal of Business and Technical Communication, 11*, 5-23.

Rogers, E. M. (1995). *Diffusion of innovations*. New York: Free Press.

Rojo, A. & Ragsdale, R. G. (1997a). A process perspective on participation in scholarly electronic forums. *Science Communication, 18*, 320-341.

Rojo, A. & Ragsdale, R. G. (1997b). Participation in electronic forums: Implications for the design and implementation of collaborative distributed multimedia. *Telematics and Informatics, 14*, 83-96.

Rooy, F. J. van. (1996). *Elektronische discussielijjsten: Een case-studie*. [Online]. Available: http://www.ubu.nl/EBU/a2-4.html.

Scholl, W. & Pelz, J. (1997). Computervermittelte Kommunikation in der deutschen Wissenschaft. In B. Batinic (Ed.), *Internet fuer Psychologen* (pp. 337-358). Goettingen: Hogrefe.

Scholl, W., Pelz, J., & Rade, J. (1996). *Computervermittelte Kommunikation in der Wissenschaft*. Muenster: Waxmann.

Taubes, G. (1994). Peer review in cyberspace. *Science, 266*, 967.

Tombaugh, J. W. (1984). Evaluation of an international scientific computer-based conference. *Journal of Social Issues, 40*, 129-144.

Traore, N. & Landry, R. (1997). On the determinants of scientists' collaboration. *Science Communication, 19*, 124-140.

Turoff, M. & Hiltz, S. R. (1998). Superconnectivity. *Communications of the ACM, 41*, 116.

Walsh, J. P. (1998). Scientific communication and scientific work: A survey of four disciplines. *Internet Research, 8*, 363-366.

Walsh, J. P. & Bayma, T. (1996a). Computer networks and scientific work. *Social Studies of Science, 26*, 661-703.

Walsh, J. P. & Bayma, T. (1996b). The virtual college: Computer-mediated communication and scientific work. *The Information Society, 12*, 343-363.

Walther, J. B. (1995). Relational aspects of computer-mediated communication: Experimental observations over time. *Organization Science, 6*, 186-203.

Weedman, J. (1993). On the "isolation" of humanists. A report of an invisible college. *Communication Research, 20*, 749-77.

Whittaker, S. & Sidner, C. (1997). E-mail overload: Exploring personal information management of e-mail. In S. Kiesler (Ed.), *Culture of the Internet* (pp. 277-295). New Jersey: Lawrence Erlbaum.

Zaltman, G. (1974). A note on an international invisible college for information exchange. *Journal of the American Society for Information Science*, 113-117.

Ziesemer, A. (1996). *Verändert die Nutzung des Internet die Kommunikationsräume von Wissenschaftlern?* Unpublished manuscript. Gerhard-Mercator-University Duisburg, Germany.

Ziman, J. (1994). *Prometheus bound. Science in a dynamic steady state*. Cambridge: University Press.

23 Empirically Quantifying Unit-Nonresponse Errors in Online Surveys and Suggestions for Computational Correction Methods

Gerhard Lukawetz

Quantifying unit-nonresponse errors is in any case an extensive task. Two ways are commonly used:

1. Comparative methods: The same population is surveyed using two different methods: one which is to be examined, and another known to possess a good reliability. In the case of online research, typically, the results of a telephone survey are compared to the results of the online study.
2. Calibration with highly reliable sources: The results obtained online are compared with another source of well-known high reliability (e.g., the census).

Advantages and disadvantages of the two methods are complementary. Comparative studies rely on the (limited) quality of the empirical procedure used for proof. However, they offer no or only little restriction in the examined empirical dimensions. In our example, the majority of survey questions may be asked as well in an online survey as in a telephone survey. The situation is different when employing calibration methods. Results of the demanded level of high reliability are rare and availability is limited. This limit is formed both in respect of the population (there is no such thing as a census of online users) and to the availability of indicators. Comparative methods are indeed often found in the literature (Findlater & Kottler, 1998; Comley, 1996).

To eliminate answer biases totally from affecting our measurement of nonresponse errors, a third concept, called "Reproduction Fidelity Method," had to be developed[1] especially for our purposes. It uses only automatically machine-recorded data: the amounts of time users were spending online from the logfiles of the online system to be investigated. In the short term, the distribution of online time spent from the total-

---

[1] Even though there are similarities between our developed method and the one we call "Calibration" method, examples of similar procedures in online research have not yet been found. The author appreciates any direction to the appropriate literature which might be provided by the reader.

ity of users was compared to the distribution observed from only the responding users. The measure for nonresponse error is the fidelity of the reproduction (generated by the usage patterns of the survey respondents) of the original usage profile of the online system. This concept will be described and discussed more detailed later in this chapter. For further investigation, a comparative study utilizing a telephone survey was also completed. Some experiments utilizing weighting methods were completed in order to correct observed nonresponse errors.

23.1 Background of the Research Project

The context of this research project is of some importance and will be described here briefly. The goal of this study was to obtain information about the users of an online community: "Black-Box" founded in 1992, is one of Europe's oldest free-nets. When the survey was conducted, it used a graphically enhanced bulletin-board-system software (then SoftArc's "FirstClass") and had nodes in Vienna, Linz, Graz (all in Austria) and one in Brussels (Belgium, for use of the headquarters of some European youth organizations). "Black-Box" offered an Internet e-mail address for free. In the time the survey was conducted (1995), full Internet access was rare in nonacademic areas in Austria. Less than 6% of the users claimed Internet as their most important online account. The survey results should provide information for advertising purposes, specifically, media-planning. The questionnaire was closely oriented to that of the Austrian "MediaAnalyse," a survey conducted periodically of newspaper and magazine usage.

The principal design and field work for this study were already completed in 1995. At this time, the first online surveys were around, nearly all using self-selected respondents. The author of this research report was among those many who felt very uncomfortable because of the then uninvestigated selection effects and biases. In order to control for these effects, this research design was developed.

23.2 Empirical Research Design Outline

As the primary empirical source, an e-mail-based[2] online survey was carried out. An important design feature was the use of a true random sample (N = 600) drawn from

---

[2] However it used some specifics of the "FirstClass"-software used as technological basis for the online community. So the original questionnaire form was located outside the mailbox in a special folder on the online desktop and was already self-addressed. It did not use design elements typical for web-based surveys and mostly resembled an e-mail-based questionnaire in appearance.

the user directory[3] of the online community instead of selecting respondents with the self-selection approach. This allowed for the employment of common methods to increase sample coverage: advance notification e-mail to all selected users and two reminder mails (which also included the whole questionnaire again) to those who did not answer within a given time.

For all units of the sample, the online usage time for a period over two months was calculated using the logfile information of the community-server. This is necessary information for applying the "Reproduction Fidelity Method" for nonresponse-error measurement.

To obtain detailed comparative data from nonrespondents of the online survey, a random subsample of these community-users was selected for telephone interviews[4]. By this way the "Comparison Method" for nonresponse error checking could be employed. The original online questionnaire was shortened for the telephone-survey, but contained all dimensions of the user's information including interests, demography, and self-reported online usage. This allowed estimation of the amount of nonresponse error independent of specific dimensions surveyed.

23.3 Hypotheses and Assumptions about Nonresponse Errors

The main idea of this study is that the amount of nonresponse error varies independent of the dimensions or topics covered by a survey. Another important assumption is that the probability that a person will respond to an online survey is closely related to specific variables of online usage – primarily time spent online but also computer skills, and other factors.

Thus, we expect a broad variety of nonresponse errors. We expect high effects with regard to the reproduction of the usage profile of the surveyed online system and relatively strong effects on variables closely related to the dimension "online use". We expect individually lower effects for measurement of most other variables like attitudes and socio-demographic indicators.

Hypotheses about the possibilities of computational corrections will be discussed later.

---

[3] This survey covered only users of the Vienna-based node of Black-Box online community, which was always the biggest, the predecessor of the now existing web-based second generation "Black-Box.NET".

[4] Phone numbers where available from the user directory of the online community. Although access to the community-network was always free, member data were roughly checked before full access was approved. Therefore in most (but not all) cases, correct user information was available.

23.4 Empirical Results: Online Media Usage Dramatically Over-Estimated

It is important to remember that the results presented in this section of the chapter are solely based on the logfiles of the online system. They illustrate how the selection of respondents is skewed due to and with regard to usage behavior. Usage data presented here was computed using the logfiles of the month preceding the online survey (when sampling took place).

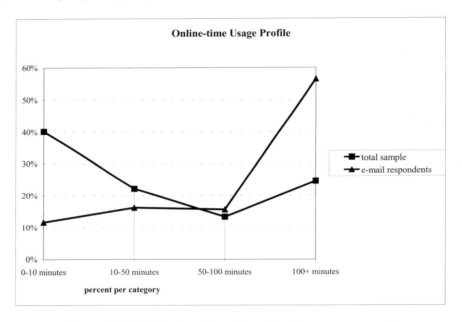

Figure 23.1: Distribution of monthly online time among users of the online system ("usage profiles")

The graph in Figure 23.1 shows the distribution of time spent online monthly by the users of the online community. The whole range starts at 0 minutes per month (inactive users) and goes up to 5,000 minutes per month. This range is divided into four categories: One from 0 to 10 minutes ("mostly inactive"), another from 10 to 50 minutes per month ("light usage or offline-readers"[5]), another from 50 to 100 minutes per month ("medium use") and the last category covering users spending more than 100 minutes online ("heavy users"). There is a small amount of people (about 2%) who spend about 1,000 minutes (nearly 17 hours) and sometimes much more online at the commity network.

The frontmost, darker graph shows the usage profile for the whole initial random-sample drawn from all registered users of the online system. It shows a skewed u-formed distribution with a big portion (40.2%) of mostly inactive users, who applied for an account at one time but rarely use it. Light and medium usage accounts for 22.1% and 13.3% of all users, and "heavy use" is the second category in size and covers 24.4% of all users.

Of high significance is the second, lighter graph. It shows the usage distribution of the respondents of the e-mail survey. All results were calculated from 154 people who completed the questionnaire. Clearly, heavy users are highly over-represented among the e-mail respondents. It also shows that mostly inactive users are strongly underestimated while light users are somewhat underestimated. Observed medium online usage is only slightly overestimated. In general, respondents of the online survey with definitely low fidelity and a strong bias towards heavy online usage reproduce the original usage distribution. For higher lucidity, both results are compiled in the following table 23.1.

Table 23.1: Distribution of online usage (total sample vs. e-mail respondents)

Online usage per month	0-10 minutes	10-50 minutes	50-100 minutes	100+ minutes
total sample	40%	22%	13%	24%
e-mail respondents	12%	16%	16%	56%

23.5 Effects of Response Time

The effect of response time is investigated next. Online surveys are often called a fast method. It is important, though, to find out what effects to expect when an e-mail based survey is carried out fast and with only a short field time.

---

[5] "Offline readers" are persons who utilize software which loads e-mails and all messages of (previously selected) discussion forums to the user's computer and uploads newly created messages to the online system. This enables a user to read and write offline not only mail but also contributions to discussion forums. This method significantly reduces online time and saves connection costs when using dial-in access. Examination of the logfiles showed that about 8 percent of all users employ offline reading methods.

For this reason, we divided the online usage profile derived from e-mail respondents according to the timeframe between the initial start of the survey (first distribution of the questionnaire) and the day the completed questionnaire was returned. The results show clearly that to reach a significant amount of low-intensity users, we needed a field time of at least 14 days. Even after a full 26 days of response time, this user group was still under-represented. While in the first two days 81% of all respondents belonged to the group of heavy users and only 10% to the mostly inactive or light users, it took about 10 days to collect higher amounts of the latter class. The relationship between response time and observed usage is statistically significant (Pearson's $r = -.24$, $p = .004$), giving a linear regression coefficient B of -7.6 (significant at .004). Therefore, for each day our survey is in field, a respondent's average monthly online usage time should be 7.6 minutes lower than that observed the day before.

The figure below (Figure 23.2) should provide a good impression of the effects. However, one must take into account that, due to relatively small group sizes (about 38 persons each), the observed distributions are subject to serious statistically caused deviation.

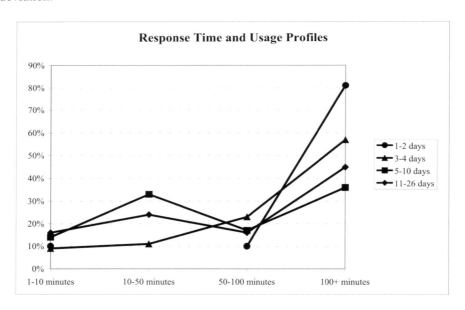

Figure 23.2: Distribution of monthly online time ("usage profiles")
among respondents of the online survey, broken down to
response time

Table 23.2 shows the increasing amount of time necessary for a significant gain in response level (first and rightmost row). It took only 4 days to collect 51% of all questionnaires ultimately returned. Yet, it took 22 days to collect the remaining 49%. The total return rate of the online survey was 25%, which is reflective of typical values reported in literature. As mentioned above, usual measures were taken to increase the completion rate: personal advance notification messages from the administrator of the online system and two reminder messages.

Table 23.2: Distribution of online usage with breakdown by response time; response rate of the online survey (based on total completed questionnaires received)

	1-10 minutes	10-50 minutes	50-100 minutes	100+ minutes	percent completed
1-2 days	10%		10%	81%	28%
3-4 days	9%	11%	23%	57%	51%
5-10 days	14%	33%	17%	36%	75%
11-26 days	16%	24%	16%	45%	100%

23.6 Nonresponse Effects and Attitude Measurement

Since the questionnaire developed for the online study was closely oriented to an advertisement study, it also included an item battery to investigate information interests. The original item battery (over 35 indicators) was reduced to 9 items located on different dimensions resulting in only very low internal correlation. These items were included both in the original online questionnaire and in the telephone survey of the nonrespondents. Different to the data about online usage, comparative data came only available by conducting another, a telephone-survey. Nevertheless this is an often-used approach for testing a new survey method.

Figure 23.3 shows a comparison of results between e-mail survey results and computed values. This comparison is estimation for the total sample. These estimations are a weighted (by response rate) combination of e-mail survey data ("respondents") and telephone-interviews ("nonrespondents"). For comparison reasons, online use, as described before, is also displayed. As suggested by Gabler (1994), chi-square tests are displayed to demonstrate the similarities or dissimilarities of the two results. Chi-square tests were calculated from e-mail survey data versus telephone survey data to make differences clearer and to avoid working with weighted data. Figure 23.3 includes only a subset of the full item battery, but enough to demonstrate the effects. We see clearly that none of the data gathered by survey techniques show as high a difference between the groups of respondents and the total results than time spent online. Two items did show significant differences. First, interest in "health and environment" (abbreviated as „health" in Figure 23.3) has the strongest, and interest in "hobbies/crafts" (not shown in Figure 23.3) is significant too, but none of these are as strong as the observed differences in online use.

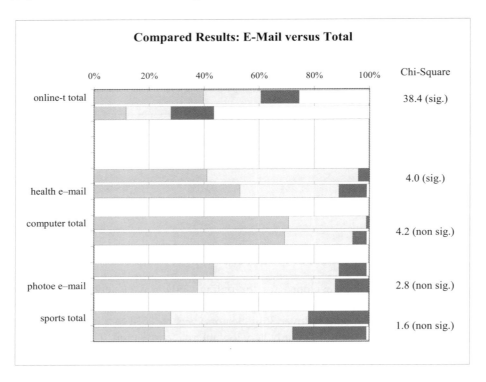

Figure 23.3: Differences in results between the group of respondents and a mathematically constructed total sample (computed from telephone and online survey data)

23.7 Discussion of the Results

The empirical findings fully support our hypotheses. The dimension "time spent online" is heavily affected by nonresponse phenomena. It is also clear that there is a big variation in nonresponse errors. We found that only one information interest "health and environment" showed a strong effect, and a much lesser effect than online use. Another item, interest in "hobbies and crafts," showed some effect. We found only nonsignificant effects in demography. However, there may be some evidence of a bias towards more educated and male respondents. These results match with those reported in the literature. For example, Kehoe and Pitkow report for the Graphics, Visualization, & Usability (GVU) WWW user survey, the "father" of all big self-selected online surveys, heavy overestimation with regard to online usage but only small deviations regarding other dimensions.

First what explanations might exist as to why the dimension "time spent online" shows such a strong nonresponse effect in our research. Possible explanations include:

1. Statistical possibility: It seems clear that a person spending more time online has a greater chance to find the introductory messages, questionnaires, and reminder messages.
2. Time budget: If the time budget for online use is higher, the time needed to complete the survey may be easier to allocate.
3. Motivational factors: More intense use of a "tool" like an online system or an online community leads to a higher identification with it, and increases the motivation to support it (e.g., by completing a survey). Our messages to the users did, in fact, appeal to this motivation.

Our observations regarding the effects of response time (we found a better match of the system's usage profile from late-arriving questionnaires) may also be caused by this explanation. The longer the field time the higher the possibility to find and react to the questionnaire, and the more requests (reminder messages) one will face. Perhaps low-intensity users with less identification to an online system need more "motivation." However, such extra time efforts definitely increase survey quality. One possible indicator of identification with the online system surveyed is whether it is the "most important one" or if it is only one of several. Indeed the results show that 61% of respondents find "Black-Box" to be the most important for them but only 48% of the nonrespondents. However, this result showed a low significance.

A more technical reason as to why online use shows such a strong nonresponse effect may be...

1. Quality of measurement: Differences show up more clearly the better the quality of the measurement is. Weak techniques will distort and bias results, leading to distorted differences, obscuring effects.

It follows a theoretical model for measurement, which makes clear that we have to distinguish between selection effects due to nonresponse and effects of the instrument used to collect this data.

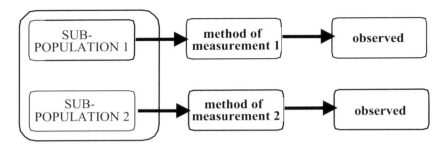

Figure 23.4: Formal model for nonresponse measurement

The model in Figure 23.4 makes clear that differences in samples due to nonresponse are influenced by the effects of the method used to collect the data. One can think of this measurement methods as complex functions expressed in a matrix. It is clear that online use has many implications which may lead to the observed effects. However, since we did not use data collection techniques derived from the social sciences but rather computer-monitored data, which are – at least in this case – highly reliable, we found the full undistorted effects in our data. Comparision methods employing two survey methods from the social sciences, here e-mail and telephone, are subject to well known methodological effects – not at least those caused by employing two different survey techniques.

In our example, the relatively high effects in the "health and environment" item make it clear that there are effects we have not previously considered. While this was not investigated directly in this study, a possible explanation exists in that the "Black-Box" online system may also act as a workgroup utility for computer supported cooperative work (CSCW). A variety of organizations including both nongovernmental organizations and political parties set up internal work groups. The biggest group is the party of the Greens which utilizes "Black-Box" not only as a mail-system but also as an instrument for internal coordination. Clearly members of this work group spend more time online and show a higher identification with this online system which leads to a higher response rate which may lead to the effects observed.

23.8 First Considerations about Correction Techniques

Our last task will be the application of what we have learned about nonresponse effects to the development of correction techniques. However, only first efforts are shown here as the consequences of the methods are still in examination.

Since we have learned that the time spent online is subject to nonresponse bias, we may consider utilizing a technique to correct this error by weighting. This would provide for reconstructing the original distribution (which is known from the logfiles). Constructing the weights for each set of data is a simple task, since we have to take care only of one dimension. Of course since the observed distortion of the original distribution is very heavy, the weights are also heavy. In our case, factors more than 3 would be necessary, exceeding any recommendation for weighting technologies. This promises bad side effects like increasing variances similar to reduced sample sizes (Rösch 1994, p.26). This procedure may be seen as a weighting by reversed estimated response probabilities. Thus, it may be called a very crude and basic form of Propensity Model (Schnell, 1997, p.249; Cassel, Särndal, & Wretman, 1983).

A second approach could use our knowledge that late respondents will form a better representation of the distribution of online use. I-Fen Lin and Schaeffer (1995) used a method for estimating the effects of nonparticipation in surveys which brought the idea for this effort. We therefore will illustrate an initial comparison of the two methods.

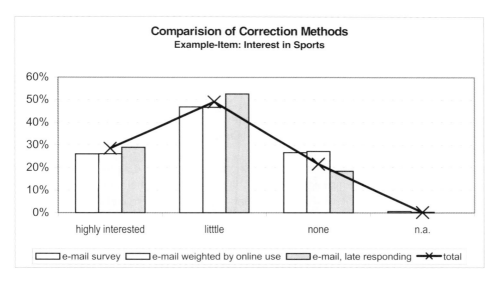

Figure 23.5: Example of the effects of two correction methods.
Distribution of one interest-item. Three kinds of results (bars) are
compared to the computed total results (line). Note the differences
of fits.

The results in Figure 23.5 indicate that using only late arriving e-mail questionnaires (rightmost bar) shows the most accurate representation of the total results (line). To select the second half of incoming e-mail questionnaires, all questionnaires were ordered in succession of arriving and only those with an arriving date higher than the median were used. Again total results were calculated using both e-mail and telephone results and weighting e-mail results down to the return rate of the e-mail-survey.

This result is somewhat disturbing since it practically advocates eliminating the first half of arriving questionnaires. This procedure is only one example, but a typical one. In any case, further research is imperative.

23.9 Summary and Conclusions

We have found that the distribution of online usage, the time respondents usually spend online, will be heavily affected by nonresponse errors. Frequent users, spending a long time online (at the surveyed system) will be overrepresented up to factors of 3 and more. Vice versa, respondents showing only small online activities will be underrepresented in the sample of completed questionnaires. Only small effects could be observed regarding other variables like demography or information interests.

Another important finding is that the length of field time – the time span available for respondents to return completed questionnaires – has a very positive affect regarding nonresponse errors. Respondents who answer late (after 7 days and more) are much more likely to be infrequent users, thus minimizing nonresponse errors considerable. In this sense, it is wrong to speak of e-mail surveys as a quick method. Although these results were derived from an e-mail survey-design, it is likely that Web-interviews will show the same tendency. This is especially true for, but not limited to, self-selected respondents in Web surveys.

Two correction methods were suggested: weighting of the data to achieve a correct distribution of online use and weighting favoring datasets belonging to the group of late answering respondents. First results show nearly no positive effects employing the first, but quite positive effects employing the latter. Further investigations must take place before recommendations may be made.

References

Batinic, B., Werner, A., Gräf, L., & Bandilla, W. (Eds.). (1999). *Online Research – Methoden, Anwendungen und Ergebnisse*. Göttingen: Hogrefe.

Bosnjak, M. & Batinic, B. (1999). Determinanten der Teilnahmebereitschaft an internetbasierten Fragebogenuntersuchungen am Beispiel E-Mail. In B. Batinic, A. Werner, L. Gräf, & W. Bandilla (Eds.), *Online Research – Methoden, Anwendungen und Ergebnisse* (pp. 141-153). Göttingen: Hogrefe.

Cassel, C.-M., Särndal, C.-E., & Wretman, J. H. (1983). Some uses of statistical models in connection with the nonresponse problem. In W. G. Madow & I. Olkin (Eds.), *Incomplete data in sample surveys* (pp. 143-160). New York: Academic Press.

Comley, P. (1996). *The use of the Internet as a data collection method.* [Online]. Available: http://www.sga.co.uk/esomar.html.

Dillman, D. (1998). *Mail and other self-administered surveys in the 21st century. The beginning of a new era.* [Online]. Available: http://survey.sesrc.wsu.edu/dillman/papers/svys21st.pdf.

ESOMAR (1999). *Guideline. Conducting marketing and opinion research using the Internet.* [Online]. Available: http://www.esomar.nl/guidelines/internet_guidelines.htm.

Findlater, A. & Kottler, R. (1998). Validating the application of web interviewing using a comparative study on the telephone. In D. Fellows-Rödl (Ed.), *The worldwide Internet seminar 1998* (pp. 59-74). Amsterdam: ESOMAR Publication Series.

Gabler, A. (1994). Eine allgemeingültige Formel zur Anpassung an Randtabellen. In S. Gabler, J. Hoffmeyer-Zlotnik, & D. Krebs (Eds.), *Gewichtung in der Umfragepraxis.* Opladen: Westdeutscher Verlag.

Hiltz, S. (1979). Computerized conferencing for opinion research. *Public Opinion Quarterly, 43,* 562-571.

Kehoe, C. & Pitkow, J. (n.a.). Surveying the territory. GVU's five www user surveys. *WWW Journal, 3.* [Online]. Available: http://www.w3j.com/3/s3.kehoe.html.

Parker, L. (1992). Collecting data the e-mail way. *Training and Development,* 52-54.

Rösch, G. (1994). Kriterien der Gewichtung einer nationalen Bevölkerungsstichprobe. In S. Gabler, J. Hoffmeyer-Zlotnik, & D. Krebs (Eds.), *Gewichtung in der Umfragepraxis.* Opladen: Westdeutscher Verlag.

Schaefer, D. & Dillman, D. (1998). Development of a standard e-mail methodology: Results of an experiment. *Public Opinion Quarterly, 62,* 378-397.

Schnell, R. (1997). Nonresponse in Bevölkerungsumfragen. Ausmaß, Entwicklung und Ursachen. Opladen.

Selwyn, N. & Robson, K. (1998). Using e-mail as a research tool. *Social Research Update, 21.* [Online]. Available: http://soc.surrey.ac.uk/aru/SRU21.html.

Walker, D. (1998). E-mail research. In ESOMAR & D. Fellows-Rödl (Eds.), *The Worldwide Internet Seminar 1998* (pp. 117-134). Amsterdam: ESOMAR Publication Series.

Walsh, J., Kiesler, S., Sproul, L., & Hesses, B. (1992). Self-selected and randomly respondents in a computer network survey. *Public Opinion Quarterly, 56,* 241-244.

Authors

Bandilla, Wolfgang, senior project director at ZUMA, center for survey research and methodology in Mannheim. Postal Address: ZUMA – Center for Survey Research and Methodology, P.O. Box 12 21 55, 68072 Mannheim, Germany. E-mail: bandilla@zuma-mannheim.de, URL: http://www.gesis.org/Forschung/Online_Res earch/mitarbeiter/bandilla/.

Batinic, Bernad, assistant professor at the department of organizational and social psychology at the faculty for business administration, economics, and social science of the University of Erlangen-Nuernberg. Postal Address: Organizational and Social Psychology, Lange Gasse 20, 90403 Nuernberg, Germany. E-mail: Bernad.Batinic@wiso.uni-erlangen.de, URL: http://wiso-psychologie.uni-erlangen .de/.

Berker, Thomas, postdoc research scholar at the department of interdisciplinary studies of culture, Center for technology and society. Postal Address: Norwegian University of Science and Technology, N-7491 Trondheim, Norway. E-mail: thomas.berker@hf.ntnu.no, URL: http://www.informatik.uni-frankfurt.de/~berker/.

Bosnjak, Michael, research fellow at the center for survey research and methodology (ZUMA) in Mannheim, Germany, working group "Online Research". Postal Address: ZUMA OnlineResearch, P.O. Box 12 21 55, 68072 Mannheim, Germany. E-mail: bosnjak@zuma-mannheim.de, URL: http://www.gesis.org/Forschung/Onl ine_Research/mitarbeiter/bosnjak/.

Brenner, Viktor, assistant professor at the Wisconsin school of professional psychology. Postal Address: Wisconsin School of Professional Psychology, 9120 W. Hampton Avenue #212, Milwaukee, WI 53225, USA. E-mail: brennerv@execpc .com, URL: http://www.execpc.com/~wspp/.

Döring, Nicola, deputy professor at the University of Erfurt (2001-2002) and assistant professor at the Ilmenau University of Technology, department of media and communication research: Communication studies. Postal Address: TU Ilmenau, IfMK, P.O. Box 100565, 98684 Ilmenau, Germany. E-mail: Nicola.Doering@tu-ilmenau.de, URL: http://www.nicoladoering.net/.

Göritz, Anja S., Ph.D. student at the department of organizational and social psychology of the University Erlangen-Nuremberg, Germany. Postal Address: University Erlangen-Nuremberg, Organizational and Social Psychology, Lange Gasse 20, 90403 Nuremberg, Germany. E-mail: anja.goeritz@wiso.uni-erlangen.de, URL: http://wiso-psychologie.uni-erlangen.de/Mitarbeiter/goeritz/.

Gräf, Lorenz, CEO at Globalpark GmbH. Postal Address: Dietrich Bonhoeffer-Str. 5, 50354 Huerth, Germany. E-mail: graef@globalpark.de, URL: http://www.glo balpark.de/.

Hertel, Guido, assistent professor at the department of work, organization, and consumer psychology at the University of Kiel, Germany. Postal Address: University of Kiel, Arbeits- Organisations- und Marktpsychologie, Olshausenstr. 40, 24096 Kiel, Germany. E-mail: hertel@psychologie.uni-kiel.de, URL: http://www.psychologie.uni-kiel.de/aom/.

Hofmann, Jeanette, academic staff at the center of science Berlin for social research (WZB). Postal Address: WZB, Reichpietschufer 50, 10785 Berlin, e-mail: jeanette@medea.wz-berlin.de, URL: http://duplox.wz-berlin/.

Janetzko, Diemar, assistant professor at the centre for cognitive science at the institute of computer science and social research at the Albert Ludwig University of Freiburg. Postal Address: Center for Cognitive Science, Institute of Computer Science and Social Research, Friedrichstr. 50, 79098 Freiburg, Germany. E-mail: dietmar@cognition.iig.uni-freiburg.de, URL: http://www.iig.uni-freiburg.de/cogni tion/team/members/janetzko/janetzko.htm.

Konradt, Udo, full professor at the department of work, organization, and consumer psychology at the University of Kiel, Germany. Postal Address: University of Kiel, Arbeits- Organisations- und Marktpsychologie, Olshausenstr. 40, 24096 Kiel, Germany. E-mail: konradt@psychologie.uni-kiel.de, URL: http://www.psy chologie.uni-kiel.de/aom/.

Klauer, Christoph, full professor for psychology at the University Bonn. Postal Address: Psychological Institute, University of Bonn, Römerstr. 164, 53117 Bonn, Germany. E-mail: christoph.klauer@uni-bonn.de, URL: http://www.psychologie. uni-bonn.de/sozial/staff/klauer/klauer.htm.

Kreutz, Stefan, studies social sciences at the University of Göttingen. E-mail: pms1@moresales.de.

Lukawetz, Gerhard, consultant for online business, specialized at online media, online research and market research. Postal Address: Huetteldorferstrasse 160/27, A-1140 Vienna, Austria. E-mail: lu@blackbox.at.

Matzat, Uwe, Ph.D. student at the interuniversity center for social science theory and methodology (ICS), department of sociology, University of Groningen (Netherlands). Postal Address: Grote, Rozenstr. 31, 9712 TG Groningen, Netherlands. E-mail: u.matzat@ppsw.rug.nl, URL: http://www2.ppsw.rug.nl/~matzat/.

McKnight, Patrick, Ph.D. in clinical psychology at the University of Arizona in 1997. Postal Address: 2110 E. Water St., Tucson, AZ 85719, USA. E-mail: pem@theriver.com, URL: http://www.mcknightconsulting.com/.

Musch, Jochen, assistant professor in social and personality psychology at the University of Bonn. Postal Address: Psychological Institute, University of Bonn, Römerstr. 164, 53117 Bonn, Germany. E-mail: jochen.musch@uni-bonn.de, URL: http://www.psychologie.uni-bonn.de/sozial/staff/musch/musch.htm.

Naumann, Sonja, psychologist. Postal Address: University of Kiel, Arbeits-, Organisations- und Marktpsychologie, Olshausenstr. 40, 24 096 Kiel, Germany.

Reinhold, Nicole, project manager at DaimlerChrysler Research and Technology 2 Lab 11. Postal Address: DaimlerChrysler Research and Technology, FT 2/K Concepts for Railsystems and Aircraft, Goldsteinstraße 235, 60528 Frankfurt, Germany. E-mail: nickk@web.de, URL: http://www.tpanel.com/.

Rietz, Ira, postdoctoral position at the deptment of educational psychology, University of Federal Armed Forces Hamburg. Postal Address: University of Federal Armed Forces Hamburg, Department of Educational Psychology, Holstenhofweg 85, 22043 Hamburg, Germany. E-mail: p_rietz@unibw-hamburg.de.

Rausch, Alexander, since 1980 research fellow at the University of Frankfurt/M (since 1981 at the centre of the university). Doctorand at the department of social sciences. Postal Address: Hochschulrechenzentrum, Graefstr. 38, 60054 Frankfurt, Germany. E-mail: rausch@rz.uni-frankfurt.de.

Reips, Ulf-Dietrich, senior researcher in experimental psychology at the University of Zürich, Switzerland. Postal Address: Experimental and Developmental Psychology, University of Zürich, Attenhoferstr. 9, 8032 Zürich, Switzerland. E-mail: ureips@genpsy.unizh.ch, URL: http://www.genpsy.unizh.ch/reips/reipspers.html.

Rössler, Patrick, full professor for media sociology and media psychology at the University of Erfurt. Postal Address: University of Erfurt, Prof. Dr. Patrick Rössler, Kommunikationssoziologie und –psychologie, Nordhäuser Str. 63, 99089 Erfurt, Germany. E-mail: patrick.roessler@uni-erfurt.de, URL: http://www.uni-erf urt.de/.

Sassenberg, Kai, postdoctoral position in social psychology at the Friedrich-Schiller University, Jena. Postal Address: Friedrich-Schiller University, Humboldtstrasse 26, 07743 Jena, Germany. E-mail: kai.sassenberg@uni-jena.de, URL: http://www. uni-jena.de/svw/socpsy/English/staff/Kai_Sassenberg.html.

Stegbauer, Christian, research fellow at the department of social sciences, Frankfurt. Postal Address: WbE Methodologie, FB Gesellschaftswissenschaften, Johann Wolfgang Goethe-Universität, Robert-Mayer-Str. 5, 60054 Frankfurt, Germany. E-mail: stegbauer@soz.uni-frankfurt.de, URL: http://www.rz.uni-frankfurt.de/~ch ris/.

Tuten, Tracy L., assistant professor of marketing and management at Longwood College in Farmville, Virginia. Postal Address: 1209 West Franklin Street, Richmond, VA 23220, USA. E-mail: tuten@visto.com.

Utz, Sonja, assistant professor at the department of work, organizational, and social psychology at the University of Chemnitz. Postal Address: Wilhelm-Raabe-Str. 43, 09120 Chemnitz, Germany. E-mail: sonja.utz@phil.tu-chemnitz.de, URL: http://www.tu-chemnitz.de/phil/psych/professuren/sozpsy/Mitarbeiter/Utz/utz.shtml.

Urban, David J., full professor of marketing at the deptment of marketing and business law at the VCU school of business, Richmond, VA. Postal Address: Virginia Commonwealth University, School of Business, P. O. Box 844000, Richmond, VA 23284-4000, USA. E-mail: djurban@vcu.edu, URL: http://www. wcb.vcu.edu/wcb/schools/BUS/mrk/durban/durban.html.

Wahl, Svenja, research position at ITIS, University of Federal Armed Forces München. Postal Address: University of Federal Armed Forces Hamburg, Dept. of Educational Psychology, Holstenhofweg 85, 22043 Hamburg, Germany. E-mail: wahl@unibw-hamburg.de.

Wilhelm, Oliver, lecturer in cognitive psychology at the University of Mannheim since 1998, visiting assistant professor at the Georgia Institute of Technology in 2000-2001. Postal Address: Lehrstuhl Psychologie III, Universität Mannheim, 68131 Mannheim, Germany. E-mail: wilhelm@tnt.psychologie.uni-mannheim.de, URL: http://www.psychologie.uni-mannheim.de/psycho2/leute/wilhelm/ow.htm.

Werner, Andreas, journalist, media consultant and –researcher. E-mail: werner@pobox.com.